CITY UNSILENCED

What do the recent urban resistance tactics around the world have in common? What are the roles of public space in these movements? What are the implications of urban resistance for the remaking of public space in the "age of shrinking democracy"? To what extent do these resistances move from anti- to alter-politics?

City Unsilenced brings together a cross-disciplinary group of scholars and scholar-activists to examine the spaces, conditions, and processes in which neoliberal practices have profoundly impacted the everyday social, economic, and political life of citizens and communities around the globe. They explore the commonalities and specificities of urban resistance movements that respond to those impacts. They focus on how such movements make use of and transform the meanings and capacity of public space. They investigate their ramifications in the continued practices of renewing democracies. A broad collection of cases is presented and analyzed, including Movimento Passe Livre (Brazil), Google Bus Blockades San Francisco (USA), the Platform for Mortgage Affected People (PAH) (Spain), the Piqueteros Movement (Argentina), Umbrella Movement (Hong Kong), post-Occupy Gezi Park (Turkey), Sunflower Movement (Taiwan), Occupy Oakland (USA), Syntagma Square (Greece), Researchers for Fair Policing (New York City), Urban Movement Congress (Poland), urban activism (Berlin), 1DMX (Mexico), Miyashita Park Tokyo (Japan), 15M Movement (Spain), and Train of Hope and protest against Academic Ball in Vienna (Austria).

By better understanding the processes and implications of the recent urban resistances, *City Unsilenced* contributes to the ongoing debates concerning the role and significance of public space in the practice of lived democracy.

Jeffrey Hou is Professor of Landscape Architecture at the University of Washington in Seattle. His work focuses on design activism, public space, and cross-cultural placemaking. He is the editor of *Insurgent Public Space: Guerrilla Urbanism and the Remaking of Contemporary Cities* (2010) and was the City of Vienna Visiting Professor at TU Wien (2013).

Sabine Knierbein is Associate Professor for Urban Culture and Public Space at the Faculty of Architecture and Planning, TU Wien. She currently coordinates the AESOP Thematic Group for Public Spaces and Urban Cultures. She is the editor of *Public Space and the Challenges of Urban Transformation in Europe* (2014) and *Public Space and Relational Perspectives: New Challenges for Architecture and Planning* (2015).

"This cutting-edge collection raises important and salient questions and provocations about urban resistance in the context of dominant neoliberal practices in many cities in the contemporary era. Its distinctiveness lies not only in its excellent critical analysis but also in its breadth of case studies, drawing insights from a variety of sites and cities across the globe. This is a must-read for urbanists and activists who recognise the crucial importance of public space for transformative urban politics."

Sophie Watson, Professor of Sociology, The Open University

CITY UNSILENCED

Urban Resistance and Public Space
in the Age of Shrinking Democracy

Edited by Jeffrey Hou and Sabine Knierbein

Routledge
Taylor & Francis Group

NEW YORK AND LONDON

First published 2017
by Routledge
711 Third Avenue, New York, NY 10017

and by Routledge
2 Park Square, Milton Park, Abingdon, Oxon, OX14 4RN

Routledge is an imprint of the Taylor & Francis Group, an informa business

Library of Congress Cataloging-in-Publication Data
Names: Hou, Jeffrey, 1967– editor. | Knierbein, Sabine, 1977– editor.
Title: City unsilenced : urban resistance and public space in the age of shrinking
    democracy / edited by Jeffrey Hou and Sabine Knierbein.
Description: New York, NY : Routledge, 2017. | Includes index.
Identifiers: LCCN 2017001672 | ISBN 9781138125803 (hardback) | ISBN 9781138125810 (pbk.)
Subjects: LCSH: Urban spaces—Political aspects. | Urbanization—Political aspects. |
    City dwellers—Political activity. | Protest movements. | Political participation.
Classification: LCC HT153 .C574 2017 | DDC 307.76—dc23
LC record available at https://lccn.loc.gov/2017001672

ISBN: 978-1-138-12580-3 (hbk)
ISBN: 978-1-138-12581-0 (pbk)
ISBN: 978-1-315-64724-1 (ebk)

Typeset in Bembo
by Apex CoVantage, LLC

Cover image
by Pak-Chai Tse

MIX
Paper from
responsible sources
FSC™ C013985

Printed in the United Kingdom
by Henry Ling Limited

CONTENTS

FIGURES

NOTES ON EDITORS AND CONTRIBUTORS

Notes on Editors

Jeffrey Hou is Professor of Landscape Architecture at the University of Washington in Seattle. His work focuses on design activism, public space, and cross-cultural placemaking. He is the editor of *Insurgent Public Space: Guerrilla Urbanism and the Remaking of Contemporary Cities* (2010) and was the City of Vienna Visiting Professor at TU Wien (2013).

Sabine Knierbein is Associate Professor for Urban Culture and Public Space at the Faculty of Architecture and Planning, TU Wien. She currently coordinates the AESOP Thematic Group for Public Spaces and Urban Cultures. Her research focuses on global urbanization, post-positivist planning theory, and the social, affective, and performative practices of urban design.

Notes on Contributors

Christina Antiporda is a San Francisco-based landscape architect committed to interdisciplinary methods of practice and discussion to enhance the value and life of public spaces. Her research centers on movement through and occupation of contested landscape spaces. She received her MLA from Harvard University's Graduate School of Design. She is a partner in CAMO Studio.

Kimberly Belmonte is a doctoral student in the Critical Social/Personality Psychology program at the CUNY Graduate Center and a researcher with the Public Science Project.

Caitlin Cahill is Associate Professor of Urban Geography and Politics at Pratt Institute. She works with youth organizers in New York City to engage in critical participatory action research to explore urgent concerns including gentrification, immigration, education, and policing. She cofounded the Mestizo Arts & Activism Collective, an intergenerational social justice think tank in Salt Lake City.

Ketty W. Chen is Vice President of Taiwan Foundation for Democracy. Her research fields include comparative politics, international security, democratization, civil societies, and social movements in Taiwan. She is a regular commentator on Taiwan's politics in media outlets such as *Wall Street Journal, Al Jazeera, New York Times, Financial Times, Voice of America*, and *BBC-World*.

Yun-Chung Chen is Associate Professor in Cultural Studies at Lingnan University, Hong Kong. His research focuses on innovation studies and critical urban studies. As community planner, he actively participates in preservation and community building projects in Hong Kong, including preservation of Queen's Pier in 2007 and rebuilding of new Choi Yuen Village in 2010.

Luciana da Silva Andrade is an architect, urbanist, and Associate Professor of the Urban Design Graduate Program at the College of Architecture and Urban Design of the Federal University of Rio de Janeiro—PROURB/FAU/UFRJ, Brazil. She received a PhD in Geography, and conducted her postdoctoral research at Bauhaus-Universität Weimar.

Silvano De la Llata is an urban designer, activist, and Assistant Professor in Geography Planning and the Environment at Concordia University. He received his PhD in City and Regional Planning from Cornell University. His dissertation explores alternative planning processes in the context of protest encampments in horizontal social movements.

Christian Dimmer is Assistant Professor for urban studies at Waseda University, Tokyo. He earned his PhD from the University of Tokyo on the intellectual history of public space in modern Japan. He is founder of the civil society initiatives Open Architecture Collaborative Tokyo Chapter (former Architecture for Humanity), Tohoku Planning Forum, and Tokyo Transitions.

Selma Djokovic is a Research Associate at the Public Science Project at CUNY Graduate Center. She received her B.A. in Forensic Psychology from John Jay College of Criminal Justice.

Anna Domaradzka is Assistant Professor at the Robert Zajonc Institute for Social Studies, University of Warsaw, Poland, where she received her PhD and MA in Sociology. Her research interests include social movements and local activism in urban context, with main focus on "right to the city" movement and social entrepreneurship in comparative perspective. She's involved in the creation of Warsaw Development Strategy 2030 as an expert on social issues.

Angelika Gabauer is a political scientist and Study Assistant at the Interdisciplinary Centre for Urban Culture and Public Space at TU Wien. Her research interests revolve around social movements, in particular pertaining to the analysis of complex relationships between social phenomena and the structure and meaning of the (urban) public space.

Melissa García-Lamarca is a postdoctoral researcher at the Universitat Autònoma de Barcelona. She holds a PhD in Geography from the University of Manchester and is a Platform for Mortgage Affected People (PAH) activist. Her research looks at housing financialization, indebted subjectivities, and the processes of political subjectivation.

João Paulo Huguenin is an architect, urbanist, and Assistant Professor at the Goiás Campus of Federal University of Goiás—UFG, Brazil. He has a master's degree from the Urban Planning Graduate Program at the College of Architecture and Urban Design of the Federal University of Rio de Janeiro—PROURB/FAU/UFRJ.

Maria Kaika is Professor of Human Geography, University of Manchester, UK. She holds a PhD in Human Geography (Oxford University) and an MA in Architecture and Planning (NTU Athens). Her research focuses on urban political ecology, and cities and crisis. She is Chief Coeditor of the *International Journal of Urban and Regional Research* and author of *City of Flows* (2005).

Lazaros Karaliotas is a Hallsworth Research Fellow at the School of Environment, Education and Development, University of Manchester. He holds a PhD in Human Geography and an MA in Development Studies from the University of Manchester. His research interests revolve around the ordering of urban spaces, the geographies of post-democratization, radical politics, urban political movements, and urban environmental politics.

Elina Kränzle investigates processes of urban development in a context of social and political change. In her research, she focuses on citizens' appropriations of public spaces and political processes in urban governance in the face of new urban crises. She is currently University Assistant at the Interdisciplinary Centre for Urban Culture and Public Space, TU Wien.

Henrik Lebuhn is Assistant Professor for Urban and Regional Sociology at Humboldt University Berlin, and Coeditor for *PROKLA—Zeitschrift für kritische Sozialwissenschaft* (Journal for Critical Social Science). His monograph *Stadt in Bewegung:. Mikrokonflikte um den öffentlichen Raum in Berlin und Los Angeles* (City in Motion: Micro-Conflicts over Public Space in Berlin and Los Angeles) was published in 2008.

Jose Lopez is the Director of Organizing at Make the Road New York. He received a BA from Hofstra University. He was appointed as a member of the President's Task Force on 21st Century Policing.

Manissa M. Maharawal is Assistant Professor of Anthropology at American University in Washington DC. Her research looks at political subjectivity, social movements, and urban space. She is the cofounder of the Narratives of Displacement and Resistance oral history project in San Francisco as part of the Anti-Eviction Mapping Project.

Amanda Matles is an urban geographer, filmmaker, organizer, and a PhD student in Geography at the CUNY Graduate Center. Amanda researches collaboratively with young people about their experiences growing up policed in NYC. Her collaborative research documents, theorizes, and builds upon their life experiences to disrupt dominant discourses and to generate social, political, and cultural transformation.

Marcus Owens is currently a PhD candidate at UC Berkeley's College of Environmental Design. Trained as an architect, his research is centered on the politics of nature and technology within design and urbanism focusing on the San Francisco Bay Area and Berlin, Germany. He is a partner of CAMO Studio with Christina Antiporda.

Adilka Pimentel is a Youth Organizer at Make the Road New York. She works to politicize black and brown youth ages 14 to 24, using political education, leadership development, and the arts.

Paula Cecilia Rosa holds a PhD in Social Sciences. She graduated with a degree in Sociology (University of Buenos Aires, 2006) and currently holds the title of Professor of Sociology at the University of Buenos Aires. She works as Research Assistant at the National Council for Scientific and Technical Research (CONICET).

Brett G. Stoudt is Associate Professor in the Psychology Department with a joint appointment in the Gender Studies Program at John Jay College of Criminal Justice and the Environmental

Psychology Doctoral Program at the Graduate Center. His interests include the social psychology of privilege and oppression as well as aggressive and discriminatory policing practices.

Mirana M. Szeto is Assistant Professor of Comparative Literature, University of Hong Kong. She publishes in critical theory, postcolonial, literary, and film journals like *Jump Cut, Journal of Chinese Cinemas, Concentric: Literary and Cultural Studies, Interventions: International Journal of Postcolonial Studies*, and collections including *Sinophone Cinemas, Neoliberalism and Global Cinema*, and *Hong Kong Screenscapes*.

María Elena Torre is on the faculty of the Critical Psychology at The Graduate Center, CUNY and is the Founding Director of The Public Science Project (www.publicscienceproject.org). Her work introduced the concept of "participatory contact zones" to collaborative research and she continues to research how democratic methodologies, radical inclusion, and notions of solidarity impact scientific inquiry.

Burcu Yiğit Turan is Assistant Professor in Department of Urban and Rural Development, Division of Landscape Architecture at Swedish University of Agricultural Sciences, Uppsala, Sweden. Her current work focuses on the emerging cultural landscapes of planetary urbanism and emancipatory planning and design practices. She holds a PhD in Urban Planning and Design from TU Wien.

Regina Vidosa graduated with a degree in Sociology (University of Buenos Aires, 2008) and currently develops her PhD dual degree in Urban Regional Studies at the National University of Cordoba, Argentina in agreement with the Bauhaus-Universität Weimar, Germany. She works as Professor of Political Economy at the Faculty of Social Sciences, University of Buenos Aires.

Darian X has fully dedicated the last 4 years of his life to community organizing and forwarding public policy in New York City. At Make the Road NY, he has been active in city wide campaigns with young people around both Education and Policing reform and is currently the Police Accountability Youth Organizer at Make the Road. Darian has also given testimony to President Obama's 21st Century Policing Task force.

ACKNOWLEDGEMENTS

The life time of a book project is such that the world around it may have shifted once the project is completed, and the shift may either have validated or invalidated the premise of the book. At the time when we started this project in 2014, the Occupy and Indignados events of 2011—the year of "dreaming dangerously" (Žižek 2012)—were still fresh in our mind. As we began the process of collating and editing the chapters in 2015, the so-called "refugee crisis" in Europe reached a new height and became publicly visible. Now, at the moment of finalizing this book, the world has been engulfed by the events of 2016—the "year of unleashing" (Kurbjuweit 2016) when xenophobia and right-wing backlashes become manifest in different world regions in which chapters of this book are rooted: Brazil faced the impeachment procedures and the dismissal of the first female president to be substituted by a far-right, ultra-conservative president; in Turkey, following the failed coup d'état, President Erdoğan began criminalizing activists, journalists, university teachers, and others, and turned the democratic state into an autocratic regime; the European Union was confronted with the economic and political impact of Brexit; and the United States would face new political and social uncertainties in the aftermath of Donald Trump's electoral win.

Whereas it seems that nationalism and xenophobia have dominated national political agendas in 2016, it is also important to point out that urban populations have voted generally in favor of equality, social justice, and lived ethnic and cultural differences. This was visible in the Social Democrats/Green Government coalition of Vienna winning the municipal election again in October 2015 (when the massive influx of refugees and a wave of solidarity gilded the neo-fascist, neo-racist and antipluralist voices in the urban political arena), and in the (repeated) presidential elections in Austria where the liberal and cross-party candidate was eventually elected. What we have witnessed across the globe, nevertheless, can be interpreted as a series of backlashes against democratic institutions which produce noteworthy tensions and debates but also polarization and stagnation—institutions that have long been undermined by neoliberal economic policies and politics. As such, one might argue that 2011 and 2016 were just two important culmination points of wider aspects of neoliberal urban restructuring that have been in place globally since the 1970s, a process that has impoverished populations in the Global South and now in the Global North, to which resistance movements have emerged in cities and regions around the world. This book project has been an aspirational effort to understand better the contexts, mechanisms, and processes that propelled these movements as well as their implications for the future of public space and democracy.

This book is also in part the outcome of an ongoing pedagogical experiment at the Interdisciplinary Center for Urban Culture and Public Space (http://skuor.tuwien.ac.at), at the Department of Spatial Planning, Faculty of Architecture and Planning, TU Wien (Austria). Directed by Sabine Knierbein, the center is an interdepartmental institution, funded by the City of Vienna to undertake innovative curriculum developments in planning and architecture schools and to influence the skills of future professionals in the field. This exceptional initiative came about in 2008 as Vienna's governmental and university institutions recognized the need to reinforce the link between planning and architectural education, social needs, cultural demands, democratic claims, and related policy fields, and decided to join forces.

The financial support of the City of Vienna enabled the founding of Visiting Professorships and inauguration of a series of international and transdisciplinary explorations, in the forms of educational training (summer schools, graduate and postgraduate teaching modules, participatory action research) and public events (lectures, symposia, and conferences). The program has been dedicated to a specific theme each year and the activities have been codesigned with the annually invited international visiting professors. The themes and invited scholars include civil society, culture, and conflict (with Thomas Sieverts and Chiara Tornaghi in 2009); state, politics, and planning (with Ali Madanipour and Aglaée Degros in 2010); markets, economy, and innovation (with Sophie Watson and Tore Dobberstein in 2011); resources, aesthetics, and materiality (with Maria Kaika in 2012); knowledge, education, and difference (with Jeffrey Hou in 2013); ways of life, everyday life, and insights (with Rob Shields and Elke Krasny in 2014); past(s), urban peace, and the welfare state (with Nikolai Roskamm in 2015); present(s), urban solidarity, and European crises (with Sybille Frank in 2016); and future(s), urban equity, and the global agenda (with Ed Wall in 2017).

This volume represents one outcome of the second half of the 2013 program led jointly by Jeffrey Hou and Sabine Knierbein. The yearlong cooperation under the theme of "Urban Culture, Public Space and Knowledge—Education and Difference" also included the realization of a European Summer School in 2014 with the theme of "Designing Places for Emancipation." The program presented an opportunity to examine and reflect systematically upon the recent wave of urban resistance around the world. Specifically, with experiential approaches to reinterpret and question the notion of urban emancipation, the event provided an opportunity for extensive discussions on the emancipatory potential of collective, urban actions. It was in this context that the topic of urban resistance and public space came into focus.

We would like to thank all colleagues and friends with whom we had rigorous discussions on public space and urban resistance that challenge the conditions of what we call "shrinking democracy." In particular, we would like to thank participants of the various educational activities realized at TU Wien and various sessions of the Association for European Schools of Planning (AESOP) Thematic Group on Public Spaces and Urban Cultures, particularly the Becoming Local meeting series in Vienna, Paris, Prague, and Oporto. The thinking behind this volume also benefitted from discussion in a number of events, including "Cities That Talk," the 8th International Conference for the Young Academics (YA) Network of the Association of the European Schools of Planning (AESOP) at the University of Gothenburg (2014); "Putting Public Space in Its Place," a conference at the Graduate School of Design, Harvard University (2013); the "Global Insurgencies—Remaking the Public City in Asia" symposium at the Asia Research Institute, National University of Singapore (2012); the "City Axioms Symposium" at the University of Stockholm (2012); and the "Freedom of Assembly: Public Space Today Redux" symposium at the Center for Architecture in New York (2012), as well as invited lectures at CUNY Graduate Center, Pratt Institute, and KTH Royal Institute of Technology.

A number of individuals and organizations have made the publication of this book possible. Specifically, the yearlong cooperation was made possible by the generous support of the

Administrative Group for Urban Development, Traffic and Transport, Climate Protection, Energy and Public Participation and the related Stadtbaudirektion—Gruppe Planung (Urban Building Directorate—Group Planning), City of Vienna, and by the Faculty of Architecture and Planning and the related Department of Spatial Planning at TU Wien. Dérive, a Vienna-based urban research NGO, and the Urban Renewal Management Office GB*5 supported our work during the Urbanize Festival 2013. The Vienna Science and Technology Fund (WWTF) provided the budget to host the summer school, which benefitted from additional support by different institutions at TU Wien. Faculty Professional Development Fund from the Department of Landscape Architecture at the University of Washington, Seattle and funds from the Vice Rectorate for Research and Innovation at TU Wien also supported the editorial work.

We are also grateful to a number of colleagues that have worked with us in various educational activities, in particular Anja Steglich, Lale Rodgarkia-Dara, Tihomir Viderman, Nina Mayerhofer, and Julia Pyszkowski, as well as a number of individuals from local associations and institutions in Vienna who also contributed to the program. We also wish to thank the anonymous reviewers and colleagues who provided comments to earlier versions of our chapters. For chapters 17 and 18, we are thankful to Elina Kränzle and Claudia Tomadoni, and to Angelika Gabauer for her comments, critique, and suggestions. Birger Schacht rescued a computer from collapsing in the last week before submission. Finally, we wish to thank Dominique Peck, Andrew Prindle, and Sally Parker. Without their competent editorial work, translations, and further support, this book would not have come to fruition.

As urban resistance cannot have happened without the actions of numerous activists and citizens in different corners of the world, this book is dedicated to their courage, resourcefulness, and determination.

Jeffrey Hou (Seattle) and Sabine Knierbein (Vienna)

References

Kurbjuweit, D., 2016. Year of Unleashing (Jahr der Entfesselung). *Der Spiegel*. Special Volume Chronicle, 7 December 2016, pp. 10–16.

Žižek, S., 2012. *The Year of Dreaming Dangerously*. London and New York: Verso.

Introduction

1

SHRINKING DEMOCRACY AND URBAN RESISTANCE

Toward an Emancipatory Politics of Public Space

Jeffrey Hou and Sabine Knierbein

2014 was a year like no other in the streets of Taipei and Hong Kong. Fewer than six months apart, political demonstrations swept through each city much like the super-typhoons that have become increasingly frequent in the region. In the night of March 18, hundreds of students and activists protested outside the National Legislature in Taipei against the passage of a trade agreement with China. To escalate the resistance, they climbed over the walls of the complex and proceeded to occupy the legislative chamber for 23 consecutive days (Figure 1.1). The unprecedented action and the strong public support for the occupation successfully stalled the agreement. Through large-scale mobilization, the event went on to transform the country's political landscape.

A few months later, hundreds of thousands of Hong Kong citizens took to the streets of Admiralty and later in Causeway Bay and Mongkok to support students and activists who staged a class boycott demanding universal suffrage, a decision that was left open by the Chinese government when the former colony was handed back from Great Britain in 1997 (Figure 1.2). The protestors accomplished what was unthinkable only weeks before: blocking major thoroughfares in this hyper-dense city. Using umbrellas to fend against pepper spray by riot police, the umbrellas became the symbol of the protest and gave it its name. The longest occupation at Admiralty lasted for two and half months. Although the movement did not succeed in achieving its immediate goals in the end, the occupations and the mobilization gave rise to a reawakened political consciousness in Hong Kong as well as emergence of new political actors and organizations.

Local and distant observers alike compared the extraordinary occupations in Taiwan and Hong Kong to other recent protests around the world, namely Arab Spring, the Indignados Movements in Spain and Greece, and Occupy Wall Street, in terms of their scale, spontaneity, and significance. The protest scenes even looked similar, with colorful tents and large yet diverse crowds mobilized through similar tactics and infrastructure, namely social media and mobile technologies that stream the events live on the Internet, which drew even larger crowds.

Despite the specificity of local issues and contexts, both of the events in Taipei and Hong Kong also operated in a political and economic milieu that has become common in cities and regions around the world. In Taipei, the trade agreement would allow large corporations to operate with no adequate oversight—a feature of neoliberalization that has undermined democratic accountability and socioeconomic stability elsewhere in the world. In Hong Kong, the Umbrella Movement came on the heel of years of urban redevelopment that favored developers and business elite over existing communities and put profits ahead of collective memories, resulting in displacement and

FIGURE 1.1 Occupation of the legislative chamber by young activists during the Sunflower Movement in Taipei in 2014

Source: Kevin-WY from Taichung, Taiwan

FIGURE 1.2 Protesters took over the streets of Admiralty in Hong Kong during the Umbrella Revolution in 2014

Source: simonwai from Taipei, Taiwan

disappearance of places and communities. Similar to their counterparts elsewhere, the cases of Taipei and Hong Kong reflect an ongoing process and outcome of global economic and institutional restructuring that finds different expressions in specific geographic and political contexts.

The Taipei and Hong Kong cases share yet another common feature with other recent protests in that public spaces became the center stage of social, economic and political struggles. Furthermore, occupation of these places in turn shaped the identity of the movements and their politics. The occupations in Hong Kong and Taipei, as in Tahrir Square in Cairo, Puerta del Sol in Madrid, Zuccotti Park in New York City, Gezi Park in Istanbul, the Stadtpark in Stuttgart, and so on, allow us to investigate the linkages and interplay between urban resistance and public space in the context of ongoing political and institutional restructuring, a sort of restructuring that has produced what we call "shrinking democracy"—a state of democracy that has become increasingly limited in producing agency and accountability. Together, these cases compel us to ask: What is the significance of urban resistance and public space in the age of shrinking democracy and increasing enclosure? What are the specific roles of public space in the recent resistance movements? What are the implications of urban resistance for the continued production of public space?

These are the broad questions that we intend to address in this book, with help from a collection of case studies around the world. But before we go further, it is important for us to first set the stage by articulating what we mean by "shrinking democracy" and by outlining both the practical and theoretical issues concerning urban resistance and public space in the context of the neoliberalizing city.

Shrinking Democracy?

> One of the defining features of democracy in modern times is its lack of democracy.
> *(Merrifield 2014, p. viii)*

It was not too long ago that democracy as a political system and preferred form of governance seemed to be an unstoppable force around the world. In what he calls democracy's third wave, Huntington (1993, p. 3) estimated that at least 30 countries made transition to democracy between 1974 and 1990, "just about doubling the number of democratic governments in the world." Prior to that, 36 countries were governed democratically in 1962 (Huntington 1993, p. 3). By the mid-1990s, the triumph of democracy, free market, and human rights around the world were celebrated by liberal political leaders, scholars, and activists (Alagappa 2004). With the collapse of Berlin Wall, Francis Fukuyama (1989) famously declared the "end of history," suggesting that the advent of Western liberal democracy has marked the endpoint of the sociocultural evolution in human history.

Today, this glossy view of political emancipation and democratic governance seems dampened by the influence of special interests and multinationals that operate above nation-states without clear oversight and direct accountability, not to mention the recent rise of demagogic political leaders. Under processes of neoliberalization and economic globalization (Peck and Tickell 2003, Brenner and Theodore 2003, Low 1997, Smith 2009), democratic states have succumbed to increasing global competition, transnational flows of capital and labor, and policies that steadily dismantled regulations and institutions that once provided necessary protection and stability for societies, as well as opportunities for democratic participation and political accountability. At the supranational scale, global entities such as the IMF, World Bank, WTO, and myriad other such organizations have "uploaded various state functions from the national scale" (Smith 2009, p. 6), thus weakening democratic control at the state level. Under these processes of globalization, Low (1997, p. 242) argues, "a politics of place no longer seems possible at the scale of the national state."

In the beginning of the 21st century, instead of long-standing state institutions, cities and regions are now governed by what Swyngedouw (2010, p. 5) describes as "a proliferating maze of opaque networks, fuzzy institutional arrangements, with ill-defined responsibilities and ambiguous political objectives and priorities." Decisions affecting local communities are being made from an unknown distance, behind closed doors, by networks of actors and entities, under laws, practices, and loopholes beyond the comprehension of ordinary citizens. Local democratic processes are only as effective as electing politicians who have limited power under a system that operates above the local institutions.

Participatory democracy and oversight, to the extent that it has existed, is replaced by new alliances of political and commercial interests. Healey (2010, p. 69) calls this "a kind of network governance, in which linkages are developed between some key government arenas," which makes it much more difficult to identify where decisions are located, resulting in a loss of transparency. Brenner and Theodore (2003, p. vi) argue that, "this multifaceted, multiscalar dynamic of neoliberalization has entailed the loosening or dismantling of the various institutional constraints upon marketization, commodification, the hyper-exploitation of workers, and the discretionary power of private capital." Likewise, Swyngedouw (2010, p. 2–3) suggests that urban governance has shifted so profoundly in the beginning of the 21st century that a new form of governmentality has risen, "one that is predicated upon new formal and informal institutional configurations— forms of governance that are characterized by a broadening of the sphere of governing, while narrowing, if not suspending, the space of the properly political."

Such systems of networked economic and political hegemony constitute what Hardt and Negri (2000, p. xi) call *empire*, a new global order, a new logic and structure of rule, "the sovereign power that governs the world," or what Swyngedouw (1996, p. 1518) describes as *new authoritarianism*, "a weakening of democratic control over key decision-making procedures and activities," and as a by-product, creating what Neil Smith (1996) calls *revanchist city*, as cities become the prime sites in which these processes take place, or as Brenner and Theodore (2003, p. ix) note, "a key arena in which the everyday violence of neoliberalism has been unleashed."

The New Authoritarian City?

Cities, or more precisely city-regions, have indeed become an important site in which processes and outcomes of neoliberalization can be vividly witnessed, including shrinking democracy and evidences of public life. Mayer (2013) outlines four dimensions of this new urban formation: (1) a process of urban upgrading driven by global developers and international investors; (2) gentrification-led restructuring of urban centers; (3) marketization of cities through branding, festivalization, mega events, and attraction of creative industries; and (4) the concurrent outsourcing of manufacturing to the Global South, coupled with the post-industrial cities of the north becoming "the playgrounds for the upper classes, serviced by armies of downgraded and increasingly precarious workers" (Mayer 2013, p. 9).

In the context of accelerating competition between city-regions and in effort to attract investment and capital, regulations have been relaxed and subsidies have been doled out to developers and investors. "Geobribes," Smith (2003, p. 80–81) argues, have been paid by the city to global corporations to attract their investment. Healey (2010, p. 11) notes that instead of responsible representatives of citizen's concerns, politicians are being "buttressed by self-interested officials and lobby groups, distanced from people's everyday lives." In many East Asian cities, including Taipei and Hong Kong, for example, city governments or redevelopment authorities have become complicit in expropriating properties for developers and bulldozing entire neighborhoods under the banner of urban renewal (Figure 1.3). In Hong Kong's Wan Chai District, for example, the once working-class neighborhood has been a site of speculation and redevelopment with the Urban Renewal Authority as the main actor in acquiring and assembling properties that allowed private developers to construct new, upmarket residential towers and commercial complexes (Figure 1.4).

FIGURE 1.3 Once a thriving neighborhood formed by refugees who came to Taiwan following the defeat of nationalists in China in 1949, the Huaguang community was bulldozed and slated for a new development modeled after the Roppongi Hills in Tokyo

Source: Jeffrey Hou

FIGURE 1.4 Everyday lived spaces in Hong Kong's Wan Chai district have been threatened by speculative redevelopment in the area

Source: Jeffrey Hou

In North American cities, the formidable *fortress cities* (Davis 1992) of the 1980s—gated environments created to defend commercial development against urban vices and undesirable populations—have been augmented by perhaps even more powerful force of segregation and displacement: gentrification. As urban places become more pleasant through both programming and upgrading, neighborhood residents and small businesses are being priced out by the next higher-paying renters or buyers. Meanwhile, remaining inner-city neighborhoods are being heavily policed, driven by the broken-window model of policing leading to oppressive practices against populations profiled for criminal behaviors. Such zero-tolerance techniques have in turn been imported and deployed by police forces around the world (Smith 2003).

In the years since 9/11, the policing of cities, cityscapes, and citizens has been further heightened by hyper-security measures including surveillance and control of both physical public spaces and cyberspaces that are meant to prevent and counter terrorist attacks (Low and Smith 2006). In the United States and some Latin American countries, municipal police now resemble paramilitary forces with high-grade gear and equipment. Police in Europe have even employed the use of drones to track down what they identify as "socially deviant behavior." These hyper-security measures are increasingly used against not only potential terrorist threats but also political dissent as protests and occupation are quickly dispersed or prevented in the first place.

For example, anti-terrorist laws have been used against housing and anti-gentrification activists in post-Katrina New Orleans, environmental opponents of London Heathrow Airport expansion, and even Critical Mass gatherings (Smith 2009). In Istanbul, many of the Gezi Park activists face court trials, bearing firsthand the effects of the criminalization of democracy. In both Istanbul and New York City, any resemblance of occupation, particularly in central and symbolic sites, would be quickly expelled.

Are we not living in democratic societies anymore? Yes and no. Democracy in its appearance may still exist, and its formalities are perhaps no less than before, as evident in elections, council assemblies, public meetings, ballot measures, and other remaining institutional arrangements. The challenge before us is that such exercises, the actually existing democracy, appear to be empty, ineffective, and no longer sufficient or adequate in holding the hegemonic economic and political dynamics accountable at either the local or state level. The diminished practices of democracy have become part of the systemic problems facing neoliberalized societies around the world.

Urban Resistance and Public Space

With communities displaced, jobs lost, pensions evaporated, costs of living rising, citizens harassed and killed by the police, and no effective or available democratic process to hold back and reverse these trends, it is not surprising that citizens and communities are taking to the streets, squares, plazas, and other types of public and quasi-public spaces to voice their grievances and to demand specific local policy changes in concert with global attempts to rearticulate general political mores. From mass assemblies in Brazilian cities, to occupation of the state capital building in Madison, Wisconsin, and protests in cities across Europe, ordinary citizens have been engaged in a new wave of passionate protests and embodied resistance. Cities, it seems, have become again catalyst for struggles to maintain, renew, and establish more radical democratic projects, as it is here where the material impacts of abstract policies so viscerally materialize.

Movement scholars have taken note of these recent protests and their specific features and significance (see Martin 2015, Konak and Özgür Dönmez 2015, Jasper 2014, Gestring et al. 2014). Mayer (2013, p. 5) suggests that today's mobilizations are distinct from the earlier urban struggles since the 1960s and operate in very different settings: "much of the conceptual and theoretical framework traditionally used for understanding the dynamics and potential of urban activism is no longer helpful." While they are also shaped by legacies of previous struggles, the recent protests address and correspond with specifically neoliberal designs and enclosures (Mayer 2012, 2013). Specifically, compared to the movements in the 1960s that reacted to the crisis of Fordism concerning collective consumption, i.e., housing, public transport, schools, and other public services, Mayer (2012, p. 66) argues that the recent movement "demanded not only improved institutions of collective consumption, but also more participation in the decision making of their design." Merrifield (2014, p. ix) suggests that what these movements have in common is "a popular dissatisfaction with current political-economic life, with a regime of capital accumulation [. . .], that dispossesses."

Compared with "old social movements" grounded in labor insurgency and organized in response to industrial capitalism, Fisher (1993) identifies five distinct elements in the movements of 1980s and 1990s that still seem relevant today. First, the new movements are based around communities of interest, not necessarily at the site of production; second, they are transclass groupings of constituencies and cultural identities; third, the ideological glue is democratic politics, and their organizational form is small, loose, and flexible; fourth, struggles over culture and social identity play a greater role; and finally, strategies focus on community self-help and empowerment. Other movement scholars have analyzed the mechanics of these movements. McAdam et al. (1996, p. 2), in particular, identifies three broad sets of factors that define the emergence and development of social movements: (1) the structure of political opportunities and constraints; (2) the forms of organizations (formal and informal) available to the insurgents; and (3) "the collective process of interpretation, attribution, and social construction that mediate between opportunities and actions."

Although Mayer (1993, p. 165) has suggested before that the field of urban social movements is "more fragmented and displays far more heterogeneous orientations," more recently, she suggests that, "all around, new types of coalitions have sprung up that join diverse groups together. . . . More often than in the past, these local mobilizations succeed in bringing together deprived and excluded groups with comparatively privileged ones that make up the anti-neoliberal or global justice movements" (Mayer 2012, p. 70–71). In an interview published in *The Observer*, Saskia Sassen argues that one distinguishing factor in recent movements is the involvement of the middle class, "who have often been the beneficiaries of the systems they are protesting against but whose positions have been eroded by neoliberal economic policies" (Beaumont 2013).

A few others have noted another important common thread among these movements—the role of public space. Merrifield (2014, p. ix) notes, "What equally unites these movements is how they've used prominent spaces of the city and new social media to express common grievance and collective solidarity. They've affirmed new forms of resistance, contesting, amongst other things, our hyperexploitative undemocratic system of global urbanism." Similarly, Lubin (2012) argues that, "by occupying public spaces, protestors forced city governments and mainstream media to acknowledge their presence." With the concept of "Global Streets," Sassen (2011, p. 573) takes stock of the recent street struggles and demonstration, and argues that, "the question of public space is central to give the powerless rhetorical and operational openings." She further distinguishes between "the classic European notion of the more ritualized spaces for public activity" and the street "conceived as a space where new forms of the social and political can be made" (Sassen 2011, p. 574), thus echoing what Asef Bayat (2010) has addressed in "Life as Politics," the role of street politics in acts of (silent) everyday resistance.

Public space, indeed, has been central to recent movements. But public spaces are also important in the recent struggles in a different sense. Specifically, public space, similar to the city, has been not only the site but also the subject of contestation and struggles against neoliberal development and policies. As Mitchell and Staeheli (2006, p. 144) note, "as cities redeveloped, public space has become a key battleground—a battleground over the homeless and the poor and over the rights of developers, corporations, and those who seek to make over the city in an image attractive to tourists, middle- and upper-class residents and suburbanites." Public spaces, including parks, plazas, and streets, are increasingly redeveloped to maximize values of surrounding properties. They are often privatized or managed through so-called public-private partnerships to offload cost of operations from municipalities strapped by austerity measures and faced with diminishing resources. As such, public spaces today face not only increasing control for order and security but also threats from financial interests from both municipalities and corporations.

As simultaneously a place for mobilization and organized resistance and as a space threatened by neoliberal urban development and policing, public space serves as an important site for examining the linkages between processes of shrinking democracy and urban resistance. As public spaces come under attack, they also serve as a vestige of the few remaining spaces of active democracy—spaces of expression, mobilization, and contestation. However, aside from the recent discussion as referenced above, the altering role of public space in the changing urban resistance remains under-theorized and poorly understood. Specifically, for many movement scholars, space remains primarily as a backdrop to discussion of movement strategies, tactics, and larger structural factors facing resistance movements. For planning and design professionals responsible for the making of contemporary public space, protests and resistance are far from their project focus. In the worst scenarios, their work is often intended to facilitate surveillance and control, if not to deter mass assemblies in the first place. For planning and design scholars focusing on public space, there remains much more work to be done in unpacking the role of public space in supporting and engendering active democracy.

It was precisely with this in mind that we undertook this project, one that brought together a diverse group of scholars and scholar/activists from different cultural and disciplinary backgrounds to examine a variety of recent resistance movements around the globe. We look for resistance movements that share a common struggle against neoliberal urban policies and shrinking democracy but with different linkages to the notion and material manifestation of public space. In taking on the subject of urban resistance and public space, we seek to build on our earlier work on the changing notions of public space (Hou 2010, 2012, 2016, Madanipour et al. 2014, Tornaghi and Knierbein 2015, Knierbein 2010, Vessler Vaz et al. 2006). By examining these cases, we are interested in addressing the questions as stated earlier in this chapter: *What is the significance of urban resistance and public space in the age of shrinking democracy and increasing enclosure? What are the specific roles of public space in the recent resistance movements? What are the implications of urban resistance for the continued production of public space?*

This Book

This volume is organized in four parts, corresponding to specific ways in which urban resistance intersects with the making and remaking of contemporary public space. Each part serves to highlight a specific set of relationships that link social movements to aspects of the built and lived environments. In doing so, we also seek to underscore the agency of space in urban resistance movements, an aspect of urban social movement that, we believe, has been under-researched.

In Part 1, **Mobilizing**, we begin by examining different forms of mobilization in public space. In the case of Movimento Passe Livre (Free Pass Movement) in Brazil, Luciana da Silva Andrade and João Paulo Huguenin examine not only the horizontal forms of movement organization and mobilization that have been common in recent social movements, but also how the movement recognizes "the importance of using the city as a means to win over the city itself", for example, through issues of public transportation to bring attention to the condition of social and economic inequality in the society. This is followed by a similar case study in San Francisco by Manissa Maharawal in which blockades of Google buses on the city streets serve to highlight both the impact of tech-driven gentrification and privatization of public resources, in this case, streets and bus stops. In the case of the Platform for Mortgage Affected People (Plataforma de Afectados por la Hipoteca, PAH) in Spain, the focus of public space takes a different turn as Melissa García-Lamarca illustrates how PAH finds solutions to mortgage problems that are typically experienced in private and makes them visible in the public sphere through weekly assemblies, blocking of evictions, and occupation of bank-owned buildings. Lastly, in the case of Argentina, Paula Rosa and Regina Vidosa take a long view by examining resistance movements against neoliberal policies under the authoritarian regime since the 1970s, and how public space serves not only as a medium but also increasingly as "a platform for resistance, debate, meeting, and learning."

In Part 2, **Reclaiming**, the chapters focus on cases in which movements to protect and reclaim public space from threats of neoliberal development, excessive policing, and privatization, also represent efforts to reclaim the political. Yun-Chung Chen and Mirana Szeto lead off with the case of the Reclaim the Public Space movement in Hong Kong, which preceded the Umbrella Movement in 2014, by examining how the movement was equally about protecting the public space as about creating a democratic space in a system increasingly dominated by political and commercial imperatives. Focusing on the Occupy Gezi Park movement in Istanbul, Burcu Yiğit Turan shows that public spaces have become both an arena for the neoliberal strategies as well as the space for political contestation and formation of new and diverse politics. Caitlin Cahill and her research team then take us to the streets of Brooklyn, New York to examine how scholarly activism can join forces with oppressed social groups, in this case inner-city youths. To act against spatial exclusions and discrimination, the researchers supported the youths to organize politically and to educate others about their human and civil rights. Lastly, focusing on a different kind of political engagement, Anna Domaradzka examines how diverse groups of urban activists scale up their operation through the formation of a nationwide coalition and emerged as influential political actors in many Polish cities.

Part 3, **Negotiating**, addresses a persistent challenge facing urban social movements—that of competing interests, identities, and agendas among movement organizations and activists. Maria Kaika and Lazaros Karaliotas examine the lasting impacts of the 2011 protests at Syntagma Square in Athens in terms of how differences and tensions were manifested and negotiated in the spatialization of politics post-2011. Similarly, Ketty Chen examines the self-organization of groups, cliques, and interest groups within the Sunflower Movement in Taiwan and how such arrangement offers new niches and room for negotiation and collective learning on issues related to tolerance, solidarity, and transparency in the movement's decision-making process. In the case of urban activism in Berlin, Henrik Lebuhn examines how campaigns on citywide referendum serve to bring together diverse grassroots organizations through focused and shared discursive frameworks. Lastly, in the case of Occupy Oakland, Marcus Owens and Christina Antiporda explore the lineage of diverse claims as well as the negotiations and maneuverings between neighbors, competing constituencies, police, city officials, and so on in the fallout of the movement.

Finally, the chapters in Part 4, **Contesting**, examine the continued struggles of urban resistance and the anti- and alter-politics inscribed in resistance tactics, specifically in the face of backlashes (including militarized policing and criminalization), rising xenophobia, and persistence of neoliberal urban policies and development. In his analysis of Operation 1DMX in Mexico City, Silvano De la Llata examines the militarization of public space and material blockades during the presidential inauguration in Mexico, and furthermore the tensions between the right to the city and rule of law in public spaces. Elina Kränzle examines the gap between the movement for alternative urbanism following the 15M Movement in Madrid and the neoliberal backlash in the form of redeveloped central public spaces in the city. In the case of Miyashita Park in Shibuya, Tokyo, Christian Dimmer offers a more nuanced view of events leading to the rebranding and redesign of a park that once was home to a homeless encampment. Lastly, Sabine Knierbein and Angelika Gabauer use a pair of cases in Vienna—Train of Hope and protests against Akademikerball—to illustrate the rise of anti-pluralism politics and the appropriation of public space through exclusionary resistance on one hand, and two forms of inclusive resistance on the other—one leaning towards anti-politics, the other suggesting a new model to organize space and society, an alter-politics. The chapter further examines the notions of "worlded resistance" aiming at enacted solidarity and embodied egalitarian differences.

These cases cover a wide range of geographic locations and sociopolitical contexts. Still, this volume is by no means exhaustive, as one may notice that some locations and contexts are glaringly missing, such as Africa and the Middle East. Similarly, one may also notice that a few well-known cases are not included here, most notably Occupy Wall Street, Stuttgart 21 Protests, and Occupy St. Pauls. We believe that such cases have been widely reported and examined in both popular media and scholarly publications already. Instead, we use our limited space to include cases that are less studied.

Toward an Emancipatory Politics of Public Space

The common threads among the recent resistance movements will be examined further in the concluding chapter of this book. But one thing is clear even as we begin: Urban resistance movements are instrumental in challenging the hegemonic, neoliberal political, and economic paradigm that governs practically every aspect of life in today's societies. Specifically, the recent resistance movements bring necessary attention to the social, cultural, ecological, economic, and political impacts of current political and economic systems today in a loud and vivid way. These movements create a space for discussion, debate, and social and political mobilization, necessary to resist the hegemonic forces. Specifically, they develop discourses and action-based coalitions that are critical to political changes. In short, whereas the politics of public space in both the literature and everyday life has predominantly focused on policing, sale, and erosion of public space (Sorkin 1992, Mitchell 1995, Low and Smith 2006), these recent resistance movements signal a distinct direction for an emancipatory politics of public space, focusing on its increasingly important role as a vehicle for active democracy.

In recent movements around the world, while neoliberal policies, urban inequality, and increasing social precarity may be the focus of resistance, it is fundamentally the diminishing democracy, specifically the shrinking capacity of democratic process, that leave protesters and ordinary citizens with no other resort than to take to the streets, the emblematic public space for reinstating democracy. As Harvey argues (borrowing from Lefebvre), while cities operate as sites of neoliberalization, "the urban [. . .] functions also an important site of political action and revolt." Furthermore, "[t]he actual site characteristics are important, and the social re-engineering of territorial organization of these sites is a weapon in political struggles" (Harvey 2012, p. 117–118). Similarly, Brenner and

Theodore (2003, p. x) argue, "[e]ven in the age of neoliberal dominance, cities remain crucially important arenas for struggles in the name of social justice, radical democracy, popular empowerment, and the politics of difference." The streets, then, represent one such arena, one that enables citizens and communities to debate, interact, find solidarity, learn, and engage in a lived democracy. Frank and Fuentas (1990, p. 142) argue, "[a]lthough social movements are more defensive than offensive and tend to be temporary, they are perhaps the most important agents of social transformation." It is this capacity for social transformation that, we argue, suggests the direction for a new, emancipatory politics of public space.

Shrinking democracy, coupled with economic restructuring, constitutes an underlying challenge facing cities and communities around the world. Public space, as a building block and medium of political engagement, represents a counter-space to systems of shrinking democracy. In its capacity as a vehicle for lived democracy and active democratization, public space in contemporary society deserves greater care, attention, and critical reflection. As many cases in this book demonstrate, resistance movements have evolved with time, necessity, imagination, and interacted with public spaces in different ways. As movements evolve to confront new challenges, explore new opportunities, negotiate with new actors and circumstances, and utilizing new technologies and platforms, our understanding of the role and agency of public space must also advance. This is precisely the objective of this book and the focus of our agenda for exploring the linkages between urban resistance and public space in the age of shrinking democracy. It is our hope that with this work and others to follow, we can continue to explore public space as sites of renewed hope and possibilities in the quest for a more just, enduring, and democratic society.

References

Alagappa, M., 2004. Introduction. *In*: M. Alagappa, ed. *Civil Society and Political Change in Asia: Expanding and Contracting Democratic Space*. Stanford: Stanford University Press, 1–21.

Bayat, A., 2010. *Life as Politics: How Ordinary People Change the Middle East*. Stanford: Stanford University Press.

Beaumont, P., 2013. Global Protest Grows as Citizens Lose Faith in Politics and the State [online]. *The Observer*, 22 June 2013. Available from: www.theguardian.com/world/2013/jun/22/urban-protest-changing-global-social-network [Accessed June 30, 2014].

Brenner, N. and Theodore, N., eds., 2003. *Space of Neoliberalism: Urban Restructuring in North America and Western Europe*. New York: Wiley-Blackwell.

Davis, M., 1992. Fortress Los Angeles: The Militarization of Urban Space. *In*: M. Sorkin, ed. *Variations on a Theme Park: The New American City and the End of Public Space*. New York: Hill and Wang, 154–180.

Fisher, R., 1993. Grass-Roots Organizing Worldwide: Common Ground, Historical Roots, and the Tension Between Democracy and the State. *In*: R. Fisher and J. Kling, eds. *Mobilizing the Community: Local Politics in the Era of the Global City*. Newbury Park: SAGE Publications, 3–27.

Frank, A. G. and Fuentas, M., 1990. Civil Democracy: Social Movements in Recent World History. *In*: S. Amin, G. Arrighi, A. G. Frank, and I. Wallerstain, eds. *Transforming the Revolution: Social Movements and the World-System*. New York: Monthly Review Press, 139–180.

Fukuyama, F., 1989. The End of History? *The National Interest*, 16, 3–18.

Gestring, N., Ruhne, R., and Wehrheim, J., 2014. *City and Social Movements* (Stadt und soziale Bewegungen). Wiesbaden: Springer VS.

Hardt, M. and Negri, A., 2000. *Empire*. Cambridge, MA: Harvard University Press.

Harvey, D., 2012. *Rebel Cities: From the Right to the City to the Urban Revolution*. London and New York: Verso.

Healey, P., 2010. *Making Better Places: The Planning Project in the Twenty-First Century*. New York: Palgrave Macmillan.

Hou, J., ed., 2010. *Insurgent Public Space: Guerrilla Urbanism and the Remaking of Contemporary Cities*. London and New York: Routledge.

Hou, J., 2012. Making Public, Beyond Public Space. *In*: R. Shiffman, R. Bell, L. J. Brown, and L. Elizabeth, eds. *Beyond Zuccotti Park: Freedom of Assembly and the Occupation of Public Space.* Berkeley, CA: New Village Press, 89–98.

Hou, J., 2016. Deadly and Lively Encounters. *In*: J. Darling, and H. F. Wilson, eds. *Encountering the City: Urban Encounters from Accra to New York.* London and New York: Routledge, 221–228.

Hou, J. and Hammami, F., 2015. On the Entangled Paths of Urban Resistance, City Planning and Heritage Conservation. *PlaNext*, 1 (1), 9–16.

Huntington, S. P., 1993. Democracy's Third Wave. *In*: L. Diamond, and M. F. Platter, eds. *The Global Resurgence of Democracy.* Baltimore and London: The Johns Hopkins University Press, 3–25.

Jasper, J., 2014. *Protest: A Cultural Introduction to Social Movements.* Cambridge: Polity Press.

Knierbein, S., 2010. *The Production of Central Public Spaces in the Attention Economy: Aesthetic, Economic, and Media Restructuring: The Example of Berlin Since 1980* (Die Produktion zentraler öffentlicher Räume in der Aufmerksamkeitsökonomie: Ästhetische, ökonomische und mediale Restrukturierungen am Beispiel Berlin seit 1980). Wiesbaden: VS Verlag für Sozialwissenschaften.

Konak, N. and Özgür Dönmez, R., 2015. *Waves of Social Movement Mobilizations in the Twenty-First Century.* London: Lexington Books.

Low, M., 1997. Representation Unbound: Globalization and Democracy. *In*: K. R. Cox, ed. *Spaces of Globalization: Reasserting the Power of the Local.* New York and London: The Guilford Press, 240–280.

Low, S. and Smith, N., eds., 2006. *The Politics of Public Space.* New York and London: Routledge.

Lubin, J., 2012. The "Occupy" Movement: Emerging Protest Forms and Contested Urban Spaces [online]. *The Urban Fringe.* Available from: http://ced.berkeley.edu/bpj/2012/09/the-occupy-movement-emerging-protest-forms-and-contested-urban-spaces [Accessed 16 June 2016].

Madanipour, A., Knierbein, S., and Degros, A., eds., 2014. *Public Space and the Challenges of Urban Transformation in Europe.* London and New York: Routledge.

Martin, G., 2015. *Understanding Social Movements.* London and New York: Routledge.

Mayer, M., 1993. The Career of Urban Social Movements in West Germany. *In*: R. Fisher, and J. Kling, eds. *Mobilizing the Community: Local Politics in the Era of the Global City.* Newbury Park: SAGE Publications, 149–170.

Mayer, M., 2012. The "Right to the City" in Urban Social Movements. *In*: N. Brenner, P. Marcuse, and M. Mayer, eds. *Cities for People, Not for Profits: Critical Urban Theory and the Right to the City.* London and New York: Routledge, 63–85.

Mayer, M., 2013. First World Urban Activism: Beyond Austerity Urbanism and Creative City Politics. *City*, 17 (1), 5–19.

McAdam, D., McCarthy, J. D., and Zald, M. N., 1996. Introduction: Opportunities, Mobilizing Structures, and Framing Processes: Toward a Synthetic, Comparative Perspective on Social Movements. *In*: D. McAdam, J. D. McCarthy, and M. N. Zald, eds. *Comparative Perspectives on Social Movements: Political Opportunities, Mobilizing Structures, and Cultural Framings.* Cambridge: Cambridge University Press, 1–20.

Merrifield, A., 2014. *The New Urban Question.* London: Pluto Press.

Mitchell, D., 1995. The End of Public Space? People's Park, Definitions of Public, and Democracy. *Annals of the Association of American Geographers*, 85 (1), 108–133.

Mitchell, D. and Staeheli, L. A., 2006. Clean and Safe? Property Development, Public Space, and Homelessness in Downtown San Diego. *In*: S. Low, and N. Smith, eds. *The Politics of Public Space.* New York and London: Routledge, 143–176.

Peck, J. and Tickell, A., 2003. Neoliberalizing Space. *In*: N. Brenner, and N. Theodore, eds. *Space of Neoliberalism: Urban Restructuring in North America and Western Europe.* New York: Wiley-Blackwell, 33–57.

Sassen, S., 2011. The Global Street: Making the Political. *Globalizations*, 8 (5), 573–579.

Smith, N., 1996. *The New Urban Frontier: Gentrification and the Revanchist City.* London and New York: Routledge.

Smith, N., 2003. New Globalism, New Urbanism: Gentrification as Global Urban Strategy. *In*: N. Brenner, and N. Theodore, eds. *Space of Neoliberalism: Urban Restructuring in North America and Western Europe.* New York: Wiley-Blackwell, 80–103.

Smith, N., 2009. Introduction: Altered States. *In*: H. Gautney, O. Dahbour, A. Dawson, and N. Smith, eds. *Democracy, States, and the Struggle for Global Justice.* London and New York: Routledge, 1–16.

Sorkin, M., ed., 1992. *Variations on a Theme Park: The New American City and the End of Public Space*. New York: Hill and Wang.

Swyngedouw, E., 1996. Reconstructing Citizenship, the Re-Scaling of the State and the New Authoritarianism: Closing the Belgian Mines. *Urban Studies*, 33 (8), 1499–1521.

Swyngedouw, E., 2010. Post-Democratic cities: For whom and for what? Paper presented in Concluding Session, Regional Studies Association Annual Conference, Budapest, 26 May 2010.

Tornaghi, C. and Knierbein, S., eds., 2015. *Public Space and Relational Perspectives: New Challenges for Architecture and Planning*. London and New York: Routledge.

Vessler Vaz, L., Knierbein, S., and Welch Guerra, M., 2006. *Public Space in Planning Policy: Studies from Rio de Janeiro and Berlin* (Der öffentliche Raum in der Planungspolitik. Studien aus Rio de Janeiro und Berlin). Weimar: Bauhaus University Press.

PART 1

Mobilizing

Taking to the Streets!

2

BETWEEN STREET AND HOME

Mobility, Housing, and the 2013 Demonstrations in Brazil

Luciana da Silva Andrade and João Paulo Huguenin

The year 2013 upended stereotypes of Brazilian culture as a politically apathetic population. Initially triggered by an increase in bus fares, public political activity subsequently swelled, compounded by widespread dissatisfaction with significant public investment in large public events, and demonstrations began happening across Brazil. Public dissatisfaction reached a new height with local frustration with bus fares and was amplified by a glut of massive public spending in major events, including the Soccer World Cup in 2014,[1] the 2016 Olympic Games in Rio de Janeiro (here on simply referred to as "Rio"), the 2013 Confederations Cup in Brazil, and World Youth Day in Rio. The demonstrations of June 2013 were unique in that they were influenced and enabled by our more interconnected world through new means of communication, allowing for perspectives beyond those of corporatized media. They mirrored many other protests including Occupy Wall Street in New York City, the Indignados Movement in Spain, and other counterparts in Greece, Turkey, and Egypt, among others.

In this chapter, we intend to analyze what and how urban conditions contributed to recent insurgencies in Brazilian cities, especially the most densely populated ones. Our main focus is how access to housing is linked to issues of mobility and transportation. We will focus on Rio both because it is the core of the second largest metropolitan region in Brazil and because of the unique aspects of its protests. While most demonstrations in Brazil were limited to the month of June 2013, the ones in Rio lasted until the end of the year and contributed to the state governor leaving office before the end of his term.

The 2013 demonstrations suggest that social movements in Brazil are undergoing a profound transformation. We believe such dramatic transformation has been catalyzed by the opportunity to connect with others through collaborative structures of social organization that are not rooted in competition. The collaboration generated new ways to counter the hegemonic power of the existing systems. We are curious what parallels may exist between other historical moments of drastic advancements in technology (e.g. the printing press, industrialization) and what implications these advancements may have for the articulation and contestation of the bourgeois public sphere (Habermas 1984).

Consequently, we ask if the 2013 protests in Brazil occurred in a context of profound transformation that points to significant sociocultural challenges to the dominance of capitalist-driven urban organization. Given that some social groups may have more power and resources than others, this perspective investigates how contemporary media and communication allow horizontal forms of social organization to challenge existing vertical hierarchies of power, and suggests other social orders such as Hardt and Negri's (2011) collaboration-driven alter-modernity where socially produced wealth is collectively appropriated and where structuration is not only based on radical redistribution, but is committed to preserving sociocultural memory and natural resources for future generations.

The Year 2013

With no effective mass rapid transportation system in Brazil, public transportation in Brazil is delivered primarily by bus with poor or nonexistent connections to other modes of transportation. "Bilhetes únicos," an integrated ticket system allowing for the integration of different lines or modes of transport, was introduced and popularized only recently in the last decade. This system allowed for continuous transportation over two hours in Rio and three hours in São Paulo. The integrated ticket system was an essential contribution to a system that already does not charge public elementary and high school students or senior citizens for public transportation. However, populations in peripheral neighborhoods are often subject to long intervals between buses, resulting in overcrowding, which is exacerbated by trip times that can last for hours. Even when there are additional forms of transportation, this does not change the situation, since these modes of transportation have either not been renovated for a long time, or have not been expanded as necessary. The largest subway system in Brazil, in São Paulo, continues to be unable to meet demand in spite of the support of the existing public bus system.

The unmet need for efficiency has contributed to the entire public transit system being heavily stigmatized. Many of the region's wealthy and social elite perceive the system as beneath them and refuse to use it, relying on expensive private helicopters to move about the city. The majority of Brazil's middle and working class reside in Rio's southern zones and some parts of northern zones of the city. The combination of social disparities and underfunded, disconnected public transit has heavily encouraged the use of automobiles. Automobile use experienced tremendous growth when tax exemptions and long-term automobile loans were issued in the 2000s. Streets and highways were also not adequately expanded to meet user needs, and transit corridors were quickly overtaken by vehicles, leading to unprecedented traffic jams.

Brazil's eagerness to fund massive global event infrastructure and simultaneous failure to manage and invest in comprehensive public transportation propelled thousands of protestors to gather in nearly every Brazilian state center in 2013. Given the critical public discontent against a 20-cent increase in ticket prices[2] first in São Paulo and then in other capitals,[3] revolts predictably ensued because of the significant impact on the lives of the poorer population. This indignation of the masses found a voice in the actions proposed by the Movimento Passe Livre (MPL [Free Fare Movement]). The MPL was founded in 2005 at the World Social Forum in Porto Alegre through the organization of different independent collectives who protested against the prior 2005 ticket price increases in many Brazilian cities. The MPL understands the importance of mobility to urban life and their goal was to implement free transportation.

By 2013, the movement had matured and recognized collective transportation as an issue that was linked with different urban problems and should be considered a fundamental right of all citizens. This movement then started to consider the importance of using the city as a means to win over the city itself. Rejecting the institutions established by the Charter of Cities,[4] such as City Councils,[5] the MPL decided to take to the streets for direct action as the main way for people to collectively take control over their own lives.

We must highlight that, due to its own nature, the MPL never acted as the "owner" of the demonstrations. MPL's decentralized organization is understood as the precedent for another form of association: horizontal association schemas where people relate in a more autonomous and collaborative way as opposed to the hierarchical structure commonly seen in labor unions or governments. They work in a decentralized way because they have flexibility built in to their organization, where each member may act autonomously so long as they are in accordance with the principles of the collective. The main achievement of MPL's June 2013 protests was the cancellation in ticket price hike for more than 100 cities in Brazil that year (MPL 2013).

Maricato (2013) suggested that whoever followed the urban dynamics in Brazil would not be surprised by the feeling of indignation that resulted in street resistance in June 2013. The initially isolated movement against increasing bus fares quickly gained popular momentum and led to a broader debate on how movements for housing and urban reform are related to these dynamics. In fact, several other urban social movements had already been self-organizing in various ways,[6] particularly in promoting demonstrations that were increasingly attracting media attention. This was true for the housing movements that came into being at the time of re-democratization and after the Federal Constitution was promulgated in 1988 by a new social movement, the Forum Nacional de Reforma Urbana (FNRU [National Forum for Urban Reform]). It exists to this date, with the purpose of fighting for an urban redistributive reform in Brazil and for the enforcement of rights assured by the nation's Magna Carta and by the specific articles pertaining to cities—the Charter of Cities, 2001.

Indeed, some of the most important urban rights achievements are the inclusion in the Federal Constitution of articles 182 and 183, addressing urban policy, and the publication of the Charter of Cities, 13 years later, which established the legal framework that enabled actions aimed at the democratization of the city. This helped create, with the PT (Workers' Party [Partido dos Trabalhadores]) in the presidency of the Republic:

- in 2003, the Ministry of Cities, and also the City Councils and the local, state, and federal Conference of Cities,
- in 2004, the National Housing Policy,
- in 2005, the first bill of law; as one of the consequences of this policy the first bill of law was created, triggered by public initiative, setting up the National System for Social Housing (SNHIS) and the National Fund for Social Housing (FNHIS), and
- in 2009, the Plano Nacional de Habitação (PLANHAB [National Housing Plan]), which guided the conduct of state and municipal plans.

However, these achievements were hindered by the interests of real estate capital markets. In addition, the ultimate failure of the National Housing Plan, a program that the housing movements had argued for in response to grassroots claims, undermined credibility for movements for a more egalitarian city. If the agenda of the National Movement for Urban Reform is systematically implemented, it may include several agendas derived from public sentiment to improve the lives of its citizens. Consequently, a few groups opted to continue to oppose urban gentrification through the occupation of abandoned buildings, participation in councils, and the organization of political events.

These movements did not play a leading role in the 2013 protests, although they did help pave the way for the demonstrations. However, many of the members found themselves in a curious position: protesting against the government that had provided the most significant social advances in the context of re-democratization.

Beyond 20 Cents

The increase in bus ticket prices happened while Brazilian cities were going through a major urban mobility crisis. PT administrations chose to implement policies that did not positively contribute to public infrastructure or quality of life but instead promoted consumption of manufactured goods. Instead of focusing on actionable elements of the public realm, particularly urban connectivity, the PT attempted to cultivate an urban fabric dependent on commodities and purchasing power. These development policies sold products like cars at very low rates but failed to create sufficient infrastructure for growing car use. Travel times increased significantly in the main metropolitan regions and spending two or more hours commuting became commonplace for the large majority of the urban population, particularly for the less affluent (Rodrigues 2013).

Since 1963, large Brazilian cities have grown according to a model that is highly exclusive and socially segregated. The extraordinary urban growth during the Military Dictatorship period worsened the situation, as new housing complexes were built in distant peripheral areas with poor connectivity to each other or urban cores. Kowarick (1979) studied the effects of this situation on people's lives and called it "urban spoliation." Although many social movements have emerged from this early period of dissatisfaction, public momentum and communicability were not enough to bring about large-scale social mobilization. It is important to remember that the repression period of the 1960s and 1970s silenced popular dissatisfactions due to fear of persecution and often violent political repression. Given that policies set in motion in the 1970s continued unabated for decades, understanding the catalytic forces of 2013 may offer insight into the interrelationships between public policy, public sentiment, and media and communication forms.

Once the PT had obtained the presidency, they created many programs that increased the consumption capability of different social groups who had been denied access to some achievements of modernity. Initially these policies seemed to increase redistribution, but they succumbed to conservative powers and populist strategies to remain in power (Cardoso and Lago 2015). Eventually, by 2007, construction work related to road recovery and urbanization of favelas were grouped under the title Programa de Aceleração do Crescimento (PAC [Growth Acceleration Program]). And in 2008, in the context of an American and European economic crisis, the federal government launched an influential program, the Programa Minha Casa Minha Vida (PMCMV [My Home, My Life Program]). The program's stated goal was to produce social housing units, as well as maintain economic growth through the civil construction industry and create jobs for the less-qualified workforce. The PMCMV was the first program in Brazilian history to promote subsidized housing for low- and very-low-income populations, but in an unfortunate twist it ended up significantly increasing the value of urbanized land and displacing citizens. Demand from international investors in real estate also began to accrue. The combination of local value increase and international attention led to the displacement of a significant number of people to less valued neighborhoods, leading to the acceleration of gentrification and social segregation (Cardoso and Lago 2015). The government's interventions that could have had a positive socio-spatial impact ended up significantly privatizing public space. The program became an example in which the state offered conditions so that a small group of entrepreneurs could profit immensely to the detriment of common good (Maricato 2013).

Even before PT came to power, there were changes in the Brazilian social structure that have slowly pointed towards cracks in the current social model. In the 1990s, the fact that youth from the favela were able to enter the best universities in Brazil made the headlines. Some of them continued their academic development, completing PhD programs, and were hired as university professors (Silva 2003). Re-democratization had contributed to major reassessment of the country's official historical narrative, leading not only to a revision of its heroes, but also to heavy politicization of its processes. The new educational policies promoted the ability to challenge the establishment. As a result, it appears obvious PT forcefully took power, even seeing as its administrations had put forward publicly empowering legislation for the lower classes over the last 12 years. Perhaps the greatest achievement was the increasing access to higher education (Rede 2014). If we add to this the high levels of dissatisfaction with urban living conditions;

the competitive and individualistic culture exacerbated by neoliberalism paradoxically rooted in the re-democratization process; and the ability to connect to and interact with the whole world through social networks, then we have the ingredients that set the basis for the acts of urban resistance triggered by the increase in urban transportation fares.

It is important to mention that Brazilians, because of a political history marked by authoritarianism and slavery, developed a culture that was supported by networks of family and friendship relations (kinship), instead of institutional ones. The economic consequences of globalization and neoliberalization contributed to significant changes in these cultural networks during the process of re-democratization of the 1980s. Neoliberal globalization weakened family and social support, giving rise to rampant individualism that social, political, and democratic institutions were not able to adapt to quickly enough.

With this background it is not surprising that, sooner or later, different sectors of the population would feel the need to make their voices heard. The straw that broke the camel's back was the increase of the bus ticket price right before the Confederations Cup, from which a significant part of the population was excluded because of ticket prices. The demonstrations then make a particular sense when the role of the government is, as we saw, complex, ambivalent, and ill-equipped for appropriate response times or channels.

"Journeys of June"

In spite of the accumulation of state-influenced gentrification and infrastructural negligence, the people of Brazil had not yet reached a critical tipping point before 2013. As mentioned before, Rio had a unique role in the 2013's demonstrations. Among the large construction projects carried out in the city of Rio starting in 2008 were the renovation of the Mario Filho Stadium, also known as Maracanã; the urban consortium Porto Maravilha, envisioned to revive the port area; and the design and construction of the Olympic Village and the construction of BRT, the Bus Rapid Transit system. This system focuses on important avenues and represents a network of buses that travel at higher than normal speeds. State actions that aimed at eliminating armed activity of drug dealers in Rio's favelas also originated at this time.

Real estate valuation in the city was consequently undergoing a considerable increase. From 2009 to 2012 the increase in the price of real estate was approximately 185%/m^2 (Maricato 2013). Faulhaber and Nacif (2013) state that these interventions emphasize the binomial center-periphery relation, because urban segregation was increased through housing policies that pushed poorer members of urban society to peripheral areas. This period of rapid growth and intense value growth resulted in an unprecedented number of families and persons being evicted and displaced. It is important to remember that, despite the visibility of many favelas in the wealthiest areas of the city, the territory of the metropolitan region of Rio de Janeiro is marked by large, sprawling peripheries with precarious services and infrastructure.

In this context, protesters in the demonstrations of 2013 stated that mobility was just one of many aspects that heavily impacted people's everyday lives and exacerbated the climate of inequality. The failure to invest in physical equity compounded feelings of social inequality on a material level (i.e. not having a service readily available) while watching foreign companies redirect investment from public infrastructure (social and material) toward massive speculative and ephemeral global projects such as the Olympics and World Cup. This interaction of local and global forces is critical to understanding the catalytic factors leading up to the June 2013 protests. We can say that this urban crisis is the result of a gradual process of increasingly denying people's right to the city, ultimately reaching a tipping point of discontent with the ticket price increase.

The initial use of heavy police force in the repression of protests failed to calm the situation and further compelled people to take to the streets. The swelling public frustration began to transcend issues of mobility or eviction and many other demands began being presented. Traditional social movements joined the new ones, swelling the ranks of polyphonic voices claiming their collective right to the city. These demonstrations were initially ignored by the national media, but as demonstrations continued to grow they began to receive national and international media coverage.

June 17, 2013 was a landmark moment: All major cities of Brazil (Rio de Janeiro, São Paulo, Brasília, and others) saw crowds take to the main streets of downtown areas. Larger protests occurred three days later. In Rio, over a million people (Almeida 2013) occupied President Vargas Avenue, a 3-kilometer-long and 60-meter-wide street. At that time, the Confederations Cup had already begun, and new demonstrations were promoted on upcoming match days. Police repression remained strong; not only were several activists arrested and protestors injured, but passers-by were hurt as well (Figures 2.1 and 2.2).[7]

On July 13, 2013, another protest occurred on the wedding day of the granddaughter of Jacob Barata, one of the most important businessmen of the transportation sector in Rio. On June 17, 2013, four companies won the 2010 bid for the right to operate all bus services, and one of them was owned by Jacob Barata.[8] Protests emerged in front of the church in downtown Rio where

FIGURE 2.1   A demonstration that took place on the last day of the 2013 Confederations Cup in Rio de Janeiro. Under the crying Brazilian flag, there is a complaint saying that the terror comes from the state.

Source: Luciana Andrade, 2013

FIGURE 2.2 On the same day, the police were taking care of Maracanã Stadium, where the last football game was going to happen. At the end of the day one of the various cases of the disproportional use of police force to repress the protests occurred.

Source: Luciana Andrade, 2013

the wedding took place, as well as in front of Copacabana Palace Hotel, where the wedding party was being held. Protestors intended to draw public attention to the fact that a few tycoons control public transport services in the city and state.

Growing public demonstrations led the authorities to fear new protests during the upcoming visit of the Pope on World Youth Day, July 23–28, 2013. Local and state authorities prepared additional repressive measures in anticipation. Because it was now forbidden to wear masks during protest, young supporters of black bloc tactics (wearing black clothing, scarves, sunglasses, ski masks, and other face-concealing items) took to the streets on July 22, 2013 showing their faces but also carrying the flag of anarchists, autonomists, and other movements. During the official welcome ceremony for the Pope, numerous police forces were deployed outside the State Government Palace (Palácio Guanabara), preventing the public from approaching the venue. At that time, a demonstrator was accused by the military police of throwing a Molotov cocktail at the riot police. It was later shown that the act had been perpetrated by a police officer in civilian clothes, to justify the use of repressive measures (for similar tactics by the authority, see also de La Llata Gonzalez, this volume).[9]

At this point the violent actions of the military police forces, previously seen as routine only in poor neighborhoods or in favelas, were now being consistently carried out at various demonstrations around the city. The only significant difference was in the bullets used: while in the streets they used rubber riot-control ballistics, in the favelas they used live ammunition. The military police and the public security agency deployed their increasingly abrasive conduct in an event that took place in Rocinha, one of Brazils' most famous favelas. The so-called Unidades de Polícia Pacificadoras (UPP [Peacekeeping Police Units]) had started to show their cruel nature:[10] public embarrassment, assault, and even murder of villagers. New protests were triggered by the disappearance of a builder named Amarildo, last seen being apprehended for questioning by UPP officers. Organized by Rocinha dwellers, one of these demonstrations met with another group of demonstrators organized by people of the middle class, close to the state governor's home, in Avenue Vieira Souto. "Where is Amarildo?" was the outcry heard in all marches that followed.[11]

The most significant pressure, however, was placed on the state governor, Sergio Cabral, who was being heavily criticized for a series of corruption cases involving the overbilling of public construction works, which demonstrated his disregard for oversight and commensurability of public money. On July 28, 2013, dozens of people camped near the governor's house in Leblon, one of Brazil's most expensive neighborhoods.[12] The movement was called Ocupa Cabral (Occupy Cabral). People from different social classes supported the movement by delivering supplies to the occupants. Furthermore, the governor's attempt to clear the area was ineffective as he had no legal backing.

Amidst a surging wave of unpopularity, Cabral resigned as governor on April 3, 2014. By resigning, Cabral managed to detach himself from deputy mayor Luiz Fernando Pezão, who later became the elected governor of Rio de Janeiro from 2015 to 2018. In spite of media attention of the demonstrations and the successful removal of Cabral, Pezão's reelection shows how complex and persistent Brazilian politics is. In this election, public education rose to critical importance. Basic and secondary education in Brazil is severely undervalued and teacher salaries are among the lowest in the world (OECD 2014). The lack of social or financial capital investment in education by the government represents a structural condition that helped galvanize critical social mobilization. Teachers are highly capable of political mobilization, which can be seen to a certain extent in the teaching methodologies used in the classroom. Classroom teaching practices helped motivate people to question politics that narrowly serve the interests of the hegemonic classes.

On August 8, 2013, teachers in state and local public schools initiated a strike in Rio. Demonstrations had been losing some of the early momentum they had in June and May, but when the teachers' demonstrations were vigorously repressed by the military police, people took to the streets in large numbers again. Collectives were expressing themselves in a variety of different ways in virtually all protests. Coletivo Projetação (Forecasting Collective) was a group that figured out how to link their media equipment through illegal connections to the state's electricity and data networks. They showed images and texts challenging the hegemonic discourse transmitted by public television channels. Media activists used the Internet to share their own alternative interpretations of what was being broadcast on the news. These practices allowed acts of police violence to be registered and mapped. Youths and teenagers used black bloc tactics to protect demonstrators from police hostility, and their graffiti left a mark in the city. Obviously, they were initially classified as vandals and troublemakers by police and media, and unfortunately by ordinary citizens as well; but after their support of the teachers' movement, they came to be respected by a significant share of the population. Predictably, however, numerous arrests of youth were made.

Protestors enjoyed the support of another collective: Advogados Ativistas (Activist Attorneys), a group of lawyers defending the right to gather and hold demonstrations. The Human Rights Commission of the Organization of Brazilian Attorneys (OAB) also participated. Health professionals set up emergency stations to care for those injured during the rallies. They offered first-aid to people affected by police aggression, aided those suffering from inhalation of tear gas and pepper spray, and helped to rapidly evacuate locations where intense clashes occurred.

Social Movements, Public Space, and Alter-Modernity?

The 2013 protests included youths from the middle class as well as those from lower classes who had improved their economic and cultural stature. The allegation that those movements would be unable to effectively represent their constituents was contradicted by how protests were organized—with an emphasis on the horizontality desired for the operation of the polis. We refer to the idea of symmetry between social and spatial relations that came to be when the bourgeois public sphere emerged. According to Sennett (1977), this would have been favored by the cultivation of diverse public spaces where people could work to promote egalitarian debate and where one's argument was respected because of its rhetoric and not according to social hierarchy. Here we go back to our initial question: how significantly do recent social movements contribute to promoting a structural transformation of sociopolitical production in Brazil?

The modern constitution of the public sphere came to be through the press's ability to disseminate ideas, which in addition to fostering information exchange also transformed news into a vital cultural product. Its power dynamics have always been at risk of serving the authorities, reaching only educated men in particular. The public sphere, therefore, was essentially constituted by bourgeois who benefited from the selective exchange of ideas that the press promoted for this social class (Habermas 1984). The development of capitalism broadened the access to knowledge for the average citizen, and in the 21st century we see a significant rupture in the control of information by capital. Even if global surveillance is a seemingly inevitable possibility, a prospect denounced by Edward Snowden in 2013 during his interviews with *The Guardian* and *Washington Post*, the Internet offers multiple possibilities and has brought together groups of people with common motivations frequently involving the radicalization of democracy. In addition to that, social networks have increased the circulation of non-hegemonic dominated thinking, allowing for diverse interpretations of global events. Meanwhile, access to education has also increased, especially in Brazil. This means that access to critical thinking is no longer restricted to spheres of realpolitik or academic areas.

Indeed, the increase of communication possibilities brought about by social media on the one hand has contributed to the escalation of conflict and "hate demonstrations" that bear a fascist nature (see Knierbein and Gabauer, this volume). Nevertheless, in spite of significant complications brought about by new communication possibilities, new modes of communication have played a fundamental counter-hegemonic role in disseminating humanitarian values, questioning prejudice, and bringing together different political groups in networks that are able to loosen the public space apathy. If the capacity of social media to propagate humanistic and collaborative ideals increases, the possibility of a crack in the capitalist system may also be found. The networks that have brought together progressive groups and communities in public space demonstrate the importance of different people recognizing the similarity in their struggles and reveals the power of collective desire to share assets to collectively combat their struggles. The combined power of both virtual and physical forms of contact, communication, and organization demonstrate that democracy in public space can, indeed, produce an alter-modernity (Hardt and Negri 2011).

Therefore, it seems to us that the trigger, the increase in bus ticket fares, was motivated by the emerging perspective of another world—more humane and collaborative—and to the perception of how inadequate the system is that promotes rampant individualism, concentrates wealth in the hands of a few, and does not offer adequate conditions for the production of civil life. The capacity to imagine the attainability of a more just world results from the rejection of representative democracy and the demand for a radicalization of the right of the multitude to exercise political power, thus rejecting hierarchies and collectively demanding equitable transformation.

In spite of the influx of conservativism after the 2014 elections, other demonstrations that reject hierarchy happened again in many cities, such as women protesting against the bill that intends to revoke the right to abortion in case of rape. Another demonstration is happening now in São Paulo as we complete the writing of this chapter at the end of November 2015: teenagers have occupied about 200 schools to reject a reform imposed by the state government that plans to close more than 90 schools. During the occupation, young people reinvented their curricula and proposed a self-managed form of curriculum development. It may be too early to tell whether or not the demonstrations that gained visibility in 2013, as well as the ones that came before and after them, represent the emergence of an alter-modernity. Nevertheless, it is possible to see that there is, as Hardt and Negri (2011, p.140) argue, "an intervention in the current power relations that tends to subvert the dominant power and to redirect forces in a certain direction," and perhaps furthermore, "a collective construction of the common."

Notes

1. The host cities were Rio de Janeiro (RJ), São Paulo (SP), Belo Horizonte (MG), Porto Alegre (RS), Brasília (DF), Cuiabá (MT), Curitiba (PR), Fortaleza (CE), Manaus (AM), Natal (RN), Recife (PE), and Salvador (BA).
2. A study conducted by the General Accounting Office of the City of Rio de Janeiro pointed to the need to reduce the ticket price from BRL$2.75 to BRL$2.50.
3. Demonstrations against the increase in transportation prices are not new in Brazil. But in Rio, the strategy of increasing ticket prices only on weekends as adopted by the Federation of Passenger Transportation Companies of the State of Rio de Janeiro (FETRANSPOR) have dampened the most expressive insurgences related to the high cost of mobility.
4. The Charter of Cities regulates the articles of the Federal Constitution that deals with urban questions.
5. The City Councils are representative and deliberative councils. As part of the Ministry of Cities they propose, implement, and assess the execution of urban policies (Article 1 of the decree 5,790, May 25, 2006).
6. "Social movements" are here defined as groups of people organized around a political action that make direct or indirect pressure on public institutions for a better redistribution of common goods.
7. It is worth mentioning that the protests triggered by the Free Pass Movement (MPL) changed over time. Demonstrations were used by conservative groups to push a nonpolitical anticorruption agenda, with the sole purpose of striking the Workers' Party in the federal government.
8. See newspaper *O Globo*, June 17, 2013.
9. The case was filed by the State Prosecutor's Office due to lack of evidence. This case was described by various media. See, for example, G1/O Globo, 2013. PM é acusada de infiltrar policial sem farda em protesto no Rio: relações públicas da polícia se diz 'enojado' com a acusação. Manifestação foi perto da sede do governo na segunda à noite. Rio de Janeiro: Organizações Globo [online], 24 July. Available from: http://g1.globo.com/rio-de-janeiro/noticia/2013/07/pm-e-acusada-de-infiltrar-policial-sem-farda-em-protesto-no-rio.html [Accessed 9 November 2015].
10. Since 2008, some favelas of Rio de Janeiro received Unidades de Polícia Pacificadoras (UPP [Peacekeeping Police Units]). The intention was to reduce the violence inside favelas, but for this the policemen work almost like they are in a war. The inhabitants, especially the young black men, are treated as if they are the enemies.
11. Amarildo was not found until May 2016.
12. One square meter costs BRL$23,493.00; approximately US$6,111.92 or 5,380.16 €. See O Estado de S. Paulo, 2015. Rio de Janeiro tem o metro quadrado mais caro do Brasil. *Estadão* [online], 15 May. Available from: http://economia.estadao.com.br/noticias/geral,rio-de-janeiro-tem-o-metro-quadrado-mais-caro-do-brasil,1688341 [Accessed 14 March 2017].

References

Almeida, F. P. M. de, 2013. Manifestação do dia 20 de junho no Rio de Janeiro: Dados, percepções no fino do espelho social [online]. *Blog da Boitempo*. Available from: http://blogdaboitempo.com.br/2013/08/22/manifestacao-do-dia-20-de-junho-no-rio-de-janeiro-dados-percepcoes-no-fino-do-espelho-social/ [Accessed 30 September 2015].

Cardoso, A. L. and Lago, L. (coord.), 2015. *Avaliação do Programa Minha Casa Minha Vida na Região Metropolitana do Rio de Janeiro: impactos urbanos e sociais.* Rio de Janeiro: Observatório das Metrópoles/IPPUR/UFRJ.

Faulhaber, L. and Nacif, C., 2013. Rio Maravilha: desapropriações, remoções e reforço do padrão de organização espacial centro-periferia. *Anais do Encontro Nacional da ANPUR.* Recife: ANPUR.

Habermas, J., 1984. *Mudança Estrutural da Esfera Pública.* Rio de Janeiro: Tempo Brasileiro.

Hardt, M. and Negri, A., 2011. *Commonwealth: El proyecto de una revolución del común.* 1st edition. Madrid: Akal.

Kowarick, L., 1979. *Espoliação Urbana.* Rio de Janeiro: Paz e Terra.

Maricato, E., 2013. É questão urbana, estúpido! *In*: Maricato, E., ed. *Cidades Rebeldes: Passe livre e as manifestações que tomaram as ruas do Brasil.* São Paulo: Boitempo/Carta Maior, 19–26.

Movimento Passe Livre, 2013. Não começou em Salvador, não vai terminar em São Paulo. *In*: E. Maricato, ed. *Cidades Rebeldes: Passe livre e as manifestações que tomaram as ruas do Brasil.* São Paulo: Boitempo/Carta Maior, 13–18.

OECD, 2014. *Education at a Glance 2014.* Paris: Organisation for Economic Cooperation and Development.

Rede, A., 2014. Número de negros em universidades brasileiras cresceu 230% na última década [online]. *Portal Fórum.* Available from: www.revistaforum.com.br/2014/11/23/numero-de-negros-em-universidades-brasileiras-cresceu-230-na-ultima-decada/ [Accessed 1 December 2015].

Rodrigues, J. M., 2013. Transformações urbanas e a crise da mobilidade urbana no Brasil: hipóteses sobre o caso do Rio de Janeiro no contexto dos megaeventos. *e-metropolis*, 14, 38–50.

Sennett, R., 1977. *The Fall of Public Man.* New York: Knopf.

Silva, J., 2003. *Porque uns e não outros? Caminhada de jovens pobres para a universidade.* Rio de Janeiro: 7Letras.

3

SAN FRANCISCO'S TECH-LED GENTRIFICATION

Public Space, Protest, and the Urban Commons

Manissa M. Maharawal

In the past few years San Francisco has experienced rapid gentrification amidst what is locally referred to as "tech boom 2.0." In turn, a diverse movement has developed to contest the processes of gentrification, privatization, enclosure, and displacement that are occurring in the city. In this chapter I analyze two struggles over public space: an altercation over a soccer field and the blockade of tech shuttle buses. Through these cases, I analyze how San Francisco residents have contested processes of privatization, enclosure, and exclusion in and through struggles over public space. In doing so I argue that such struggles are inherently linked to the colonizing logics of tech capital and that the forms of resistance it engenders can be understood as a fight for the maintenance of an urban commons. In the first section I give an analysis of the political economic conditions that form the backdrop to these struggles. I then describe how tactics of interruption were used in the cases of "Google bus blockades" and the altercation at Mission Playground to protect the urban commons. I end with an analysis of these struggles through the concepts of "implicit privatization" and enclosure, and discuss how current patterns of displacement and dispossession in San Francisco imbricate with longer histories of settler colonialism.

Eviction Epidemic: San Francisco's Tech Boom 2.0

Currently in San Francisco conflicts over public space are happening within the context of what is locally referred to as "tech boom 2.0," a venture-capital-infused bubble of technological "innovation" that has made the city one of *the premier* sites of urban capitalist speculation in the United States. Over the past few years, struggles over gentrification and public space have become increasingly charged as the city rapidly becomes more expensive and unaffordable to long-term residents, particularly for the city's Black and Latino residents and those in lower socioeconomic brackets (Truong 2015). The present tech boom, much like the previous tech bubble in the 1990s, has resulted in a rapid influx of capital into the city as valuations of private tech companies have reached unprecedented levels (Dee 2015). Investors and hedge funds have flooded money into new startups while more established companies, such as Facebook, Apple, and Google, continue to outperform other stocks with a collective net worth of approximately $1.6 trillion (La Monica 2015, Schaefer 2015, Detar 2015). At the same time newer companies, often based in a "sharing economy" model, such as Uber and Airbnb, continue to grow rapidly.

In this context of tech-led speculative capitalism (Harvey 1989), the industry has become San Francisco's newest gold rush. Ambitious young professionals increasingly choose tech careers over more "traditional" high-powered and high-income career paths in the finance sector (Alden 2013). The influx of tech capital and wealthy tech workers has in turn precipitated spectacular increases in rental and housing prices throughout the region with some of the largest increases in the country (Legislative Analyst's Office 2015). Moreover, the regional economy increasingly acts as a gravitational force on tech workers around the world, pulling in waves of new cohorts. As an acquaintance who moved from Budapest to San Francisco in order to land a job in the technology industry explained to me, "If you want to make it in tech you *must* be in San Francisco . . . after all that is where the money is".

Statistics on urban income inequality highlight the concentration of capital and inequality in the Bay Area. By almost any measure, San Francisco ranks as one of the most unequal places in the United States (Frank 2014). A 2014 Brookings Institute report found that San Francisco has one of the largest wealth gaps and the most rapidly increasing wealth gap nationwide.[1] Similarly, a report by the Human Services Agency of San Francisco found the city's Gini coefficient to be .523, well below the national average of .45 and on par with highly unequal countries (Knight 2014, Human Services Agency of San Francisco 2012).

Another indicator of San Francisco's transformation is the rapid loss of its Black and Latino populations and changing racial makeup (Truong 2015). While the general population of the city is growing, San Francisco's Black population, which was decimated by urban redevelopment and slum clearance programs in the 1960s, has been decreased by half since 1970 from 13% to 6% of the city's total population (Anti-Eviction Mapping Project n.d. a). In addition, San Francisco's Mission District (a historically Latino neighborhood) has experienced a 27% decrease in its Latino population from 2009 to 2013 (Budget and Legislative Analyst's Office 2015, see also Truong 2015).

One of the effects of the influx of tech capital into the region has been the effect on real estate. The city boasts the second highest average home sale prices in the country and has the most expensive rental market in the country, with the median two-bedroom apartment renting at $5,000 a month in 2015 (Elsen 2015). As urban real estate markets across the United States have increasingly taken up the function of absorbing or "mopping up" international capital and surplus value in the wake of the financial crisis in 2007 and 2008 (Harvey 2012), San Francisco stands out as a city where such "absorption" has precipitated a social and political crisis.

This crisis has taken the form of what housing advocates call an "eviction epidemic" (Maharawal, personal field notes, May 2014), as large numbers of long-term, rent-stabilized tenants are evicted. According to a report by the San Francisco Anti-Displacement Coalition (SFADC) evictions have steadily increased and are higher than at any point in the past decade, with a 54.7% increase in 2014. In addition such "official" counts are likely two or three times lower than the actual number of evictions taking place in the city, often through unofficial means (SFADC 2015). The city's homeless population has also risen with the percentage of older and severely unwell homeless people growing the most (Fagan and Knight 2015). In their 2014 annual report San Francisco's Coalition on Homelessness wrote: "In the midst of the housing crisis, poor people are getting hit from all sides—many are becoming homeless, and those who are homeless are facing unprecedented criminalization efforts and diminished resources" (COH 2014, p. 3). Indeed there are many connections between the city's rapid gentrification, its housing crisis, homeless population, and new anti-homeless policies.[2]

But while homelessness and evictions increase, the tech boom has also precipitated a building boom in the city with hundreds of new, almost all "market-rate" developments built in the past few years (Paragon Real Estate Group Report 2015). While the city and developers claim that the

FIGURE 3.1 "Comunidad no Comodidad" banner hung on Mission and 16th Street

Source: Manissa M. Maharawal

construction of more market-rate housing units will alleviate the housing crisis in San Francisco, activists have been sharply critical of this market-rate building boom. Particularly, they argue that building market-rate housing often precipitates speculative increases in property values in the immediate vicinity, effectively creating an upward pressure on rents, spurring more evictions and catalyzing the loss of affordable housing stock in the city. To alleviate the city's affordable housing crisis they argue that low-income housing and not just market-rate housing must be built.

These issues have been exceptionally heated in the city's Mission District, a traditionally low-income Latino/a neighborhood that has been hit particularly hard (see Figure 3.1). It is therefore not surprising that many of the key political struggles, protest actions, and everyday altercations around these issues have occurred here, including the incidents I outline here: the Google bus blockades and an altercation over the use of the Mission Playground.

"Conquistador Transportation": The Google Bus Blockades

In November 2013 in San Francisco's Mission District a group of 40 protestors identifying themselves as the "San Francisco Displacement and Neighborhood Impact Agency" unfurled banners and blocked a large "Google bus" from continuing on its way. The first in a series of "Google bus blockades" that occurred over the next few years, the bus was one of many contracted by technology companies to pick up their employees in San Francisco and take them to their jobs in Silicon Valley south of the city. The protest, organized by the Heart of the City collective, aimed to bring attention to tech-led gentrification and the city government's collusion in this process. Blocking the bus for 30 minutes with signs that read "Privatization of Public Infrastructure!" protestors also issued mock citations to the bus for its use of the public MUNI[3] bus stop and handed out flyers alleging that technology companies now owed over $1 billion to the city in fines; money they argued could be used to refurbish MUNI or build affordable housing (Maharawal 2014).

This first bus blockade action soon made national and international headlines as a symbol of the gentrification and displacement caused by the tech industry in the city (Solnit 2013). In response city officials quickly issued information about a "Commuter Shuttle Policy and Pilot Program" that put to an end the informal arrangement between tech companies and the city by charging $1 per stop to the tech buses for their use of the public MUNI stops.[4] However, this plan did not alleviate the concerns of housing advocates who claimed that the city was sidestepping the important issues of displacement and eviction along the tech shuttle routes. Indeed, mapping evictions along the tech shuttle routes, the Anti-Eviction Mapping Project found that 69% of evictions in the city occurred within four blocks of a tech shuttle stop (Anti-Eviction Mapping Project n.d. c). This research corroborated earlier findings that rental prices within a five-block radius of Google bus stops increased at a higher rate (Goldman 2013). The city's "Commuter Shuttle Policy and Pilot Program" was contentious and criticized because it not only ignored this socio-spatial impact of these new privatized transportation infrastructures but also because it effectively, through charging a nominal fee, legalized the private use of public bus stops, thereby de facto sanctioning the creation of a private corporate regional transportation system.

FIGURE 3.2 Senior and Disability Action Bus Blockade, August 1, 2014

Source: Manissa M. Maharawal

In subsequent bus blockades, Apple, Facebook, and Microsoft buses were also blocked to protest both specific evictions and the general "takeover" of the city by the tech industry. Using activism in public space, the bus blockades were a disruptive protest tactic with a dual function: that of materially interrupting tech employees on their way to work, and also symbolically bringing attention to the *social* process of the neoliberal urban restructuring (Brenner and Theodore 2005) that the buses were part of and that activists were attempting to stop.

The protests also made visible and gave articulation to the intense feelings of anger and disempowerment of those who feel increasingly excluded from the city more broadly as they provided daily reminders of the exclusion of non-tech employee residents from these new private corporate infrastructures. In public meetings at City Hall about the tech shuttle pilot program, handicapped residents spoke about how the tech shuttles dangerously swerved in and out of the bus stops while they were being picked up and others complained about how the tech shuttle buses slowed down the public buses. A common refrain from residents in the city's Mission District was the sense that the technology industry was taking over the city's public spaces, building exclusionary private transportation infrastructures and flouting laws while doing so. In the words of Roberto Hernandez, a long-time Mission activist, the buses are a kind of "conquistador transportation." This reference to longer histories of dispossession and colonialism in which conquering Spanish or Portuguese soldiers colonized much of the Americas during the 16th and 17th centuries equates the private infrastructure of the buses with a kind of colonialism and enclosure.

Dispossession at the Mission Playground

In the midst of the protests about the tech shuttle buses in early October 2014 a video titled "Mission Playground Is Not for Sale" (Mission Creek Video 2014) was posted on YouTube. The four-and-a-half-minute video, which went viral, shows an altercation between mostly Spanish-speaking youth and tech employees at the Mission Playground soccer field at 19th Street and Valencia Street. Divisions of race, class, and privilege and struggles over the changes in the neighborhood are all touched upon as the tech employees, who have obtained a permit for the field, attempt to kick the youth, off it. In response, and refusing to leave, the youth argue that the field has "always" been used for seven-on-seven pickup games.

The video has many poignant moments, one in which the main youth, Kai says, "just because you got money [and] you can pay for the field doesn't mean you can book it and take over." In response the tech employees, most of them youngish white men, imply that the youth don't understand the legitimacy that their permit grants, saying: "You guys understand this? Its pretty simple, we paid $27 to reserve the field for an hour . . . read it . . . read it!" Kai answers, "I know how to read . . . I also know that this field has always been for pickup where you play seven on seven." A few moments later Kai explicitly highlights how the tech employees are violating informal norms of the space when he asks: "How long have you been in the neighborhood bro?" To which a voice off-screen is heard saying: "Who gives a shit . . . who cares about the neighborhood?" while one tech employee replies "over a year." Kai then replies "Oh over a *year*! Over a *year*! . . . Listen I was born and raised here for 20 years . . . my whole life."

The video ends inconclusively shortly thereafter but to many its meaning was immediately legible.[5] As community groups and politicians got involved the conflict was transformed from a momentary altercation in public space into a media storm in the public sphere, and ultimately into a political debate about public space, dispossession, and belonging in the city.

About a week after the incident, the Latino Democratic Club held a protest on the steps of City Hall. Among people holding signs reading "Mission Playground Not for Sale," here the president of the Democratic Club, Edwin Lindo, said: "We were outraged that our youth were being pushed off their *ancestral* playground where they grew up" (see Figure 3.3). His use of the word "ancestral" was a deliberate reference to the way that many of the Mission's Latino/a residents felt about the process of gentrification in their neighborhood: that it was analogous to historic processes of colonialism.

At the protest one of the youth from the video, 15-year-old Hector Gomez, also spoke, explaining how the Mission Field was a safe place for him to be where his family didn't have to worry, emphasizing that it wasn't fair for him to be kicked out of this space, one he had known all his life. He ended with the plea: "I mean where else can I *be* in the neighborhood?" His comments made it clear that in the context of the rapid gentrification of the Mission neighborhood the field was not just a space for recreation but also a vital space of *belonging* in the midst of urban change.

This particular conflict over the use of public fields, and the permitting system that has facilitated their privatization, is the continuation of a citywide struggle over the charging of fees and

FIGURE 3.3   "No Eviction in the Mission" sign, October 4, 2014

Source: Manissa M. Maharawal

generating of revenue at San Francisco's parks and public spaces. While the youth maintained that seven-on-seven pickup play was the norm at the Mission Field—and it mostly was—it was also true that during "peak hours" the field was rented by the hour by the San Francisco Recreation and Parks Department (SFRP). Through the SFRP permitting system, San Francisco residents book occasional and advance use of public spaces for a $27 per hour fee.[6] Introduced in 2011, the shift to this pay-to-play model (at particular places and times) was met with opposition by residents and community groups who saw it as a move away from treating parks and open spaces as vital public assets, maintained with public tax revenue, towards treating public space in the city as privatized goods that are dependent on wealthy donors, pay-to-play, and licensing revenue, and are increasingly leased to private organizations.[7]

At the Mission Field the implementation of pay-to-play fees during "peak hours" was first introduced after the field's renovation from concrete to artificial turf in 2012. At that time it drew protests from its mostly Latino, Spanish-speaking users and a petition went around asking the city to change the permitting policy. People were particularly upset about the field being rented to for-profit groups like SF Pickup Soccer,[8] which used the app Meetup and charged people $5 to $10 to reserve spots for pickup games (McElroy 2014). Indeed many of the field's Latino users were unaware or unclear about the permitting policy,[9] confused as to how it was enacted, and upset that people—most of them white, young, affluent, corporate tech employees—could show up and kick them off the field because they had paid to reserve it or used an app to gain access to the space.[10] In short, what the video and the subsequent protests made clear was that the permitting system was working to dispossess one community from the space, while granting access to another, a process that was (momentarily) disrupted when a few youth filmed themselves refusing to leave the field.

Settler Colonialism, Pseudo-Privatization, and the Urban Commons

Threading through the incidents described here are narratives of belonging that explicitly draw connections between gentrification and histories of settler colonialism. Whether this is Roberto Hernandez's "conquistador transportation" comment or Edwin Lindo calling the Mission Playground stolen "ancestral" land, Latino residents in the Mission District often interpreted what was happening to their neighborhood through the lens of colonial histories. Understanding settler colonialism as a "structure, not an event" (Wolfe 1999, p. 12, see also Rose 2001) that is grounded in expropriative sets of property relations, I contend that by using this lens residents were doing more than constructing a simple dichotomy between "natives" and "settlers." Rather, to Edwin Lindo, Roberto Hernandez, and other Mission residents, gentrification and settler colonialism are comingled and similar historical projects.

By taking this claim seriously and thinking these projects together we can understand their shared logic as part of a larger system of capitalist dispossession, deeply intertwined with primitive accumulation and "the bloody violence of expropriating the commons and exploiting the commoners" (Sharma and Wright 2008, p. 132). As the testimonies of the youth soccer players attest, their struggle was about more than the new paid permitting system, but rather about being dispossessed of a community space that they thought of as "another home." For these youths the Mission Playground functions as an *urban commons* in which their shared practices created and reproduced the space as collective and common good.

In contrast to "public space" which is (among other things) a legal category that stands in relation to "private" space, the concept of the "commons" explicitly refers to social practice (Susser and Tonnelat 2013, Linebaugh 2009, Blackmar 2006). According to Gidwani and Baviskar (2001), the commons can be understood as "a variegated form of social wealth . . .

governed by emergent custom and constantly negotiating, rebuffing and evading the fixity of law" (p. 42, cited Thompson 1993). As such, it is dependent on the people and practices of "commoning" through which it is produced, reproduced, and maintained (Linebaugh 2009, Gidwani and Baviskar 2011, Siefkes 2009). Understood this way, it is clear that the struggles outlined here were not just for legally defined public space but for spaces that are held and produced *in common* through social practices of commoning practiced for and by an existing community.

In contrast to the youth practice of using the field as an urban commons (for example through seven-on-seven pickup as a way of sharing access to the field with anyone who wished to play), the pay-to-play model, which turns the field into a commodity, operates through colonial logics of enclosure and cultural erasure. As Erin McElroy, of the Anti-Eviction Mapping Project, writes: "Instead of getting to know the existing culture of the seven-on-seven pickup games in the park and slowly integrating, these newly arrived settlers seek to bypass existing culture altogether, claiming sovereignty through access to government—and an app" (McElroy 2014). One of the principles of common rights is that they are embedded in particulars and local knowledge (Sharma and Wright 2008). In the case of the Mission Playground, the actions of neighborhood youth and the subsequent public outcry can be read as a political claim for precisely such a kind of common rights.

It is no coincidence that tech capital and tech-led gentrification had come into conflict with such common rights and existing urban commons. Tech startup culture has flourished through strategies of commodifying and enclosing that which was previously free and commonly and publicly accessible (Wong 2014). Following this logic, tech-led gentrification has created ever more exclusionary public spaces—effectively enclosing the urban commons. In turn these public spaces, whether playing fields or bus routes, have become crucial spaces for politics of dissent and urban resistance (Low and Smith 2005, Mitchell 2003). Disruptive action in these public spaces—such as refusing to leave a field or blocking a bus—have become popular "repertoires of contention" (Tarrow 1993) through which residents reclaim these spaces, while also provoking larger public conversations about dispossession in the city (see Figure 3.4). These conflicts and protests, which occurred within the context of a growing anti-eviction and housing rights movement, should thus be read as part of broader *class struggles* through which San Francisco residents seek to reclaim their "right to the city" (Lefebvre 1996, Purcell 2002, Mitchell 2003, Harvey 2012). In both of the incidents outlined here, protestors framed their discontent using language in which they accused the city of being "for sale" through practices of privatization operating through the nexus of tech capital and governmental collusion. While these two incidents became flashpoints, they did not occur in isolation. Later the same year the Anti-Eviction Mapping Project released a map that outlined numerous other examples of the "Loss of Public Space" ranging from the rental of City Hall and Civic Center Plaza to companies such as SalesForce for conferences and events to efforts to "clean up" public spaces such as the Powell Street BART station by removing homeless people (Anti-Eviction Mapping Project n.d. b) While the enclosure of public space highlighted by the Anti-Eviction Mapping Project is not unique to San Francisco but indicative of a neoliberal entrepreneurialism model of urban governance that privileges the stimulation of corporate investment and real estate development above all other interests (Brash 2011), it does have unique aspects. These particularities relate to the political economy of the technology industry in the region and its use of San Francisco as the testing ground for new privatizing technologies—often at the margins of legality. These new privatizing technologies include apps for gaining access to pickup soccer games and the construction of private corporate infrastructures such as the Google buses for certain residents at the exclusion of others.

FIGURE 3.4 "Smash Gentrification" banner, October 4, 2014

Source: Manissa M. Maharawal

It is in this context that activism carried out in public space has become the privileged means of resisting the disenfranchisement of working and middle-income residents of the city. Tech-led hyper-gentrification in San Francisco has transformed previously public or noncommodified spaces into *implicitly privatized* spaces. I am using the term "implicitly privatized" in a similar vein to Don Mitchell's definition of spaces "that are formally owned by the state, by the public, but that are subject to control and regulation by private interests" (1995, p. 153). Both the private bus infrastructure and encroachment on Mission Playground can be understood as versions of this form of implicit privatization, resembling Mitchell's case of sidewalks governed by Business Improvement Districts or conservatories. In the San Francisco Bay Area, however, such implicit privatizations are part of a wider tech strategy for capital accumulation that, using the city as a testing ground, pushes the limits of city regulation and public tolerance over how the tech industry can "disrupt" various parts of everyday life, from housing to transportation. These services, many of them app-based and part of the booming "sharing economy," are often openly antagonistic to regulation by the government, which it considers "slow, staffed by mediocrities, ridden with obsolete rules and inefficiencies" (Packer 2013).

The parking apps MonkeyParking, Sweetch and ParkModo, which all facilitated people bidding for and selling their public parking spots, are examples of explicit attempts to privatize public space for profit (Streitfeld 2015). While deemed illegal by city officials (Weise 2014), they represent an example of implicit private space in which private interests do not *de jure* control public space, but rather private companies mitigate access to such spaces and therefore have the potential to *de facto* control it. What is happening in San Francisco is not necessarily outright privatization in the traditional sense, but rather a struggle over the practices that constitute an urban commons or those which commodify space through a process of enclosure. Here the Mission Playground incident and the Google bus blockades were protests against the privatization of public space and struggles against a particular form of tech control over these spaces that is inherently exclusionary. As one resident who testified against the city's tech-bus plan said to me: "Tech companies want to do whatever they want and change everything . . . as if the rest of us aren't here!" Such comments correctly identify a process of enclosure, one that Rebecca Solnit described during the first tech boom of the 1990s, as the city "delivered vacant" (Solnit 2000) to the industry.

Through transforming mundane objects such as buses and permits into visible and pressing political issues, the Google bus protests and the Mission Playground incident achieved important disruptions of the implicit privatization and enclosure of space in San Francisco. In doing so the urban commons were defended, and something akin to what Jeff Hou describes as "insurgent public space" that is "brought into being by those who appropriate, reclaim or occupy to express their opinions" (Hou 2012, p. 92) was created. By creating such insurgent spaces to contest processes of enclosure, residents also politicized and made visible the rapid gentrification and the attendant "eviction epidemic" in the city and made connections between spatial transformations, economic dispossession and personalized stories of displacement and humiliation. In doing so they contributed to the broader housing movement in the city while also countering "the mirror of gentrification" (Schulman 2012), in which gentrification is normalized as an inevitable process in which "only the gentrified get their stories told in mass ways" (Schulman 2012, p. 28).

Coda: For Alejandro Nieto

On March 21, 2014, Alejandro Nieto, a 28-year-old City College student who had grown up in the Mission, was shot and killed by the San Francisco Police Department (SFPD) in Bernal Heights Park. His friends told the media that he often went up Bernal Hill, with its wind-swept views of the city, when he needed some space to think. It was there that someone called 911, reporting him as a "suspicious person" in the park "acting erratically" (Ho 2014). In the wake of his death, feelings of anger and loss reverberated through the Mission and critical conversations were had about the ways in which the city's intense gentrification and the attendant transformation of its public spaces caused people of color to be criminalized for merely *being* in public space. At a march in his honor some held signs that read "Gentrification = Police Brutality" and as people grieved, they spoke about how Nieto had been killed by the police *and* gentrification (see Figure 3.5).

I write about Alejandro Nieto here to highlight the deadly intensity of struggles over public space in San Francisco. His death is a reminder that the "colonial" logic of gentrification is not merely rhetorical but often enacted with lethal force on the bodies of Mission residents, destroying communities and homes through displacement, and ending life with police gunfire.

But if the violence of gentrification in San Francisco is unrelenting, so too are the protests and everyday acts of resistance which contest it. Protests, rallies, packed city hall meetings, and direct actions occur regularly—sometimes daily. These protests draw connections between inequality, wealth and evictions, and homelessness, and police violence, city policy, and histories of colonialism. I am deeply indebted to these struggles for my analysis here, which is in many ways the product of my participation in these protests.

FIGURE 3.5 Street Memorial for Alejandro Nieto outside Red Poppy Art House

Source: Manissa M. Maharawal

Acknowledgement

Funding for the research and writing for this contribution was provided by the Wenner–Gren Foundation for Anthropological Research and the American Council for Learned Societies.

Notes

1. Using American Community Survey data, the 2014 report analyzed nationwide 95/20 ratios, finding that San Francisco ranked second with a ratio of 16.6, had the largest increase in its ratio from 2007–2012 and the largest increase nationwide for its 95th percentile households (Berube 2014).
2. Some of these anti-homeless policies include the "cleaning up" of the Powell Street BART station of homeless people (Anti-Eviction Mapping Project, n.d.) and the hosing down of streets that homeless people slept on especially in the Mid-Market area (Hayoun 2014).
3. MUNI is the colloquial shorthand for San Francisco Municipal Railway, a public transportation network consisting of buses, light rail, and trolleys. It has the seventh largest ridership in the country and is one of the slowest and most expensive to operate. For more information see American Public Transportation Association reports available at www.apta.com/resources/statistics/Pages/RidershipArchives.aspx [Accessed 10 March 2017].
4. The full report from the San Francisco Municipal Transport Authority is available at www.sfmta.com/sites/default/files/agendaitems/1-21-14%20Item%2014%20Private%20Commuter%20Shuttle%20policy.pdf [Accessed 10 March 2017].
5. It was later reported that the two groups resolved the conflict by splitting the field.
6. To be eligible for resident fees proof of identification and proof of residency is required. In 2014 the fee was increased to $29.

7. This shift required city officials to update the primary policy document for Open Space in the Recreation and Open Space Element (ROSE) of the of the city's General Plan (Jones 2011).
8. As reported in Mission Local: "SF Pickup Soccer is an organizer which has contracted with us to utilize the site on Tuesdays from 7 to 9 p.m. to encourage the community to get involved and play soccer," says Connie Chan, deputy policy director for the parks department. SF Pickup Soccer uses a mobile app to let users sign up in advance to play soccer on available fields. "It is an experiment with new mobile app technology," says Chan (Hoffman 2014).
9. A contributing factor is that the signs about policies governing the field are exclusively in English.
10. The field is no longer rented to SF Pickup Soccer.

References

Alden, W., 2013. For a High-Powered Career, It's Finance vs. Tech [online]. *DealBook*. Available from: http://dealbook.nytimes.com/2013/10/30/for-a-high-powered-career-its-finance-vs-tech/ [Accessed 13 February 2016].

Anti-Eviction Mapping Project, n.d. a. Loss of Black Population, Bay Area [online]. *Anti-Eviction Mapping Project*. Available from: www.antievictionmap.com/demographic-maps#/loss-of-black-population-bay-area/ [Accessed 13 February 2016].

Anti-Eviction Mapping Project, n.d. b. San Francisco for Sale [online]. *Anti-Eviction Mapping Project*. Available from: www.antievictionmappingproject.net/publicspace.html#0 [Accessed 13 February 2016].

Anti-Eviction Mapping Project, n.d. c. Tech Bus Stops and No-Fault Evictions [online]. *Anti-Eviction Mapping Project*. Available from: http://www.antievictionmap.com/tech-bus-stops-and-no-fault-evictions/ [Accessed 13 February 2016].

Berube, A., 2014. All Cities Are Not Created Unequal [online]. *The Brookings Institution*. Available from: www.brookings.edu/research/papers/2014/02/cities-unequal-berube [Accessed 15 September 2015].

Blackmar, E., 2006. Appropriating "The Commons": The Tragedy of Property Right Discourse. *In*: S. Low and N. Smith, eds. *The Politics of Public Space*. New York: Routledge, 49–80.

Brash, J., 2011. *Bloomberg's New York: Class and Governance in the Luxury City*. Athens, GA: University of Georgia Press.

Brenner, N. and Theodore, N., 2005. Neoliberalism and the Urban Condition. *City*, 9 (1), 101–107.

Budget and Legislative Analyst's Office, 2015. *Displacement in the Mission District*. San Francisco, CA: City and County of San Francisco, Board of Supervisors, Policy Analysis.

Coalition on Homelessness, 2014. *Building Power Fighting Back: Annual Report 2014*. San Francisco, CA. Available from: http://www.cohsf.org/wp-content/uploads/2014/12/COH2014Report.pdf [Accessed 10 March 2017].

Dee, S., 2015. Why You Shouldn't Lose Sleep Over the Tech Boom [online]. *Forbes*. Available from: www.forbes.com/sites/greatspeculations/2015/08/13/why-you-shouldnt-lose-sleep-over-the-tech-boom/ [Accessed 13 February 2016].

Detar, J., 2015. Facebook, Google Lead 3 Top-Rated Big-Cap Internets [online]. *Investor's Business Daily*. Available from: www.investors.com/stock-lists/facebook-google-netease-big-cap-leaders-list/ [Accessed 13 February 2016].

Elsen, T., 2015. The Median Rent for an SF Two-Bedroom Hits $5,000/Month [online]. *Curbed SF*. Available from: http://sf.curbed.com/archives/2015/10/09/the_median_rent_for_an_sf_twobedroom_hits_5000month.php [Accessed 13 February 2016].

Fagan, K. and Knight, H., 2015. S.F. Homeless Population Getting Sicker, Older, Survey Says [online]. *SFGate*. Available from: www.sfgate.com/bayarea/article/S-F-homeless-population-getting-sicker-older-6387308.php [Accessed 13 February 2016].

Frank, R., 2014. Cities with the Most Millionaires Per Capita [online]. *CNBC*. Available from: www.cnbc.com/2014/07/22/cities-with-the-most-millionaires-per-capita.html [Accessed 13 February 2016].

Gidwani, V. and Baviskar A., 2011. Urban Commons. *Economic and Political Weekly*, 46 (50), 42–43.

Goldman, A., 2014. The "Google Shuttle Effect": Gentrification and San Francisco's Dot Com Boom 2.0. Master's thesis, University of California, Berkeley.

Harvey, D., 1989. From Managerialism to Entrepreneurialism: The Transformation in Urban Governance in Late Capitalism. *Geografiska Annaler: Series B, Human Geography*, 71 (1), 3–17.

Harvey, D., 2012. *Rebel Cities: From the Right to the City to the Urban Revolution*. New York: Verso.

Hayoun, M., 2014. Activists Say San Francisco Trying to Wash Away the Homeless [online]. Available from: http://america.aljazeera.com/articles/2014/2/18/san-francisco-tensionbetweenhomelessandsecond techboomers.html [Accessed 13 February 2016].

Ho, V., 2014. Man Killed by S.F. Police Was "Inspiration" But Had Troubles [online]. *SFGate*. Available from: www.sfgate.com/crime/article/Man-killed-by-S-F-police-was-inspiration-but-5344159.php [Accessed 24 January 2016].

Hoffman, A., 2014. Petitioner fights pay-to-play in Mission Soccer. *Mission Local*. Available from: http://missionlocal.org/2012/10/petitioner-fights-pay-to-play-in-mission-soccer/ [Accessed 10 March 2017].

Hou, J., 2012. Making Public, Beyond Public Space. *In*: R. Shiffman, R. Bell, L. J. Brown, and L. Elizabeth, eds. *Beyond Zuccotti Park: Freedom of Assembly and the Occupation of Public Space*. Oakland, CA: New Village Press, 89–98.

Human Services Agency of San Francisco, 2012. *Demographic and Poverty Trends in San Francisco*. San Francisco, CA. Available from: http://www.sfhsa.org/asset/ReportsDataResources/HSABrownBag101812v4. pdf [Accessed 10 March 2017].

Jones, S., 2011. Parks Inc. *48 Hills,* 12 July 2011. Available from: http://48hills.org/sfbgarchive/2011/07/12/parks-inc/ [Accessed 10 March 2012]

Knight, H., 2014. Income Inequality on Par with Developing Nations [online]. *SFGate*. Available from: www.sfgate.com/bayarea/article/Income-inequality-on-par-with-developing-nations-5486434.php [Accessed 15 September 2015].

LaMonica, P. R., 2015. Facebook Now Worth More Than Walmart [online]. *CNNMoney*. Available from: http://money.cnn.com/2015/06/23/investing/facebook-walmart-market-value/index.html [Accessed 13 February 2016].

Lefebvre, H., 1996. *Writings on Cities*. 1st edition. Cambridge, MA, USA: Wiley-Blackwell.

Legislative Analyst's Office, 2015. *California's High Housing Costs: Causes and Consequences*. Sacramento, CA: Legislative Analyst's Office.

Linebaugh, P., 2009. *Magna Carta Manifesto: Liberties and Commons for All*. Berkeley: University Press Group Ltd.

Low, S. and Smith, N., eds., 2005. *The Politics of Public Space*. New York: Routledge.

Maharawal, M., 2014. Protest of Gentrification and Eviction Technologies in San Francisco. *Progressive Planning*, 199, 20–24.

McElroy, E., 2014. Soccer, Airbnb, and the Colonization of the Mission. *48 Hills*. Available from: http://48hills.org/2014/10/13/soccer-airbnb-colonization-mission/ [Accessed 10 March 2017].

Mission Creek Video, 2014. "Mission playground is not for sale" (video). Available from: https://www.youtube.com/watch?v=awPVY1DcupE [Accessed 10 March 2017].

Mitchell, D., 1995. The End of Public Space? People's Park, Definitions of the Public, and Democracy. *Annals of the Association of American Geographers*, 85 (1), 108–133.

Mitchell, D., 2003. *The Right to the City: Social Justice and the Fight for Public Space*. New York: Guilford Publications.

Packer, G., 2013. Change the World: Silicon Valley Transfers Its Slogans—and Its Money—to the Realm of Politics [online]. *The New Yorker*, May 27. Available from: www.newyorker.com/magazine/2013/05/27/change-the-world [Accessed 5 July 2016].

Paragon Real Estate Group, 2015. San Francisco New-Home Construction & Development Paragon Real Estate [online]. Available from: www.paragon-re.com/San_Francisco_Housing_Development_Report [Accessed 24 Jan 2016].

Purcell, M., 2002. Excavating Lefebvre: The Right to the City and Its Urban Politics of the Inhabitant. *GeoJournal*, 58 (2–3), 99–108.

Rose, D. B., 2001. Settler Colonialism and the Transformation of Anthropology. *Postcolonial Studies*, 4 (2), 251–261.

Schaefer, S., 2015. Google Guys Worth Billions More Thanks To Stock's Earnings Surge [online]. *Forbes*. Available from: www.forbes.com/sites/steveschaefer/2015/07/17/google-stock-surge-brin-page-billions/ [Accessed 13 February 2016].

Schulman, S., 2012. *The Gentrification of the Mind: Witness to a Lost Imagination*. Berkeley: University of California Press.

SFADC, 2015. San Francisco's Eviction Crisis. Report by the San Francisco Anti-Displacement Coalition. Available from: http://www.antievictionmappingproject.net/EvictionSurge.pdf [Accessed 10 March 2017].

Sharma, N. and Wright, C., 2008. Decolonizing Resistance, Challenging Colonial States. *Social Justice Journal*, 35 (3), 120–138.

Siefkes, C., 2009. The Commons of the Future: Building Blocks for a Commons-Based Society. *The Commoner*. Available from: www.commoner.org.uk/wp-content/uploads/2009/03/siefkes_future-commons.pdf [Accessed 5 July 2016].

Solnit, R., 2000. *Hollow City: The Siege of San Francisco and the Crisis of American Urbanism*. London: Verso Books.

Solnit, R., 2013. Diary. *London Review of Books*, 7 February, 34–35.

Streitfeld, D., 2015. Parking Apps Face Obstacles at Every Turn [online]. *Bits Blog*. Available from: http://bits.blogs.nytimes.com/2015/06/10/parking-apps-face-obstacles-at-every-turn/ [Accessed 24 Jan 2016].

Susser, I. and Tonnelat, S., 2013. Transformative Cities: The Three Urban Commons. *Focaal: Journal of Global and Historical Anthropology*, 2013 (66), 105–121.

Tarrow, S., 1993. Cycles of Collective Action: Between Moments of Madness and the Repertoire of Contention. *Social Science History*, 17 (2), 281–307.

Thompson, E. P., 1993. *Customs in Common: Studies in Traditional Popular Culture*. New York: The New Press.

Truong, K., 2015. Historically Latino District in San Francisco on Track to Lose Half Its Latino Population [online]. *Mashable*. Available from: http://mashable.com/2015/10/30/san-francisco-mission-latino-population/ [Accessed 13 February 2016].

Weise, E., 2014. SF City Attorney: No Renting Out Public Parking Spaces [online]. *USA TODAY*. Available from: www.usatoday.com/story/tech/2014/06/23/san-francisco-rent-public-parking-space-monkey-parking-sweetch-parkmondo/11263723/ [Accessed 20 January 2016].

Wolfe, P., 1999. *Settler Colonialism and the Transformation of Anthropology: The Politics and Poetics of an Ethnographic Event*. London and New York: Cassell.

Wong, J. C., 2014. Dropbox, Airbnb, and the Fight Over San Francisco's Public Spaces. *The New Yorker*, October 23. Available from: http://www.newyorker.com/tech/elements/dropbox-airbnb-fight-san-franciscos-public-spaces [Accessed 10 March 2017].

4

RECONFIGURING THE PUBLIC THROUGH HOUSING RIGHTS STRUGGLES IN SPAIN

Melissa García-Lamarca

In the wake of the 2008 housing-financial crisis, the United States and several European countries, including Spain, poured billions of public (taxpayer) funds into numerous banks teetering on the brink of collapse. Public discourse—from politicians, mainstream economists, and the media—largely depicted these bailouts as necessary, or at least a necessary evil (e.g. elEconomista.es 2012). While there may be broad agreement around the need to protect everyday savers, bailing out financial institutions that created and invested in speculative financial commodities, and the people driving these practices, is hotly contested. At its base, the conflict revolves around whose interests, and in whose benefit, the state (supposedly in the name of the public) acts to rescue financial systems: people or capital?

This contestation brings into sharp focus the role of the state and what is public. Beyond the idealized Habermasian account of the public sphere these are ultimately questions related to democracy (Fraser 1997). In the urban realm in particular, these questions have become heated in recent decades as restrictions in and control over the public sphere, closely related to the privatization of public space, have been growing under neoliberal regimes (Low and Smith 2006). As a democratic act, seizing central urban space was at the core of the Spanish *indignado* 15M plaza occupations in May 2011, often cited as an emblematic urban resistance in recent years. Spurred by skyrocketing unemployment, increasing precarity, bailouts for the banks, and austerity for the people, hundreds of thousands occupied plazas for weeks across Spain, placing the political and financial class at the center of their critique and demanding "real democracy NOW!" While many see the fruits of the 15M ripening in the form of new political parties (e.g. Podemos) and the success of leftist municipal platforms in the May 2015 elections (Kassam 2015, The Economist 2015), these institutional transformations are in their infancies. Indeed, deep democratic change has a long and challenging road ahead, requiring a reconfiguration of social relations towards placing people at the center, not the endless growth of capital. Actions towards this end would, for example, strive to disrupt the predominant political and economic consensus that seeks to maintain neoliberalism and its broader capitalist social order.

This chapter focuses on struggles around housing, a key aspect of society and life in the urban realm. It looks at how contestations related to the public have emerged in Spain through the actions of the housing rights movement known as the Platform for Mortgage Affected People (la Plataforma de Afectados por la Hipoteca [PAH]). I argue that their actions make visible the inegalitarian nature of the country's financial system bailout as they unfurl processes that materially and discursively reconfigure what is considered the public in Spain today. In the context of Spain's housing-financial crisis, focus is placed on how the movement appropriates the assets (i.e. houses) of partially or fully rescued (e.g. nationalized) banks for people, not capital, reflecting on what this means for notions of the public, the public sphere, and public space. Working from an understanding that the public sphere is enmeshed in historical and political practices, and that "the spatiality of the public sphere transforms an understanding of the politics of public space" (Low 2015, p. 4), I reflect on how capturing the spatiality of the public sphere raises fundamentally important questions about the political dimensions of public space. I examine public space and the public sphere through a dialectical approach that begins with social relations in space and their material arrangements to then link to abstract thought in order to critically ground my analysis (Knierbein 2015).

The focus on housing is an important one, particularly in the Spanish context. The PAH is one of the strongest housing rights movements in Europe, founded in 2009 in Barcelona in response to a waterfall in foreclosures and evictions upon the burst of the country's 1997–2007 real estate bubble. Grounded in local assemblies collectively advising people unable to pay their mortgages or facing rental or squatting eviction, the PAH deploys a range of actions including blocking evictions, organizing bank blockades and occupations, promoting popular legislative initiatives to change Spanish law, and recuperating (occupying) empty bank-owned housing, among others. The PAH fights to change the legal and structural roots of housing dispossession taking place in Spain where over 695,000 foreclosures and over 327,000 evictions have taken place between 2008 and 2016 (CGPJ 2017). Rising unemployment and plummeting housing prices have been compounded by Spanish mortgage law requiring that the contracted outstanding debt must be repaid even after one's home is auctioned off. This has left hundreds of thousands of people not only homeless but also indebted for life (Colau and Alemany 2012).

This chapter draws on empirical research conducted from October 2013 to September 2014, including 21 in-depth interviews with mortgage affected people, 14 semi-structured interviews with key informants from the policy and banking sector, and participant observation at assemblies and actions of Barcelona's and Sabadell's PAHs, as well as my engagement in the PAH as an activist post–September 2014. In my research I approached the PAH as a situated source of knowledge: the PAH generates its own analysis, concepts, experiences, and practices (Casas-Cortés et al. 2013, Clair 2012). In terms of methodology, this underlined the need for an engaged ethnographic approach that involves "blurring established social scientific boundaries and promoting a more relational-symmetrical approach" (Casas-Cortés et al. 2008, p. 17).

The chapter unfolds in four sections. The first explains the PAH's emergence within the context of the political economic foundations underlying Spain's most recent housing boom that has left a legacy of dispossession amidst 3.5 million empty housing units across the country (INE 2013). The second section details the PAH and its activities, demonstrating how it reconfigures housing problems experienced in the private, household sphere into collective, public concerns. The third focuses on the campaign that recuperates (occupies) housing with and for families with no housing alternative, called *Obra Social* (social work), as an emblematic reconfiguration of the public sphere in Spain. Closing thoughts and reflections are provided in the conclusion.

From Housing Boom to Crisis: The Emergence of the PAH

The real estate sector, historically important in Spain, was established as a generator of economic growth under the 1939–1975 Franco dictatorship (Charnock et al. 2014). In 1950 over half the Spanish population lived as renters, and a key strategy of the dictatorship was to create a nation of homeowners as a tool of "stability" and control (Colau and Alemany 2012). But the country's

1997–2007 housing boom was the third and most extensive one in the country's history. During a decade, one-quarter of Spain's land area was built up and the country became the European leader in the consumption of cement (Naredo et al. 2008). Housing prices climbed over 200% and close to 7 million housing units were built, in peak years surpassing the combined totals of France, Germany, and Italy (López and Rodríguez 2011).

The state was a key agent in making the financialized homeownership model spread. Indeed, the 1997–2007 housing boom was possible thanks to the carefully calculated deregulation of land, banking, and mortgage financing-related policies during the 1980s and 1990s, under both Conservative and Socialist party rule, deregulation that was also driven by European Union membership requirements. At the same time, the devolution of housing and urban planning-related tasks to regional and local governments in the 1980s was not accompanied with sufficient funding to implement projects. Both broader deregulation and devolution combined with historical and material factors to make real estate an attractive and lucrative source of local tax revenue, engendering rampant corruption. This occurred in a context where Spanish housing policies "have been shaped more by a desire to stimulate economic activity than by social policy per se" (Hoekstra et al. 2010, p. 129).

Upon adopting the euro, which diminished fears of monetary devaluation, unprecedented amounts of capital began flowing into Spain in the late 1990s. Financial entities, in particular Spain's 45 (private) savings banks, granted 9.3 million mortgages from 1997–2007. Inflated housing appraisals meant that loans were offered not for 80% of the market price as stipulated by law, but 80% of the *appraised* value of the home in the expectation that housing prices would keep rising (Garcia Montalvo and Raya Vilchez 2012). Mortgages were repeatedly granted despite the fact that 30% of existing employment contracts were temporary and that workers' average salaries fell by 10% between 1995 and 2007 (López and Rodríguez 2010).

To contest the difficulty in accessing housing due to skyrocketing housing prices and declining real wages, previous to forming the PAH several of its founders participated in a group named Miles de Viviendas (Thousands of Houses) that sought to popularize squatting in 2003, albeit unsuccessfully and amidst differences and conflicts within the squatting movement (Mir García et al. 2013). Miles de Viviendas organized a workshop against real estate and urban violence (Taller VIU) from which V de Vivienda (H for Housing) mobilizations emerged (Mir García et al. 2013). V de Vivienda, an allegory for V for Vendetta, became one of the militant sectors of the Spanish-wide Movement for Dignified Housing, a movement that began in 2003 to fight for better access to housing and more sustainable urban planning (Aguilar Fernández and Fernández Gibaja 2010). V de Vivienda in particular was able to rally thousands of people in Barcelona and Madrid in a 2006 protest under the emblematic slogan "You'll never own a house in your whole fucking life" (Prieto Serrano 2014). Yet despite sit-ins, protests, and parodies over the next few years, V de Vivienda's communication, framing, and tactics largely mobilized youth and students and failed to reach immigrants and others with difficulties accessing housing during the boom (Aguilar Fernández and Fernández Gibaja 2010). Neither it, nor the Movement for Dignified Housing, were able to transform the situation. As two of the PAH's founders note, V de Vivienda was a minority movement pushing against a largely homeownership-based society that during the boom saw its patrimony (housing) steadily increase in value (Colau and Alemany 2012).

Indeed, this was the story told during the boom through references to the enormous increase in the net "wealth" of households in Spain. But virtually the entire surge in net wealth corresponded to property wealth (see Naredo et al. 2008). A former Catalan secretary of housing explained that, "[after the 1990s] the financial establishment hurled itself on families so that they would ask for [mortgage] credit" (personal communication May 7, 2014). While financial institutions competed for clients through aggressive marketing campaigns the Spanish population continuously heard how the price of housing never falls and that housing is a safe investment from the public administration, estate agencies, developers, builders, financial institutions, and the mass media (Garcia Montalvo 2008). Homeownership was also equated with a certain status in society, where media representations depicted home ownership as almost a Spanish genetic predisposition (Palomera 2014). This push for homeownership was reinforced by an increasingly expensive and unstable rental market and a marginal social housing stock, standing at 1.5–2% of total housing (Pareja Eastaway and San Marín Varo 2002).

But the "increase" in household "wealth" that occurred upon becoming a mortgaged home-owner actually corresponded to a real increase in household debt, dependent upon speculatively driven increases in housing prices. In other words, the supposed increase in wealth was based on deepening debt and over-inflated housing prices. Indeed, indebtedness rose significantly during the boom amidst workers' declining real wages. The amount of debt people held was four times higher in 2006 than it was in 1990, where in 2006, 42% of people over the age of 20 held debt, well over half of which was mortgage related (Banco de España 2007). By 2006 the ratio of household debt to net disposable income stood at 125% (Banco de España 2007). This means that, in aggregate, households owed €1.25 for every euro of monthly net salary. Spain ranked among the top countries worldwide in regards to the highest percentage of long-term household mortgage debt with respect to disposable income (Naredo et al. 2008).

The burst of the real estate bubble unmasked this indebted reality. Unemployment climbed, housing prices dropped, and many mortgaged families faced increased monthly mortgage installments. The bust obliged V de Vivienda to reinvent itself, both to respond to the wave of mortgage evictions and to verify the failure of the model that created it (Colau and Alemany 2012). Mortgages were particularly problematic in a country where prior to the crisis nearly 85% of the population was a homeowner. As housing prices have fallen dramatically, most mortgaged households have a debt for life upon foreclosure and eviction as the sale price does not cover the amount of the original mortgage. Due to Spain's Mortgage Law, established in 1946, people are legally bound to pay, or to have their goods and salary (above a €967 monthly minimum) appropriated to repay their debt.

The PAH: How the Private Realm of the Household Becomes Collective and Public

The first PAH assembly was organized in Barcelona in February 2009 in a neighborhood association in the city center, attracting 40 people facing mortgage foreclosure, largely immigrants (Blanchar 2014). Learning through trial and error, what finally worked were "collective and open assemblies to generate a space of confidence, where people lose their fear, empower themselves and verify that alone they can't but together they can" (Blanchar citing Domingo 2014, n.p.).

The PAH has spread across Spain, with 236 local nodes. Each is unique in many ways, but all are united through the same organizational principles and demands. The 15M plaza occupations in May 2011 were fundamental in extending the PAH's social reach and legitimacy (Antentas 2013, Colau and Alemany 2013). As a PAH activist explained to me: the 15M was a sort of "liquid implosion" without clear and defined lines of action, whereas the PAH required specific and direct action to solve urgent social needs, like blocking an eviction (personal communication, October 29, 2013). In other words, the PAH pointed to immediate material acts in the context of ongoing (and some would say endless) deliberating in 15M plaza assemblies and can be considered as an outlet to move from plazas to other urban spaces where urgent housing problems were unfolding. The links between the 15M and the PAH are thus strong, although the spatial and organizational interconnections between the two vary per locality depending on the social and political movements existing previous to or emerging from the 15M.

The PAH has thus subsequently been built as a free, horizontal, and non–party-affiliated movement. It both denounces the state of affairs that has made thousands of families unable to pay their mortgage and face foreclosure and eviction and seeks to make housing accessible and affordable for all. The PAH has built campaigns around three minimum, nonnegotiable demands: (1) to change Spain's mortgage legislation so that during foreclosure proceedings the bank cancels all outstanding mortgage debt in exchange for the house (*dación en pago*); (2) to immediately stop all evictions where it is the family home and sole property; and (3) to transform empty houses held by rescued financial institutions into social housing, where families would pay a social rent of no more than 30% of their income (PAH 2014).

As the PAH has faced insufficient responses from national, regional, and local levels of government to these demands, they address urgent material needs by enacting solutions themselves. Regular actions include blocking evictions, recuperating (occupying) empty bank-owned housing for families that have no other housing alternative (*Obra Social*), and bank actions/occupations to demand solutions for mortgage negotiation cases at a standstill, alongside a myriad of other periodic actions such as denouncing politicians at public events or in front of their homes (*escraches*) and occupying real estate fairs or city halls.

But before, or at least alongside, these actions, problems related to mortgage default, foreclosure, and eviction, as well as rental and squatting evictions, are first made visible through weekly assemblies, an activity at the heart of the PAH (Figure 4.1). Interviews and participating in assemblies revealed how mortgage problems instilled deep-seated feelings of guilt, fear, and shame, family and health problems, depression, suicidal thoughts, or in a some cases even suicide attempts. Upon coming to the PAH, many interviewees spoke about feeling relief and hope, and over half spoke specifically of how they no longer felt alone once they began their struggle with the PAH to solve their situation. Such experiences are exemplified by a person who noted how "before coming to the PAH I thought my world had fallen apart, that I was the only one who has this problem. However, no, when I went there [to an assembly], well millions of us are affected

FIGURE 4.1   PAHC Sabadell assembly, September 18, 2014

Source: Emma Giné

and we are in the same boat, fighting for the same things, because there is strength in numbers" (personal communication, 28 August 2014).

With regular, weekly support from the assembly as a base, PAH members begin their struggle with the bank for debt forgiveness in exchange for giving the home back to the bank and/or social rent, and engage in collective actions. In this way, through different forms of being-in-common (García-Lamarca 2015), solutions are found for shared housing problems experienced in the individualized, private realm of the household, bringing the collective, and public, nature of these problems to light. Applying Mitchell's (2003) understanding of public space as a space of struggle, we can conceptualize how, at least for a brief period, the PAH—by mobilizing along sidewalks and streets in front of homes whose inhabitants face eviction (Figure 4.2) or rallying together in the private space of a bank as dozens occupy it to demand debt forgiveness for a comrade—converts these spaces into public spaces. At the very least, they politicize the spatiality of the public sphere, making debates and above all disagreement (Rancière 1999) visible in space. They are examples of relational counter spaces, "where alternative paths of urban development beyond capitalist growth scenarios can be imagined, invented and explored" (Knierbein 2015, p. 53).

Furthermore, the socialization of both debt and guilt is rejected by the PAH, as is the state's objective to privatize banks and real estate assets that were nationalized during the financial system rescue and restructured from 2010–2012. During this period both Socialist and Conservative governments focused their efforts on rescuing and restructuring 21 (private) savings banks, whose books were bloated with defaulted real estate debt and assets, with billions of euros of public funds. These 21 entities were either merged and sold to banks or nationalized and run as private banks. The PAH rejects the narrative often repeated by prominent politicians and economists that "we have lived beyond our means, now it's time to tighten our belts" (Tranche 2013). Through

FIGURE 4.2 Blocking an eviction in Barcelona, January 2014

Source: Melissa García-Lamarca

collective processes, demands, and actions, the PAH signals those responsible for the crisis, the government and the financial sector, and demands that what has been made "public" actually benefits people, not capital. For example, empty flats owned by rescued financial entities should become social housing, as detailed in the subsequent section.

The PAH's *Obra Social* Campaign: Occupying Housing, Recuperating What's Public

This campaign originated in the autumn of 2011 where, as one of its founders explained, "it was born in the street in a very intuitive way" (personal communication November 5, 2013). The first occupation took place in September 2011 when the PAH was unable to stop the third eviction of a family with an open eviction order in Montcada i Reixac, a city in the Barcelona metropolitan area, and the city council provided no alternative, so the family occupied their former flat that was now owned by the bank (personal communication November 5, 2013). Collective occupations of empty bank-owned housing blocks to rehouse multiple families started in Terrassa, a city in the Barcelona metropolitan region, at the end of 2011, where the *Obra Social* campaign was officially launched (Figure 4.3).

Obra Social seizes the social function of housing, ensuring that families engaged with the PAH who are facing eviction and have exhausted all housing options are not left living in the street, and pressures the public administration at different levels to guarantee the universal right to housing. In both collective and individual occupations, the aim is to regularize a family's situation by negotiating a social rent with the bank, ideally in the same flat/building. As the former spokesperson for the *obra social* explained, through this campaign the PAH normalizes and positivizes squatting from an ideological point of view towards generating a squatting movement of a new order (personal communication October 29, 2013). Close to 50 buildings have been collectively recuperated across Spain and in total over 2,500 people rehoused and thousands have been individually recuperated by PAH members. While this is a small amount in relation to the total number of evictions in Spain since the start of the crisis, recuperations are important in making the housing problem visible in the public sphere, pressuring banks to offer social rent, and signaling the incapacity of the administration to deal with the scale of the problem despite an abundance of (publicly rescued) empty housing.

Empty bank-owned flats or entire buildings are the exclusive targets of PAH occupations. Particular focus is placed on the properties from financial entities bailed out with over €61 billion in public funds, part of the legacy of over half of the country's 45 savings banks that were crushed under the weight of nonperforming real estate loans granted to developers and households during the boom. In the third part of a three-phased rescue and restructuring of the Spanish financial system from 2010–2012, one of the European Commission's conditions to release funding to Spain was the creation of an asset management company, also known as a "bad bank" (Byrne 2015). Founded in November 2012 and 45% state-owned,[1] Spain's bad bank is called the Management Company for Assets Arising from Bank Reorganization (SAREB). It is where the "toxic assets" of nine nationalized and semi-nationalized banks were transferred for less than half their original price in exchange for both Spanish government guaranteed bonds and European rescue funds (Eurostate 2014). After the socialization of the financial system's losses, the SAREB is a 45% publicly backed bet to recover part of these funds. So far at least €36 billion is unrecoverable, most of which has gone to benefit and strengthen existing banks (de Barrón 2014).

In the context of making private (financial sector) losses public, and subsequently partially privatizing profits, the PAH's position is that "the SAREB is ours, and so are its houses!" In other words, housing rescued with public funds is public, and should be used to meet the needs of

FIGURE 4.3   A PAH *Obra Social* housing block, occupied February 2015 in Barcelona

Source: Melissa García-Lamarca

people, not capital. On the one hand, the PAH demands that housing from the SAREB and other banks rescued with public funds is converted into social housing, with affordable and stable rents. But since neither the SAREB, banks, nor the state take sufficient action to avoid people living on the streets, the PAH squats—framed as occupying, recuperating or liberating—housing themselves. As one activist explained, the PAH attempts "to give it [squatting] a language, new in the sense that we don't focus on the house but rather put what has happened at the centre: they have robbed rights and housing from us, so we recover it; they've evicted us so we rehouse" (personal communication November 5, 2013).

The *Obra Social* is thus a political act that challenges the very foundation of the existing political economic system; as its former spokesperson remarked in an interview, "it lets us illustrate the contradictions of systemic accumulation and domination more than other campaigns" (personal communication October 29, 2013). In the words of another activist, it shows the "absolute contradiction" between the PAH's collective solidarity-based practices and the values of the capitalist liberal democratic system grounded in individualism, competition, and personal benefit (Jiménez 2013). This statement is reflected in Dean's (2014, p. 270) remark that "occupation is a divisive tactic that expresses the fundamental division on which capitalism depends." Housing, in other words, is de-privatized, and becomes a form of common or public space—a contested space for struggle. Occupying vacant housing asserts the use value of housing over the exchange value and profit-driven focus of the SAREB, disrupting the core dynamics of urban capital accumulation that it hopes to (re)instigate (see García-Lamarca 2017). Furthermore, it challenges and reconfigures what can be considered the public by literally occupying it and putting it to a social use. Occupations exemplify how the logic of submission is subverted and becomes an embodied spatial practice (Moore 2013). As framed by Hoskyns (2014, p. 4), "the spaces of democracy (spaces for the practice of democracy) and the democracy of space (democratic relations in the production of space) are intertwined."

Virtually all interviewees perceived the *Obra Social* as important and necessary and as a logical action responding to an urgent need. Several expressed how squatting is the only way to make the government do something. In this light, it enacts an immediate need and produces a new way of inhabiting. This is illustrated in the following quote from a mortgage-affected Ecuadorian PAH member (personal communication, 11 June 2014):

> If the political authorities think they are in their right and we elect them to represent us, and they don't represent us, they don't do what they need to do, well then we have to do it! You know, make ourselves heard. I think it [*Obra Social*] is good, because if they evict you from your house, you are a person, you have not committed any crime. . . . And there are people responsible for this situation, they are the responsible ones, so they need to pay for this, because they auction off your house and who takes it? The bank, public entities. You have a family, you are a human being, you have a right. The constitution says that everyone has a right to housing, to a dignified salary, and they have to apply it. But they don't, they do things for themselves. I would go to all the places that need to be occupied, because there is no right to what they do.

In this way, recuperating housing that has been "rescued" by the state is a deeply political act. While the capitalist state is "so fully complicit with the program of capital" (Mitchell 2003, p. 25) in general, struggle and direct action has always been critical in wresting and winning rights and urban space—and taking/making the public for the people. This is the essence of the *Obra Social*.

Conclusions

In the context of Spain's housing-financial crisis, this chapter sought to illustrate how the PAH disrupts and reconfigures dominant notions of the "'public'" and the public sphere. The brief sketch of the political economic dynamics around housing in Spain, where the emergence of the PAH and its precursors is explained, show how the country's 1997–2007 housing boom was built on household indebtedness, both directly and indirectly furthered through housing policy and discourse. The way that the PAH brings housing problems experienced by hundreds of thousands of people from the individualized, private realm of the home to the public sphere was illustrated, through both collective assemblies and actions. Focus was then placed on one campaign in particular, the *Obra Social*. While meeting urgent housing needs through recuperating (occupying) empty housing owned by banks bailed out by the state with and for families with no housing alternative, the *Obra Social* makes visible the fact that the Spanish financial sector's (private) debt crisis post-2008 has been purposefully turned into a public crisis by the Spanish state and the EU. It reclaims housing rescued by public funds for the people (the public) by squatting empty housing that has been left for speculation.

The PAH exemplifies how "the public" can be and is politicized, both materially and discursively. Capturing urban spaces for the short or long term, be it through streets while blocking evictions, occupying bank branches, or recuperating housing owned by the SAREB or other rescued banks, the PAH appropriates them, both spatializing and politicizing the public sphere. As explained in looking at the genealogy and emergence of the PAH, the 15M plaza occupations were an important dynamic through which the PAH multiplied and was consolidated across Spain, expanding to over 235 local branches. If we consider public space as a space of struggle (Mitchell 2003), some of the spaces taken in the PAH's actions can be conceptualized as becoming public, albeit temporarily; in the very least they deeply blur the boundaries between the private and the public. Either way, the PAH's acts contest the idea of full-fledged financial system rescue as a "necessarily evil" and that people "lived beyond their means," at the same time that buildings rescued by the public purse are taken to be lived in, not speculated with, to benefit people over capital. The PAH simultaneously continues to demand a stop to all evictions of a household's principal home, to change Spain's mortgage law so a household's debt is forgiven in exchange for giving their home back to the bank and to hand over the housing stock of the SAREB and all rescued banks to the hands of citizens, to create public housing with affordable and stable rents. The PAH's actions bring to light how moves by the government, supposedly in the name of the "public", have overwhelmingly benefited the banks at the expense of the people. The PAH thus expresses its action very clearly: we rescue people, not banks.

As an ideological construction, just as the false ideal of public space being open to all can become a "rallying point for successive waves of political activity" (Mitchell 1995, p. 117), the ideal of the public can be used to recuperate spaces in the name of (supposedly universal) rights. The PAH uses the constitutional right to housing as a rallying call towards its materialization by recuperating (occupying) housing that has been rescued with public funds, at the same time that they demand rights be guaranteed through legal changes. This suggests that Mitchell's (2003) proposition that space becomes public through actions and purposeful occupation also means that the public for the people, not capital, is won through struggle. In other words, we can never assume that rights or any idealized public will ever be automatically fulfilled—as Marx famously stated, "between equal rights, force decides" (Marx 1976 [1867], 344)—but can only struggle to create the spaces for the public to happen.

Further Information

Colau, A. and Alemany, A. 2013. *Mortgaged Lives: From the Housing Bubble to the Right to Housing*. Los Angeles: Journal of Aesthetics and Protest Press. (More information about the Platform for Mortgage Affected People [PAH] from two of its founders.)

"La PAH presenta: de la burbuja a la Obra Social," 2013. [online video]. Available from: www.youtube.com/watch?v=TkrM-zBGjBQ [Accessed 30 September 2015]. (An 8-minute didactic video about the PAH's *Obra Social* campaign, with English subtitles.)

"#LaSAREBesNuestra," 2015. [online video]. Available from: www.youtube.com/watch?v=aIA7cNnj938 [Accessed 25 January 2016]. (A 5-minute video about the PAH's campaign to reclaim Spain's bad bank, the SAREB, in Spanish.)

Note

1. The state is the the largest single owner of the SAREB, with 22 private banks and insurance companies constituting the remainder.

References

Aguilar Fernández, S. and Fernández Gibaja, A., 2010. El movimiento por la vivienda digna en España o el porqué del fracaso de una protesta con amplia base social. *Revista Internacional de Sociología*, 68 (3), 679–704.

Antentas, J., 2013. La Indignación, tras la explosión inicial. El 15M en Catalunya durante 2012. *In*: L'Observatori del Conflicte Social, ed. *Anuari del Conflicte Social 2012*. Barcelona: Universitat de Barcelona, 263–274.

Banco de España, 2007. *Informe anual 2006*, Madrid. Available from: www.bde.es/bde/es/secciones/informes/Publicaciones_an/Informe_anual/2006/ [Accessed 5 August 2015].

Blanchar, C., 2014. Sí, pudieron [online]. *El País*, 21 February. Available from: http://politica.elpais.com/politica/2014/02/21/actualidad/1393010178_488272.html [Accessed 2 March 2014].

Byrne, M., 2015. Bad Banks: The Urban Implications of Asset Management Companies. *Urban Research & Practice*, 8 (2), 255–266.

Casas-Cortés, M., Osterweil, M., and Powell, D. E., 2008. Blurring Boundaries: Recognizing Knowledge Practices in the Study of Social Movements. *Antropological Quarterly*, 81 (1), 17–58.

Casas-Cortés, M., Osterweil, M., and Powell, D. E., 2013. Transformations in Engaged Ethnography: Knowledge, Networks, and Social Movements. *In*: J. S. Juris, and A. Khasnabish, eds. *Insurgent Encounters: Transnational Activism, Ethnography, and the Political*. Durham and London: Duke University Press, 199–228.

CGPJ, 2017. Datos sobre el efecto de la crisis en los órganos judiciales por Provincias hasta Cuarto Trimestre 2016. Consejo General del Poder Judicial, Madrid. Available from: http://www.poderjudicial.es/stfls/ESTADISTICA/FICHEROS/Crisis/Datos sobre el efecto de la crisis en los organos judiciales 4T 2016 PROVINCIAS.xls. [Accessed 10 March 2017].

Charnock, G., Purcell, T., and Ribera-Fumaz, R., 2014. *The Limits to Capital in Spain: Crisis and Revolt in the European South*. London: Palgrave Macmillan.

Clair, R. P., 2012. Engaged Ethnography and the Story(ies) of the Anti-Sweatshop Movement. *Cultural Studies ↔ Critical Methodologies*, 12 (2), 132–145.

Colau, A. and Alemany, A., 2012. *Vidas hipotecadas: De la burbuja immobiliaria al derecho a la vivienda*. Barcelona: Cuadrilátero de Libros.

Colau, A. and Alemany, A., 2013. *¡Sí se puede!*. Barcelona: Ediciones Destino.

Dean, J., 2014. After Post-Politics: Occupation and the Return of Communism. *In*: J. Wilson, and E. Swyngedouw, eds. *The Post-Political and Its Discontents: Spaces of Depoliticization, Spectres of Radical Politics*. Edinburgh: Edinburgh University Press, 261–278.

de Barrón, I., 2014. ¿Cuánto dinero se ha inyectado en la banca? ¿cuánto se ha perdido? *El País*, 21 November. Available from: http://economia.elpais.com/economia/2014/11/21/actualidad/1416599768_030102.html [Accessed 25 August 2015].

The Economist, 2015. Los Indignados in Power [online]. *The Economist*. 4 July. Available from: www.economist.com/news/europe/21656735-left-wing-parties-are-taking-over-cities-los-indignados-power [Accessed 10 July 2015].

elEconomista.es, 2012. España, 'rescatada': 'préstamo' de hasta 100.000 millones sin condiciones para sanear a la banca. *Eleconomista.es*, 9 June. Available from: http://www.eleconomista.es/espana/noticias/4031557/06/12/Espana-va-pedir-el-rescate-para-sanear-sus-bancos-y-el-Eurogrupo-lo-aceptara-segun-Afp.html [Accessed 10 March 2017].

Eurostate, 2014. *Sareb, Europe's Largest Property Fund Manager Starts Liquidation Process*, Barcelona [online]. Available from: www.eurostate.com/Eurostate_Spanish Bad Bank_ENG.pdf [Accessed 20 July 2015].

Fraser, N., 1990. Rethinking the Public Sphere: A Contribution to the Critique of Actually Existing Democracy. *Social Text*, 25/26, 56–80.

García-Lamarca, M., 2015. Insurgent Acts of Being-in-Common and Housing in Spain: Making Urban Commons? *In*: M. Dellenbaugh, M. Kip, M. Bieniok, A. K. Müller, and M. Schwegmann, eds. *Urban Commons: Moving Beyond State and Market*. Berlin: Birkhäuser, 165–177.

García-Lamarca, M., 2017. From Occupying Plazas to Recuperating Housing: Insurgent Practices in Spain. *International Journal of Urban and Regional Research*. DOI 10.1111/1468-2427.12386.

Garcia Montalvo, J., 2008. *De la quimera inmobiliaria al colapso financiero: crónica de un desenlace anunciado.* Barcelona: Antoni Bosch.

Garcia Montalvo, J., 2015. Situación y perspectivas del saneamiento inmobiliario del sector financiero español. *Cuadernos de Información Económica*, 248, 71–87.

García Montalvo, J., and Raya Vilchez, J.M., 2012. What Is the Right Price of Spanish Residential Real Estate? *Spanish Economic and Financial Outlook*, 1(3), 22–28.

Hoekstra, J., Heras Saizarbitoria, I., and Etxezarreta Etxarri, A., 2010. Recent Changes in Spanish Housing Policies: Subsidized Owner-Occupancy Dwellings as a New Tenure Sector? *Journal of Housing and the Built Environment*, 25 (1), 125–138.

Hoskyns, T., 2014. *The Empty Place: Democracy and Public Space.* Abingdon: Routledge.

INE 2013. *Censos de Población y Viviendas 2011* [online]. Edificios y viviendas. Datos provisionales. Madrid. Available from: www.ine.es/prensa/np775.pdf [Accessed 6 July 2016].

Jiménez, A., 2013. ¿La PAH, es de derechas o de izquierdas? ¿Importa? *Rotekeil* [online]. Available from: http://rotekeil.com/2013/06/07/la-pah-es-de-derechas-o-de-izquierdas-importa/#more-132 [Accessed 23 February 2014].

Kassam, A., 2015. Manuela Carmena Set to Lead Spain's "Indignados" to Power in Madrid [online]. *The Observer*. 30 May. Available from: www.theguardian.com/world/2015/may/30/madrid-next-mayor-ex-communist-judge-manuela-carmena [Accessed 4 June 2015].

Knierbein, S., 2015. Public Space as Relational Counter Space—Scholarly Minefield or Epistemological Opportunity? *In*: C. Tornaghi, and S. Knierbein, eds. *Public Space and Relational Perspectives: New Challenges for Architecture and Planning.* London: Routledge, 42–64.

López, I. and Rodríguez, E., 2010. *Fin de ciclo: Financiarización, territorio y sociedad de propietarios en la onda larga del capitalismo hispano (1959–2010).* Madrid: Traficantes de Sueños.

López, I. and Rodríguez, E., 2011. The Spanish Model. *New Left Review*, 69, 5–29.

Low, S., 2015. Public Space and the Public Sphere: The Legacy of Neil Smith. *Antipode*, 49 (S1), 153–170.

Low, S. and Smith, N., 2006. Introduction: The Imperative of Public Space. *In*: S. Low, and N. Smith, eds. *The Politics of Public Space.* New York: Routledge, 1–16.

Marx, K., 1976 [1867]. *Capital: A Critique of Political Economy*, Vol. 1. Ben Fowkes, trans. New York: Penguin Books.

Mir Garcia, J., França, J., Macías, C., and Veciana, P., 2013. Fundamentos de la Plataforma de Afectados por la Hipoteca: activismo, asesoramiento colectivo y desobediencia civil no violenta. *Educación Social: Revista de Intervención Socioeducativa*, 55, 52–61.

Mitchell, D., 1995. The End of Public Space? People's Park, Definitions of the Public, and Democracy. *Annals of the Association of American Geographers*, 85(1), 108–133.

Mitchell, D., 2013. *The Right to the City: Social Justice and the Fight for Public Space.* New York: The Guilford Press.

Moore, S., 2013. Taking Up Space: Anthropology and Embodied Protest. *Radical Anthropology*, 7, 6–16.

Naredo, M., Carpintero, Ó., and Marcos, C., 2008. *Patrimonio inmobiliario y balance nacional de la economía española (1995–2007).* Madrid: Fundación de las Cajas de Ahorros.

PAH, 2014. Libro Verde de la PAH: Una guía básica sobre la PAH [online]. Barcelona: Plataforma de Afectados por la Hipoteca. Available from: http://afectadosporlahipoteca.com/wp-content/uploads/2014/01/LibroVerde-PAH-32.pdf [Accessed 5 February 2014].

Palomera, J., 2014. How Did Finance Capital Infiltrate the World of the Urban Poor? Homeownership and Social Fragmentation in a Spanish Neighborhood. *International Journal of Urban and Regional Research*, 38(1), 218–235.

Pareja Eastaway, M. and San Marín Varo, I., 2002. The Tenure Imbalance in Spain: The Need for Social Housing Policy. *Urban Studies*, 39 (2), 283–295.

Prieto Serrano, D. 2014. Producción del espacio urbano y participación ciudadana. El "habitar" la ciudad de los movimientos sociales en Madrid. *In*: E. Serrano, A. Calleja-López, A. Monterde, and J. Toret, eds. *15MP2P: Una mirada transdisciplinar del 15M.* Barcelona: INE/UOC, 255–272.

Rancière, J., 1999. *Disagreement: Politics and Philosophy.* Minneapolis: University of Minnesota Press.

Tranche, R., 2013. Vivir por encima de nuestras posibilidades [online]. *El País*. 16 May. Available from: http://elpais.com/elpais/2013/05/07/opinion/1367943599_530998.html [Accessed 12 August 2015].

5

URBAN RESISTANCE AND ITS EXPRESSION IN PUBLIC SPACE

New Demands and Shared Meanings in Argentina[1]

Paula Rosa and Regina Vidosa

The implementation of neoliberal policies in Argentina began in the 1970s, and as a consequence of critical infringements on democratic public space, a new form of urban resistance has begun. Public space has been essential for the protest against neoliberal policies for two essential reasons, first being the basic democratic open exchange and debate amongst citizens, and secondly as a platform for unfolding diverse strategies for consolidation of their organizational forms. In this sense, public space "refers to the shape and to politics [. . .] it is not a pre-existent scenery nor an epiphenomenon of the social organization or the political culture, it is the public space as long as a social experience goes over it, while at the same time it organizes that experience and it shapes it" (Gorelik 1998, p. 19–21).

The crisis that Argentina has blithely cultivated since the mid-1970s makes the emergence of alternative social logics in public space possible, particularly when the accumulated cost of state policies causes the collapse of class identity distinctions (Tejerina 2005, p. 73). The collapse of prior social hierarchies is owed to the devaluation of work as a social integrator, and this collapse has a reverberating effect resulting in protest extending beyond spheres of private production and in collective demand for changes in a variety of spheres: sustainability, environment, and gender and human rights. In addition, broad and class-transcending levels of unemployment have led to new forms of collective resistance.

"Movements of the unemployed" arise as a result of a loss of identity through the loss of the ability to work. The loss of the workplace as a social sphere pushes people into public space:[2] people are no longer expressing frustrations at work with members of their same social class but, through the collective loss of unemployment, become exposed to each other in public space. Furthermore, the similarity of their demands across a variety of platforms allows for the building of social momentum. Thus, public space turned into an area for popular resistance: through road blockades and massive protests in the most important plazas of the city.[3]

Social class and worker identity have been important in Argentinean society. Citing Gregory (1984, p. 137), Sznol (2007, p. 28) suggests, "spatial structure is not, then, just the arena where class conflicts are expressed, but the territory within which—and partly, through which—class relationships are constituted." Tyler (2015, p. 496) suggests that, "class analysis is properly concerned with developing approaches and methods which might allow us to better understand and address the effects of class-based inequalities and the forms of exploitation which accompany and enable inequalities to be sustained and reproduced," and that contemporary society is not necessarily characterized by a "capitalism without classes" in which social inequalities can be seen in an "individualized" way (Tyler 2015, citing Willms 2004, Paton 2014, citing Beck 1992). Consequently, it can be said that being identified as a "worker" is central to both individual and collective personal identity. The loss of labor entails the loss of personal and social vindication across class structures in response to the regressive conditions of neoliberal politics.

Within this framework, the following chapter analyzes some specific experiences of urban resistance in the neoliberalization of Argentina. The consolidation and attending consequences of these urban resistances has unfortunately been met with several regressive public policies and practices. This chapter focuses on the main characteristics of the resistance, including how demands, identities, organizational modalities, and its ways of appropriation of the public space have remained consistent across the decades as seen in the present forms of organization and resistance. Accordingly, this chapter offers a historical view, going over the first implementation of neoliberal policies in Argentina, the context of a social, economic, and political crisis in 2001, and contemporary observations of the present urban resistance.

Neoliberalism and Urban Resistance

In the middle of the 1970s, a cruel military dictatorship undertook significant economic restructuration towards a *market economy*, focused on financial capital, deindustrialization, and dissolved stability of the work market. Such economic changes implicated problematic connections to political purposes where popular groups of cooperating members from different working classes were forced to close down (Azpiazu and Schorr 2010). The loss of functioning syndicates, political parties, and organizations meant gathering, political action, and, above all, collective action spaces were shut down. The military junta institutionalized a systematic and strategic repression plan which led to *state terrorism* for the purposes of battling so-called subversion. The tactics adopted by the state, with compliance and active participation of capital and church sectors, went from censorship and kidnapping, to torture in concentration camps, disappearances, and murder.

In spite of this, resistance and organization did not cease to exist completely. As a result of the dismantling of productive and inclusive urban policy institutions in the 1980s and restrictions placed on social citizenship, civil society gained renewed importance. Since then, social actors and new collective actions regarding women's, generational, urban, ethnic, and human rights movements, among others, became visible. The most emblematic resistance group against the military junta were Mothers and Grandmothers of Plaza de Mayo, who emerged with the purpose of fighting for the return of detained and disappeared people (especially their children), as well as the prosecution of those who were responsible for crimes against humanity. During the military dictatorship, they started to march around the Pyramid at Plaza de Mayo and demanded their kidnapped children be returned alive (see Figure 5.1). Public space was the platform from which their demands could be revealed to their fellow citizens, as well as political and military leaders.

The end of the last military dictatorship (1976–1983) ushered in a period for recovering social and political rights. The debate and the actions of that time were focused on the role of the state in politics, the construction of democracy, and the vindication of human rights. In this period, remaining human rights organizations were consolidated into politically significant and institutionalized social movements with great importance across country. Public space continued to serve as a territory for expressing the increasingly popular demands of these burgeoning institutions.

The 1980s ended, however, with an eroding and unstable economy (recession, hyper-inflation, and high poverty and unemployment rates, among others). Neoliberal measures have thus been strengthened and recapitulated since the early 1990s. The state began to act "more specifically

FIGURE 5.1 Round, Mothers of the Plaza de Mayo founding line. March of Resistance, 2011

Source: Sub.Coop

as territorial conditioner and promoter, according to the new needs of the private capital" (Ciccolella 2009, p. 46). The city gradually became an *exclusive* space reserved for social groups with high purchasing power. There is an increase in the cost of *inhabiting the city* as a result of "public-private investment initiatives within urban reform; higher privatized public services costs and huge private investments on new elite residential typologies in peripheral areas, which modify the housing and urban land market" (Cravino et al. n.d., p. 1). In this way, one can see in a series of highly visible, gentrifying, self-defining, and self-excising territories a troubling sign of growing social inequalities. Country clubs and gated communities were placed in suburbanized areas usually inhabited by low-income sectors—cheap lots, informal settlements, and shanty towns—showing a deep social divide between them and their surroundings in spite of their physical proximity. These high-friction adjacencies created demands related to basic services provision, occupation of land for a living place, and struggles for legal recognition of the occupied lots, leading to the formation of cooperatives and neighborhood councils (González Bombal 1998). Urban social movements were consolidated by undertaking "resistance not only based on pursuing survival, but also by building an alternative system to the neoliberal one through popular organization, focusing on the recuperation of urban space" (García Calderón 2011, p. 5). The systems and methods of recuperation were different, peripheral locations focused on the occupation of parcels of land while central urban areas focused on the appropriation of public and abandoned spaces or buildings. One of the most well-consolidated urban social movements since the end of the 1980s is Movimiento de Ocupantes e Inquilinos (Occupants and Tenants Movement [MOI]), which organized occupation of buildings in Buenos Aires and the creation of housing cooperatives for working families and/

or low income families. Coordinadora de Inquilinos de Buenos Aires (Buenos Aires Tenants Coordination [CIBA]) originated slightly earlier in the 1970s and acted as adviser and organizer for people facing eviction or trying to form a housing cooperative. Even though these social movements focused on housing claims, their demands were not so different from the problems workers or the unemployed had to face (e.g. losing a job, low salaries, sub-employment, losing working rights).

The deepening of neoliberal policies in the 1990s led to massive layoffs of workers, both state workers (through privatization and reduction of public spending) and the private industrial sector. This situation was exacerbated by the subsequent loss of membership from traditional bodies of protection and advocacy: work and labor unions. In this context, as a response to high unemployment rates, there was an emergence of unique forms of urban resistance. Among them, the activity of the Unemployed Workers' Movement (Movimiento de Desocupados or "Piqueteros") between 1996 and 1997 stood out. This group represented an important evolutionary step for Argentinean resistance by creating new forms of protest and organizational modalities. Further, through the articulation of the Piqueteros as a social identity organized around the popularization of demands to work again, the group gave "way to an important transformation in the repertoires of mobilization and in the appropriation of the public space by the Argentine society" (Svampa 2005, p. 238). In relation to this, Caparrós (2002) states that for "more than a century, the workers who wanted to make a claim were organized around their working place: strikes, or even occupation of the place, were the usual ways" (Caparrós 2002, p. 180). But now that they are unemployed, the only space where they can manifest themselves as citizens, viable workers, or protestors is the public space. Road blockades, meetings at plazas, and marches through the city's main avenues, among other measures, make up the forms of social protest carried out in public space as a way to make their claims visible and to win support.

In 2001, the Piqueteros' movement expanded beyond their local boundaries and became a national platform composed of different organizations.[4] As the scope of these movements increased, the need grew for meetings between delegates and leaders of the organizations to build consensus and collectively manage the resistance process. The primary agreements between the organizations involved questioning the legitimacy of the model of accumulation and the rejection of the national government's plan of adjustment. The resistance still has, as it did when it began, a horizontal way of organization, holding general assemblies called "Piqueteros National Assemblies." These meetings became the space for debate, decision making, and designing forms of collective action. At the assemblies, "the debate was about which kind of road blockades should be made—total [blockage] or leaving alternative accesses—and about employing sticks and hoods" (Natalucci 2007, p. 3).[5] There was also a proposal to create a political program in the future. The spontaneity of the first blockades and manifestations began to give way to more organized and formal methods of protest.

Another important form of urban resistance against unemployment and social inequalities brought along the first cases of "factories recovered by their workers."[6] In these cases, apart from horizontal and assembly decision making, production was collectively organized through cooperatives. Specifically, workers reactivate paralyzed businesses affected by commercial deregulation (e.g. slaughterhouses, textiles, transportation, and manufacturing) that were about to go bankrupt or be abandoned by their managers. Recovering these businesses implicates transition towards a new juridical regime where workers take hold of production by making agreements with suppliers and/or clients in order to ensure certain work capital as well as setting the minimum wage for their work (Palomino 2010). In these practices, (previous) workers do not abandon their jobs as a way of protest and organization but they occupy through the operation of the factory facilities themselves. According to Moore (2013), we see a phenomenon in which social movements' claims are crystallized by spatial and corporeal actions; eventually, the occupation or spatial emplacement led to physical interventions (acts of resistance) through "human" barriers, physical barriers, or more importantly, the formation of alter-networks of production and communication. In these cases, the "performative body" could intervene in the spaces in order to habilitate new forms of politics and popular demands.

Crisis of the Neoliberal Model and New Scenery for Urban Resistance

The prolonged recession propelled by expanded neoliberalization in the 1990s meant that, by the end of 2001, social protest was becoming increasingly encompassing. Under a "state of siege"[7] where state-sanctioned armed forces were deployed for repression, a mass of citizens from different socioeconomic sectors went into the streets, plazas, and sidewalks banging their pots (this form of protest was called *cacerolazo*[8]) under the slogan of "¡Que se vayan todos!" (see Figure 5.2). This expression referred to "throwing all the politicians out of government." The *corralito*, a restriction on the withdrawal of money from banks, was the final trigger. Citizens spontaneously mobilized themselves in public space, without any influence from political parties, syndicates, or institutionalized social organizations. Plaza de Mayo was once again witness to acts of urban resistance in the public space and severe police repression, leading to the death and detention of several protestors. Finally, these protests led to President Fernando de la Rúa's resignation, bringing about greater social, economic, and political instability, which would continue for several years.[9]

FIGURE 5.2 *Cacerolazo* protests, December 19–20, 2001

Source: Sub.Coop

There are numerous theories as to the causes that gave birth to this crisis. Neoliberal economists state that the neoliberal reforms carried out in the previous decade were not deep enough—especially the deregulation of the labor market and public spending reduction; that is, the political class was responsible for the crisis because they were incapable of implementing effective neoliberal reform. Another theory suggests that the model was simply untenable as demonstrated by the collective social fallout and attending advancement of serious socioeconomic concerns regarding the neoliberal model's effects on the general public (Bonnet 2002). There is then a third vision, with which we agree, which perceives the 2001 crisis as an *organic crisis*, originating in the decay of the neoliberal accumulation regime and a simultaneous crisis of political representativeness (Basualdo 2003, Lozano 2003, Castellani and Schorr 2003).

According to Rodríguez (2013, p. 2), "the general mobilization during the period between 2000 and 2001 represents a generalized reaction in response to the model and its political class. Struggles gained significant importance and through them, new social movements emerged, which demonstrated a crisis of the traditional forms of participation, such as syndicates and political parties, [which were being] exceeded by spontaneous actions of the population." As a result, the movements of the unemployed and the recovery of factories were consolidated and numerous "popular assemblies" were created.[10] In the public space (streets, corners, and plazas) neighbors began gathering to exchange ideas, sing, engage in political debates, and to work against the degradation of social and political rights. Through face-to-face interactions, these "neighborhood assemblies" made clear the need for action in response to the hopelessness which filled the political environment. "Popular pots" and "barters clubs" were thus organized, making it possible to exchange food and objects in a horizontal way to demonstrate solidarity and to unburden those most affected by unemployment and poverty.

These novel forms of public space appropriation offer a strong contrast with the extended commercialization and privatization of the 1990s. The neighborhood assemblies' claims were based on social rights associated with the collective appropriation or reappropriation of public spaces through collective management (e.g. community dining rooms, cooperatives) and cultural interventions (e.g. cultural activities, training courses, film libraries) (Palomino 2010). At this point, the assemblies re-politicized public spaces and social relations outside the traditional channels for political participation and the state logic of politics (Retamozo 2011, p. 28).

However, strong currency devaluation propelled a regressive shock exploited by dominant economic groups for maximized self-benefit at the expense of responding to preexisting social and economic demands of the already disenfranchised. It seemed that the crisis was again resolved through a remarkable advance of the benefits granted to the owners of capital over the welfare of workers, in spite of the important level of protest in the first term of 2001 (Castellani and Schorr 2003, p. 18).

As Palomino (2010) states, new emergent movements in the public since December 2001 in Argentina demonstrate that efforts for reconstructing social links created new forms of organization. Such organization forms and communication channels allowed for the visibility and legitimacy of all political groups to grow dramatically after the 2001 crisis. The changes made at this point in public policy for advances in income distribution and expansion of social rights had an important precedent to work from. This precedent was the horizontal process through which all the forms of resistance were collectively organized and the physical expression of their demands. All the resistance which arose in response to neoliberal policies—from the Movement of the Unemployed to the neighborhood assemblies—has left an important legacy in regard to organizational and communicative channels. This can be seen nowadays in the fact that every syndical, student, neighbor, professional, or artist sector uses street blockades in order to render themselves visible, or popular assemblies as a horizontal organization space (Barrera 2011).

Urban Resistance in the Face of Recent Economic and Political Contexts

Since 2003, Argentina has undergone significant changes in growth patterns. Between 2002 and 2010, the country reached one of the highest cumulative growth rates (7.6%) in recent history, as well as significant results in the job market: the creation of more than 4 million jobs, the reduction of unemployment and sub-employment rates to one digit, a low increase of registered employment, and a reduction in the incidence of informal employment (CIFRA 2011, p. 2). During this period, salary negotiation tactics were revitalized achieving a record of signed collective agreements.

Retamozo (2011, p. 16) states that the government showed support for old methods of political intervention (syndical, neighborhood, and student actions) and incorporated the political concerns of other publics by relying on activists involved in social movements. Hence, a number of organizations evaluated the possibility of becoming part of the National Popular Party under either the direction of Néstor Kirchner or Cristina F. de Kirchner. This decision might have suggested a degree of resigned autonomy as the organization's collective action did not take the form of protest and their mobilizations were framed within the national government's directives.[11]

Yet, according to Retamozo (2011, p. 16) there was growing social resistance against Kirchner as well. The government fostered opposition in groups who aspired for substantial changes in income distribution and those who demanded the complete end of the present economic model. These groups perceived these models as based on the devastation of natural resources through exploitation by huge national and international corporations. As a result, the protection of natural resources as common goods was expressed through protest against devastating environmental effects, habitat destruction, and forced displacement of populations. At the same time, protest was strengthened by questioning the effects and the model of private appropriation of the resources and the benefits which result from exploiting them (Seoane 2006). Within this context in which local, regional, and global modes of criticism became connected, the resistance expanded in both urban and rural spaces, broadly cultivating and galvanizing public sentiment to steward natural resources in a variety of contexts: water contamination because of large-scale mining projects, substitution of regional products for soybean monoculture, environmental contamination due to the use of unmonitored use of agricultural chemicals, and general problems for the land titling.

These new popular sentiments have incorporated new modalities through the use of digital means of communication in order to make arguments known, denounce certain situations, find others with similar dispositions, and to enhance their collective visibility. At this point, rural movements have incorporated some communication forms of the urban movements, like the use of social networks and large-scale forms of communication, and even mobilization in urban areas for higher visibility. Giarracca (2002, p. 49) states, "the advance of communication technologies, mainly the Internet, contributed to breaking isolation and favoring the circulation of such speeches even in the most geographically remote regions." Previously, many protests were extremely localized and few of these demands were "heard" by the resident population in major urban centers. The specific circumstances of rural areas were shared through social networks and thus gained sufficient support to make the issues a part of the country's larger conversation.

One of the central issues has been the expansion of agricultural and livestock systems whose aspiration for higher profitability has led to rapid deforestation, massive use of agrochemicals, and an increase in soybean monocultures (see Figure 5.3). This situation often causes the displacement of populations and threats of eviction for peasant communities, leading to the creation of several forms of resistance. In the last few years, they have gained great visibility due to their forms of protest. One can observe forms of political organization that are characteristic of the previous period such as direct action, road blockades, and horizontal decision making in assemblies. One

FIGURE 5.3 Camp Congress: Day of the food sovereignty, November 20, 2014

Source: Sub.Coop

of the major movements is MOCASE (Peasant Movement in Santiago del Estero) in Santiago del Estero province, which is comprised of around 9,000 organized families.

Another case indicative of these emerging tactics is the conflict Esquel, a city in the Patagonia region, had with the Canadian mining industry Meridian Gold. On March 23, 2003, 81% of the voting citizens in Esquel rejected the exploitation of a gold and silver field. More than ten years after the plebiscite, no mining industry could carry out the exploitation of the fields in the province, while resistance against large-scale mining operations grew throughout the Andes Mountains. In all the cases, the mobilizations were heterogeneous, with a strong presence of middle classes and frequently involved the professional sectors (teachers, technicians, and so on).

Conclusions

The case of Argentinean protest history and the consequences of neoliberal implementations have given birth to a variety of demands and protests. They expanded beyond the physical sites of factories into urban public space and eventually into the far rural regions of the country. Originally catalyzed by unemployment, public space gained relevance as a platform for resistance and democratic discussion and as a way for displaying solidarity around popular issues—through road blockades and demonstrations. In this sense, the exclusion of workers created an inflection point because it galvanized the resistance against job insecurity, underemployment, and poverty. What this chapter has worked to demonstrate is that analysis centered on class struggle is pertinent because "being" a worker is still a central analytical category to understanding resistance displayed in the public space as the socially organized recapitulation of labor against the authority. Even though neoliberalism had modified social structure, it did not incur the cessation of demands based on inequalities between social classes. This was illustrated by the fact that many protests linked to the job market, which initially arose spontaneously and with almost no organization, persisted and eventually led to the institutionalization of their demands, becoming a fully articulated social movement. In this way, through the evolutions of the organizational processes, one can realize that even though initial demands centered on employment, other demands were added in order to articulate broader goals involving other common interests (e.g. better conditions for all the workers, better pensions, higher salaries). This "expansion" of demands was possible because demonstrations and resistance were practiced beyond the physical limits of the factory space into the broader public spaces, both physical and digital.

In regards to this evolution of urban resistance, the crisis of 2001 became an inflection point in Argentine history. The political and social outbursts of this period originated as reactions to the social consequences produced by neoliberal policies, propelling the development of increasingly organized urban resistance. Public space gained great importance as the territory where many social sectors organized themselves against state-adopted measures. Many of these strategies of using public space left an important legacy that continue to inform present forms of organization and demand.

In spite of state actions initiated in 2003 that aimed at helping Argentina correct the serious social, economic, and political consequences created by neoliberal policies, there was still a great deal to be done to continue improving living conditions for many social classes. This is why new forms of resistance continue to be found, particularly where there are demands for higher relevance and visibility of those associated with natural resource exploitation. These new forms of protest have incorporated new modes of communications, especially digital communication, allowing for the expansion of their demands to a wider audience. Yet, in spite of these advancements, physical public space remains the primary arena for social protest. The struggles against predominant inequalities continue to be expressed there. As such, the present analysis makes it possible to argue that in spite of advancements in organization, tactics, and communication, physical public space continues to have a central role for urban resistance from the 1970s to the present day in Argentina.

Notes

1. All translations of citations from Spanish into English were made by Rosario Palau Posse.
2. This reinforces the idea that dynamics of class exploitation are not limited to the workplace (Harvey 2013, p. 188)
3. For a detailed analysis of roadblocks to enhance protest visibility, see Scribano (1999).
4. After preparing the plan of struggle in July 2001, the first road blockade was made. An estimated 100,000 people participated in 200 road blockades. "The closure for 48 hours of blockades and protests was a march towards Plaza de Mayo, in which around 50,000 people took part" (Natalucci 2007, p. 4)
5. Employing self-defense tools (carrying sticks and covered faces) established a deep identity. These practices were increasingly adopted due to police persecution and violence. Hoods are used for self-protection against possible legal accusations and sticks are employed to form a cordon for self-defense during marches (Corsiglia Mura 2013, Almada 2013).
6. Between 2002 and 2013, the recovered factories grow from 33 to 311 in the whole country (Ruggeri 2014).
7. On December 19, 2001 there were major lootings of supermarkets and other kinds of shops in different parts of *boneaerense* suburbs. That night President De la Rúa declared a state of siege which granted security forces special powers for repression.
8. Many of the balconies and windows were spontaneously filled with the noise of people clanging pots and pans as a way of protest and resistance against that presidential order. The state of siege's purpose was preventing the population from leaving their homes for manifestation; the *cacerolazo* showed opposition against this measure, and it led thousands of people and families to "occupy" the urban public space.
9. Between 2001 and 2002, the unemployment rate stayed around 15%, while the suboccupation involved approximately 20–25% of the economically active population. The average real salary fell by 20%

compared to rates at the end of 2001, while the salary cost was reduced almost 50%. The population under the poverty line reached 55%, while those people who cannot even satisfy their basic needs (indigent) represented 26% of total population (Rapetti 2005).

10. In August 2002, there were 122 assemblies in the City of Buenos Aires and 329 throughout the country (Triguboff 2015, p. 13)

11. Since 2005, several Piqueteros leaders occupied government positions, especially as the secretaries related to social and community action, both in the national and provincial governments (Svampa 2007).

References

Almada, J. S., 2013. Piqueteros, Luchas de Poder e Identidades. *Astrolabio*, (11), 292–310.

Azpiazu, D. and Schorr, M., 2010. Tu pasado te condena [online]. *Página 12*. Available from: www.pagina12. com.ar/diario/suplementos/cash/33-4311-2010-05-10.html [Accessed 7 June 2015].

Barrera, S., 2011. Las Asambleas Populares del 2001–2002: La primavera de la autoactividad de las masas [online]. *Herramienta*, 46. Available from: www.herramienta.com.ar/revista-herramienta-n-46/las-asambleas-populares-del-2001-2002-la-primavera-de-la-autoactividad-de-l [Accessed 12 January 2016].

Basualdo, E. M., 2003. Las reformas estructurales y el Plan de Convertibilidad durante la década de los noventa. [online]. *Monografias.com*. Available from: www.monografias.com/trabajos901/reformas-estructurales-argentina-convertibilidad-noventa/reformas-estructurales-argentina-convertibilidad-noventa.shtml [Accessed 15 January 2016].

Beck, U., 1992. *Risk Society: Towards a New Modernity*. London: Sage.

Bonnet, A., 2002. La crisis de la convertibilidad [online]. *Theomai*, 99. Available from: www.redalyc.org/pdf/124/12490103.pdf [Accessed 10 December 2015].

Caparrós, M., 2002. *Qué país*. Buenos Aires: Editorial Planeta.

Castellani, A. and Schorr, M., 2003. ¿Crisis . . . qué crisis? Notas sobre la debacle del régimen convertible en la Argentina, *Sociology Conference of UNLP*.

Ciccolella, P., 2009. Buenos Aires: una metrópolis postsocial en el contexto de la economía global. *In*: P. Pírez, ed. *Buenos Aires, la formación del presente*. Olachi: Quito, 35–62.

CIFRA, 2011. CIFRA: Informe de coyuntura No 7, el nuevo patrón de crecimiento [Argentina 2002–2010] [online]. Available from: www.centrocifra.org.ar/ [Accessed 2 March 2016].

Corsiglia Mura, L., 2013. *Jóvenes Piqueteros y Encapuchados*. De la Plata: Editorial de la Universidad Nacional de La Plata.

Cravino, M. C., Wagner, F. R. and Varela, O., n.d. *Notas sobre la política habitacional en el AMBA en los años '90* [online]. Available from: www.infohabitat.com.ar/web/img_d/est_30072009230802_n30072009230627. pdf [Accessed 3 March 2016].

García Calderón Pavón, I., 2011. *Transformación del espacio urbano y movimientos sociales en Argentina tras la crisis de 2001: El caso del Movimiento Territorial Liberación*. Madrid: Complutense University of Madrid.

Giarracca, N., 2002. Movimientos sociales y protestas en los mundos rurales latinoamericanos: nuevos escenarios y nuevos enfoques. *Sociologías*, 8, 246–274.

González Bombal, I., 1998. *La visibilidad pública de las organizaciones de la sociedad civil*. Buenos Aires: CEDES.

Gorelik, A., 1998. *La grilla y el parquet*. Buenos Aires: National University of Quilmes.

Gregory, D., 1984. *Ideología, Ciencia y Geografía Humana*. Barcelona: Oikos-Tau.

Harvey, D., 2013. *Ciudades rebeldes: Del derecho de la ciudad a la revolución urbana*. Madrid: Editorial Akal.

Lozano, C., 2003. *Apuntes sobre la etapa actual*. Buenos Aires: Instituto de Estudios y Formación de la CTA.

Moore, S., 2013. Taking Up Space: Anthropology and Embodied Protest. *Radical Anthropology*, 7, 6–16.

Natalucci, A. L., 2007. La unidad de los que luchan: las asambleas nacionales piqueteras (2001). *Questión*, 1 (16), 1–8.

Palomino, H., 2010. La Argentina hoy. Los movimientos sociales [online]. *Herramienta*, 27. Available from: www.herramienta.com.ar/revista-herramienta-n-27/la-argentina-hoy-los-movimientos-sociales [Accessed 13 February 2016].

Paton, K., 2014. *Gentrification: A Working Class Perspective*. Farnham, Burlington: Ashgate.

Rapetti, M., 2005. La macroeconomía argentina durante la post-convertibilidad: evolución, debates y perspectivas. *Policy Papers Series*, New York: Economics Working Group, The Argentina Observatory, Graduate Program in International Affairs, New School University.

Raschke, J., 1994. Sobre el concepto de movimiento social. *Zona abierta*, 69, 121–134.

Retamozo, M., 2011. Movimientos sociales, política y hegemonía en Argentina. *Polis. Revista Latinoamericana*, 10 (28), 243–279.

Rodríguez, S. L., 2013. Los movimientos sociales en la Argentina a partir de la década del 90. Paper presented at XVIII Encuentro Nacional de Economía Política, organized by the Brazilian Society of Political Economy SEP.

Ruggeri, A., 2014. Informe del IV relevamiento de Empresas Recuperadas en la Argentina. 2014: las empresas recuperadas en el período 2010–2013. 1a ed. Ciudad Autónoma de Buenos Aires: Cooperativa Chilavert Artes Gráficas [online]. Available from: www.recuperadasdoc.com.ar/Informe_IV_relevamiento_2014. pdf [Accessed 21 August 2015].

Scribano, A., 1999. Argentina cortada: "Cortes de ruta" y visibilidad social en el contexto del ajuste. *In*: M. López, ed. *Lucha popular, democracia, neoliberalismo: protesta popular en América Latina en los años del ajuste*. Venezuela: Maya Editora, Nueva Visión, 45–71.

Seoane, J., 2006. Social Movements and the Defense of Natural Resources in Latin America: Reaction Against the Neoliberal Model and the Construction of Alternatives. *Sociedade e Estado*, 21 (1), 85–107.

Svampa, M., 2005. *La sociedad excluyente. La Argentina bajo el signo del neoliberalismo*. Buenos Aires: Taurus.

Svampa, M., 2007. Las fronteras del Gobierno de Kirchner: entre la consolidación de lo viejo y las aspiraciones de lo nuevo [online]. *Cuadernos del CENDES*. Available from: www.redalyc.org/articulo. oa?id=40306502 [Accessed 2 March 2016].

Sznol, F., 2007. Geografía de la Resistencia. Protesta social, formas de apropiación y transformación del espacio urbano en la Argentina (1996–2006). *Theomai*, (15) primer semestre, 21–34.

Tejerina, B., 2005. Movimientos sociales, espacio público y ciudadanía: Los caminos de la utopía. *Revista Crítica de Ciências Sociais*, (72), 67–97.

Triguboff, M., 2015. *Asambleas populares: Movilización social, trayectorias y prácticas políticas en Buenos Aires (2001–2006)*. Buenos Aires: Imago Mundi.

Tyler, I., 2015. Classificatory Struggles: Class, Culture and Inequality in Neoliberal Times. *The Sociological Review*, 63 (2), 493–511.

Willms, J., 2004. *Conversations with Ulrich Beck*. Cambridge: Polity Press.

Websites

Movimiento de Ocupantes e Inquilinos (MOI). Interview with Néstor Jeifetz. OSERA N°3. Available from: http://webiigg.sociales.uba.ar/empresasrecuperadas/PDF/PDF_03/Movimiento%20de%20ocupantes% 20e%20Inquilinos.pdf [Accessed March 3, 2016].

PART 2

Reclaiming

From Public Space to the Political

6

RECLAIMING PUBLIC SPACE MOVEMENT IN HONG KONG

From Occupy Queen's Pier to the Umbrella Movement

Yun-Chung Chen and Mirana M. Szeto

On September 28, 2014, protesters in Hong Kong launched the largest protest in the city's history—later named the Umbrella Movement or Umbrella Revolution. The protests and occupation of streets and public space took place in multiple locations throughout the city, drawing more than 100,000 demonstrators at any one time. The longest occupation in Causeway Bay lasted for 79 days. While the movement was unprecedented in its scale in Hong Kong, using direct action to reclaim public space is not new to the city. Precedents date back to the 97-day occupation of Queen's Pier in 2007, which led to other Reclaim the Public Space movements in the city. This chapter explains the transformation of movement implications, scale, and form by drawing on our viewpoint as activists who have participated in both movements.[1]

Occupy Queen's Pier emerged as a movement in 2007 to preserve the historical Queen's Pier from demolition (Community Cultural Concern 2007, Chen 2009). Young activists challenged the colonial port city imagination of Hong Kong as "borrowed place, borrowed time" (Hughes 1976), a transient space of capital and opportunism. More than just protecting the historic site, the movement strived to gain agency in the development and planning of the city that has long been denied to the locals. The movement was especially meaningful for those who chose to stay in Hong Kong despite the handover to China in 1997, particularly working-class residents unable or unwilling to emigrate. For them, the Queen's Pier was the only remaining accessible harborfront public space in the central business district. Occupy Queen's Pier was therefore a movement to "reclaim our city" against bulldozer-style neoliberal development.

The scale and scope of Reclaim the Public Space movement exploded exponentially in the Umbrella Movement of 2014. With the slogan "Hong Kong is ours, only Hong Kong people can save Hong Kong," the movement manifests a new Hong Kong political subjectivity and a desire for uncompromised autonomy and democracy (J. Chan 2014, S. Chan 2015, Ortmann 2015, Veg 2015). Occupying the throughways of the most economically vibrant districts of Admiralty, Causeway Bay, and Mongkok, activists and citizens went beyond merely reclaiming public space to also reclaim political agency that has been gradually taken away from Hong Kong people by the Beijing authority.

From Protestival to Occupy

Before comparing and analyzing these two movements—Occupy Queen's Pier and the Umbrella Movement—it is necessary to position them in relation to recent global movements to reclaim public space. Reclaiming public space as collective action can be traced back to 1969 in central

Stockholm, when environmentalists temporarily blocked the street for non-car users. "Reclaim the Streets" (RTS) movement was thus coined. Strategic street blockade expanded globally on May 16, 1998, when Global Street Parties were organized in 30 cities around the world to protest against the G8 meetings in Birmingham, England and the WTO ministerial meeting in Geneva the following week. Again on June 18, 1999, during the world economic summit in Cologne, "protestivals" were organized in 40 cities (Leitner, Peck, and Sheppard 2007). These protestivals demonstrate "a resurgence of autonomism, anarchism and direct democracy [. . .] developing within the context of global opposition to neo-liberalism" (St. John 2008).

However, RTS or protestivals are typically short-term actions emphasizing creativity more than sustained and transformative resistance. They often remain ambiguously stuck between protest and carnival. At worst, when swung more towards creativity than resistance, these activities can be easily co-opted into the "cultural diversity and attractiveness of neoliberal" city branding (Mayer 2007, p. 97). Occupy Wall Street (OWS) in 2011, which lasted for almost two months, was perhaps an attempt to break away from the short-lived, protestival-style occupation. Furthermore, it showed how "direct democracy" could be enacted through assemblies and collective decision making.

The above comparison is not intended to suggest a dichotomy. Rather, it illustrates the spectrum of public space movements within which most hybrid examples fall. Hong Kong's Reclaim the Public Space movement, for example, presents a hybrid example that combines long-term occupation, political-economy analysis, vibrant carnivalesque actions, and utopian imaginations.

Occupy Queen's Pier: Reclaiming Our City

The Reclaim the Public Space movement in Hong Kong first emerged after the demolition of Star Ferry Pier (50 meters away from Queen's Pier) in December 2006. When the Housing and Transportation Bureau (known as the Development Bureau since July 1, 2007) hurriedly demolished the Star Ferry Pier at Victoria Harbor on December 13, 2006 to make way for land reclamation in the harbor, they did not realize that their "routine" action would ignite a new social movement. That night, 14 "activists" who barely knew each other engaged in direct action to stop the bulldozers at the Star Ferry Pier. Most of them had never taken part in a confrontation with the police before. Soon 200 citizens rallied outside in support after receiving text messages or viewing live footage online with protestors being rounded up. The protesters were arrested. But upon release, they returned to the demolition site to launch a hunger strike. Subsequently, they teamed up with anti-urban-renewal groups, concerned artists, civil reporters, poets, bloggers, social workers, anarchists, cultural commentators, and scholars, and formed a new alliance called Local Action to continue the movement. This earlier process set the stage for Occupy Queen's Pier.

Queen's Pier was built in 1953 as part of Edinburgh Place, a cluster of modern architecture and public space built on the then-new harborfront reclamation area in Central District (called "Central" hereafter), the financial center of Hong Kong. The pier had been outside the public radar in Hong Kong due to its quotidian low profile. To preservationists, however, Queen's Pier was important historically as it functioned both as a ceremonial pier for the symbolic landing and departure of British royalties and colonial governors and as a public pier for cruises. However, the Development Bureau insisted on demolition to make way for land reclamation and the construction of an underground bypass to ease traffic. As activists, we exposed the hidden agenda behind the stated transportation needs: to create land for luxury grade-A commercial office towers, shopping malls, and the military berth of the People's Liberation Army (PLA) Headquarters (Figure 6.1).

On April 25, 2007, only a few months after the demolition of Star Ferry Pier, the Hong Kong government announced the closure of Queen's Pier. Before the government could fence it off,

FIGURE 6.1   Queen's Pier at the heart of Hong Kong's Central District

Source: Pak-Chai Tse

Local Action activists occupied the soon-to-be demolished Queen's Pier to prevent the government from cordoning it off, so that the public could continue to enjoy this public space. Between April 25 and August 1, 2007, activists camped there for a total of 97 days to demand that this public space be kept and to prevent further commodification and militarization of Victoria Harbor.

As a neocolonial city dominated by neoliberal discourses and practices (Purcell 2008, Brown 2015) with little attention to preservation of cultural heritage, we argue that the significance of the Occupy Queen's Pier movement goes beyond merely preserving a historical site or public space. Instead, its purpose was to "reclaim our city" for future generations of Hong Kong. The main contributions of the movement are summarized below.

Reclaiming the Historical Origin of Edinburgh Place as a Civic Space

Queen's Pier was an integral part of the Edinburgh Place complex (together with Star Ferry Pier, City Hall, and Hong Kong's first public carpark), which was constructed during a paradigm shift in Hong Kong urban planning (Hong Kong City Hall 1962a, 1962b, 1967). Before World War II, the public space in the city's commercial heart that housed the previous generations of piers was not accessible to grassroots populations, thus denying them opportunities to turn them into "lived" spaces (Ng et al. 2010, p. 411). The new Edinburgh Place in the Central District, together with Victoria Park in Causeway Bay, represented a new paradigm of building large public spaces on expensive reclamations. Some scholars suggested that the provision of public spaces was still top-down because the colonial government was meeting the needs of the industrializing economy by providing "inclusive" civic spaces for the general public (Ng et al. 2010, p. 411). The construction of large public spaces on harborfront reclamation in the 1950s could therefore be seen as the colonial government's response to provide more recreational space for reproduction of labor and to calm the social unrest among grassroots populations. As such, it was also meant to regain legitimacy of colonial rule through means of social control against the spread of Mao's socialist ideology in Hong Kong. Occupy Queen's Pier was therefore an effort to reaffirm the continuation of the civic space tradition embedded in Edinburgh Place and to protect the evidence of colonial state response to local discontent and disenfranchisement.

Reclaiming the History of People's Resistance

As a civic space and major transportation hub by design and as a symbolic space of colonial rule, Queen's Pier has been a popular site for demonstrations in Hong Kong. Because of its symbolism and convenience, there was no better site to stage an anti-colonialism and anti-imperialism protest than here. Major social movements that took place here included a hunger strike against a Star Ferry price hike in 1966 (that led to the 1966 Riots), the Campaign for Chinese as Official Language in 1970 (signaling the rise of local identity politics among the post-WWII locally born generation), and Protect the Diaoyutai Movement in 1970–71 (against post-WWII British colonialism and Japanese and American imperialism). Various labor and social rights movements since 1970 also started here, including the anti-imperialism movement by left-wing Filipina domestic workers since the mid-1980s. Unlike conservative local historians who argued that histories can be preserved in museums, Local Action activists argued that none of the subaltern histories would be mentioned in museums or textbooks, and that the history of Queen's Pier would be best preserved if it were still alive and continued to be "lived" by existing and new users. They argue that the struggle to reclaim Hong Kong people's history can best be achieved by reclaiming public space (Harvey 2012, Mitchell 2003).

FIGURE 6.2 Local Action holding a meeting at Queen's Pier

Source: Pak-Chai Tse

Reclaiming a Lived Multicultural Space

Queen's Pier was also a multicultural public space open to all. During our 24-hour occupation shifts, we witnessed a full range of civic activities on Queen's Pier. In the morning, people of all ages and races would come to exercise, perform Tai Chi, or dance. At noon, both blue-collar and white-collar workers would eat their lunches while enjoying the sea breeze. In the afternoons, retirees from different ethnicities gathered here to play chess. At night, bikers would stop for a cigarette break before continuing their journey. Mongolian traders skipped expensive hotels and stayed here overnight before returning home. During weekends, Filipina domestic helpers would gather here for all sorts of functions including picnics, dance practices, forums, and family reunions. Wedding couples would come to have pictures taken after marriage registration at City Hall. Young couples and students would hang out and go on dates. Middle-aged men come to fish, chitchat, read, and take afternoon naps. Street performers and underground bands perform here occasionally. Filmmakers loved to do location shooting here because no permission was needed. Many celebrities, like actor Chow Yun Fat, expressed support for preserving Queen's Pier because of their fond memories here. Multiculturalism was never a norm in Hong Kong, but Queen's Pier was one place to actually witness existing multiculturalism in the city.

Reclaiming the Site of Resistance Against the Landscape of Power

Behind the scene, through research-based activism, Local Action combed through government archives and discovered many hidden agendas buried under promotional booklets. Publicly distributed leaflets by the government mislead the public and Legislative Council (LEGCO) members concerning the proposed 400-meter-long, 10-story-high "groundscraper" (nicknamed by

FIGURE 6.3 Occupy Queen's Pier: Reclaim the Public Space as a project of decolonization and democratization

Source: Pak-Chai Tse

government technocrats), a "skyscraper" stretching horizontally from the Central MTR Station to the new Star Ferry Pier. Camouflaged in green to approximate a hilly landscape, the floor area of the "groundscraper" would be similar to the tallest building in Hong Kong, the International Financial Center (IFC). In the future, Star Ferry passengers would be forced to walk through this luxury shopping mall from the Central MTR Station to reach the pier. In addition to the ground-scraper, the reclamation project also included a secretive plan to build a 300-meter-wide military berth in Central and directly in front of the PLA Headquarters. In addition to losing such precious open space, the co-location of the government offices, PLA Headquarters, and IFC at the heart of Central was also an image we asked the public to question. Occupy Queen's Pier was therefore an attempt to stop the consolidation of the finance-military-state complex.

Reclaiming the Politics of Emancipation

Refusing to become a new colonial subject under an authoritarian regime, Local Action aimed to nurture a new local subjectivity with the agency to plan our own city (see the first note). Occupy Queen's Pier represented a demand for decentralizing the decision-making process in urban development. The systematic manipulation of the consultation process through "fake con-sultations" was exposed, as no consultation was actually done on the demolition of the piers. The collusion of the planning authority and the developers in Hong Kong had worsened after the financial crisis in 1997 as corporations and business elites forced the state to speed up urban redevelopment that would subsidize the accumulation of private capital.

Although Occupy Queen's Pier eventually failed to preserve the pier, the spirit of Reclaim the Public Space as a project of decolonization and democratization has spread to other community resistances. Reclaiming the Blue House (2006 to present) was the first case of "living heritage conservation" in Hong Kong where existing tenants could continue to stay. Reclaiming the public parks by Freedom Ball (2007) was a project also aiming at loosening the tight government con-trol over the use of public parks. Reclaiming Lee Tung Street (2007) was an attempt to protect a quotidian heritage community and printing cluster from urban redevelopment. Reclaiming Times Square actions (2008) succeeded in loosening up the strict control on activities such as street performance and public gatherings at this privately managed public space in Causeway Bay. Similar to Reclaim the Public Space movements elsewhere, local efforts in Hong Kong have tried to rebuild urban commons that have been enclosed by privatization and bureaucratic con-trol (Ng 2013). What is significant about Hong Kong's movement was that it went further than reclaiming the commons and improving the quality of life by directly challenging the expansion of real-estate-led redevelopment through multi-site resistances against the authoritarian regime.

Umbrella Movement: Reclaiming Our Way of Life

Although Reclaim the Public Space movements grew in Hong Kong after the demolition of Queen's Pier in 2007, the outcomes were still limited. The main reason lies in the difficulty of fighting[2] powerful real estate tycoons who control most urban spaces. Furthermore, the pro-real-estate government became even more hard-line against democratization after Beijing decided to delay parliamentary democracy in Hong Kong. Under an increasingly authoritarian rule, Hong Kong people are losing not only control of their public spaces but also other aspects of their everyday lives, including free press (Lee 2015). An important turning point for the shift from the "reclaiming our city" discourse to that of "reclaiming our way of life" was the Anti-Express Rail Movement that began in 2009. The project is a 26-km-long railway that will link Hong Kong Station at West Kowloon, crossing the border to Shenzhen to connect with the national high-speed rail grid planned by Beijing. Transportation projects were once regarded as *local* development under the full control of the Hong Kong government. The construction of the Express Rail, however, was elevated to a national project on which Beijing had the final word. As such, the Anti-Express Rail Movement now represents a direct confrontation with the Beijing authority. In short, the Reclaiming Public Space Movement, once a *local* social movement, now jumps scale to become a movement against authoritarian Beijing. The collapse of local and national spaces of activism pushes social activists and pan-democrat politicians into the same corner against the same Beijing authority.

On September 22, 2014, the Hong Kong Federation of Students (HKFS)[3] announced a week-long boycott of classes at Tamar, the newly built Hong Kong government headquarters and the Legislative Council (LEGCO) complex (site of the harbor reclamation) to demand genuine direct election for the head (chief executive or CE) of the Hong Kong Special Administration Region. Roughly 5,000 university students participated in a five-day boycott of classes to protest against the 170 to 0 vote by the Beijing authority, via its National People's Congress Standing Committee on August 31, 2014 in favor of shutting down all election reform proposals for CE election in Hong Kong in 2017 and beyond. The boycott was also a protest against the occupation strategy proposed by the Occupy Central committee that was deemed too slow (Occupy Central planned to occupy the Central District on October 1, 2014) and too conservative (they gave up the original action to paralyze the financial district, and merely prepared supporters for arrest under minor offenses as a way to raise public sympathy).[4]

From the perspective of movement participants, this was how the Umbrella Movement came to be. On September 26, 2014, the last day of the boycott, another student organization, Scholarism,[5] joined HKFS to organize their own one-day high school student boycott. Around 500 high school students in school uniform showed up at Tamar. The same night, Joshua Wong, convener of Scholarism, suddenly announced their intent for direct action to reclaim the Civic Square at Tamar.[6] This direct action had been discussed secretly for months among HKFS and Scholarism, but seemed to have escaped the watchful eyes of the Hong Kong police who were often accused by activists for illegally tapping their phones and meetings. Over 200 students and young protestors rushed to reclaim Civic Square. They forced open the gate and confronted the police, resulting in many being pepper sprayed by the riot police. The image of the confrontation was widely broadcasted on both mainstream and social media, inspiring many people to rush to the site to support the students and young protestors trapped by heavy police force. The police made multiple attempts to besiege the stage set by HKFS outside Civic Square and arrested HKFS student leaders who used loudspeakers to mobilize the crowd. The move to silence the student leaders backfired as more protestors came to surround the police and block them from taking students away.

The next day, more people gathered at Tamar to support the students who were either under police custody or still trapped in Civic Square by the police. They demanded the release of the students and the reopening of Civic Square, and blocked the passageway to prevent more police from entering. As riot police tried many times to disperse the crowds by frantically using pepper spray and batons, nonviolent protestors in the frontline opened umbrellas as shields to block the pepper spray, with some success. The untrained protestors formed over eight defense lines, and continued to pass colorful umbrellas from the back to the front to protect protestors from pepper spray. Riot police forcefully pulled away the umbrellas, but the supply of umbrellas continued unbroken. Some umbrellas even parachuted from the overpass like flowers falling from the sky, creating a stunning visual impact that excited the crowds and encouraged them to hold their ground and continue to block the riot police from clearing Tamar.

To prevent the police from taking back the occupied Tamar at night, over 1,000 protestors equipped themselves with umbrellas, covered their faces with plastic wrap and goggles, and stayed vigilant through the night behind various barricades built on the streets. Such images soon flooded social media. The everyday nature of umbrellas, plastic wrap, and goggles ubiquitous in Hong Kong but deployed in a completely new and unique manner vividly crystallized the image and naming of the Umbrella Movement as a massive and endearingly quotidian effort (Veg 2015). On September 28, 2014, more diverse people rushed to support the protestors and demand immediate release of Scholarism and HKFS student leaders. To prevent the crowds from reaching Tamar, the police sealed off the overpasses from Admiralty MTR Station to Tamar, forcing the angry crowds to spread across Harcourt Road opposite Tamar. Angry protestors simultaneously occupied main roads of Mongkok in Kowloon and Causeway Bay on Hong Kong Island, turning the two most important shopping districts and transportation hubs into Umbrella Squares.

The Umbrella Movement as it was internationally witnessed was neither a planned event nor an accident. It was in fact a continuation of the 30-year-old democracy movement in Hong Kong that turned increasingly desperate, resulting in radical evolution of protest by a new generation of activists calling themselves "Umbrella Soldiers."[7] Direct actions in civil disobedience, mass mobilization, and prolonged occupation are not unusual in Hong Kong social movements. Mass mobilization routines also include the annual First of July rally for democracy and the June Fourth Vigil to commemorate victims of the 1989 June 4th Tiananmen Massacre in Beijing. What was new in the Umbrella Movement was how direct actions, prolonged occupation, and mass mobilization were comprehensively deployed together by the activists, with an estimated 1.2 million people at the three main sites during the Umbrella Movement. Specifically, the Umbrella Movement is significant as outlined in the next sections.

FIGURE 6.4 Umbrellas and tent communities at the Admiralty occupied zone where the Umbrella Movement started

Source: Pak-Chai Tse

The Emergence of a New Generation of Umbrella Activists

The recorded 87 tear gas canisters fired into the crowd on September 28, 2014 brought large numbers of Hong Kong residents out into the streets. Many of them had never demonstrated before. Outraged by the police brutality against nonviolent protestors, these first-time protestors walked out of their everyday comfort zone to become the backbone of the Umbrella Movement during the 79-day occupation. The newbie protestors, labeled by mainstream media as "yellow ribbon" or self-labeled as "Umbrella Soldiers," have been eagerly looking for new and more effective methods of protest that are drastically different in order to maintain efficacy in fighting for genuine democracy and defending the erosion of their way of life.

The Emergence of a Self-Help Mentality: Do-It-Together Culture

Witnessing the systemic failure and the inability of the pan-democrat politicians to make changes, Hong Kong people have arrived at the conclusion that they themselves have to protect their society from further deterioration. This self-help mentality manifested beautifully in the creation of "umbrella villages" at the three occupied zones. "Our Hong Kong, We Save" became not only the slogan, but also the motivation for many people to take part or contribute to the occupation. Office workers brought drinks and lunch boxes to the site. Homemakers offered hot soup and homemade bread to protestors. Van drivers provided free transportation of materials. Students took shifts to help other protestors (by setting up stations for recharging cellphones, recycling, receiving and managing donated materials, public forums, art projects, etc.). Carpenters built

FIGURE 6.5 Do-It-Together culture at Occupy Mongkok: collectively made makeshift dialogue zone and cardboard communal sitting room

Source: Pak-Chai Tse

FIGURE 6.6 An "umbrella village" at occupied Mongkok

Source: Pak-Chai Tse

furniture for students to study at the "Umbrella Square." Self-organized marshals took shifts to guard the "frontier"[8] and block police and alleged thugs hired by the ruling establishment from entering the occupied zones. The defensive nature of the barricades did not preclude occupiers from turning them into an explosion of installation art, sculptures, mountings of paintings, poetry, banners, and plenty of other forms of creativity. What endeared the world to the Umbrella Movement is the creative, cultural "weapons," quotidian "armors," and communitarian Do-It-Together culture of Umbrella "Soldiers." All these altruistic community-building efforts transformed the occupied areas filled with strangers into "villages" where protestors began to build strong bonds and friendships that continued into the post-Umbrella era.

The Emergence of a "Protect Our Own Culture and Language" Mentality

In Hong Kong, so-called mainlandization has spilled over from the economy to politics and everyday lives. Gradual integration with and competition from Chinese cities, coupled with immigration from China, have contributed to an erosion of Hong Kong's way of life perceived by a growing number of people. Due to the asymmetrical scale between the colossal Chinese consuming/investing public and the local market, Hong Kong finds itself overwhelmed by Chinese mainlanders coming for real estate, health care, clean food, and places in its liberal education system. Mainlandization is also perceived in a xenophobic manner through the infiltration of negatively perceived mainland cultural habits, the increase in corruption and decrease in consumer/citizen rights, as well as the invasion of global brand-name chain stores serving mainland tourists and pricing out quotidian mom-and-pop stores. To navigate daily life without reference to China as the hegemony and "mainlandization" as an imperative (Szeto 2014, Szeto and Chen 2011, 2015) is a luxury that Hong Kong can no longer afford. A survey of Umbrella Movement occupiers shows that besides true universal suffrage, their second most important concern is Hong Kong–China relations.[9] Mainlandization is obvious also in the government's failed attempt to implement the National Education Guide (Patriotic Education) in 2012. The Cantonese-speaking majorities in Hong Kong are fiercely opposed to implementing simplified Chinese writing and spoken Mandarin in school curriculum. They are afraid that the local Cantonese language (and its cultures) will be marginalized and gradually replaced. Meanwhile, the protection of Cantonese language and culture has also been used by right-wing *localists* in Hong Kong to breed ethno-nationalist sentiments. For example, any Chinese-looking person who speaks Cantonese with a strong accent is now unwelcome or even accused of being a spy. Many new immigrants who supported and volunteered during the Umbrella Movement share unpleasant experiences of being mistaken by right-wing localists as spies, and being humiliated in public or even castigated in the umbrella villages.

The Growth of Ethno-Nationalist Sentiments and the Pro-Independence Movement

It is important to note that the localist discourses split into Left and Right during the Umbrella Movement. While "Hong Kong is not China" and "Hong Kong people should have first priority" remained shared discourses between the two camps, they were divided by a major difference in their attitudes towards Chinese immigrants from mainland China. The Left accepted Chinese immigrants as part of Hong Kong society. "Your parents are all immigrants from China," they say, and "should not be discriminated." The inclusive politics of the Left would not leave out the rights of immigrants, migrant labor, and racial minorities and Chinese immigrants (Chen and Szeto 2015a, 2015b). The Right however, wants to restrict Chinese immigrants because they regard them as burdens of Hong Kong society who compete for jobs and social welfare. The ultra-right go even further to accuse every immigrant of being a spy of the Chinese Communist Party (CCP), and they consider immigration to be an ethnic cleansing conspiracy of the CCP to make Hong Kong people a minority. Intensified political repression from the Beijing authority helps flame this Hong Kong nationalism and the pro-independence movement, transforming them into a cultural hegemony within the localist movement, pushing left (progressive) localism to the margins.

Prefigurative Politics versus the Emergence of Violent Resistance

Accusations of police violence and collaboration with hired intruders have reached record highs in Hong Kong today. Over 1,000 protestors have been arrested and some prosecuted since the Umbrella Movement. The nonviolent resistance of the liberal and left-leaning Umbrella Movement leadership and regular occupiers was heavily criticized by the right-wing militant participants for failing to stop police violence and to disrupt government operation. In place of nonviolence, violent resistance against police brutality and disruption of social order gradually became dominant discourses. The clash between police and protestors during the Lunar New Year in February 2016 set a precedent for violent resistance in the future. In the so-called Fish Ball Revolution, protestors fought back against the police crackdown on street vendors using whatever they could find on the streets, including bricks. The clash resulted in serious injury on both sides. Over 80 people (including innocent bystanders) were arrested and prosecuted. The momentum of violent resistance and anti-China sentiments built up during the Umbrella Movement, and thus cast a dark shadow over the movement.

Post-Umbrella Prefigurative Politics: From Occupying the Streets to Occupying Communities

We understand that appreciation of the Umbrella Movement soon turned sour due to a predominantly skeptical and defeatist discourse about the lack of any demonstrable "outcomes" or "successes." Like the post-Occupy sentiments elsewhere, people ask: How much difference had it really made? Had it lead to more democracy (van de Sande 2013)? Even proponents of radical democracy like Chantal Mouffe focused on the failure of Occupy movements to "secure any substantial political change" or improvement of daily lives (Mouffe 2013, van de Sande 2015). Rather than understanding the significance of the movement through reductive neoliberal logic, which economizes politics and all other aspects of life into short-term stated goals and demonstrable outcomes (Brown 2015, van de Sande 2015), we propose to re-evaluate the movement through notions of "prefigurative politics," "micro-utopia," and "acting as if one is already free" (Baker, 2016, Graeber 2009, p. 210, 257), a Do-It-Together culture that emphasizes prefigurative participatory democracy and the collective sense of community resistance and building. The struggle for a different society must create that society through its forms of struggle (Holloway 2010). In future research, we will approach the cultural significance of the Umbrella Movement on its own terms. Perhaps, in the face of Beijing's colossal stability maintenance machine and the immense and continuing dominance of national politics and neoliberal governance, only such a utopian, prefigurative cultural logic can keep a community hopeful and driven in the long run.

Even though the Umbrella Movement failed to achieve genuine democratic reform for the chief executive election in 2017 and beyond, the positive prefigurative spirit accumulated during the Umbrella Movement has turned into a "new community movement" in the post-Umbrella era. In the local district council election in November 2016, more than 50 Umbrella activists registered as independent candidates. Eight were elected, and others captured over 30% of total votes. It was a surprisingly good result for independent rookie candidates with no assistance from political parties. Apart from participating in local elections, many Umbrella activists also created their own ways to "occupy their own community." "Our Community, We Save" is the slogan of a new community movement, echoing the "Our Hong Kong, We Save" slogan of the Umbrella Movement. One example in this camp has been the Community Citizen Charter movement that offers training and resources for Umbrella activists to create autonomous community plans in every neighborhood. Their signature activity is the weekly "book floating" stations set up at multiple sites across Hong Kong to promote ideas of sharing while attracting residents to talk about the problems in their neighborhood, and hopefully, to organize residents to launch autonomous community plans to serve their own community.

Conclusions

As we had demonstrated in Occupy Queen's Pier and the Umbrella Movement, this chapter focuses on how the Reclaim the Public Space movement in Hong Kong can fundamentally change the operational logic of the political practices and how citizens can be empowered to reclaim the history and subjectivity of the city. The acts of resistance denounce the undemocratic decision by the state through direct actions that resist demolition of a place and/or silencing of the freedom of expression. Reclaiming public space is thus critical to protecting the space for continuous struggle against the neoliberal and authoritarian regime. The acts of reclaiming public space write, create, and preserve histories of democratic struggles in public space. They remake the space into a civic space for sustaining freedom of expression and political assembly. Through reclaiming and occupying the selected space of power, the activists could expose the collusion and unjust consolidation of political and economic power under neoliberal regimes. In other words, in order for the people to speak in the face of power, one must reclaim space that matters, by either paralyzing it through direct actions or revitalizing it through collective civic disobedience. During occupation, activists built extended networks of civic spaces both on the ground and on the Internet to enlarge political space and sustain the struggle against the undemocratic regime. In the worst-case scenario where the state takes back the place by force, the extended networks ensure that the movement continues in other mediums. The occupation of public space in Hong Kong, in this sense, has been a means for political mobilization and building of civic and political subjectivity in a context of growing political repression. As the intense neoliberal restructuring on the global scale has undermined the democratic institutions everywhere, the experience in Hong Kong may offer insights on the resistance to the biopolitics of neoliberalism. As such, voices to reinstate or deepen democracy elsewhere might converge with those fighting for democratization in an authoritarian city-state like Hong Kong.

Notes

1. When the authors use "we" and "our," it indicates their taking an activist position.
2. The militaristic language we use to articulate the activism here comes from the actual language and self-conception of the protestors.
3. Hong Kong Federation of Students (HKFS), founded in 1958, is a student organization formed by the student unions of universities in Hong Kong. With membership during the Umbrella Movement at over 80,000, its purpose is to promote student movements and to enhance students' engagement in society.
4. Occupy Central is a civil disobedience campaign initiated by Benny Tai Yiu-ting, Associate Professor of Law at the University of Hong Kong. It formed Occupy Central with Love and Peace (OCLP) in March 2013, which sought to fight for equal suffrage through civil disobedience, namely the nonviolent occupation of Central.
5. Scholarism is a Hong Kong secondary school student activist group formed in 2011. Its first campaign was to protest against the establishment of Chinese Moral and National Education as a required subject in the secondary school curriculum. With this highly successful campaign, Scholarism is recognized as a core political force. Its membership, fundraising, and mobilization power are larger than even most local political parties.
6. Civic Square was so named after the Anti-National Education Movement organized by Scholarism that occupied this public square in 2012. Soon after that occupation, the government fenced off this square, and a six-meter-tall iron fence was erected.
7. This is what Umbrella Movement participants called themselves. "Umbrella Soldier" is the literal translation of the Chinese term 傘兵, which also means parachuter. As a colony/neo-colony, Hong Kong is not responsible for its military defense and does not have a military culture. Thus, "soldier" in local popular culture refers to Hong Kong people's self-image as toiling "soldier" and "worker" bees, persistent, hardworking, and dedicated to communal duties. The image also conveys a tinge of modest pride and gallantry.
8. The "frontiers" refer to the barricades at the borders of occupied zones made from movable fences seized from the police and public trash bins on the streets.
9. According to the Civic Council, 62% of Hong Kong people wanted the government to control One-Way Permits (for mainlanders to emigrate to Hong Kong); 54% wanted to limit the number of mainland individual travelers by withdrawing multiple-entry permits (Civic Council 2014).

References

Baker, M., 2016. The Prefigurative Politics of Translation in Place-Based Movements of Protest: Subtitling in the Egyptian Revolution. *The Translator*, 22 (1), 1–21.

Brown, W., 2015. *Undoing the Demos: Neoliberalism's Stealth Revolution*. New York: Zone Books.

Chan, J., 2014. Hong Kong's Umbrella Movement. *The Round Table: The Commonwealth Journal of International Affairs*, 103 (6), 571–580.

Chan, S. C., 2015. Delay No More: Struggles to Re-Imagine Hong Kong (for the Next 30 Years). *Inter-Asia Cultural Studies*, 16 (3), 327–347.

Chen, Y. C., 2009. Petition: Preserving Edinburgh Place as a Monument [online]. *Hong Kong Independent Media*. Available from: www.inmediahk.net/node/1005092 [Accessed 9 November 2009].

Chen, Y. C. and Szeto, M., 2015a. In-Your-Face Multiculturalism: Reclaiming Public Space and Citizenship by Filipina Immigrant Workers in Hong Kong. *In*: D. P. S. Goh, ed. *Worlding Multiculturalisms: The Politics of Inter-Asian Dwelling*. London and New York: Routledge, 55–74.

Chen, Y. C. and Szeto, M., 2015b. The Forgotten Road of Progressive Localism: New Preservation Movement in Hong Kong. *Inter-Asia Cultural Studies*, 16 (3), 436–453.

Civic Council, 2014. Civic Questionnaire, 5–9 November. Available from: www.facebook.com/media/set/?set=a.565329333610953.1073741840.556597047817515&type=1 [Accessed 3 January 2015].

Community Cultural Concern, 2007. *Preserving Edinburgh Place as a Monument.* Hong Kong: Heritage Watch, October 9, 2007.

Graeber, D., 2009. *Direct Action, an Ethnography.* Edinburgh and Oakland: AK Press.

Harvey, D., 2012. *Rebel Cities: From the Right to the City to the Urban Revolution.* New York: Verso.

Holloway, J., 2010. *Crack Capitalism.* London: Pluto Press.

Hong Kong City Hall, 1962a. *The City Hall 1962–1999.* Hong Kong: Government Printer.

Hong Kong City Hall, 1962b. "Hong Kong City Hall—Introduction," Hong Kong Government Website [online]. Available from: www.lcsd.gov.hk/CE/CulturalService/CityHall/50/en/index.php [Accessed 1 March 2016].

Hong Kong City Hall, 1967. *City Hall: The Cultural Centre of Hong Kong: 1967, Fifth Anniversary.* Hong Kong: Government Printer.

Hughes, R., 1976. *Borrowed Place, Borrowed Time: Hong Kong and Its Many Faces.* London: Andre Deutsch Ltd.

Lee, E., 2015. Space of Disobedience: A Visual Document of the Umbrella Movement in Hong Kong. *Inter-Asia Cultural Studies,* 16 (3), 367–379.

Leitner, H., Peck, J. and Sheppard, E.S., eds., 2007. *Contesting Neoliberalism: Urban Frontiers.* New York: Guilford Press.

Mayer, M., 2007. Contesting the Neoliberalization of Urban Governance. *In*: H. Leitner, J. Peck, and E. Sheppard, eds. *Contesting Neoliberalism: Urban Frontiers.* New York: Guilford Press, 90–115.

Mitchell, D., 2003. *The Right to the City: Social Justice and the Fight for Public Space.* New York: The Guilford Press.

Mouffe, C. 2013. *Agonistics: Thinking the World Politically.* London: Verso Books.

Ng, A., 2013. Fighting Inequality in Hong Kong: Lessons Learned From Occupy Hong Kong. *Radical Criminology,* 2013 (2), 47–68.

Ng, M. K., Tang, W. S., Lee, J. & Leung, D., 2010. Spatial Practice, Conceived Space and Lived Space: Hong Kong's 'Piers Saga' Through the Lefebvrian Lens. *Planning Perspectives,* 25 (4), 411–431.

Ortmann, S., 2015. The Umbrella Movement and Hong Kong's Protracted Democratization Process. *Asian Affairs,* 46 (1), 32–50.

Purcell, M., 2008. *Recapturing Democracy: Neoliberalization and the Struggle for Alternative Urban Futures.* London: Routledge.

Sande, M. van de, 2013. The Prefigurative Politics of Tahrir Square—An Alternative Perspective on the 2011 Revolutions. *Res Publica,* 19, 223–239.

Sande, M. van de, 2015. Fighting with Tools: Prefiguration and Radical Politics in the Twenty-First Century. *Rethinking Marxism,* 27 (2), 177–194.

St. John, G., 2008. Protestival: Global Days of Action and Carnivalized Politics in the Present. *Social Movement Studies,* 7 (2), 167–190.

Szeto, M. M., 2014. Sinophone Libidinal Economy in the Age of Neoliberalization and Mainlandization: Masculinities in Hong Kong SAR New Wave Cinema. *In*: A. Yue, and O. Khoo, eds. *Sinophone Cinemas.* Hampshire and New York: Palgrave Macmillan, 120–146.

Szeto, M. M. and Chen, Y. C., 2011. Mainlandization and Neoliberalism with Postcolonial and Chinese Characteristics: Challenges for the Hong Kong Film Industry. *In*: J. Kapur, and K. Wagner, eds. *Neoliberalism and Global Cinema: Capital, Culture, and Marxist Critique.* New York: Routledge, 239–260.

Szeto, M. M. and Chen, Y. C., 2015. Hong Kong Cinema in the Age of Neoliberalization and Mainlandization. *In*: E. M. K. Cheung, G. Marchetti, and E. C. M. Yau, eds. *A Companion to Hong Kong Cinema.* Chichester, UK and Malden, MA: Wiley-Blackwell, 89–115.

Veg, S., 2015. Legalistic and Utopian: Hong Kong's Umbrella Movement. *New Left Review,* 92, 54–73.

7

OCCUPY GEZI PARK

The Never-Ending Search for Democracy, Public Space, and Alternative City-Making

Burcu Yiğit Turan

On May 31, 2013 a small-scale protest in Istanbul against the destruction of a public park to make way for the construction of a shopping mall transformed into a nationwide uprising. The peaceful demonstrations in support of this desire to protect Gezi Park and its trees were met by brutal attacks from the police. News of the events spread through social media by individuals calling for solidarity and resistance. Many who had never before been politically active breached their long "silence" by pouring into the streets, parks, and squares. The protestors raised a variety of issues, ranging from the state's neoliberal top-down policies regarding cities, nature, culture, and agriculture, to policies on women, fertility, belief, education, economy, labor, and so on, issues and voices that had long been suppressed by the government through its exclusionary, homogenizing, and marginalizing discourses and practices. By breaching their silence, the protestors raised demands for freedom of speech, access to public spaces, justice, inclusive democracy, and pluralistic politics. Dissent against politics practiced during the period of AKP government became the focus of this resistance and occupation. The social and political practices that arose from those spaces of occupation and resistance would eventually shape new spatial and political understanding.

Throughout the protests, different space-making and political practices popped up and then faded away, both in and beyond Gezi Park. The design community questioned and experimented with its own role, tactics, methods, and tools within the context of a new urban social movement which demanded the right to the city and to democracy. However, the processes of the creative exploration of true democracy and of city-making generated by "Occupy Gezi" was suppressed by the government through a combination of police brutality and the use of media that distorted the movement's meaning in the eyes of the general public. After Occupy Gezi, all urban space became militarized; protestors and activists were marginalized and suppressed and the physical marks of the movement were erased from both Gezi Park and Taksim Square. However, despite its ephemeral nature, Occupy Gezi has come to influence different fields and different groups in their search for true democracy, public space, and city-making.

Focusing on the case of the Occupy Gezi Park movement, this chapter explores the reclaiming of public space by an "unsilenced city" and the politics generated by social and spatial occupation practices. It analyzes the political and spatial dialectics of the Gezi protests and occupation at the global, national, and local scales. The chapter further examines the political, social, and spatial crisis that occurred before, during, and after the urban resistance movement. Lastly, this chapter traces the influences of the movement on the political, social, and spatial practices and suggests that the Occupy Gezi Park movement continues to evolve in different ways. While some aspects fade away entirely, the movement has not ended. It has influence on both the physical and political space in different, albeit fragmented, forms.

The Emerging Dialectic between Politics and Space: Urban Resistance in the Context of "Neoliberal Urbanism"

The recently emerging dialectic between politics and space, at least in the case of the Occupy Gezi Park movement in Turkey, is part of a phenomenon defined as "planetary urbanism" or "neoliberal urbanism." This phenomenon has occurred across a broad, global context and promises the creation of stable, developing economies. It offers a traditionally liberal concept of democracy based on the creation of consensus and has thus influenced the political landscape of many countries (Mouffe 2000). In this system, opposition should be sacrificed for the sake of the majority; politics and political practice are for the concealment of truth, and political appearances are also an illusion (Rancière 1999). The system of traditionally liberal democracy has constructed an intricate process to selectively enforce silence in societies. With the power of monist politics, decisions regarding every realm of life are made according to a singular mind-set, and are always top-down. Meanwhile, "construction" and urbanization become both the source and the facilitator of capitalist development. The alliance between the state and capitalist enterprise starts to alter places at any scale regardless of territory or characteristics. This transcends the physical limits of cities, and through privatization and deregulation imposes the infrastructures, socio-spatial conditions, cultures, and ecologies of capitalism as planetary phenomena (Harvey 1996, Amin and Thrift 2002, Brenner 2013). From a spatial perspective, this situation has resulted in monolithic power and the imposition of a particular imagination over spaces and cultures, thereby erasing the general public's connection to their own right to imagine, contest, or practice spatiality.

The political, economic, and spatial exclusion and homogeneity created by global capitalism have in turn created unrest in societies. This unrest has raised a variety of issues neglected by ordinary political systems and has provoked the eruption of urban resistance movements for "the right to the city" that have emerged all over the world (Brenner 2013). These movements, particularly the Occupy movement, have given a voice to the silent masses, and have deciphered and connected all the symptoms of capitalism that infiltrate every single aspect of life (privatization of nature, genes, water, seeds, urban spaces, and so on) and which generate increasing levels of inequality (Shepard 2012). Moreover, the movements have created truly public spaces by making dissent and difference visible (Arendt 1998, Rancière 1999, Lorey 2014), which stand in contrast to the landscapes of neoliberalism or planetary urbanism. The inclusive power of these urban resistance movements has brought together disparate and previously mutually exclusive groups (Pell 2014). These movements have produced diverse landscapes and enabled an autonomous remaking of parts of the city by ordinary people. In addition, they have created a fruitful platform for the critical engagement of cultural production (including diverse practices from political philosophy to planning as well as design and art). Consequently, they have produced a new political imagination, opening forms and practices of subjectivization and have engendered dissent towards real politics and the political (Rancière 1999).

Neoliberalism's Touch on Turkey: Urbanism, Cultural Politics, and Public Space in Istanbul

Peck and Theodore (2012) emphasize the fact that there is no singular formula for how neoliberalism will adjust to different geographical contexts since it gains particular shapes according to the cultural and political peculiarities of every location to achieve the political legitimacy it requires. After the 2001 economic crises, the AKP (Adalet ve Kalkınma Partisi, or Justice and Development Party) came to power by promising political stability and economic development through the implementation of

IMF-crafted policies to cut public spending, control wages, significantly roll back agricultural sub-sidies, and privatize state-owned enterprises, lands, and natural resources. Most importantly for the expansion of capitalist accumulation, rent-seeking and speculative construction initiatives constituted the backbone of the AKP's political economy (Patton 2006). In 2013 alone, 36.2 million square meters of land were opened for construction (Turkstat 2014). The decision-making process for urban projects was centralized, transferring the authority of local municipalities to central state ministries. The Housing Development Administration of Turkey (TOKI) began to play a major role in urban regeneration (Lovering and Türkmen 2011). Meanwhile, an emerging Islamic bourgeois started to exercise a hegemony through the use of media power and the opening of private schools and universities. In Turkey, neoliberalism became legitimized through Islamic conservative codes (Tugal 2007, Blad and Koçer 2012). This led to a significant decline in civil liberties and political rights for non-AKP groups and brought Islamic social interventionism and concomitant restrictions on secular lifestyles (Gürcan and Peker 2015). These developments created a massive authoritarian biopolitic which tells people how and where they will live, what they will eat and drink, how many children they should have, and what they should learn and believe. This is a hegemony over every possible aspect of biological, mate-rial, and intellectual existence; every landscape was realigned to the phenomenon of planetary (neolib-eral) urbanism. With changes to the law (Butunsehir Yasasi, or Whole City Law 2013), all villages fell under urban jurisdiction; agriculture within rural settlements was banned, common land was privat-ized, and capitalistic urbanism infiltrated the very heart of every village. In addition, over 500 rivers and creeks were diverted for hydroelectric power plants (Enerji Atlasi 2015), thereby diverting water away from everyday use, the agricultural production of individual farmers, and from nature itself.

In such a context, Istanbul became the most intensive theater of the emerging political and economical framework of the government. In particular, the gentrification of housing districts and cultural centers, the occupation and privatization of public spaces through an increasing number of shopping malls, gated communities, and theme parks, and the intensive semiotization of urban landscapes as viewed through the lens of the government's ideology changed Istanbul immensely. The urban fabric that previously consisted of complex authentic cultural and natural networks of formal and informal developments started to dissolve (Kurtuluş 2005, Adaman and Keyder 2006, Bartu Candan and Kolluoğlu 2008, Karaman and Islam 2012). The unsterile and dynamic aesthetics of everyday urbanism that were constantly being produced by different sub-jectivities were replaced by artificial ones reflecting the singular ideology of the government and the meanings given to them by the developers.

Alongside the everyday piecemeal alterations of urban space in the city, the government announced megaprojects to be implemented without public approval and without any consider-ation of the social, cultural, and ecological phenomenality of a place or the well-being of society. These included a third bridge and a new airport, a new satellite city, Channel Istanbul, a meeting area in Yenikapi (a vast coastal infill area far away from the city center, devoted to mass meetings and political party gatherings), a grandiose mega-mosque on the Çamlıca Hills, and the Taksim Pedestrianization Project. Any criticism of the projects was immediately and publically discred-ited, and alternative ideas were marginalized.

The Spatial Context of Occupy Gezi: Taksim Square and Gezi Park

In the early 19th century, there were almost no settlements in the Taksim area. *Taksim* means "allocation" and it took its name from the water distribution chamber completed in 1839 during the reign of Mahmut II. An artillery barracks and courtyard were constructed between 1803 and 1806 and required rebuilding and renovation on several occasions due to fires and damage from uprisings (Kubilay 1994). As an extension of the Grand Rue de Pera, the district was developed under the influence of a non-Muslim bourgeoisie and foreign inhabitants. With the expansion of the city, new residential areas for Muslim populations, infrastructure, and public buildings were created and the area gradually became more diversified. By the 19th century it had become "Ottoman cosmopolitan" (Çelik 1993) and at the turn of the 20th century Taksim was an urban juncture connecting newly developing areas with the historical peninsula. After WWI, Taksim Square became an important natural locus for the Kemalist regime, which was looking to create spaces to disseminate Western ideas and discourses on modernism, republicanism, civic rights, progress, and secularism (Baykan and Hatuka 2010). In 1940, the military barracks and the Armenian cemetery were demolished and a public park, Gezi Park and Esplanade, was planned according to the modernist urban principles of the time by French urbanist Henri Prost (Bilsel 2010).

A giant multipurpose cultural center and opera house, the Atatürk Cultural Center, was added in 1969. In the 1970s, Taksim Square became part of the real democratic political terrain by serving as a meeting place for dissent, in particular highly organized protest demonstrations by the Turkish Left. After a massacre of protestors on May 1, 1977, International Labor Day, Taksim became the symbol of a working-class struggle for justice and democracy in Turkey (Baykan and Hatuka 2010). Taksim Square, Gezi Park, and its environs gradually evolved into a rich social place with diverse everyday practices and political events for a variety of people, particularly minorities, largely because of its hard-won secular and liberal atmosphere. In such a context, redeveloping the Taksim area carried much deeper meanings for then–Prime Minister Erdoğan. The government's tactics were to leave the Atatürk Cultural Center, Gezi Park, and Taksim Square to decay and to ban all political protest. In 2012, the Taksim Pedestrianization Project was declared. This included the rebuilding of the military barracks as a shopping mall and luxury residence in the neo-Ottoman style on the Gezi Park location, the demolition of the Atatürk Cultural Center, and the construction of the Taksim Republican Mosque, a History of Religions Museum, and massive traffic interventions on the major routes around Taksim Square. Meanwhile, the district municipality would attempt to ban outdoor seating for local restaurants and pubs, and new regulations were imposed to limit alcohol consumption. According to Gürcan and Peker (2015, p. 72–73), the Taksim project was a conservative attempt to eliminate Taksim as a center of entertainment, leisure, and political protest.

With its social, architectural, aesthetic, and urban characteristics, and also the apparent level of its design quality, the project became the focus of criticism from local inhabitants, professionals, intelligentsia, and artists. It also attracted the close attention of organized groups from several counter-urbanism movements. As the proposed military barracks would function as a shopping mall and luxury residence, the whole public park would be privatized. It would also carry a neo-Ottoman aesthetic, thereby erasing the modernist landscape of the Early Republican Era. The vast hardscape of its surroundings would be ornamented with green, tulip-shaped patches similar to other landscape design examples in the Gulf Region. Traffic circulation would be put below street level, dividing and separating the streets, and narrowing the pedestrian sidewalks. Furthermore, a futuristic, orientalist mosque and a "religions center" would be erected. Through these arrangements, pedestrian circulation would be limited and taken under control, public spaces would be privatized, and access would be limited. The park's natural habitat would be erased, and consequently there would be no place left for political demonstrations and meetings.

Soon after the announcement of the project, Taksim Platform, a civic organization supported by neighborhood foundations and professional groups, was established to express the public values of the Taksim area and Gezi Park, to expose the negative outcomes of the project to the general public, and to constitute a participatory organization within which artists, professionals, intellectuals, and local inhabitants could collectively imagine the future of the area. In this context, urban planning and design professionals explored different ways to become involved in the process by inventing new social practices.

Through various events and studies, Taksim Platform attempted to act as a constructive agent by using positive language focused on spatial, social, and ecological values rather than criticism

aimed at the government or the municipality; it wrote letters to the mayor of the greater municipality of Istanbul to invite him for a Sunday walk in the park (Taksim Platform 2012); well-
known artists, writers, and parliament members adopted the trees of the park which had been
marked to be cut down; and a Taksim symposium was organized to discuss the characteristics of
the project and the future of the area with experts. With "Kayıtdışı" workshops and site installations, students went to the Taksim area to highlight how pedestrian circulation would be affected
by the project (Arkitera Mimarlık Merkezi 2012). A foundation called Herkes İçin Mimarlık
(Architecture for All) began to organize weekly festivals in Gezi Park in order to enrich the social
and cultural life and attract people's attention to the park. This was a key way the civic organizations challenged the government's media discourse, which trivialized the role of the park (Herkes
için Mimarlık 2012). Civil organizations appealed to the Ministry of Culture and the Higher
Board of Protection of Cultural Heritage, countering municipal decisions with expert reports
presented at legal platforms.

Despite all these efforts, Prime Minister Erdoğan did not wait for the outcome of the judicial
process. During the launch of the third bridge construction, he stated: "Whatever you do, we
made a decision for that place, and we will do it" (Erdoğan 2013a). On May 27, construction vehicles entered the park, trees were uprooted, and urban and environmental activist groups started
to gather and encamp in order to stop the destruction. The uprooting of a few trees unleashed
the accumulated frustration felt against the socio-ecological traumas occurring throughout the
landscapes of Turkey (Figure 7.1).

FIGURE 7.1 The encampment area in Gezi Park; the motto on the banner reads, "Do not touch my
neighborhood, my square, my tree, my water, my soil, my house, my seed, my forest, my village, my
city, my park!"

Source: Burcu Yiğit Turan

Occupy Gezi Park: Reclaiming and Exploring "Public Space," "Democracy," and "City-Making"

On the morning of Friday, May 31, the encampments of the activists were destroyed, the police evicted people from the park using tear gas, and the park itself was sealed off. The police then obstructed a press conference organized by professional and civic organizations. A sit-in by around 600–700 people began in Taksim Square, but this was soon met by the police force and several protestors were severely injured. This was the limit for the silent masses. Through social media, the ongoing incidents were communicated to the wider public while the mainstream media reported nothing. Most of the social media messages focused on the violent suppression of the peaceful demonstrations, and after leaving their schools and workplaces, thousands of people from all over Istanbul started to march to Gezi Park shouting "enough is enough." Those who could not go encouraged the others by banging together pots and pans on their balconies and out of their windows, shouting "resist Gezi, resist Turkey!" The city was no longer "silent."

By the morning of Saturday, June 1, people had occupied Gezi Park and the Taksim area after brutal struggles with the police, and similar events had spread and escalated into nationwide anti-government protests. All over Turkey, millions of people occupied open urban spaces to express their demands for democracy and their rights to their own cities and nature. These events led to a broader realization of how profoundly a society needs public space and that the citizens should have the right to access it.

For Yörük and Yüksel (2014), the social profiles of the people involved in the protests and occupation activities in Gezi Park could not be explained by an examination centered on social class or a singular ideological tendency, but rather through an understanding of the diverse political and cultural orientations that became united against the urban, social, environmental, economic, and cultural policies of the government. Young people and women constituted the majority of the protestors; their education level was very high, with over 40% having university and higher degrees. Significantly, many protestors would later state that they had never been involved in a political demonstration before (Yörük and Yüksel 2014).

As soon as the protestors reoccupied the park, they cleared away the spent tear gas canisters and other garbage. A volunteer group of medical doctors established a medical room, and volunteer veterinarians started to check the injured street dogs and cats. In the middle of the park, people started to leave food to help each other. Much of the sociopolitical discourse at the park revolved around this sentiment: It was all because the people were deprived of freedom of expression. Gezi would be the opposite. Everyone could express his/her thoughts, feelings and demands. Within a short time there were small-scale occupations of the park that became full of encampments by various groups, including the Ecology Initiative, Taksim Solidarity, the Gezi Park Beautification Foundation, the Union of Chambers of Turkish Engineers and Architects, Anti-Capitalist Muslims, LGBT movements (LGBT Bloc, Kaos LG), People's Houses, the Youth Union of Turkey, Çarşı and other football fan clubs, feminist groups (the Socialist-Feminist Collective and the Women's Coalition), the Animals' Rights Movement, and many other groups, artists, intellectuals, and thousands of individuals. All made their own individual narratives or created their own humorous expressions. No one interfered, and everyone became visible. An alternative world and a united community had taken shape under the trees of Gezi Park.

The emergent landscapes of Gezi Park evolved informally and according to the changing needs and agendas of the protestors. The whole Taksim area was truly pedestrianized as the traffic was blocked by barricades. The damaged part of the park was repaired and trees and flowers were planted. The Ecology Initiative established an orchard to grow vegetables to attract attention to the issue of food justice. A spot was marked as a free speech corner. Armenian protestors highlighted a forgotten heritage of the park, the Armenian Cemetery, which had been bulldozed while the park was being built. Tents were erected and a library was set up to circulate books to be read during encampments. Many other spontaneous spatial organizations were set up to meet functional needs or to send political messages alongside art installations, graffiti, banners, and posters. During its two weeks of existence, forums were organized for people to express their thoughts and reach decisions on the issues of everyday life in the park or on the much broader political issues regarding the protests (Figure 7.2). In the forums, communication, management, negotiation, and decision-making processes and methods were explored to achieve true democracy.

Individuals became politicized through the subjectification of themselves and others by learning how to socialize across different perspectives. Yogis and yoginis organized yoga sessions in the mornings, artists gave concerts, ballet dancers performed, and pianist Davide Martello came to play for the mothers of protestors who had come to protect their children. Experts and communities established informative circles to talk about contemporary problems, particularly urban issues and human rights, and the members of the Herkes İçin Mimarlık (Architecture for All) foundation helped with the temporary spatial interventions of the people and documented the emergent structures under the theme of #Occupy Gezi Architecture (Gündoğdu 2013). There were art courses for children. Food was collected and cooked in the park and commercial activities were banned. The street children were included and given food, shelter, and friendship and

FIGURE 7.2 One of seven forums established in Gezi Park discussing the terms of negotiation with Prime Minister Erdoğan one day before the brutal evacuation by the police, June 14, 2013

Source: Burcu Yiğit Turan

were integrated in the events. An independent television channel, Çapul TV, was established, since the mainstream media initially did not break their schedules to report this major protest and police actions in the center of Turkey's most populous city. Millions of tweets and Facebook posts spread the word of Gezi to the whole world (Demirhan 2014). The people of Gezi Park became a "whole," and Gezi Park became more than a physical entity through these organic articulations of people (Gambetti 2014), spaces, performances, actions, and expressions. The hope was that people would make the city, democracy, and public space their own by realizing their dreams in the utopian world of Gezi as a critique of the existing socio-spatial order.

After Occupy Gezi Park

On Saturday, June 15, the police evacuated the park with excessive force on the orders of Prime Minister Erdoğan (Erdoğan 2013b). On Sunday, June 16, the European Union Integration Minister Egemen Bağış stated, "Whoever comes to Taksim will be treated as a terrorist" (Bağış 2013). In the following weeks the protests gradually faded away. Nationally, 10 people were killed and over 8,000 were injured (Amnesty International 2013). The processes of the creative exploration of true democracy and of city-making generated by Occupy Gezi were suppressed by the government through a combination of police brutality and the use of mainstream media, in which the movement's meaning was distorted in the eyes of the majority. Protestors and activists were marginalized and suppressed. The whole Taksim area became militarized and the municipality erased all signs of occupation from the landscape of Gezi Park through the homogenization of its aesthetics and by rolling out ready-made grass. The gravestones of lost protestors were instantly removed.

However, despite its ephemerality, Occupy Gezi has influenced different fields and different groups in their search for true democracy, public spaces, and city-making. Occupy Gezi was not only a material entity fixed to a singular space. The experiences, knowledge, emotions, and solidarity prevailed. People established "park forums" in their own neighborhoods, sticking with the same principles that were developed in Gezi. The forums connected with each other via the Parklar Bizim (Parks Are Ours) blog and communicated to establish possible collaborations for urban, social, and political productions (Parklar Bizim 2013). National and international social and intellectual forums were developed to highlight and discuss critical issues. Professionals, medical doctors, sociologists, teachers, architects, etc. established their own forums to explore how best to fit into their new roles and emerged with new perspectives provided by Gezi. Academic meetings and events were organized to better comprehend the phenomenalities of Gezi and to further build on them. The largest LGBTI parade in Turkish history was organized on June 30, 2013 on Taksim Istiklal Street in answer to a call by the LGBTI block of Gezi Park, which invited the whole of society to stand with them against oppression, violence, and discrimination. Despite the high risk of police brutality, thousands of people attended the parade with the motto of "There is no emancipation alone: either all together, or no one" (LGBT Blok 2013).

The freedom of expression in the park paved the way for emerging empathy among very different groups. A retired man painted a famous flight of steps in the Cihangir district in rainbow colors to give a message of solidarity, and all over Turkey, steps started to be painted in similar fashion. During Ramadan, the Anti-Capitalist Muslims, hand-in-hand with secularists, organized "Earth Tables" on Istiklal Street to stress "unity against discrimination," "diversity against the homogenization of society," "simplicity against vanity," "fertility against scarcity," and "sharing against self-serving" (Anti-Kapitalist Müslümanlar 2013). After being inspired by Gezi, several inhabitants of the Yeldeğirmeni neighborhood squatted in an empty building and filled it with artistic and intellectual content (Doğanoğlu 2013). Architects, urbanists, and designers realized how spatial design is a social act capable of producing complex phenomena. *XXI Magazine of Architecture, Design and Space* (published in Turkish) devoted two special issues to Occupy Gezi Park: *Gezi Parkı Mimar(sız)lığı* (The Architect(less) Architecture of Gezi Park) (July/August 2013) and *Yeni Bir Mimarlığa Doğru mu?* (Towards a New Architecture?) (September/October 2013), in which architects and designers expressed their fascination with the remaking of public space and democracy in its true sense by ordinary citizens, and also described their attempts to find new roles for themselves after Occupy Gezi Park. The Taksim Platform turned itself into a new group, Istanbul Hepimizin (Istanbul Belongs to All of Us), and prepared a manifesto for the local elections of March 2014. Left-wing opposition party members brought the messages of Gezi into their parties. Criticizing the absence of localness in urban politics, the group called on all the candidates from all political parties to work according to the principles mentioned in their manifesto, and emphasized the citizens' rights to all aspects of the city (Aktar 2015).

The expression of dissent, once represented in city squares and streets, in Taksim and on Istiklal Street in particular, found new unexpected spaces. For instance, football matches became protest events. Football fans sent political messages through mass media with chants and banners until ways to silence them were found.

Conclusions

Starting with dissent against the destruction of a public park in the middle of Istanbul, the Occupy Gezi Park movement became a uniting platform for all groups who stood against government policies on many aspects of life. People realized that to take back control of their lives and of their living environments it was essential to reassert themselves politically regardless of how absent they may have been from politics. Gezi Park became a truly public space and for two weeks enabled people to express their thoughts, feelings, experiences, and dreams about the politics and just city-making. Novel forms of direct democracy were explored and experimented with. Different groups established strong empathies and alliances, raising awareness about the injustices that they experience. People produced various socio-spatial practices based on conflict, negotiation, and consensus. An urbanism emerged within the agonistic patches of landscape which were appropriated by different groups. Consequently, new social and political identities were constituted by those in search of a means of relating themselves to the social context through their professional skills and agencies.

This two-week interruption of the general silence and rehearsal of democratic politics and city-making showed us the social and political potential of public space. Furthermore, it proved that there should be a foundation of agreement on freedom of "expression" (verbal, bodily, spatial, artistic, etc.) that will enable true pluralism. This pluralism is not a stable one, however. As Mouffe (2000) stresses, it is agonistic. Furthermore, through explorations of novel forms of direct democracy, Occupy Gezi Park proved that ordinary people have the capacity to remake the city and the politics with their autonomous, conflicting, but negotiable acts of insurgency. Within these acts, a fascinating, ever-changing landscape emerges with a multiplicity of meanings related to the subjective heritage, everyday culture, lifestyle, memories, and dreams. Consequently, this landscape makes space both public and political with its semiotic and physical incompleteness, and it also has a complexity that stands for social and ecological justice against the landscapes of neoliberalism.

On the other hand, however, this short interruption of political silence in Turkey reinvigorated the historical paradox of the conflict between hegemony and anti-hegemonic formations. Today, monist politics has consolidated and brought massive suppression of free speech and the media. This situation has drastically reduced any opportunity for political influence, academic knowledge production and dissemination, and socio-spatial practices. In addition, the commercial development project that will destroy Gezi Park is still continuing. Public dissent either physically or in cyberspace is now managed through regulations, court cases, city permits, police practices, and media diversions. Therefore, and as witnessed in the aftermath of many other movements such as Tahrir Square, Los Indignados, or Occupy Wall Street, there has been no immediate transformative influence of Occupy Gezi Park on the current political system or the institutional city-making process in Turkey. On the contrary, there has been an increasing erosion of freedom, rights, and participation in decision making. Despite this erosion, the Occupy Gezi Park resistance left a rich heritage of experience and sentiment, particularly for urban planners and designers who are learning how to mobilize against specific injustices in their own realm. Therefore, its legacy is not directly connected with its physical ephemerality or with any particular political group formation. The Occupy Gezi Park movement continues to multiply; its different aspects continue to evolve in different ways. While some aspects have faded away entirely, the movement's influence has not ended. It will reclaim both the physical and political space in many different albeit fragmented forms until the silence is once again interrupted by voices raised by a unifying call for democratic politics, city-making, and public space.

References

Adaman, F. and Keyder, C., 2006. *Poverty and Social Exclusion in the Slum Areas of Large Cities in Turkey*. European Commission, Employment, Social Affairs and Equal Opportunities DG, No. VC/2005/0155.

Aktar, C., 2015. Resources and Shortcomings of Pluralism in Today's Turkey: Gezi Park Protests in the Light of Pluralism. *Philosophy & Social Criticism*, 41 (4–5), 465–471.

Amin, A. and Thrift, N., 2002. *Cities: Reimagining the Urban*. 1st edition. Cambridge: Polity Press.

Amnesty International, 2013. Turkey: Gezi Park protests: Brutal Denial of the Right to Peaceful Assembly in Turkey [online]. Available from: www.amnesty.org/en/documents/document/?indexNumber=EUR44%2f022%2f2013&language=en [Accessed 13 February 2016].

Anti-Capitalist Muslims [online], n.d. Available from: www.antikapitalistmuslumanlar.org [Accessed 6 August 2015].

Antikapitalist Müslümanlar, 2013. Earth Tables. Available from: http://www.antikapitalistmuslumanlar.org [Accessed 6 August 2015].

Arendt, H., 1998. *The Human Condition*. 2nd edition. Chicago: The University of Chicago Press.

Arkitera Mimarlık Merkezi, A. M., 2012. Kayıtdışı'nın Taksim Operasyonu [online]. *Arkitera.com*. Available from: www.arkitera.com/haber/6771/kayitdisinin-taksim-operasyonu [Accessed 13 February 2016].

Bağış, E., 2013. Egemen Bağış: Taksim'e çıkan terörist muamelesi görür—#Politika [online]. *Radikal*. Available from: www.radikal.com.tr/politika/egemen-bagis-taksime-cikan-terorist-muamelesi-gorur-1137822/ [Accessed 13 February 2016].

Bartu Candan, A. and Kolluoğlu, B., 2008. Emerging Spaces of Neoliberalism: A Gated Town and a Public Housing Project in İstanbul. *New Perspectives on Turkey*, 39, 5–46.

Baykan, A. and Hatuka, T., 2010. Politics and Culture in the Making of Public Space: Taksim Square, 1 May 1977, Istanbul. *Planning Perspectives*, 25 (1), 49–68.

Brenner, N., 2013. Theses on Urbanization. *Public Culture*, 25 (1), 85–114.

Çelik, Z., 1993. *The Remaking of Istanbul: Portrait of an Ottoman City in the Nineteenth Century*. Berkeley: University of California Press.

Demirhan, K., 2014. Social Media Effects on the Gezi Park Movement in Turkey: Politics Under Hashtags. *In*: B. Pătruţ, and M. Pătruţ, eds. *Social Media in Politics*. New York: Springer International Publishing, 281–314.

Doğanoğlu, T., 2013. In-depth interview, 20 November 2013. *ekşi sözlük*, 2016. 30 haziran 2013 lgbt onur yürüyüşü [online]. Available from: https://eksisozluk.com/30-haziran-2013-lgbt-onur-yuruyusu-3871382 [Accessed 13 February 2016].

Enerji Atlasi, 2015. The Number of Hydroelectric Power Plants in Turkey [online]. Available from: www.enerjiatlasi.com/hidroelektrik/ [Accessed 1 August 2015].

Erdoğan, R. T., 2013a. Gezi Parkı için karar verdik [online]. *Hürriyet*. Available from: www.hurriyet.com.tr/gezi-parki-icin-karar-verdik-23390657 [Accessed 5 August 2016].

Erdoğan, R. T., 2013b. Erdoğan: Güvenlik güçlerimiz parkı boşaltmasını bilir—#Türkiye [online]. *Radikal*. Available from: www.radikal.com.tr/turkiye/erdogan-guvenlik-guclerimiz-parki-bosaltmasini-bilir-1137753/ [Accessed 5 August 2016].

Gambetti, Z., 2014. Occupy Gezi as Politics of Body. *In*: U. Ozkirimli, ed. *The Making of a Protest Movement in Turkey*. New York: Palgrave Macmillan, 89–102.

Gündoğdu, E., 2013. In-depth interview, July 11, 2013.

Gürcan, E. C. and Peker, E., 2015. *Challenging Neoliberalism at Turkey's Gezi Park*. New York: Palgrave Macmillan.

Harvey, D., 1996. *Justice, Nature and the Geography of Difference*. 1st edition. Cambridge, MA: Blackwell.

Herkes İçin Mimarlık [online], 2012. Available from: http://herkesicinmimarlik.org/portfolio/gezi-parki [Accessed 5 August 2015].

Karaman, O. and Islam, T., 2012. On the Dual Nature of Intra-Urban Borders: The Case of a Romani Neighborhood in Istanbul. *Cities*, 29 (4), 234–243.

Kubilay, A. Y., 1994. Topçu Kışlası, Dünden Bugüne Istanbul. *Ansiklopedisi* 7, 274.

Kurtuluş, H., 2005. *İstanbul'da Kentsel Ayrışma: Mekansal Dönüşümde Farklı Boyutlar, İstanbul, Bağlam Yayıncılık*, 307 sayfa. 19 YTL.

LGBT Blok, 2013. June 30 2013 LGBT Honor March https://eksisozluk.com/30-haziran-2013-lgbt-onur-yuruyusu--3871382 [Accessed 5 August 2015].

Lorey, I., 2014. The 2011 Occupy Movements: Rancière and the Crisis of Democracy. *Theory, Culture & Society*, 31 (7–8), 43–65.

Lovering, J. and Türkmen, H., 2011. Bulldozer Neo-Liberalism in Istanbul: The State-Led Construction of Property Markets, and the Displacement of the Urban Poor. *International Planning Studies*, 16 (1), 73–96.

Mouffe, C., 2000. *The Democratic Paradox*. London, NY: Verso.

Parklar Bizim, 2013. Available from: http://parklarbizim.blogspot.com.tr [Accessed 5 August 2015].

Patton, M. J., 2006. The Economic Policies of Turkey's AKP Government: Rabbits from a Hat? *Middle East Journal*, 60 (3), 513–536.

Peck, J. and Theodore, N., 2012. Reanimating Neoliberalism: Process Geographies of Neoliberalisation. *Social Anthropology*, 20 (2), 177–185.

Pell, S., 2014. Mobilizing Urban Publics, Imagining Democratic Possibilities. *Cultural Studies*, 28 (1), 29–48.

Rancière, J., 1999. *Disagreement: Politics and Philosophy*. 1st printing edition. Minneapolis: University of Minnesota Press.

Shepard, B., 2012. Occupy Against Inequality. *Socialism and Democracy*, 26 (2), 26–29.

Taksim Platform, 2012. Invitation of Mayor of Greater Istanbul Municipality Kadir Topbaş to a Sunday Walk in Gezi Park, 4 November 2012 [online]. Available from: www.taksimplatformu.com/basin aciklamalari/04.11.2012-topbasa%20davet.docx [Accessed 1 August 2015].

Tugal, C., 2007. NATO's Islamists: Hegemony and Americanization in Turkey. *New Left Review*, 44, 5–34.

Turkstat, 2014. 2013 Total amount of constructed land [online]. Available from: www.turkstat.gov.tr/UstMenu.do?metod=temelist# [Accessed 1 August 2015].

Yörük, E. and Yüksel, M., 2014. Class and Politics in Turkey's Gezi Protests. *New Left Review*, 89. Available from: http://newleftreview.org/II/89/erdem-yoruk-murat-yuksel-class-and-politics-in-turkey-s-gezi-protests [Accessed 6 August 2015].

8

THE RIGHT TO THE SIDEWALK

The Struggle Over Broken Windows Policing, Young People, and NYC Streets

Caitlin Cahill, Brett G. Stoudt, Amanda Matles, Kimberly Belmonte, Selma Djokovic, Jose Lopez, Adilka Pimentel, María Elena Torre, and Darian X

> We do not want our children to be exempt from the law or above the law, what we are saying is we don't want them to be tried on the sidewalk (#BlackLivesMatter).

Introduction

> One morning I was on my way to school and the cops pulled up and he said, "Can I see your ID." And I gave him my ID. And before I walked away, he said, "You're beautiful." And I'm like, "Thank you." So, then he was like, "You look like, you've been doing bad things. Should I put you in hand-cuffs?" So I looked at him like, "Are you serious?" When I was walking away I was scared. As if he was going to come out of the van and grab me from behind and drag me into the van. 'Cuz like, I have younger siblings, and I wouldn't want them to be stopped by cops, and be disrespected, how they disrespected me.
>
> *Brittany, age 18, Brooklyn*

> I was walking. I had a hoodie on, and the cops just started looking at me weird. He came up to me, went in my pockets. And, like in my pocket, in my left pocket, he put his hand in there and then he started patting me down, putting the flashlight around me, started searching me with the flashlight to see if he could find anything, and didn't—so they left. The cops said I looked suspicious. I was like thirteen years old and I felt uncomfortable, it was, like, a bad experience. When the officers searched me that time I wish they could've talk to me first about how I looked suspicious, instead of just searching me. He could've just told me the reason why I look suspicious, and ask me if I had anything on me, things like that.
>
> *Jesus, age 15, Brooklyn*

Jesus and Brittany were on their way to and from school when they were each stopped by the police. Their encounters with the police did not escalate. No one was arrested, no one was hurt, and no one was killed. This is a routine stop and question, a routine frisk and search, examples of the securitization of everyday life for young people of color growing up in New York City. Marked by a convergence of policing, surveillance, and social-spatial exclusions, the sidewalk is a key site to both understand and challenge carceral geopolitics. By focusing on the struggle for "the right to the sidewalk" we call attention to how space is continually contested through power dynamics. In the act of bravely sharing their encounters with the police in public testimonials, both Brittany and Jesus speak back to the state, calling attention to violations of their rights, and reframing the experience on their own terms. Our work draws upon Michelle Billies's (2016) scholarship, who argues that the lens of collective struggle places emphasis upon what she identifies as an "epistemology of survival." She states: "For, if oppressions act in concert, so do forces of liberation, like so many hands tearing open a net" (Billies 2016). In this paper we focus on how this contestation takes shape over time, space, bodies, policies, and discourse in the historical present on the streets of New York City.

Over a million young people have been stopped by the New York Police Department over the past few years (2010–2014), mostly Black and Latino young men. Tracing the struggles over public space, we focus on young people's experiences negotiating the contradictions of broken windows policing in the context of the gentrifying spectacle of sparkling office towers, new condos, and hipster bars in New York City. Drawing upon the intergenerational participatory action research project Researchers for Fair Policing, we offer insights into the social and spatial exclusions of the aggressively policed neoliberal city and its resistance. The young people we work with are organizing politically, protesting, and educating other young people about their rights. "The right to the sidewalk" is variously experienced as the right to walk to the corner to get milk without being stopped (Zekavat 2015), the right to not be harassed while listening to music in front of your own house, and the right to hang out in the neighborhood with friends after school. Common experiences of New York youth offer a lens for analyzing the everyday geopolitics of accumulation by dispossession (Harvey 2003) in a heavily surveilled public sphere.

The right to the sidewalk is inspired by, and related to, the "right to the city," Lefevbre's "cry and demand" for "the right to freedom, to individuation in socialization, to habitat and to inhabit" (1996, p. 173). As Don Mitchell (2003, p. 25) argues, rights provide "an institutionalized framework, no matter how incomplete, within which the goals of social struggle can not only be organized, but also attained." While the capaciousness of the right to the city is its theoretical and practical strength (Mitchell and Heynen 2009, p. 616), by focusing on the sidewalk, we want to call attention to the tightening, "garretted" geography of confinement young people of color negotiate in their everyday lives (McKittrick 2006). This is not, as feminist geographer Katherine McKittrick (2006, p. 62) reminds us, a space of the margin, but instead a "paradoxical space" that is central to how we know, understand, and negotiate urban space, even if it goes unrecognized.

The sidewalk is an extension of what Rashad Shabazz (2015, p. 2) identifies as the *prisonized landscape* of carceral power that takes shape via the daily "mechanisms of normalization" (Foucault 1975) and disciplinary systems of control that operate through policing, urban development, city policy, and planning institutions. We want to extend this analysis to consider how the prisonized landscape is also a *privatized landscape*, drawing parallels between real estate space and carceral space. Engaging a political economic historical analysis, we follow Stuart Hall et al.'s work (1978) to understand how "the crisis" of crime is connected with and produced in a context of neoliberal urban policies (policing, housing, urban development) across time and various scales.

Our project is both concrete and aspirational. The struggles over sidewalk space may potentially lead to forms of imprisonment and all that is lost, stolen, and destroyed (including income, job security, school, housing, children, etc.), or end in premature death (Gilmore 2007, Alexander 2012). As Darian X, a youth researcher/organizer, who at the age of 18 had been stopped over 100 times in his young life, noted, "At any moment during those interactions, my life could have also been stripped away." The stakes are high indeed. This is at the heart of contemporary social movements in New York and across the nation, protesting state violence, the prison industrial complex, and the ongoing criminalization of communities of color.

Background

Researchers for Fair Policing is an intergenerational participatory project. Our name reflects the contradictory desire that originally motivated the project: to think through just what "fair policing" might look like in communities of color in New York City (we are now changing our name to reflect our concerns focused on alternatives to policing). We began our research in 2012, the year after the peak of "stop-and-frisk" in the city under the tenure of Mayor Bloomberg, with the goal of documenting the human cost of the New York Police Department's (NYPD) long history of broken windows policing policies, and specifically the impact upon young people. We wanted to understand the experience of growing up policed, and importantly, to mobilize our research to stop this (Stoudt et al. forthcoming, 2011). Our research developed in the context of the New York City police reform movement, informed by young and old activists, who were organizing to protest the police state in NYC.

Significantly, while our research was part of the burgeoning movement in New York City, it documents a political moment before Ferguson, and before the Black Lives Matter movement captivated national attention and significantly reframed the conversation on racism and state violence for a broader public. Black Lives Matter is "rooted in the experiences of Black people in this country who actively resist our de-humanization, #BlackLivesMatter is a call to action and a response to the virulent anti-Black racism that permeates our society" (www.blacklivesmatter.com). Launched after the acquittal of George Zimmerman for the murder of 17-year-old Trayvon Martin, Black Lives Matter has since broadened in the subsequent extrajudicial police killings of Mike Brown, Eric Garner, Tamir Rice, Akai Gurley, Rekia Boyd, and far too many others. These social movements inform our research and analysis. Our critical consciousness has shifted as grief, outrage, and collective engagement challenge and evolve how we understand the purpose and possible publics of our work.

The Researchers for Fair Policing is a collaboration of researchers and organizers from Make the Road (MTR) and the Public Science Project (PSP). Make the Road New York (www.maketheroad. org) builds the power of Latino and working-class communities to achieve dignity and justice through organizing, policy innovation, transformative education, and survival services. Specifically, we worked with the organizers from the Youth Power Project of MTR, who have been addressing discriminatory policing for almost a decade, doing extensive research and outreach, educating their peers on policing and civil rights, and organizing young people to stand up for their rights in schools and in their communities. The Public Science Project (www.publicscienceproject. org) conducts and supports critical participatory action research (PAR) with communities. In the tradition of critical PAR, we document the uneven structural distribution of opportunities and injustice, in this case, focusing on the carceral geographies of young people's everyday lives. Our work aims to shift what we define as "problems" off the backs of individuals and onto systems, structures, and policies (Torre et al. 2012), by refocusing on the geopolitical structures of state violence and urban development policies that collude to criminalize everyday life.

We engage with critical PAR as method of abolition geography with a desire to end the carceral state (Gilmore 2007, Loyd et al. 2012). Working with those who are most impacted by policing, we collaborate with young people whose voices and perspectives have been conspicuously absent from not only the research and theorization about policing and criminology, but also from the policymaking table (see Stoudt et al. 2016, forthcoming). We began our inquiry with the stories of young people's encounters with the police to inform and shape research questions, methods, how we collect data, engage in analysis, interpret our findings, and translate our research into action. The young people at MTR are first and foremost organizers around complex and interconnected issues and struggles; this informs our commitment to be accountable to, and in dialogue with social, racial, gender, and economic justice movements and struggles.

The Researchers for Fair Policing project started with the decision to develop a large-scale survey so that our research might enlighten decision makers and impact city policy in the context of the 2013 mayoral election. We collected over 1,000 surveys from young people of color across the city focused on their experiences with the police between 2010 and 2013 (Stoudt et al. 2016, forthcoming). We developed the participatory documentary short "Who's Impacted by Stop & Frisk?" and an archive of video testimonials of young people's experiences of being policed (see www.researchersforfairpolicing.org) as a commitment to public scholarship as both a process and way of engaging with diverse broader publics, particularly young people. We also engaged with creative methodologies that include comics and spoken word performances, as well as sharing our findings and video research in the pop-up exhibition "More Than a Quota" (2014). Our research is being mobilized for policy, organizing, and activism, as we shall discuss. In addition, our findings and white paper are featured on our website as part of our public scholarship commitments, and our desire to connect with other young people in particular.

"Eyes (& Hands) on the Street"

Neighborhood streets are significant urban spaces for working-class communities in New York City. Historically, neighborhood public spaces were an extension of the home, a sort of outdoor "living room" where you meet friends, children play, and elders watch from the stoop or window. Jane Jacobs (1961) called the street and the sidewalks "the most vital organs" of the city—"a city sidewalk is nothing by itself. It is an abstraction." What makes sidewalks come to life are the people that use them—this use is at the heart of building and making community. Jacobs (1961, p. 51–52) famously identified this as an "intricate sidewalk ballet," "which maintains the safety of the streets and the freedom of the city" through an informal network of "eyes on the streets" that watch over a vibrant street life. Broken windows policing also engages in everyday surveillance strategies, but to the opposite effect (Harcourt 2005). Instead of facilitating community-building, here the "eyes on the street" are not neighbors watching out for each other but the criminogenic eyes of the carceral state (Hall et al. 1978, p. 41–42), and too, the hands of the state, as we shall discuss.

Broken windows policing was originally adopted by the New York Police Department (NYPD) as a strategy to "reclaim the public spaces of New York" in the early 1990s. The policy, which became known as the "quality of life initiative," was instituted by Mayor Giuliani and Police Commissioner Bratton "specifically to address the visible signs of a city out of control, a city that cannot protect itself or its children." Drawing from Wilson and Kelling's theorizing (1982), broken windows policing focuses on order maintenance, aggressively cracking down on minor offenses such as jumping the turnstile, selling loosies, open containers, and biking on sidewalk. It is defined by reliance upon the frequent use of surveillance practices such as "stop, question, and frisk" and asking for IDs. Notably, the policy was developed in the 1980s, in the disinvested post-industrial city, the city that was abandoned by both the state and capital. The subject of much scholarly debate, critical criminology scholars argue that the "broken windows" theory of policing is not evidence-based, but a "false promise" (Harcourt 2005) that instead produces a way of "seeing disorder" that further reproduces urban racial inequalities (Smith 2001, Sampson and Raudenbush 2004). To this end, in 2013 a federal court decision determined that the NYPD's practice of "stop-and-frisk" was unconstitutional and racially biased (*Floyd, et al. v. City of New York*). Our research confirms this and asks how the policy is experienced by young people of color in particular, as more than half of all people stopped by the police are under the age of 25.

In fact, teenagers hanging out on the street were identified by both Wilson and Kelling (1982) and Giuliani and Bratton (1994) as a "sign of disorder" in their writing and police practices.

While the race and gender of the teenager was not made explicit in their writing, "urban youth" was coded as black and brown in the disinvested city. Young people of color, particularly young men, are and always have been subject to criminalization; broken windows policing is no exception. This is deeply felt by the youth who participated in our research. Of those who took our survey, 74% said they felt targeted by the police, an overwhelming majority. Some respondents explained that this was because of "how I look" or a combination of "how I look and where I live," echoing two of the most commonly reported reasons by the NYPD for stops: suspicious movements and context. For example, Gio, 20, shared an incident in his video testimonial where he received a summons from a policewoman for riding his bike the wrong way against traffic:

> She called me a delinquent just because of the way I was dressed. I was just dressed, like you know, in regular jeans, a t-shirt and a hat. They said 'look, another delinquent,' and I took that disrespectful. I didn't want to argue with her because I know it will escalate the situation and just let it be.

Gio's story and others demonstrate how young people of color are produced as broken windows in the eyes of the state. In this way the disinvestment of the "ghetto" is projected onto their bodies (discussed further below). At the same time this is a very public production, as broken windows policing functions as a spectacle of both criminalization and order maintenance. Lisa Marie Cacho (2012, p.6) argues that in this way young people are *ontologized* as criminal, even if they aren't doing anything illegal, as in "you fit the description," and "even if the evidence is not actually evidence" (see Cahill et al. 2015).

Broken windows policing purports to create order and a better quality of life, yet, our research unsurprisingly demonstrates the opposite—that it can produce "disorder" for young people and their families, sever community relationships, curtail both the freedom of movement and the freedom to "stay put" (Newman and Wyly 2006), and create an overall hostile environment in neighborhood public spaces. This is clearly expressed by Markeys, 18:

> They told us they stopped us because "we fit the description." That meant, dark skinned, Latino, with, um, their pants sagging. They were like, "Oh," that we were sagging. They described our sneakers. They described our hair. Like, they would like say little slick stuff, like, "You fuckin faggot," and "Oh, you spicks always think that you can do what y'all want . . . That makes me feel, like, unsafe and insecure. It makes me feel like I shouldn't even come outside anymore if I'm just gonna get harassed by a policeman that's supposed to be protecting me.

In this case, Markeys sheds light on how the police create a hostile state of everyday terrorism (Pain 2014) that drives young people out of their neighborhood public spaces. And yet the reality is, of course, not so straightforward. Markeys's narrative challenges the discourse of total control and compliance to the state (Billies 2016). Young people, including Markeys, are still in public spaces and while they may be surveilled, disciplined, and subject to violence, this does not go uncontested. Our project offers insights into how young people negotiate, rework, and construct knowledge in the struggle over the sidewalk. Analyzing Markeys's story alongside our quantitative analysis of our data, for example, raises critical questions about the purpose of broken windows policing in this current context of gentrification where instead of the broken windows of 1980s New York (Figure 8.1), the mirrored windows of new condos (Figure 8.2) reflect the public schools across the street where Markeys, Darian, Gio, and others must pass through metal detectors every morning on their way to class.

FIGURE 8.1 View from a social studies classroom window, Bushwick, Brooklyn, NY

Source: Meryl Meisler, 1982

FIGURE 8.2 10 Montieth Street, Brooklyn, NY

Source: ODA Architecture, 2015

While communities of color have historically endured aggressive policing in New York, the intensification of police presence and police-initiated contact with people of color in the first decade of the 21st century is noteworthy. The number of stop-and-frisks increased over 600% during the tenure of Mayor Bloomberg (2002–2013), topping off at nearly 700,000 stops in 2011. More than half of all stopped people were younger than 25, and 83% of those were Black or Latino men. Most were innocent: 89% stopped were neither arrested nor summoned, and for those that were, most did not result in a conviction. Mapping the NYPD data of police stops from 2003 to 2012 (Figure 8.3, see the video of the geography of stop-and-frisk, which can be found at http://researchersforfairpolicing.org), our analysis reveals the scope and unevenness of policing across the city, clearly showing a disproportionate targeting of neighborhoods where residents are poor and working-class communities of color.

These are the very same neighborhoods that were redlined, abandoned, and disinvested by the state, and are now heavily policed and gentrifying. Consider, for example, the neighborhood of Bushwick, Brooklyn (Figures 8.1 and 8.2). The image from the early 1980s is a stark reminder of what disinvestment looks and feels like. While the image is dramatic, it is not an exceptional part of a pattern of disinvestment in communities of color across the city experiencing housing abandonment and the cutting off of state services including fire, police, and hospitals. Bushwick almost burned to the ground in the 1970s. After weathering decades of white flight and disinvestment, the neighborhood began to stabilize in the early 2000s thanks to the ongoing work of community-based organizations, including Make the Road New York. The images illustrate the cycles of disinvestment and gentrification processes. Named by *Vogue* magazine (Remsen 2014) as the "7th Coolest Neighborhood in the World," rising rents and real estate speculation is putting pressure on long-time residents. Predominantly Latino/Hispanic (65%), the neighborhood has a median household income of $36,683 and 1 in 3 households live below the federal poverty line (Pratt Sustainable Communities Studio 2014).

A glance at the geography of stop-and-frisk (Figure 8.3) reveals that Bushwick, along with the nearby historic African-American neighborhood Bedford Stuyvesant, is one of several neighborhoods aggressively policed, as defined quantitatively by the NYPD data in terms of numbers of stops. The data presents strong correlations between the dramatic increase in police stops in the Bloomberg years and the equally dramatic increase in real estate development. We are not making a cause-and-effect argument, but instead offering a political economic analysis that considers how the relationships between parallel processes of urban development and the imperatives

FIGURE 8.3 Location of all innocent stop-and-frisks in 2011 (mapped from NYPD data)

Source: Brett Stoudt, 2013

for aggressive policing intertwine and are co-constitutive. Focusing on the historical present, we consider how at the same time that young people were being stopped on an everyday basis in their home communities, 40% of the city was rezoned and over 40,000 new buildings constructed during the Bloomberg administration.

This is not the panopticon (Foucault 1975). The sheer quantity of stops demonstrates an excessive amount of resources and manpower mobilized to produce the spectacle of stop-and-frisk as normative, obscuring strategies required by neoliberal capitalism. The spectacle and everyday routinization of Black and Latino young men being stopped redirects the gaze from structural conditions of inequality by reproducing the criminalization of young men of color and their communities. The spectacle is employed as a mode of governance which produces criminalization and disorder, and thus the appearance of order. This is what Neil Smith (2001) discusses as a "social cleansing," sweeping the sidewalks "clean" through zero tolerance policies and everyday militarized spatial control as part of the new urban strategy of gentrification. In turn, the cycle of discipline and disappearing (and incarcerating) young men works to generate economic value for developers and investors (Cahill et al. 2015, Cahill 2006, Wright 2006).

The public spectacle of policing is experienced in very personal ways by many young New Yorkers. Our research documents the constant presence of police in the most intimate spaces of their everyday lives—homes, neighborhoods, streets, and schools. Of the young Black and Latino people we surveyed, 89% had some *personal* contact with police. This involved police stops (53%) and being asked to move or show their ID by police (62%). Of those who were stopped, 76% were stopped more than once and 57% were stopped inside or in front of their building. In his testimonial, Devonne, 21, shares with us his experience of being handcuffed to his banister with his little sister and brother watching from the window. The sidewalk might here be understood along the lines of what Jenna Loyd (2011) discusses as the militarized domesticities of the home front. Jane Jacobs (1961) reminds us the sidewalk is not an abstraction, but the connective tissue of the community—it is where community life is enacted. While Devonne's experience of being stopped and handcuffed in front of his home is intimately personal, it is also a public part of the community's experience of policing, surveillance, and state-sanctioned invasions of privacy.

Our analysis reveals that while the police focus their attention on young men of color, that scrutiny is experienced collectively as a community under siege. Even some of those young people who have had no contact with the police, or no explicitly negative contact, report feeling targeted. This is perhaps not surprising when 87% of participants have witnessed police stop friends, family, and/or strangers. This informs our argument that we need to expand our understanding of policing beyond a focus upon young men of color, and consider the impact upon family members—mothers who worry about their sons, kids watching their big brother being searched, teachers who know when their students are late to school that they may have been detained or picked up for truancy, and grandmothers opening the door to the police.

Young people and their families' encounters with the police are not experienced in a vacuum, but as part of a larger set of structural dispossession. Economic inequality in New York City is the highest in the nation, while the US itself is amongst the most unequal nations in the world (Wilkinson and Pickett 2011, p. 15). At the same time that young black and brown people in New York are subjected to intensified police scrutiny in the neighborhood streets, rents are going up and families are being displaced from their homes. There is also an alarming increase of police working in schools and of schools implementing harsh, "zero tolerance" punishment characterized by a reliance on suspension, expulsion, and even arrest, to solve social conflicts (Advancement Project 2000, 2003, Mukherjee and Karpatkin 2007). The corresponding low graduation rates in schools that heavily police their students (Advancement Project 2003), and few living-wage jobs for young people and their family members reduce the life chances for young people of color on multiple fronts. Policing, mass criminalization, and the carceral landscapes of many NYC neighborhood streets and sidewalks are thus experienced and understood by young people and their families as part of the racialized context of the gentrifying, privatized landscapes of New York City. The aggressive policing and heavy surveillance contribute to an overall feeling of dispossession and a sense that people no longer feel as if they have rights to, or ownership of, their communities. With this in mind, we suggest that we need to radically reframe the debate about police reform as community development and an investment in equitable social reproduction (Cahill et al. 2015).

Conclusion

Darian X, one of our youth organizers/coresearchers, testified at the New York City Council's Committee on Public Safety (2015) hearing focused on community policing policies. After sharing data from our study, he called for "the total reinvestment in our communities of color:"

> I feel like graduation rates, a great way to track outcomes. Are more of our young people graduating? Are less of our young people in prison? . . . Are the suspension rates going down? These are trackable ways of seeing if improvement is really happening in our community.

Do more people have access to jobs then they did when we started this program? . . . Right now we can see that people are underemployed, undereducated, overworked, under accredited with humanity and dignity as a person. So, can we track human dignity? No we cannot. But we can definitely track a community's progression and growth. Are there more institutions that support this community? Are there more banks that give loans to developers that build low-income houses in this community? How are we progressing as a people totally and holistically?

Darian's testimony is in line with our analysis that suggests that the "disorder" that broken windows policing seeks to "contain" and manage are deep structural issues that would be best addressed within and by communities, using an assets-based approach to strengthening communities and building capacity (Kretzmann and McKnight 1996). Calling for a complete reorganization of the state's relationship to communities of color, Darian widens the scope of debate. Flipping the script, he also challenges stereotypes of poor people not caring about their community, shifting the gaze back to state accountability.

Much has changed since we began our research in 2012. Young people at the forefront of organizing against state violence are engaged in a national conversation and movement addressing carceral power, the role of the state, intersectionality, the extrajudicial killings of black and brown people everywhere, and the many other ways that people of color are rendered powerless by the state (see www.blacklivesmatter.com). As organizers in the Black Lives Matter movement state, "This is not a moment, it's a movement." With this in mind, we consider how our scholarship might contribute to activism, and how social movements are informing research regarding young people's experiences of being policed and the ways communities resist the police state, and alternatives to it.

As Darian's testimony demonstrates, some of us continue to advocate and actively work for policies addressing much-needed police reform in New York City and the US (*Floyd vs. the NYPD*, the Community Safety Act). Members of our research team continue to study and agitate against broken windows policing initiatives that have been sold as kinder, gentler alternatives to stop, question, and frisk, such as "pioneering neighborhood policing strategies." Community policing's feel-good name and seemingly progressive philosophy elides the further enmeshment of the police in the daily lives of New Yorkers who need jobs and schools, not more cops with guns and arrest powers (Beck and Matles 2015).

Young black and brown people are still "being tried on the sidewalk" (see opening quote). The right to the sidewalk, cannot, as Robin D.G. Kelley (2016) reminds us, be addressed with the "right" legal strategy when the system has been designed to protect white privilege, white property, and white personhood. The streets of New York City have changed dramatically over the last few years, reflective of shifting demographics that are whiter and wealthier, in gentrifying New York. In this context, the struggle for the sidewalk takes on even greater significance.

Over the past few years, following the police killings of Mike Brown, Eric Garner, Akai Gurley, and many others, thousands of New Yorkers have joined together taking over streets in citywide protests, sometimes laying down together side by side in silence on sidewalks and prominent public spaces to call attention to the deadly and persistent injustices of racialized state violence and the militarization of everyday life (Figure 8.4). In so doing, protesters transformed prisonized and privatized landscapes into truly public spaces. This taking back of the street, as architect and scholar Anthony Vidler (2001, p. 4, cited in Mitchell 2003) suggests, is what makes the

> urban life worth living [. . .] the street as a site of interaction, encounter, and the support of strangers for each other [. . .] the corner store as a communicator of information and interchange. These spaces still define an urban culture, one that resist all effort to 'secure' it out of existence.

FIGURE 8.4 Eric Garner's eyes by artist JR, during the Millions March NYC, December 13, 2014

Source: The All-Nite Images

We would add that "securing the street out of existence" in this case involves pushing young people of color, their families, and their communities out of the neighborhood. Disappearing young people of color from the public spaces, like Markeys, who stays home to stay safe, is one example; the subsequent displacement of his family is another. In this way, our analysis suggests that the right to the sidewalk is indeed the right to the city; or as Mitchell and Heynen (2009, p. 616) suggest "the right to urban life [. . .] is to say the right to be part of the city—to be present, to be."

Acknowledgements

The Researchers for Fair Policing are grateful to all of the young people who have been involved in this project over many years, who shared their stories and took the time to engage with others in collective analysis. We are thankful to the editors Jeffrey Hou and Sabine Knierbein for their thoughtful editorial engagement with our chapter. This research would not be possible without the support of the Adco Foundation; Antipode Foundation; Graduate Center, CUNY; Institute for Human Geography; John Jay College of Criminal Justice, CUNY; Pratt Institute; Taconic Fellowship, Pratt Center for Community Development; and the Sociological Initiatives Foundation.

References

Advancement Project, 2000. *Opportunities Suspended: The Devastating Consequences of Zero Tolerance and School Discipline.* Cambridge, MA: Harvard Civil Rights Project.

Advancement Project, 2003. *Derailed: The Schoolhouse to the Jailhouse Track*. Washington, DC: Advancement Project.

Alexander, M., 2012. *The New Jim Crow: Mass Incarceration in the Age of Colorblindness*. New York: The New Press.

Beck, B. and Matles, A., 2015. Opinion: We Need Fewer NYPD Officers—Not More, *AM New York*. [online]. Available from: www.amny.com/opinion/we-need-fewer-nypd-officers-not-more-1.10575625 [Accessed 5 November 2015].

Billies, M., 2016. Impossible Compliance: Policing as Violent Struggle Over Bodies and Urban Space—Metropolitics [online]. *metropolitics.eu*. Available from: www.metropolitiques.eu/Impossible-Compliance-Policing-as.html [Accessed 21 May 2016].

Cacho, L. M., 2012. *Social Death: Racialized Rightlessness and the Criminalization of the Unprotected*. New York: NYU Press.

Cahill, C., 2006. "At Risk"? The Fed Up Honeys Re-Present the Gentrification of the Lower East Side. *Women Studies Quarterly*, 34, 334–363.

Cahill, C., Stoudt, B. G., Matles, A. D., Belmonte, K., Djokovic, S., Lopez, J., Pimentel, A., Torre, M. E., and X, Darian, 2015. A Blade of Grass: Young People, Slow Violence, and the Struggle over Social Reproduction. The Gender, Place, and Culture Jan Monk Distinguished Feminist Geography Annual Lecture, Annual Association of American Geographers, April 2015, Chicago, IL.

Floyd, et al. v. City of New York, 2013. United States District Court, NY: Southern District of New York.

Foucault, M., 1975. *Discipline & Punish: The Birth of the Prison*. New York: Vintage Books.

Gilmore, R. W., 2007. *Golden Gulag: Prisons, Surplus, Crisis, and Opposition in Globalizing California*. Berkeley: University of California Press.

Giuliani, R. W. and Bratton, W. J., 1994. Police Strategy No. 5: Reclaiming the Public Spaces of New York: New York City Police Department.

Hall, S., Roberts, B., Clarke, J., Jefferson, T., and Critcher, C., 1978. *Policing the Crisis: Mugging, the State, and Law and Order*. London: Palgrave Macmillan.

Harcourt, B. E., 2005. *Illusion of Order: The False Promise of Broken Windows Policing*. Revised. Cambridge, MA: Harvard University Press.

Harvey, D., 2003. The Right to the City. *International Journal of Urban and Regional Research*, 27 (4), 939–941.

Jacobs, J., 1961. *The Death and Life of Great American Cities*. New York: Vintage Books.

Kelley, R. D. G., 2016. Robin D.G. Kelley presents Mike Brown's Body: Meditations on War, Race and Democracy Archives [online]. *Princeton African American Studies*. Available from: http://aas.princeton.edu/lecture-series/toni-morrison-lectures/toni-morrison-2014-2015/ [Accessed 21 May 2016].

Kretzmann, J. and McKnight, J. P., 1996. Assets-Based Community Development. *National Civic Review*, 85 (4), 23–29.

Lefebvre, H., 1996. *Writings on Cities*. 1st edition. Cambridge, MA, USA: Wiley-Blackwell.

Loyd, J. M., 2011. "Peace Is Our Only Shelter": Questioning Domesticities of Militarization and White Privilege. *Antipode*, 43 (3), 845–873.

Loyd, J. M., Mitchelson, M., and Burridge, A., eds., 2012. *Beyond Walls and Cages: Prisons, Borders, and Global Crisis*. Athens: University of Georgia Press.

McKittrick, K., 2006. *Demonic Grounds: Black Women and the Cartographies of Struggle*. 1st edition. Minneapolis: University of Minnesota Press.

Mitchell, D., 2003. *The Right to the City: Social Justice and the Fight for Public Space*. New York: Guilford Publications.

Mitchell, D. and Heynen, N., 2009. The Geography of Survival and the Right to the City: Speculations on Surveillance, Legal Innovation, and the Criminalization of Intervention. *Urban Geography*, 30 (6), 611–632.

Mukherjee, E. and Karpatkin, M., 2007. *Criminalizing the Classroom: The Over-Policing of New York City Schools*. New York: New York Civil Liberties Union.

Newman, K. and Wyly, E. K., 2006. The Right to Stay Put, Revisited: Gentrification and Resistance to Displacement in New York City. *Urban Studies*, 43 (1), 23–57.

Pain, R., 2014. Everyday Terrorism Connecting Domestic Violence and Global Terrorism. *Progress in Human Geography*, 38 (4), 531–550.

Pratt Sustainable Communities Studio, 2014. *Keeping Bushwick, Bushwick! Strategies to Preserve Neighborhood Affordability*. Brooklyn, NY: Pratt Institute City & Regional Planning Program.

Remsen, N., 2014. Global Street Style Report: Mapping Out the 15 Coolest Neighborhoods in the World [online]. *Vogue*. Available from: www.vogue.com/slideshow/1080625/fifteen-coolest-street-style-neighborhoods/ [Accessed 15 April 2015].

Sampson, R. J. and Raudenbush, S. W., 2004. Seeing Disorder: Neighborhood Stigma and the Social Construction of "Broken Windows." *Social Psychology Quarterly*, 67 (4), 319–342.

Shabazz, R., 2015. *Spatializing Blackness: Architectures of Confinement and Black Masculinity in Chicago*. 1st edition. Urbana: University of Illinois Press.

Smith, N., 2001. Global Social Cleansing: Postliberal Revanchism and the Export of Zero Tolerance. *Social Justice*, 28 (3/85), 68–74.

Stoudt, B. G., Cahill, C., Belmonte, K., Djokovic, S., Lopez, J., Matles, A., Pimentel, A., Torre, M. E., and X, Darian, 2016. Participatory Action Research as Youth Activism. *In*: J. Conner and S. Rosen (eds), *Contemporary Youth Activism: Advancing Social Justice in the U.S.* Santa Barbara, CA: Praeger, 327–346.

Stoudt, B. G., Cahill, C., Torre, M. E., Matles, A., Lopez, J., Pimentel, A., Belmonte, K., Djokovic, S. and X, Darian, forthcoming. *The Punishments, Insecurities and Contradictions of Growing Up Policed in NYC*. 1st edition. Make the Road New York & the Public Science Project.

Stoudt, B. G., Fine, M., and Fox, M., 2011. Growing Up Policed in the Age of Aggressive Policing Policies. *New York Law School Law Review*, 56, 1331.

T. D. Jakes (@BishopJakes), 14 December 2014. https://twitter.com/bishopjakes/status/544155241172971521

Torre, M. E., Fine, M., Stoudt, B. G., and Fox, M., 2012. Critical Participatory Action Research as Public Science. *In*: H. Cooper, P. M. Camic, D. L. Long, A. T. Panter, D. Rindskopf, and K. J. Sher, eds. *APA Handbook of Research Methods in Psychology, Vol 2: Research Designs: Quantitative, Qualitative, Neuropsychological, and Biological*. Washington, DC, US: American Psychological Association, 171–184.

Vidler, A., 2001. Aftermath; a City Transformed: Designing "Defensible Space." *The New York Times*, September 23.

Wilkinson, R. and Pickett, K., 2011. *The Spirit Level: Why Greater Equality Makes Societies Stronger*. New York: Bloomsbury.

Wilson, J. Q., and Kelling, G. L., 1982. Broken Windows: The Police and Neighborhood Safety. *The Atlantic Monthly*, (3), 29–38.

Wright, M. W., 2006. *Disposable Women and Other Myths of Global Capitalism*. New edition. New York: Routledge.

X, Darian, 2015. New York City Council's Committee on Public Safety. New York: City Council Public Meeting Testimony.

Zekavat, S., 2015. NYPD, Omnipresence and People's Right to the Street Corner. *Urban Cusp*. Available from: http://www.urbancusp.com/2015/02/nypd-omnipresence-peoples-right-street-corner-2 [Accessed: 11 March 2017].

9

LEVELING THE PLAYFIELD

Urban Movement in the Strategic Action Field of Urban Policy in Poland

Anna Domaradzka

The influx of global capital to Polish cities has resulted in significant and uneven growth. Poland's transformation from a centrally regulated communist regime to a proto-neoliberal state has created a growing crisis for the welfare state. The substantial effects on public space and communities have resulted in urban issues gaining significant importance. The intensification of negative social processes, as well as residents' increased awareness, has led to growing discontent and mobilization in many urban areas. Specifically, both large- and middle-sized cities in Poland became the arena for new types of civic activism in the form of neighborhood initiatives and urban grassroots, building local and national networks and coalitions. In recent years, this new kind of urban grassroots movement (Andretta et al. 2015, Domaradzka and Wijkström 2014, 2015, Jacobsson 2015) became one of the most vibrant aspects of the nation's civil society. In this chapter I will explain how the evolution of this social mobilization has affected changes in the physical urban environment as well as a shift in the political field of urban policy.

The interests of urban movement activists are often hyper-local, linked to specific spatial or social conflicts, yet these activists also draw inspiration and frame their actions using global concepts of "right to the city" (Lefebvre 1968, Harvey 2012), "urban democracy" (Appadurai 2001), and "spatial justice" (Soja 2010). Interestingly, the "right to the city" framework has been adopted by very different groups—from squatters, who reject the "capitalistic order of space," to inhabitants of gated communities, who want to influence the way their semi-private or semi-public spaces are organized and managed (Polańska 2013, Polańska and Piotrowski 2015, Domaradzka 2014, 2015). Given the social diversity of Polish cities, unlikely alliances are sometimes being forged around spatial issues, including middle-class house owners, precarious youth, and low-income tenants or squatters concerned about the same neighborhood or residents' rights.

Recently, these diverse groups of urban activists emerged as an influential political opposition in many Polish cities, including Warsaw, Poznań, Gorzów Wielkopolski, Kraków, or Gdańsk (see Figure 9.1). Grassroots pressure on local governments took many different forms: from lobbying and watchdog activities on an everyday basis, through organizing referenda against ruling mayors, to urban activists running in local elections. Due to the strong media support and successful coalition building, those new civil society actors gained some influence over political decisions as well as on the functioning of local and national administration. In several Polish cities, urban movement candidates were officially elected to the city council or as mayors with urban movement support.

FIGURE 9.1 Map of Polish cities where urban activists emerged as an influential political opposition

Source: Dominique Peck

The breakthrough, in respect to the networking of grassroots groups, was the organization of the first Urban Movements Congress in 2011, which was entirely dedicated to networking and sharing of experiences between local activists from cities all over Poland. Originally organized by a group of Poznań activists to exchange experiences with their counterparts from other cities, it grew into a nationwide network of grassroots organizations, finally becoming a formalized coalition of associations in 2016. The Congress, as an active network, became an organizational platform (Finnemore and Sikkink 1998) linking pragmatic local activists with intellectuals and researchers who popularized new global definitions of processes taking place in contemporary cities.

From a theoretical point of view, this chapter examines the changing roles of a particular type of civil society actors—namely the urban movement—in challenging the existing "strategic action field" of urban policy in Poland. Using a theory of fields developed by Fligstein and McAdam (2011, 2012), we can perceive recent changes in urban policy as a result of a norm cascade (Finnemore and Sikkink 1998) provoked by challengers' mobilization and successful lobbying. To illustrate the role of urban initiatives in the contestation of the practices of the local administration and the possible wider effect of the urban movement on relevant parts of the public sector, qualitative data collected in case studies in Warsaw and Poznań are used, focusing on neighborhood initiatives and urban movement organizations.[1] Data from individual interviews with representatives of grassroots groups (32 interviews) as well as Urban Movements Congress leaders (three interviews) was first collected in 2012 and 2013 and then supplemented with additional interviews in 2014 and 2015 after the local elections (four formal and several informal interviews). To describe the goals as well as the history of the urban movement initiatives and their context, various materials, including books, press articles, and online publications were used.

Through the reactions of the local authorities, institutions, and organizations to some of those initiatives (based on observations, interviews, and documents analysis), the processes within the local administration during and after the elections have been further understood. Rich qualitative data were also gathered during participatory observations of three consecutive Urban Movements Congresses in 2012, 2013, and 2015 (each hosting between 100 and 300 representatives of urban initiatives from all over Poland), government workshops and seminars concerning national urban policy in 2013 and 2014, as well as various local and national meetings gathering activists, experts, and local administration representatives.

Urban Policy Field

Following Fligstein and McAdam's (2011, 2012) theory of fields, we define urban policy as a strategic action field, where the activity of actors influences each other as well as the development of the field in terms of norms, practices, power structure, and general goals (see also Domaradzka and Wijkström 2016). According to the theory, a strategic action field is composed of incumbents, challengers, and internal governance units (IGUs) (Fligstein and McAdam 2011, p. 5). Using those concepts, we can analyze the recent changes in the urban policy field in Poland as a result of interplay between new urban movement actors (as challengers) and local governments (as incumbents), with the Department of Spatial Planning in the Ministry of Infrastructure and Development playing the role of internal governance unit on the national level.

The idea of social movement actors as challengers was introduced by Gamson (1990), who explained the distinction between "members" and "challengers" as "being inside or outside of the polity. Those who are inside are members whose interest is vested—that is, recognized as valid by other members. Those who are outside are challengers. They lack the basic prerogative of members—routine access to decisions that affect them" (Gamson 1990, p. 140). Therefore, the challengers' main mode of existence is governed by the search for an opportunity to reshape existing power structures though contention of an existing order and resistance to mainstream rules. As Tilly (1978) stresses, the "opportunity" and "threat" are distinct catalysts of challengers' mobilization. Therefore, the state facilitation and repression practices are of critical importance in shaping the dynamics of contention. Along the same lines, McAdam (1982, p. 48) argued that the "structural potential" for a movement is defined by favorable political opportunities and access to mobilizing structures (established groups or networks) independent of elite control.

In this specific field, the control over urban space is what is at stake—with urban activists renegotiating the boundaries of the urban political field situated in between a retreating city-level public sector and the general expansion of transnational corporations and private sector. In most of the cases of grassroots activity, mobilization is aimed at protecting space defined as "common good" of local residents (e.g. green squares between the buildings, neighborhood parks, or noncommercial buildings and their surroundings) from planned construction and redevelopment (either by commercial developers or public investors).[2] Here, urban space is defined as a "common-pool resource," in line with existing debate about the commons and their alleged tragedy (Hardin 1968, Ostrom 1990). The result of the ongoing "game of the city" in which incumbents defend their dominant position and control over space, while challengers seek to introduce new values and behaviors concerning urban policy, is the reshaping of the practices and narratives defining the field.

The Roots of Recent Urban Mobilization in Poland

Economic transformations, mobility, and demographic shifts have brought about some significant changes in the social structure of Polish cities in recent decades: there is now a growing group of urban residents who are aware how other cities in Europe and beyond are governed. Many of these residents often have professional expertise related to some of the processes taking place in the city. From the standpoint of public administration, it means that the "clients" or "recipients" of services and government regulations become more demanding, aware of their own rights, and often more knowledgeable in a given field than the average official. Characteristically, this is also the group that expects to be involved in decision-making processes related to their immediate environment. The increasingly active group of residents desires to have real influence over municipal decisions and investment priorities, and to participate in the planning and implementation of various urban policies related to transport, housing, culture, education, revitalization, etc. The baseline argument here is that residents are the main users and therefore owners of the city, and as such should be consulted over all issues influencing their quality of life (Mergler and Pobłocki 2010).

Until recently, the Polish municipal governments did not offer residents many possibilities for participation. Meanwhile, the residents became more and more dissatisfied with a passive role of "consumers of the city services" (interview with one of the urban leaders, July 2013). The period between 2012 and 2015, however, has brought drastic changes in this area, mainly related to the introduction of new mechanisms involving citizens in decision making (such as participatory budgeting or social consultation of revitalization programs) as well as a wider use or improvement of existing mechanisms of participation (consultation of the zoning plans, social dialogue councils, referendums on local issues). While this process was first facilitated by the need to comply with European Union requirements with regard to democratization and implementation of the various programs funded by EU, the growing political power of grassroots groups demanding greater participation enabled the EU-forced measures to become real tools in democratization of the cities' management.

These changes also respond to the challenges faced by contemporary Polish cities, stemming from the increasing complexity of the problems and needs of the residents, as well as suburbanization combined with depopulation of city centers and the rising costs of maintenance of public infrastructure. Changing attitudes and needs of residents, who became better organized and connected through modern technologies, force public institutions to reform their measures and answer those new challenges. One of them is to ensure the residents' right to participation in decision making, authorizing them to both benefit and bear the burdens of responsibility for the management of development of urban areas (Kelly 1998). The state and municipal authorities are not made exempt from their statutory duties (including provision of necessary services, development of the local economy, and protection of the natural environment), but must also ensure that decision-making processes are open and transparent as the public and civic sectors learn how to work with each other.

Given the substantial social diversity of urban residents in Poland, it is worth considering who are those that engage in urban movement and why they want to influence city development. In his book *Poznań of Conflicts*, Mergler (2008) speaks of the "pissed-off citizens groups" as the main driving force of urban movement in Poland. This definition is accurate as it points out the fact that a majority of grassroots urban initiatives started as protests against some undesirable investment or change in the urban space. Mergler argues that residents' frustration and anger is usually the result of inept and unsatisfactory urban policy introduced by city rulers, who put the interests of developers over the welfare of the residents (Mergler 2008). In practice, this means that one of the impulses for urban activity is the desire to defend the interests of tenants and small private owners (of apartments, houses, and land plots) from large private investors (developers, global companies, and dominant institutions like the army). While the protection of individual property and local quality of life may be at the roots of some urban initiatives, the urban movements' slogans are usually much broader in scope—overcoming the NIMBY ("not in my backyard") logics and relating to the residents' rights to the city, protection of their quality of life, and the need for greater participation in urban management.

On the national level, various demands related to social policy or housing policy have been put forward by the Urban Movements Congress, in coalition with tenants and squatter movements (Polańska and Piotrowski 2015). Inclusion of those particular demands into the Urban Movements Congress agenda created a new opening for a discussion on housing policy issues (eviction law, municipal housing investments, etc.) and defined the group of public housing tenants as well as welfare recipients as important interest groups whose claims should be included in urban policy measures. Other goals of the movement include the change in the municipal rent policy to promote the creation of accessible meeting places (including cheap eateries, neighbor clubs, local services, or groceries) instead of seeking to maximize profits for the city budget. These and other social demands are clearly present among the slogans proclaimed by the urban movements. However, they gain less publicity than issues related to specific conflicts over spatial investments or development plans. It also seems easier to mobilize public support for issues such as zoning plans, protection of the green areas, or removal of ads covering the facades of buildings, than for a better housing policy or more public investments in transport and revitalization.

In other words, urban movements are more successful in areas where changes can be fast and relatively easy to implement (e.g. introducing a participatory budget covering 0.5% of the municipal budget), without creating a huge budgetary burden. It seems that urban activists have a significantly smaller impact on the matters that require long-term funding and legal changes, like better access to housing, creating walkable solutions and high-quality public space, as well as stopping chaotic suburbanization and "wild" reprivatization[3] of municipal housing stock. In those more resource- or time-consuming issues changes are much less impressive, and the real effects remain to be seen in the nearest future.

Entering the Playfield

According to the definition of strategic fields of action, we can distinguish different stages of urban movement development in terms of its role as an actor in the field of urban policy. At the first stage, certain specific problems and needs at the local level become an impulse for the creation of a local strategic action field. At this stage a relatively small group of people (neighbors, residents of the area) comes to the conclusion that they have a common goal (often to fight a common enemy) and decide to act for its implementation. Subsequently, those local strategic action fields, defined around the leaders and grassroots mobilization, tend to merge and form local networks, usually in the same city or district. Finally, with the growing number of initiatives and through the emergence of socially skilled leaders (Fligstein 2001, Fligstein and McAdam 2012), the transition phase is reached, when local actors establish a national network by defining common goals and strategies. From this stage, we can talk about the existence of a common framework of action (as defined by Benford and Snow 2000) and the appearance of the social movement network structure (Diani 2015). In other words, we can say that urban grassroots initially define their strategic action fields very locally, but in time their scope widens, until finally they—as an urban movement network—enter the strategic action field of national urban policy. Those phases of development are often stimulated by external incentives like EU policies, activities of norm entrepreneurs, and popularization of global "right to the city" ideas.

Studies on urban enclaves of grassroots activity (Henzler 2009, Domaradzka 2015) show that spontaneous initiatives usually occurred as protests against local authorities after the announcement of an investment or action plan, which would be realized at the expense of local residents' quality of life. Those acts of urban resistance often had a strong spatial aspect of "taking over" a given place (through planting, occupying, painting over, or organizing public events and gatherings) to underline its social function and common "ownership." The interviewed activists underscored that through participation in several protests they usually reached the conclusion that a single group of residents have no influence on the decisions of municipal authorities, so they proceeded to create local coalitions and networks to build support for their claims. In turn, this led to a redefinition of their strategic action field boundaries—from the local to the national or even global level (through the ideas of the global "right to the city" movement).

Some intellectuals played the important role of "norm entrepreneurs" (Finnemore and Sikkink 1998), introducing the concepts of "right to the city" (Lefebvre 1968, Harvey 2012), "uneven development" (Smith 2010), or "deep democracy" (Appadurai 2001) into the urban movement narrative as well as media debate. The practitioners eventually came upon the idea of "concrete narrative" introduced by Mergler (2008), which gained the status of a buzzword, often repeated and used to define an effective framework for action at the local level. Of similar importance were the 9 Urban Theses (Urban Movements Congress 2011), formulated at the first Congress and containing key movement demands for democratization and de-commercialization of urban development strategies (see Figure 9.2). Four years later, during the fourth Urban Movements Congress (see Figure 9.3), they were updated and developed into 15 Urban Theses (Urban

FIGURE 9.2 "Right to the City" Election Committee in Poznań with 9 Urban Theses

Source: Lech Mergler, 2014

FIGURE 9.3 The fourth Urban Movements Congress in Gorzów

Source: Lech Mergler, 2015

Movements Congress 2015). All these terms have become part of the common discourse on urban movements, popularized in particular through intensive publishing (e.g., Pobłocki 2010, Mergler and Pobłocki 2010, Kusiak 2011, Celiński 2012, Leder 2013, Pluciński 2013), social media use, and networking on the national level.

Leveling the Playfield

The traditional model of public administration gave it particular authority, based on specific competences, over a citizen who was perceived as less competent and therefore subservient to the bureaucratic system. However, with increases in the levels of education in Poland, this distinction has blurred. Also, with the public administration's tasks becoming more complex and their budgets shrinking, the role of external experts and subcontractors has been growing. The budgetary crisis leads to a situation in which politicians and city administrators become increasingly willing to share responsibility for difficult decisions with citizens, as well as involve them (through civil society organizations) in social services delivery. This evolution implies a greater openness of the system to influences from outside, including input from individual citizens, civic organizations, and other interest groups, creating opportunities for investors and entrepreneurs, but also social activists willing to influence bureaucratic and political practices.

Specifically, the EU's influence paralleled the grassroots pressure on both local and national governments, where EU policies created a necessary opportunity structure (Tarrow 1998, Meyer 2004) offering civil society actors a better leverage for their claims.

It can be also argued that the New Public Management (NPM) reforms (Hood 1991, Kelly 1998) as well as New Urban Policy agenda (Swyngedouw et al. 2002) had a strong impact on redefining the role of cities and the functioning of their administration in Poland. The NPM model developed in response to the increasing welfare state burden through decentralization of management, strategic planning, and the use of market mechanisms to ensure greater effectiveness of public sector organizations, and therefore save budgetary resources. However, the resulting "marketization" and "digitization" of public administration does not necessarily lead to the realization of values such as social cohesion or equality of access, or to an improved democracy. However, while NPM has been criticized as a part of neoliberal package weakening the role of the state, it has also created opportunities for more direct engagement of civil society actors in Polish urban politics.

The New Urban Policy or "new urbanism" (Salet and Gualini 2007) focused on reshaping the urban environment to make cities more attractive to potential investors, as a way to transform them into "urban growth machines" (Logan and Molotch 1987, Nawratek 2012), which led to an increase in business imperatives (Levine 1989) as a defining trait of new "urban regime" (Stone 1993). This philosophy resulted in a growing gap between the less-affluent residents' needs and what the city can offer, leading to gentrification, increasing exclusion, and marginalization. On the other hand, as a result of commercialization of common areas and shrinkage of open green spaces, the middle-class residents also started to experience a decline in their quality of life, as well as their property values.

Interestingly, grassroots urban activism emerged as a reaction to the negative effects of such urban growth policies. Its emergence was facilitated by new "participatory" processes introduced by the managerial and technocratic NPM regime implemented both by local and national civic bodies. Given the growing level of competences and expectations of urban residents, it is not surprising that they have developed a critical attitude towards neoliberal public management. Therefore, the postulation of new urban policy measures based on democratic participation appeared more and more often in the public debate. Yet, the implementation of solutions ensuring greater participation of residents in city management faces difficulties. One of the reasons is the lack of political will among those in power, the other being the underdeveloped civil society structures and civic competences related to the understanding of citizens' rights, as well as opportunities and ways to influence administrative decisions. Those who oppose the democratization of urban management processes emphasize that citizen participation is often limited to shortsighted criticism, blocking all kinds of public initiatives for egoistic reasons, which in the long run severely hinders the implementation of important urban plans or regulations. Although levels of civic competence has slowly grown in the last decade in Poland (despite the absence of civic education), what still hinders the culture of participation is a high level of distrust towards the authorities and public institutions (Siemieńska et al. 2011) and negative stereotypes concerning public administration (Domaradzka 2015). It seems, however, that the organizational culture of Polish administration and its lack of know-how are poorly adapted to conducting constructive dialogue with citizens.

Meanwhile, in the recent rhetoric of local politicians and city officials, the new narrative of "engaging the potential of residents" to build solutions for the cities' socioeconomic development has started to increasingly appear. Earlier research shows that there are cases of successful cooperation between the administration and the residents' groups for the implementation of new solutions to problems arising in urban areas. Some of these grassroots initiatives even become institutionalized as part of the social services system, as it was in case of several "neighbors clubs" or "moms clubs" in Warsaw (Domaradzka 2015, Domaradzka and Matysiak 2015).

Using Fligstein and McAdam's (2011, 2012) concepts we can therefore state that the actors of the public sphere—the incumbents—begin to change their behavior. At the same time, the challengers—grassroots residents groups—acquire new competences and shape their strategies to act effectively in the urban policy strategic action field. The main requirements of full participation are the ability for long-term commitment of activists and a certain level of expertise, which leads to a growing professionalization of the urban initiatives and their intensive coalition building. Movement leaders often have substantial experience participating in various kinds of urban conflicts as well as advisory forums, working along local government institutions (e.g. local social dialogue councils). With the establishment of the Urban Movements Congress network, various meetings and online forums became the arena of continuous exchange of experience and know-how about methods of effectively influencing local urban politics. The Congress also became a venue for bringing together the experts in various fields related to urban policy—administrative law, transport, urban planning, sustainable development, or housing—who are willing to advise grassroots activists in their efforts.

One material outcome of the urban movement professionalization is the publication of *Spatial Anti-Helplessness Guide: Right to the City in Action* (Mergler, Pobłocki, and Wudarski 2013), which both presents the idea of the right to the city and describes several examples of relatively successful battles for space conducted by Poznań activists in the years 2009 to 2013. This guide for urban activists popularizes practical knowledge about specific opportunities to influence the decisions of the authorities and investors (in other words, resident rights), while also promoting the idea of grassroots mobilization against unsatisfactory policies of the city authorities, to establish the residents' influence over urban space. Presently, many members of Urban Movements Congress actively participate in the political life of their cities, in the role of city or neighborhood councilors, as well as candidates in municipal elections. In recent years several urban activists became employed in the local administration, introducing a bottom-up perspective of bureaucratic practices.

This blurring of the distinction between urban activists and local policy makers is an interesting phase of development of the urban policy strategic action field in Poland. It can be interpreted as the beginning of the urban movement actors' shift from challenger to incumbent positions in the field. It can also signify serious co-optation mechanisms at work, and the beginning of the end of urban activists' political influence. It also begs the question of legitimacy and whose interests are being represented by most prominent urban activists, and whether stronger relationships with often criticized public actors help the establishment of a more democratic urban policy, or rather weakens the demands of grassroots groups, co-opted by public institutions or political parties. According to the most recent observations, neither the most optimistic nor pessimistic scenario seems to be the case. While some level of co-optation or moderation of activists' claims is visible, the strength of the Congress's network and its reforming spirit preserves the original goals and helps the movement to remain politically relevant and effective.

FIGURE 9.4 Urban movement coalition candidates outside Warsaw City Hall in 2014

Source: Porozumienie Ruchów Miejskich press materials

Conclusions: The Changing Roles of Urban Movement Actors?

In recent years, intensifying activities of urban residents became clearly visible in Polish cities within the frame of the "new urban movement." One of the main reasons for grassroots mobilization was the visible domination of money-not-people-driven investments, along with the lack of a clear vision for the cities' socially sustainable development. As I argue here, the movement's emergence indicates both a shift in people's perception of their urban environment—with public space defined as a common good—and rising expectations for greater participation in local planning and decision making. In the wider context of Polish civil society, this development can be interpreted as new phase of democratization as well as a reaction to the dominant neoliberal logic. However, those processes may also cultivate the risks of hollowing out civic inclusion in the state and the instrumentalization of civil society through shifting the responsibility from the public to private sphere. Nevertheless, the changes as described here have brought new norms into play, leveling the field of urban policy to include claims for greater participation and recognition of residents' needs.

Presently, new urban policy practices are being shaped in Poland, in a meeting between neighborhood activists around a "concrete narrative" (Mergler 2008) of particular space—defined as a common-pool resource—and local needs. In the changing context of local and national administration priorities and inspiration from internationally connected "norm entrepreneurs" (Finnemore and Sikkink 1998) local conflicts are being linked to the global dispute over the right to the city. In short, active residents' groups belonging to the wider urban grassroots movement network are taking advantage of existing opportunities to enter into more central positions in the field. As one of the interviewed leaders summarized, this strategy can be described as "fracking" of the established power structure through activists' constant pressure and exploration of the "cracks" (Lehtovuori et al. 2014) in the existing institutions and decision-making processes (interview with one of the urban leaders, December 2013).

Urban grassroots movement actors described in this chapter make an interesting case to be analyzed in terms of their changing roles in the strategic action field of urban policy. In line with the definition of challengers, one of the main characteristics of the urban movement is opposition towards existing political and administrative practices that negatively influence public space and quality of life for urban residents. In the case of the Polish urban policy field, local governments and existing public institutions play the role of incumbents defining and managing the realization of city development strategies with support of internal governance units, like Department of Spatial Planning in the Ministry of Infrastructure and Development. Challengers, on the other hand, can be found in less-privileged niches within the field with little influence over it and often represent different sets of norms and values than incumbents (Fligstein and McAdam 2012). But even if challengers conform to the prevailing order, as Fligstein and McAdam (2012, p. 13) noted, "They often do so grudgingly, taking what the system gives them and awaiting new opportunities to challenge the structures and logic of the system."

At this point, after the partial success of introducing urban grassroots movement representatives into local government structures in several Polish cities, the movement faces an important challenge of recapitulating its role. One of the possible developments is a shift from direct opposition to the more cooperative approach, involving compromises on the political level in exchange for bigger influence in the field. From a theoretical point of view, it would mean a shift from challengers toward incumbent positions, which might be at odds with the watchdog role that some of the urban activists attribute themselves. On the other hand, formalized political involvement is perceived as the only effective strategy to introduce real urban change at any level. The case of the Poznań "Right to the City" committee shows that some level of constructive cooperation between local governments and activists is possible and leads to the introduction of urban movement postulations into the city management. However, despite positive examples, some of the activists fear both their independence and legitimacy would be lost through co-optation, while the power elites will try to "use and discard" them. This only shows how urban movement's differential influence from one city to another depends on the local level of transformative social capital, stemming from residents' frustration, as well as available social skills and networking capabilities.

In the wider context, the processes described here illustrate another wave of Polish urban policy change. After the wave of market-driven "post-socialist city governance" (Koch 2009, Nawratek 2012), followed by the "new public governance" wave stemming from the welfare crisis, there now seems to be another wave, characterized by the strive for more "collective governance" in the name of the residents' right to the city. The pessimistic interpretation of recent changes would point to the "neoliberal urban capitalism" patterns of decentralization and outsourcing the responsibility for public tasks to the civil society. For now, however, those ambiguous development paths seem to overlap where different actors of urban policy field coexist in a mixture of alliances, codependencies, and conflicts that are no less complex than the cities themselves.

Notes

1. Research was conducted in 2015 in the framework of the project financed by Polish National Science Centre, research grant DEC-2013/09/D/HS6/02968.
2. Examples include the initiatives to defend the city or neighborhood parks and squares from highway or housing construction, struggles to clean the surrounding areas of graffiti and rubbish, and protests against investments that negatively influence the quality of life in the given neighborhood (airports, highways, and factories, but also nightclubs, etc.).
3. Reprivatization means retrieval of land and/or buildings by pre-war owners (whose property was nationalized after the war) and their heirs. Reprivatization often leads to speculation—with legal firms buying rights from heirs and retrieving the buildings from the municipality to sell them on the market, after forcing out the "unwanted" tenants.

References

Andretta, M., Piazza, G., and Subirats, A., 2015. Urban Dynamics and Social Movements. *In*: D. Della Porta, and M. Diani, eds. *The Oxford Handbook of Social Movements*. Oxford: Oxford University Press, 200–215.

Appadurai, A., 2001. Deep Democracy: Urban Governmentality and the Horizon of Politics. *Environment and Urbanization*, 13 (2), 23–43.

Benford, R. D. and Snow, D. A., 2000. Framing Processes and Social Movements: An Overview and Assessment. *Annual Review of Sociology*, 26, 611–639.

Celiński, A., 2012. Prawo do miasta, prawo do polityki. *Res Publica Nowa*, 209, 4–10.

Diani, M., 2015. *The Cement of Civil Society: Studying Networks in Localities*. New York: Cambridge University Press.

Domaradzka, A., 2014. *Tamed City? Warsaw Enclaves of Social Activism and Their Origins*. Report submitted to National Science Center.

Domaradzka, A., 2015. Changing the Rules of the Game: Impact of the Urban Movement on the Public Administration Practices. *In*: M. Freise, F. Paulsen, and A. Walter, eds. *Civil Society and Innovative Public Administration*. Baden-Baden: Nomos Publishers, 188–217.

Domaradzka, A. and Matysiak, I., 2015. Pushing for Innovation—the Role of Citizens in Local Housing and Childcare Policies in Warsaw. *In*: M. Freise, F. Paulsen, and A. Walter, eds. *Civil Society and Innovative Public Administration*. Baden-Baden: Nomos Publishers, 302–324.

Domaradzka, A. and Wijkström, F., 2014. New Urban Movement Entrepreneurs Re-Negotiating the Public-Private Borderland: The Case of Polish Urban Politics. Paper presented at the 11th ISTR Conference, 22–25 July 2014, Munster.

Domaradzka, A. and Wijkström, F., 2016. Game of the City Re-Negotiated: The Polish Urban Re-Generation Movement as an Emerging Actor of a Strategic Action Field. *Polish Sociological Review*, 3, 309–325.

Finnemore, M. and Sikkink, K., 1998. International Norm Dynamics and Political Change. *International Organization*, 52 (4), 887–917.

Fligstein, N., 2001. Social Skill and the Theory of Fields. *Sociological Theory*, 19 (2), 105–125.

Fligstein, N. and McAdam, D., 2011. Toward a General Theory of Strategic Action Fields. *Sociological Theory*, 29 (1), 1–26.

Fligstein, N. and McAdam, D., 2012. *A Theory of Fields*. New York: Oxford University Press.

Gamson, W. A., 1990. *The Strategy of Social Protest*. Belmont, CA: Wadsworth Publishing.

Hardin, G., 1968. The Tragedy of the Commons. *Science*, New Series, 162 (3859), 1243–1248.

Harvey, D., 2012. *Rebel Cities: From the Right to the City to the Urban Revolution*. New York: Verso.

Henzler, P., ed., 2009. *Aktywni mieszkańcy—inicjatywy sąsiedzkie w praktyce*. Warsaw: CAL.

Hood, C., 1991. A Public Management for All Seasons? *Public Administration*, 69 (spring), 3–19.

Jacobsson, K., 2015. *Urban Grassroots Movements in Central and Eastern Europe*. Farnham: Ashgate.

Kelly, R. M., 1998. An Inclusive Democratic Polity, Representative Bureaucracies, and the New Public Management. *Public Administration Review*, 58 (3), 201–208.

Koch, F., 2009. Housing Markets and Urban Regimes—The Case of Warsaw. *In*: F. Eckardt, and I. Elander, eds. *Urban Governance in Europe*. Berlin: Berliner Wissenschaftsverlag, 333–357.

Kusiak, J., 2011, Rewolucyjny pośpiech, stoicka cierpliwość: miejski aktywizm i opór struktur. *Kultura Liberalna* [online]. Available from: http://kulturaliberalna.pl/2011/02/22/kusiak-rewolucyjny-pospiech-stoicka-cierpliwosc-miejski-aktywizm-i-opor-struktur [Accessed 11 March 2017].

Leder, A., 2013. Kto nam zabrał tę rewolucję? *Dziennik Opinii*, 19 April 2013.

Lefebvre, H., 1968. *Le Droit à la Ville*. Paris: Anthropos.

Lehtovuori, P., Kurg, A., Schwab, M., and Ermert, S., 2014. Public Spaces, Experience and Conflict: The Cases of Helsinki and Tallinn. *In*: C. Tornaghi, and S. Knierbein, eds. *Public Space and Relational Perspectives: New Challenges for Architecture and Planning*. London and New York: Routledge, 125–143.

Levine, M. L., 1989. The Politics of Partnership: Urban Redevelopment Since 1945. *In*: G. Squires, ed. *Unequal Partnership*. New Brunswick, NJ: Rutgers University Press, 12–34.

Logan, J. R. and Molotch, H. L., 1987. *Urban Fortunes: The Political Economy of Place*. Berkeley: University of California Press.

McAdam, D., 1982. *Political Process and the Development of Black Insurgency, 1930–1970*. Chicago: University of Chicago Press.

Mergler, L., 2008. *Poznań Konfliktów*. Poznań: Wydawnictwo Lepszy Świat.

Mergler, L. and Pobłocki, K., 2010. Nic o nas bez nas: polityka skali a demokracja miejska. *Res Publica Nowa*, 201–202/2010, 9.

Mergler, L., Pobłocki, K., and Wudarski, M., 2013. *Anty-Bezradnik przestrzenny: prawo do miasta w działaniu*. Warsaw: Res Publica Nowa.

Meyer, D. S., 2004. Protest and Political Opportunities. *Annual Review of Sociology*, 30, 125–145.

Ministry of Infrastructure and Development, 2014. *Krajowa Polityka Miejska—projekt, wersja I* [online]. Available from: www.mir.gov.pl/fundusze/Fundusze_Europejskie_2014_2020/Documents/Krajowa_Polityka_Miejska_wersja_I_27032014.pdf [Accessed 13 July 2016].

Nawratek, K., 2012. *Holes in the Whole: Introduction to the Urban Revolutions*. Winchester, UK: Zero Books.

Ostrom, E., 1990. *Governing the Commons: The Evolution of Institutions for Collective Action*. Cambridge and New York: Cambridge University Press.

Pluciński, P., 2013. Miejskie (r)ewolucje. Radykalizm retoryki a praktyka reform. *Praktyka Teoretyczna*, 3 (9), 133–157.

Pobłocki, K., 2010. Prawo do miasta. *Tygodnik Powszechny*, 4 April, 28.

Polańska, D. V., 2013. Gated Housing as a Reflection of Public-Private Divide: On the Popularity of Gated Communities in Poland. *Polish Sociological Review*, 181, 87–102.

Polańska, D. V. and Piotrowski, G., 2015. The Transformative Power of Cooperation Between Social Movements: Squatting and Tenants' Movements in Poland. *City: Analysis of Urban Trends, Culture, Theory, Policy, Action*, 19 (2–3), 274–296.

Salet, W. and Gualini, E. eds., 2007. *Framing Strategic Urban Projects: Learning from Current Experiences in European Urban Regions*. London and New York: Routledge.

Siemieńska, R., Domaradzka, A., and Matysiak, I., 2011. Local Welfare in Poland from a Historical and Institutional Perspective. WILCO Publication no. 09 [online]. Available from: http://www.wilcoproject.eu/wordpress/wp-content/uploads/WILCO_WP2_reports_09_PL1.pdf [Accessed 11 March 2017].

Smith, N., 2010. *Uneven Development: Nature, Capital, and the Production of Space*. Athens and London: University of Georgia Press.

Soja, E. W., 2010. *Seeking Spatial Justice*. Minneapolis: University of Minnesota Press.

Stone, C. N., 1993. Urban Regimes and the Capacity to Govern. *Journal of Urban Affairs*, 15, 1–28.

Swyngedouw, E., Moulaert, F., and Rodriguez, A., 2002. Neoliberal Urbanism in Europe: Large-Scale Urban Development Projects and the New Urban Policy. *Antipode*, 34 (3), 542–577.

Tarrow, S., 1998. *Power in Movement*. New York: Cambridge University Press.

Tilly, C., 1978. *From Mobilization to Revolution*. New York: Random House.

Urban Movements Congress, 2011. *9 Tez Miejskich* [online]. Available from: http://kongresruchowmiejskich.pl/tezy-miejskie/ [Accessed 13 July 2016].

Urban Movements Congress, 2015. *Tezy Miejskie 2015* [online]. Available from: http://kongresruchowmiejskich.pl/15-tez-o-miescie-kongresu-ruchow-miejskich/ [Accessed 13 July 2016].

PART 3

Negotiating

Urban Resistance and Emerging (Counter) Publics

10

ATHENS' SYNTAGMA SQUARE RELOADED

From Staging Disagreement Towards Instituting Democratic Spaces

Maria Kaika and Lazaros Karaliotas

Since the outbreak of a more-than-economic crisis in the Global North, urban politics and public spaces have undergone profound transformations. On one hand, the dominant response to the crisis revolves around the implementation of austerity policies and the closing down of urban public spaces where political disagreement can be expressed (Swyngedouw 2014). On the other hand, urban public spaces stubbornly retain their role as the stage for processes of re-politicization and massive urban uprisings beginning in 2011. During that "year of dreaming dangerously" (Žižek 2012) the initial insurgencies in Tunis and Cairo soon leapfrogged to Barcelona, Madrid, Athens, and Thessaloniki and moved to North America and the European North, from the heart of London to smaller towns in the south of Germany and beyond. In the following years Taksim Square in Istanbul became the pivot point for an uprising that defended Gezi Park from Erdoğan's "urban neoliberalism with Islamic characteristics" (Karaman 2013a, Yiğit Turan, this volume), whilst an increase in public transport fares at São Paulo led to extensive urban uprisings in São Paulo, Rio de Janeiro, and other Brazilian cities that persisted during Brazil's 2014 Football World Cup.

Although unfolding within historically and geographically variegated sites and despite their heterogeneity in spatial, discursive, and organizational repertoires, these uprisings can be seen as part of a broader planetary circulation of ideas and revolts wherein *the people* reclaim urban public spaces to stage discontent with the state of affairs and experiment with new ways of being and acting in-common (see also Merrifield 2013). The squares uprising—the early summer protests of 2011—in Greece was one of the nodal points in this political sequence. From the end of May to the end of July 2011 a heterogeneous multitude of protesters organized through social media networks and occupied Syntagma Square in Athens and many other public spaces across the country to stage political dissent and enact direct democratic practices. The squares' occupations constituted a peak in the struggle primarily against the austerity measures implemented by Greek political and economic elites, the European Union, the International Monetary Fund, and the European Central Bank.

However, as we shall argue in this chapter, the uprising at the squares was more than just protest against austerity; it also constituted a break with "traditional" modes of political mobilization and urban resistance that had characterized contentious politics in Greece over the past four decades. It was the moment when urban resistance moved beyond a critique of everyday life under austerity and into *the political*; engaging with the socially and spatially embedded institution of practices for reclaiming the commons and staging equality (Rancière 1999).

Although the squares uprising attracted significant media and scholarly interest (see among many others Giovanopoulos and Mitropoulos 2011, Dalakoglou 2012, Leontidou 2012, Stavrides 2012, Douzinas 2013, Sotirakopoulos and Sotiropoulos 2013), much of this literature seems to be polarized between "positive appraisals of the horizontal character of the square movements" and "questioning the political efficiency of the alternative modes of organization" (Prentoulis and Thomassen 2013, p. 168). In this contribution, penned four years after the eruption of the squares uprising, we unearth how protesters in the squares moved beyond the mundane materialities of an ephemeral presence/protest in public space and into generating a multiplicity of often conflicting repertoires of resistance politics. Building on this, we explore how differences and tensions were often manifested in different ways of organizing public space under occupation (Kaika and Karaliotas 2014, Karaliotas 2017). In so doing, we seek to understand the emergence of novel resistance practices within the squares and explore the insights that the squares uprising might offer for democratic politics.

The remainder of this chapter is arranged in four sections. The first one gives a brief account of the rich urban resistance history associated with Athens' Syntagma Square. The second section explores the novel practices of resistance introduced in 2011 at Syntagma, focusing particularly on how these practices challenged the dominant ordering of urban public spaces and experimented with producing new spaces in-common. The third section focuses on the tensions between two conflicting sociopolitical imaginaries and two organizational logics that marked the 2011 uprising at Syntagma Square. The concluding section highlights the legacies that the resistance in the squares left behind in instituting democratic spaces.

Syntagma Square (Constitution Square): A Space Weaved Together with the History of Urban Resistance in Greece

Syntagma (translated as "Constitution") Square is located directly in front of the Greek Parliament at the heart of the Athens city center. The square was once called "Royal Palace Square," but was renamed into "Syntagma Square" in 1843 after the revolutionary events of September 3, 1843 that took place there. The 1843 uprising put forward demands for replacing the then-absolute monarchy in Greece with constitutional monarchy through the provision of a written constitution and the institution of a democratically elected House of Parliament. Since then, Syntagma Square acquired a central place in the Greek public imaginary and history books as an emblematic space for staging democratic demands. And it retained this place well into the 20th century. After undergoing a period of "silence" during the military junta (1967–1974) when all protests were banned, Syntagma Square resumed its protagonistic role in staging urban resistance and public discontent. Located directly in front of the Greek Parliament the square became the nodal point for mass public demonstrations and protests after the end of the junta. These were mainly organized by political parties and trade and student unions and focused predominantly on sectoral demands. As Vradis (2011, p. 216) suggests, after the end of the dictatorship the "ephemeral presence of people in public space" became the "spatial contract" of political mobilization in Greece.

Since the mid-1990s, however, public spaces in and around Athens started changing. Leading up to the organization of the 2004 Athens Olympic Games, emphasis was put on implementing urban mega-infrastructure projects, whilst privatization of public land and services became one of the key drivers of the imaginary of "a Strong [competitive] Greece." During that period, the area surrounding Syntagma Square changed character significantly. From a place for staging discontent it steadily became the epicenter of an extensive process of commodification of urban space through the introduction of high-end retail stores, tourist catering services, and banks. This was coupled by the significant increase in real estate prices in and around the square. As a result, the area became engulfed by pockets of space catering for global tourism and international capital.

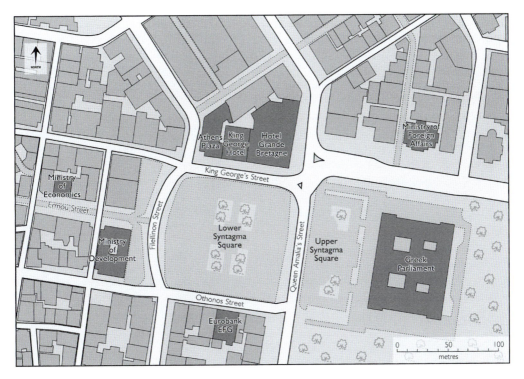

FIGURE 10.1 Syntagma Square and its surrounding area

Source: Compiled by authors, based on OpenStreetMap (openstreetmap.org)

This was the spatial expression of a new set of sociopolitical power relations articulated around a utopian vision for continuous economic growth coupled with increased glamour and enjoyment that accompanied Athens' successful Olympic bid in 2004.

During the same period, the Athenian city center was also becoming an increasingly polarized space with headquarters of administrative, financial, and judiciary authorities and wealthy neighborhoods interspersed with poor immigrant neighborhoods and increasing social unrest (Petropoulou 2010). Already in 2004, a number of nascent urban social movements articulated around "the right to the city" raised concerns over the privatization of urban land and blocking access to what used to be urban public spaces (Leontidou 2010). These movements drew their repertoire from the alter-globalization movement (op. cit.) and experimented with practices of networked horizontal organization and the formation of social centers. They organized political mobilizations in different neighborhoods across Athens, particularly ones immediately affected by the Olympic Games infrastructure projects. Yet, the forms of political mobilization orchestrated by these movements retained only a fleeting presence in urban public space and very little in Syntagma Square itself, which was sparingly used by trade union protests.

December 2008 brought new scope and aim to urban resistance practices in Greece, when mass riots were ignited by the killing of 15-year-old Alexis Grigoropoulos by a police officer at Exarcheia, a neighborhood in central Athens that had traditionally been the nexus of alternative and radical political experiments. Within a few hours of Grigoropoulos's death massive urban riots were organized through digital media and spread from Exarcheia to the whole of Athens lasting for over 15 days. Syntagma Square became one of the centers of riots. The image of a Christmas tree at Syntagma Square set in flames during the riots became the symbol of the uprising of Greek youth and immigrants that unfolded just before the outbreak of the "Greek crisis."

Syntagma Square Reloaded: Producing Open Democratic Spaces in and Through the Squares

By the time the 2008 economic crisis hit Greece in earnest, Syntagma Square served as a node for an urban *melange* consisting of occasional riots, transient migrants looking for jobs, curious tourists, elite shoppers, and habitual patrons of nearby cafes and restaurants. Hence, when the mass urban resistance started at Syntagma Square in 2011, the Athenian city center was a heavily polarized space (Kaika 2012). The gentrification of some neighborhoods in the Athens city center (e.g. Metaxourgeio) was going hand in glove with neo-Nazi pogroms against immigrants in other neighborhoods (e.g. Agios Panteleimonas) (Dalakoglou 2012).

The first large post-crisis gathering in Athens' Syntagma Square was organized on May 25, 2011 in the aftermath of a mobilization outside the Spanish embassy in solidarity with the Spanish Indignados movement. The call was issued through a Facebook event page created by three anonymous young men on May 20 to express indignation against the dominant policies in Greece (Indignants in Syntagma 2011). The call succeeded in mobilizing a large and diverse constituency beyond people who belonged to established political parties (both government and opposition) or existing social movements. Within a few days the page attracted over 7,500 members and when it was relaunched in the form of a new social media group on May 25, it attracted 12,500 members in a matter of hours (To Vima 2011). Similar initiatives proliferated in other Greek cities giving birth to the squares uprising.

During the first days, the gatherings at Syntagma were limited to ritualistic moaning and cursing against corrupt politicians in front of the parliament. Initially, the Indignants declared (via Internet pages, banners, and open cries) their commitment to exclude all political party ideologies from the square. All flags, symbols, or other insignia of political parties were banned. Everybody was welcome to the square insofar as they came in their capacity as political subjects only; as citizens "naked" from political party flags insignia and ideologies. Only Greek flags were allowed to enter the square.

This early stance led many commentators and political organizations (including the Greek Communist Party and many anarchist groups) to deem the movement apolitical. However, during the brief period of its life (two months, until July 30, 2011 when municipal police "cleared away" the protest camp) the resistance evolved into a massive heterogeneous movement that articulated and staged dissent like never before in post-junta Greek history. Whereas it is impossible to know the exact numbers of previously "invisible" citizens who became publicly "visible" by participating in the squares occupation, opinion polls indicate that it could have been a total of over 2 million (Douzinas 2013). Especially on the days of general strikes, on June 15, 28, and 29, hundreds of thousands of people protested in Syntagma and the surrounding streets.

Although the 2011 uprising drew some of its repertoire and modus operandi from the 2008 December Riots and the international urban social movements that unfolded before them, it undoubtedly moved beyond these in participation numbers, scope, organization, and articulation of demands. Its unprecedented massive character and more importantly its performative experimentation with new modes of urban being and acting in-common constituted a radical break with all previous patterns of urban resistance in this historic public space.

Just a few days after the initial gathering, a Popular Assembly was instituted in Syntagma Square. During its first meeting the Assembly articulated a clear political message:

> For a long time decisions have been made for us, without us [. . .] We are here because we know that the solutions to our problems can come only from us. [. . .] In these public squares we will shape our claims and our demands together. [. . .]

DIRECT DEMOCRACY NOW!
EQUALITY—JUSTICE—DIGNITY

(Popular Assembly Vote 2011a, emphasis in original)

Protesters in the squares (the Indignants as they came to call themselves following their Spanish counterpart) were a socioeconomically and ideologically heterogeneous multitude (Sotirakopoulos and Sotiropoulos 2013, Kioupkiolis 2014) who "differed in the minutiae of their social situations, coping strategies, and narratives of blame" (Athanasiou 2014, p. 3). By coming together in the squares, the protesters moved beyond their established identities "predicated on a transsubjective, broadly shared but differently situated sense of vulnerability to the injuries of injustice" (Athanasiou 2014, p. 3). This diverse multitude reclaimed the square as a public space (Butler 2011) and a signifier of democracy (Douzinas 2013). The protesters' continuous (24 hours a day, 7 days a week) presence in the public spaces (see Arendt 1998) in and around Syntagma moved beyond an "ephemeral presence of people in public space" (Vradis 2011, p. 216). This tactic of continuous reappropriation embodied "the desire of the protesters to dissociate their occupied public spaces from existing networks of power" (Kambouri and Hatzopoulos 2011, np). Alongside disrupting the everyday allocation of space to the mobility of capital, power, and tourists, this occupation had a further symbolic dimension that stemmed from the square's history, name, and position directly in front of the Greek House of Parliament. As Douzinas notes, two centuries after providing the spatial outlet for putting forward radical claims for freeing Greece from the then-tyranny of the Royal Palace, the same square served in 2011 as a spatial outlet for articulating the demand to "free Greece from neo-liberal domination, political corruption and post-democratic malaise" (2013, p. 153).

However, unlike what happened two centuries ago, the contemporary protests at Syntagma Square did not put forward one singular demand for change. The space directly in front of the Parliament—the "upper square"—remained the key niche for expressing indignation and anger. But Syntagma Square proper—the "lower square" (Figure 10.1)—was transformed into a "network of connected micro-squares" (Stavrides 2012, p. 588) hosting a series of thematic groups and collectives as well as the General Popular Assembly. The Assembly became the key space for collective deliberation and dialogue amongst people at Syntagma. It instituted thematic discussion groups and held meetings and debates every evening on the causes of the "Greek crisis" and ways out of it, the short and long-term goals of the uprising, ways to influence institutional politics, and effective ways to spread the practices of Syntagma in popular urban neighborhoods and workplaces. As the presence of protesters in Syntagma became continuous and prolonged, the Assembly also instituted a number of collectives to sustain and support the everyday life of urban resistance: solidarity kitchen, first-aid center, social media, cleaning and maintenance, coordination of neighborhood actions, and arts performances (Popular Assembly Vote 2011b).[1]

As Butler writes on the occupy movement:

> They were there sleeping and eating in the public square, constructing toilets and various systems for sharing the space, and so not only refusing to be privatised—refusing to go or stay home—and not only claiming the public domain for themselves—acting in concert on conditions of equality—but also maintaining themselves as persisting bodies with needs, desires and requirements.
>
> *(2011, np)*

This embodied and collectively organized act of urban resistance was performatively opening up spaces for the political by challenging and redefining the horizon of politics (Moore 2013,

Kaika and Karaliotas 2014). A new political community and a "new world" were debated and constructed here (Karaliotas 2017). In this sense, the occupation of Syntagma—and other squares across the world—put a "new world" in confrontation with *the police*; the "world" of existing institutions and existing order. For Rancière, this disruptive engagement with *the police* order is precisely what (democratic) politics is about (Rancière 1999, Dikeç 2013). The inscription of the name of the Indignants in the discursive horizon and the collective opening of a podium for articulating dissent against austerity politics was at the core of the democratizing processes that the squares resistance enacted. A resistance that revolved around the people's claim to be counted as equals, to have an (equal) voice. Following Rancière, we read the squares as the opening of democratic spaces: a reconfiguration of time and space, a process by which those who used to be invisible and played no part became visible and audible by performatively staging their egalitarian existence (Rancière 1999, Swyngedouw 2014).

Negotiating Heterogeneity in the Square

Since the early days of the occupation, the process of creating a political community and opening up democratic spaces at Syntagma was riddled with tensions and differences. These manifested not only in different mottos and discourses but also in different embodied practices, different ways of spatializing politics and ways of organizing space. In what follows, we focus on two of these tensions: the articulation of nationalist vs. egalitarian discourses and the coexistence of vertical and horizontal organizational practices within the square.

We as Greeks or We as Equals?

As noted earlier, the space directly in front of the Parliament—the "upper Syntagma Square"—became the niche for expressing anger and indignation against members of the Parliament (MPs). The number of protesters in the "upper square" varied significantly daily. But the repertoire of mottos and performative actions remained similar throughout the occupation. The most common chants were: "Thieves!" and "Traitors!" and were addressed directly to the MPs. The most common discursive point of reference to struggles of the past was that of the Greek National War of Independence against the Ottoman Empire (1821). The symbolic repertoire of these references included Greek flags and flyers, banners reciting 1821 war heroes, even people dressed up in 1821 warlord costumes (Sotirakopoulos and Sotiropoulos 2013). This symbolic matrix was complemented by ritualistic collective moaning and cursing against contemporary corrupt politicians, rude gesticulations to the walls of the Parliament, and a row of gallows awaiting "traitor" MPs.

Both right-wing (300Greeks, Greek Mothers) and left-wing (Spitha) groups came together in the "upper square" under this common nationalistic narrative that blamed equally corrupt MPs and foreign centers of power for bringing Greece to a crisis. As Kaika and Karaliotas (2014) analyze, despite differences in their mottos, all groups in the upper square portrayed the crisis as an unfair treatment against a Greek nation that had been betrayed by corrupt political elites and foreign "colonizers." Demands for "jobs for Greeks" (Greek Mothers 2011) and for ousting the [corrupt] "colonial government" (Karampelias 2011) were posited here as the way out of the crisis. However, it is important to note that the "upper square" never became host to extreme right-wing or neo-Nazi groups or discourses. Indeed, the neo-Nazi formation "Golden Dawn" openly denounced the mobilizations at Syntagma and focused instead on orchestrating racist attacks in other parts of Athens during the time of the protests (Dalakoglou 2012).

The discourses and repertoires of the "lower square" were quite different. Here, equality, justice, and dignity were the key signifiers of the resistance (Popular Assembly Vote 2011a, 2011b, 2011c).

Although most protesters in "lower square" were sympathetic to left-wing, anti-authoritarian, and anarchist groups, the "lower square" drew in a very large crowd that came from a much wider political spectrum. Here too, there were references to previous emancipatory struggles in Greece, but these were much wider than the 1821 national revolution, and included the communist-led WWII anti-Nazi resistance (EAM), the resistance against the 1967–1974 dictatorship, and the December 2008 riots (Sotirakopoulos and Sotiropoulos 2013). While anger and indignation were equally present in the "lower square," protesters there also sought to move beyond protest and beyond the existing capitalist police order (2011b, 2011c):

> the fight that started here, and for over a month, continues. [. . .] The organization and dissemination of a long-term general strike together with the struggle in the squares and the neighborhoods will be the beginning of the end of today's world of exploitation and alienation. For a society of solidarity and justice. Direct Democracy Now!
>
> *(Popular Assembly Vote 2011c, np)*

Although the upper and lower parts of the square acted as podiums for staging quite distinct performative acts and in effect, politics, we need to note here that the "barrier" between the two parts of the square was not rigid or clearly demarcated or policed. They both acted as fluid and porous spaces and protesters moved with ease from one to the other. Indeed, the partition between "upper square" and "lower square" almost disappeared during days of mass mobilizations (Kaika and Karaliotas 2014).

Yet, at times when nationalism and extreme right-wing parties are on the rise across Europe, it is important to highlight the coexistence of these conflicting logics within the occupied squares. While not all of the participants in the "upper square" shared similar ideological agendas, they were nonetheless carving out a space for an exclusionary collective that labeled itself "We: the Greeks." On the contrary, participants in the "lower square" presumed equality and inclusion for all in the spaces of their emerging political community: "We as Equals." Anger and indignation against the state and current affairs provided the common ground for the emergence of each one of these conflicting narratives, which came to coexist in the squares. However, as Jacques Rancière argues, a genuinely democratic politics revolves around the presumption of equality for each and everyone, but also around "the process of [the] differentiation [of the demos] from the ethnos [the nation]" (2011a, p. 5). In other words, a genuine democratic politics refuses to identify the *demos* of democracy with any closed community determined by origin, language, nationality, and so on.

Organizing Democratic Spaces

The novel organizational practices that the squares uprising introduced are one of its characteristics that attracted scholarly attention. Indeed, the horizontal and nonhierarchical collaborative practices of self-organization that flourished in the squares performatively enacted a critique of the existing representational and hierarchical institutions of liberal democracy (Douzinas 2013). Such practices have often been described as purely spontaneous and horizontal either to be celebrated as *the* model of 21st century politics or to be criticized for their inefficiency in achieving institutional change. Yet, once we take a closer look at the organizational practices within the squares, a far more complex landscape surfaces.

The organizational logic of the squares has built upon the presupposition of equality, the ability of all to act politically, and the belief that collective deliberation of *the people* is the proper mode of organizing democratic politics. Proposals to the Popular Assembly for instituting new thematic groups and collectives in the "lower square" could come from either individual participants or groups of people. The instituted groups and collectives maintained a level of autonomy but directly cooperated in formats decided through their own initiative or through collective decisions at the Assembly. However, all of the groups and collectives in the squares had to comply with the decisions of the Assembly (Stavrides 2012). In this sense, whilst spontaneous actions and horizontal autonomous organization held a central role in the squares, the "autonomy and horizontality" in the squares was "instituted" rather than being "natural or immediate" (Prentoulis and Thomassen 2013, p. 181).

Indeed, the everyday operation of the Popular Assembly, the thematic groups and the collectives of Syntagma required the institution of rules that guaranteed the equal participation of all. For example, each participant's turn to speak at the Assembly was decided through a draw and each participant was only allowed a minute and a half to develop their positions (Douzinas 2013). The function of the thematic groups was also organized around rules detailing practices of mutual respect amongst participants, processes of decision making within the groups, the role of the co-coordinator of group discussions, and the election and role of groups' representatives at the Assembly (Thematic Group on Direct Democracy 2011). Similar rules were instituted regarding the division of labor within the collectives that attended to the daily needs of Syntagma's occupy camp or those who sought to spread its voice and practices beyond the square. Such rules and procedures aimed to construct a space of mutual recognition and respect among the participants and, in doing so, to guarantee their autonomous and horizontal participation in the Assembly and the thematic groups.

However, given the heterogeneity of participants and the presence of conflicting viewpoints and strategies, the Popular Assembly became the stage of an unstable symbiosis between two conflicting organizational logics and imaginaries: a horizontal, loosely coordinated mobilization averse to established institutions, parties, and political programs; and a more structured form of organization articulated around fixed programs, coherent representation, and central coordination (Popular Assembly Minutes 2011a, 2011b). Of course, disagreement and conflict also existed within the collectives and thematic groups themselves. These would not only revolve around strategic orientations and ideological differences but also around everyday activities and organizational questions. Such conflicts were resolved through continuous deliberations for building consensus. If the issue was not resolved within the group, different viewpoints would be presented at the Popular Assembly where participants would deliberate and eventually vote on the issue under discussion. This mode of dealing with conflict as well as the wider coexistence of the heterogeneous collective of the squares uprising would have been impossible without "an 'agonistic respect' of different outlooks" amongst participants (Kioupkiolis 2014, p. 154). This ethos served as a basis for a dialogue between plural, and at times competing, political imaginaries, strategies, and logics that opened up a fertile terrain of strategic experimentation and revision.

The preceding analysis highlights that the democratic spaces that were opened up in the squares, while based on the principle of horizontal organization, were also ruled by institutionalized norms of behavior. As Prentoulis and Thomassen argue, "the very realization of equality [was] only possible through some representational space, and such a space unavoidably involve[d]" the institution of rules and some form of centralized/vertical organization (2013, p. 181).

Conclusion: Tracing the Legacies of the Squares in Instituting Democratic Spaces

The approval of the second memorandum with Greece's creditors by the majority of the Greek Parliament was followed by massive protests and violent police raids at occupied squares across

Greece. On July 30, 2011, municipal police "cleared away" the collective organizational infra-structure at the "lower square." Since then, the squares movement never recovered its momentum and mass participation.

Writing this chapter more than four years after the violent end of the occupation of Syntagma Square gives the opportunity to move beyond accounts that had either glorified the organizational and spatial repertoires of the squares as the model for 21st century political praxis or condemned these as apolitical and populist bubbles with insignificant or even dangerous results. The occupation of Syntagma and other squares in Greece during the summer of 2011 was a form of urban resistance that disrupted the order of *the police* and sought to reclaim and redefine "democracy" outside hegemonic discourses in two ways (Douzinas 2013, Athanasiou 2014): first through the collective production of spaces where the part that previously had no part could now have an equal voice, and second through experimenting with new ways of being and doing in-common. The squares in general, and Syntagma Square in particular, were an urban political "event that punctuate[d] the flow" of emancipatory politics and "open[ed] up [new] temporalities" (Rancière 2011b, p. 80).

Although it did not evolve into a long-lasting, solidified, formal social movement, its legacies for Greek politics can be traced both in institutionalized politics and in everyday urban political experiments and initiatives. In terms of institutionalized politics, the delegitimization of "bailout agreements" and austerity policies that the squares achieved played a major role in SYRIZA's (Coalition of the Radical Left) consecutive electoral victories in 2015 and the "no" vote in the July 2015 referendum concerning Greece's "bailout agreement" proposed by the country's creditors. In an interesting manner, the uneasy coalition between the right-wing nationalist party ANEL (Independent Greeks) and the left-wing SYRIZA reflects the uneasy coexistence of both these tendencies in Syntagma Square.

But the legacy of the squares can also be found in the everyday emancipatory practices and imaginaries that still exist and proliferate through a plethora of ongoing urban political experiments. "Actively discovering other ways of co-producing space" (Karaman 2013b) and the staging of equality inspired and fuelled the "ongoing efforts to create forms of being in common different from the ones offered from the state, the [post-]democratic consensus and so on" (Rancière 2011b, p. 80). In the aftermath of the squares, the Greek urban landscape is dotted by such socio-spatial practices and experimentations: neighborhood assemblies that collectively deliberate on local problems, social solidarity, health clinics, social groceries and initiatives evolving around buying food "without middlemen," social currencies, solidarity support networks for immigrants, refugees, and the homeless, as well as occupied factories and cooperatives of all sorts (Hadjimichalis 2013). For Swyngedouw, these socio-spatial experiments are part of "the slow but unstoppable production of new forms of spatialization quilted around materializing the claims of equality, freedom and solidarity" (2014, p. 133) initiated by the staging of equality in the squares. Together with drawing their inspiration from "incipient ideas expressed [and performed] in the event" (Swyngedouw 2014, p. 134), these initiatives are also populating their ranks with a new generation of activists forged through the squares. The embodied political solidarities that developed in the squares are evolving into lasting bonds and engagements with performatively seeking new forms of urbanity. Interestingly enough, similar, albeit geographically differentiated, experiments have emerged in the aftermath of most of the recent urban uprisings: from the convergence between the Indignados and the movements against housing dispossession in Spain (García-Lamarca, this volume), through the Strike Debt platform initiated by Occupy movement activists in the US (Ross 2013, Owens and Antiporda, this volume) to squats, social centers, and neighborhood assemblies in Turkey (Yiğit Turan, this volume).

Undoubtedly, some of these experiments will fail in the face of the various challenges and risks that they face. For example, the initiatives that emerge in the aftermath of the squares might end up becoming confined at the limits of "parochialist politics" (Harvey 1996, p. 324) if they remain localized and issue-based. In turn, this could lead some of the communities created through initiatives like social centers, neighborhood assemblies, and solidarity support networks to define themselves as closed self-reproducing entities, something that would result in new forms of enclosure (De Angelis and Stavrides 2010, p. 12). Besides, SYRIZA's second electoral victory (2015) adds a further twist on the question of the relationship between such experiments and the state when the latter is not (at least not from the outset) against them. Of course, the political coordinates in Greece are still rapidly shifting and answers to such challenges cannot be offered through theoretical analysis alone. We do, however, hope that the preceding analysis of the democratic spaces of the squares can offer some tentative insights regarding these challenges.

In order to avoid being confined into parochialist politics and becoming self-enclosed entities, these socio-spatial experiments need to always be open to "'newcomers', [to] allow new objects to appear as common concerns and new voices to appear and be heard" (Rancière 2010, p. 60). This attitude could, in turn, draw from the ethos of agonistic respect and embodied solidarity that was forged through the occupation of the squares. At the same time, questions around the relations between such experiments and the state—as well as the coexistence of SYRIZA and ANEL in power—point towards the always-present tension between democratic politics and the police as well as the need to differentiate the demos from the ethnos.

Negotiating such relations and navigating through these tensions is no straightforward task. Yet, tracing possible paths from an emancipatory democratic perspective would nevertheless require fidelity to the presupposition of equality (Hallward 2006). In other words, it would entail "to take sides, to declare fidelity to the egalibertarian practices already pre-figured" (Swyngedouw 2011, p. 378) in events like the squares uprising and their legacy. In doing so, we insist that it is important to explore the internal contradictions and limitations of this legacy alongside its strengths. We see these contradictions and limitations not as reasons to devalue the legacies of the squares but as signals of a struggle for emancipation that moves beyond staging disagreement requires rigorous, continuous, and organized efforts to construct conceptual, affective, and material democratic spaces (Stavrakakis 2010, p. 8). In turn, compounding these spatial tactics into a broader practice of democratic politics is a matter of continuous and persistent struggle, (re)negotiation, and effort.

Acknowledgements

This chapter draws upon: Kaika, M. and Karaliotas, L. 2014. The Spatialization of Democratic Politics: Insights from Indignant Squares. *European Urban and Regional Studies* [online first] May 8, 2014. DOI: 10.1177/0969776414528928; Kaika, M. and Karaliotas, L. 2014. Spatializing Politics: Antagonistic Imaginaries of Indignant Squares. *In*: J. Wilson, and E. Swyngedouw, eds. *The Post-Political and Its Discontents; Spaces of Depoliticization, Spectres of Radical Politics*, Edinburgh University Press, 244–260; and Karaliotas, L., 2017. Staging Equality in Greek Squares: Hybrid Spaces of Political Subjectification, *International Journal of Urban and Regional Research*, doi: 10.1111/1468-2427.12385. Many thanks to Graham Bowden for the cartographic support.

Note

1. We return to how the practices of these groups and collectives were organized and coordinated in the following section.

References

Arendt, H. and Canovan, M., 1998. *The Human Condition*. 2nd edition. Chicago: The University of Chicago Press.

Athanasiou, A., 2014. Precarious Intensities: Gendered Bodies in the Streets and Squares of Greece. *Signs: Journal of Women in Culture and Society*, 40 (1), 1–9.

Butler, J., 2011. Bodies in Alliance and the Politics of the Street [online]. *European Institute for Progressive Cultural Policies (EIPCP)*. Available from: www.eipcp.net/transversal/1011/butler/en [Accessed July 25, 2016]

Dalakoglou, D., 2012. Beyond Spontaneity. *City*, 16 (5), 535–545.

De Angelis, M. and Stavrides, S., 2010. On the Commons: A Public Interview with Massimo De Angelis and Stavros Stavrides | e-flux. *An Architektur*, 23, 4–27.

Dikeç, M., 2013. Beginners and Equals: Political Subjectivity in Arendt and Rancière. *Transactions of the Institute of British Geographers*, 38 (1), 78–90.

Douzinas, C., 2013. *Philosophy and Resistance in the Crisis: Greece and the Future of Europe*. London: Wiley.

Giovanopoulos, C. and Mitropoulos, D., 2011. *Democracy Under Construction: From Streets to Squares* [Δημοκρατία Under Construction: Α ό τους δρόμους στις πλατείες]. Athens: A/synexeia.

Greek Mothers, 2011. Greek Mothers to the Popular Assembly of Direct Democracy in Syntagma Square [online] [Ἑλληνίδες Μάνες πρός τήν Λαϊκή Συνέλευσι τῆς "Ἄμεσης Δημοκρατίας" τῆς Πλατείας Συντάγματος], *Spitha Thriasiou*. Available from: http://spithathriasiou.blogspot.com/2011/07/blog-post_19.html [Accessed 25 July 2016].

Hadjimichalis, C., 2013. From Streets and Squares to Radical Emancipation? Resistance Lessons from Athens During the Crisis. *Human Geography*, 6 (2), 116–136.

Hallward, P., 2006. Staging Equality: Rancière's Theatrocracy. *New Left Review*, 37, 109–129.

Harvey, D., 1996. *Justice, Nature and the Geography of Difference*. 1st edition. Cambridge, MA: Blackwell.

Indignants in Syntagma, 2011. About Indignants [online]. Facebook. Available from: www.facebook.com/AganaktismenoiStoSyntagma/info [Accessed 25 July 2016].

Kaika, M., 2012. The Economic Crisis Seen from the Everyday. *City*, 16 (4), 422–430.

Kaika, M. and Karaliotas, L., 2014. The Spatialization of Democratic Politics: Insights from Indignant Squares. *European Urban and Regional Studies*, 23(4), 556–570.

Kambouri, N. and Hatzopoulos, P., 2011. The Tactics of Occupation: Becoming Cockroach [online]. *Nomadic Universality*. Available from: http://nomadicuniversality.wordpress.com/2011/11/26/the-tactics-of-occupation-becoming-cockroach/ [Accessed 25 July 2016].

Karaliotas, L., 2017. Staging Equality in Greek Squares: Hybrid Spaces of Political Subjectification. *International Journal of Urban and Regional Research*. doi: 10.1111/1468-2427.12385.

Karaman, O., 2013a. Urban Neoliberalism with Islamic Characteristics. *Urban Studies*, 50(16), 3412–3427.

Karaman, O., 2013b. Intervention—"Defending Future Commons: The Gezi Experience" by Ozan Karaman [online]. *Antipode*. Available from: http://antipodefoundation.org/2013/08/27/intervention-defending-future-commons-the-gezi-experience-by-ozan-karaman-2/ [Accessed 25 July 2016].

Karampelias, G., 2011. Spitha and the Indignants [online] [Η Σπίθα και οι Αγανακτισσμένοι]. *Mikis Theodorakis Kinisi Anexartiton Politon*. Available from: www.mikis-theodorakis-kinisi-anexartiton-politon.gr/el/articles/?nid=1029 [Accessed 25 July 2016].

Kioupkiolis, A., 2014. Towards a Regime of Post-Political Biopower? Dispatches from Greece, 2010–2012. *Theory, Culture & Society*, 31 (1), 143–158.

Leontidou, L., 2010. Urban Social Movements in "Weak" Civil Societies: The Right to the City and Cosmopolitan Activism in Southern Europe. *Urban Studies*, 47 (6), 1179–1203.

Leontidou, L., 2012. Athens in the Mediterranean "Movement of the Piazzas" Spontaneity in Material and Virtual Public Spaces. *City*, 16 (3), 299–312.

Merrifield, A., 2013. *The Politics of the Encounter: Urban Theory and Protest Under Planetary Urbanization*. Athens, GA and London: University of Georgia Press.

Moore, S., 2013. Taking Up Space: Anthropology and Embodied Protest. *Radical Anthropology*, 7, 6–16.

Petropoulou, C., 2010. From the December Youth Uprising to the Rebirth of Urban Social Movements: A Space–Time Approach. *International Journal of Urban and Regional Research*, 34 (1), 217–224.

Popular Assembly Minutes, 2011a. Syntagma Popular Assembly Minutes 3rd of June 2011 [online] [Πρακτικά της Λαϊκής Συνέλευσης Συντάγματος—3 Ιουνίου 2011]. Available from: http://real-democracy.gr/minutes/2011-06-03-praktika-laikis-syneleysis-syntagmatos [Accessed 25 July 2016].

Popular Assembly Minutes, 2011b. Syntagma Popular Assembly Minutes 30th of May 2011 [online] [Πρακτικά της Λαϊκής Συνέλευσης Συντάγματος—30 Μαῖου 2011]. Available from: http://real-democracy.gr/minutes/2011-05-30-praktika-laikis-syneleysis-syntagmatos [Accessed 25 July 2016].

Popular Assembly Vote, 2011a. Syntagma Popular Assembly Vote 28th of May 2011 [online] [Ψήφισμα της Λαϊκής Συνέλευσης του Συντάγματος—28 Μαῖου 2011]. Available from: http://parallhlografos.wordpress.com/2011/05/28/ [Accessed 25 July 2016].

Popular Assembly Vote, 2011b. Syntagma Popular Assembly Vote 3rd of June 2011 [online]. [Ψήφισμα της Λαϊκής Συνέλευσης του Συντάγματος—3 Ιουνίου 2011] Available from: http://real-democracy.gr/votes/2011-06-03-apofaseis-laikis-syneleysis-plateias-syntagmatos [Accessed 25 July 2016].

Popular Assembly Vote, 2011c. Syntagma Popular Assembly Vote 30th of June 2011 [online]. [Ψήφισμα της Λαϊκής Συνέλευσης του Συντάγματος—30 Ιουνίου 2011]. Available from: http://real-democracy.gr/votes/2011-06-30-psifismata-laikis-syneleysis-30062011 [Accessed 25 July 2016].

Prentoulis, M. and Thomassen, L., 2013. Political Theory in the Square: Protest, Representation and Subjectification. *Contemporary Political Theory*, 12 (3), 166–184.

Rancière, J., 1999. *Disagreement: Politics and Philosophy*. Minneapolis: University of Minnesota Press.

Rancière, J., 2010. *Dissensus: On Politics and Aesthetics*. Translated edition. London and New York: Bloomsbury Academic.

Rancière, J., 2011a. The Thinking of Dissensus: Politics and Aesthetics. *In*: P. Bauman, and R. Stamp, eds. *Reading Rancière*. London: Continuum, 1–17.

Rancière, J., 2011b. Democracies Against Democracy. *In*: G. Agamben, ed. *Democracy in What State?* New York: Columbia University Press, 76–81.

Ross, A., 2013. Dossier from Strike Debt. *South Atlantic Quarterly*, 112 (4), 782–783.

Sotirakopoulos, N. and Sotiropoulos, G., 2013. "Direct Democracy Now!": The Greek Indignados and the Present Cycle of Struggles. *Current Sociology*, 61 (4), 443–456.

Stavrakakis, Y., 2010. On Acts, Pure and Impure. *International Journal of Žižek Studies*, 4 (2), 1–35.

Stavrides, S., 2012. Squares in Movement. *South Atlantic Quarterly*, 111 (3), 585–596.

Swyngedouw, E., 2011. Interrogating Post-Democratization: Reclaiming Egalitarian Political Spaces. *Political Geography*, 30 (7), 370–380.

Swyngedouw, E., 2014. Where Is the Political? Insurgent Mobilisations and the Incipient "Return of the Political." *Space and Polity*, 18 (2), 122–136.

Thematic Group on Direct Democracy, 2011. Functioning of Thematic Group [online]. [Λειτουργία της Θεματικής Ομάδας]. Available from: http://real-democracy.gr/teamvotes/2011-08-17-leitourgia-thematikis-omadas-amesis-dimokratias [Accessed 25 July 2016].

To Vima, 2011. Dozens of New Members in the Indignants Group [Δεκάδες νέα μέλη συγκεντρώνει η σελίδα των Αγανακτισμένων]. Available from: http://www.tovima.gr/society/article/?aid=402691 [Accessed 12 March 2017].

Vradis, A., 2011. Breaching the Spatial Contract [Σπάζωντας το χωρικό συμβόλαιο]. *In*: C. Giovanopoulos, and D. Mitropoulos, eds. *Democracy Under Construction: From Streets to Squares* [Δημοκρατία Under Construction: Από τους Δρόμους στις Πλατείες]. Athens: A/synexeia, 211–218.

Žižek, S., 2012. *The Year of Dreaming Dangerously*. London: Verso Books.

11

DEMOCRACY, OCCUPY LEGISLATURE, AND TAIWAN'S SUNFLOWER MOVEMENT

Ketty W. Chen

On March 31, 2014, two weeks after young activists accessed the main chamber of Taiwan's Parliament, the Legislative Yuan, half a million Taiwanese citizens flooded the streets of Taipei to demonstrate their support for the young activists who remained in the chamber.[1] The demonstrators crowded Ketagalan Boulevard, a ceremonial road in front of the Presidential Office. The demonstration permeated the surrounding streets extending northbound to the Legislative Yuan[2] and southward to Liberty Square and the National Central Library. The occupation of the Legislative Yuan by students and activists, mostly youths and young professionals in their twenties and thirties, would ultimately last 23 days. Known as the "Sunflower Movement," the event signaled a new stage of urban resistance and popular political movement in Taiwan.[3]

Known for its vibrant political oppositions, the modern history of Taiwan was not short of protests, street marches, and political rallies. In fact, political dissidents often defied the 38-year-long Martial Law era (1949–1987) and took to the streets to advocate for political reform and freedom. Environmental, labor, and political protesters would often march or conduct sit-ins without permits. Such behavior became even more prevalent in recent years, as protesters began engaging in similar behavior to what Moore (2013) calls "Taking Up Space"—using their bodies to "fill in" the space in and around government buildings and refusing to leave in demand of government response or concession on a variety of issues, ranging from industrial pollution and energy policy to labor rights and land expropriation.

As the largest political protest and longest occupation of a government building in the country's recent history, the Sunflower Movement marks a critical juncture of Taiwan's democracy in many ways and deserves attentive research and scrutiny. First, the Sunflower Movement inspired a much-needed societal debate on the state of democracy and democratic institutions in Taiwan after years of steady erosion with the return of Kuomintang (KMT) Party that ruled Taiwan during the authoritarian era after World War II. Secondly, the Sunflower Movement signifies the ripening of a Taiwan-centric identity, distinct from China, particularly among younger generations of Taiwanese. In other words, the Sunflower Movement solidified Taiwan's democracy as central to its politics, identity, and way of life.

Through a large-scale social mobilization, the Sunflower Movement also reinvigorated and reanimated Taiwan's civil society groups, which during the last decade have been disheveled, pessimistic, and combative with one another partly in competition for limited resources, difference in politics, and with a lack of common causes to unite under. The Sunflower Movement provided a rare, overarching platform for civil society groups to communicate, cooperate with and, for the least, identify each other, despite differences of their agenda and political orientations. The urgency of the movement and high political stakes, along with a limited window of political opportunities (McAdam, McCarthy, and Zald 1996), forced the groups to unite under a common purpose, despite the persistent differences and tensions between them.

The goal of this chapter is multifaceted. It will first elucidate the genesis of the Sunflower Movement and provide an explanation for the occupation of the Legislature in an escalation of protests against the Cross-Strait Service Trade Agreement (CSSTA). Then, I will examine the actual occupation by the Sunflower activists and, more importantly, the cliques and tribes that emerged during the 23-day occupation of the Legislature and the extent to which the groups were able to coexist and co-occupy the space. Lastly, the chapter explores the aftermath and lingering effects of the Sunflower Movement, the splinter groups that emerged after the movement and their goals, and how political activism emerged from the movement has been transformed into engagement in electoral politics and campaigns, leading to the defeat of the ruling, pro-China KMT Party in the most recent election in 2016. The chapter concludes by linking the processes and outcomes of the Sunflower Movement to a discussion on democracy and politics of public space.

Sowing the Seeds of Sunflower

Taiwan's transition from an authoritarian regime to a democracy over the past decades has been saturated with social and political movements, rallies, and demonstrations. The largest political opposition, that just won the 2016 presidential and legislative elections by a landslide, in fact, emerged from a political opposition movement called the "Dangwai."[4] In Taiwan, political resistance or protests manifest in many forms. Though many protests took place in the streets in marches and rallies, major protests by university students also included occupations and sit-ins, with students using their bodies to take over a public area and refuse to depart unless their demands were met. Examples included the Wild Lily Movement of 1990, where more than 6,000 university students sat in the square at the Chiang Kai-shek Memorial, and the Wild Strawberry Movement of 2008, where students occupied the same space, as well as the entrance of the Executive Yuan,[5] to protest against the oppressive Parade and Assembly Law that severely limits the freedom of assembly and expression, and thus political dissent.

In short, the occupation of public space by civic activists is not new to Taiwan. As early as May 1986, a few months prior to the official establishment of the Democratic Progressive Party (DPP), democracy activists occupied the courtyard of the popular Longshan Temple in Taipei with a sit-in to demand the lifting of Martial Law. The occupation lasted more than ten hours with the protesters surrounded by riot police. Supporters, concerned that the protesters would become hungry, threw meat buns inside the closed gates of Lungshan Temple to feed the protesters. In another instance, during a farmers' rally in 1988, protesters stormed the Legislative Yuan and took down its sign. More recently, when Miaoli County Commissioner Liu Cheng-hung expropriated the properties of local residents and demolished their homes to make way for a technology park, protesters occupied the entrance of the Executive Yuan in Taipei to plead with the Premier. After demanding that the government return the land and homes to the residents, the protesters surprised law enforcement by taking a detour and occupying the nearby Ministry of the Interior (MOI) (Figure 11.1). The occupation lasted 48 hours without any clear organization. The activists sat with the Miaoli residents whose homes were demolished by the government. They stuck stickers and spray-painted the ground of the MOI courtyard. As Professor Frida Tsai recounted, however, the mood at the site seemed "a bit strange," as she had a difficult time deciphering whether

FIGURE 11.1   The occupation of the Ministry of Interior, August 18, 2013

Source: Ketty W. Chen

the individuals entering and exiting the protest ground were supporters or infiltrators. The lack of systematic organization of the occupation served as a lesson for the protesters, especially the leaders. Many of the student activists present at the MOI occupation would later participate in the occupation of the Legislative Yuan. These earlier protests provided the experiences necessary for the students to organize and escalate their struggles that later became the Sunflower Movement.

CSSTA and the Sunflower Movement

The origin of the Sunflower Movement can be traced back to June 2013, when approximately 20 students and members of NGOs protested outside of the Executive Yuan, the day after the CSSTA was signed. Activists from organizations including the Taiwan Democracy Watch, the Taiwan Association for Human Rights, Taiwan Labor Front, Taiwan Teachers Union, and the Awakening Organization stood in front of the gate of the Executive Yuan under the scorching sun chanting slogans and delivering speeches to alert the Taiwanese of the danger of signing such an agreement with China. However, less than five local media outlets were present. No journalists from international media answered the activists' call for a press conference.

According to Show-ling Jang (2014), Professor of Economics at the National Taiwan University, among Taiwan's approximately 935,000 firms in the service sector, 99.7% are medium and small enterprises and 85% of the small enterprises are micro-enterprises with less than five employees. These medium and small enterprises in Taiwan would not be able to compete with the large enterprises from China. Hence, according to Jang (2014), the CSSTA would directly affect 4 million employees in the service industries and indirectly affect 2 million employees in the manufacturing industries. The Taiwan government was seeking to open 14 categories of the nation's service industries, including communications, construction, and commerce to health, society, finance, travel, environment, transportation, distribution, entertainment sports, wholesale, retail, and consignees. With such large-scale impact, the CSSTA would affect not only employment opportunities for the Taiwanese, but also national security through increasing economic dependency on China, which still considered Taiwan as a renegade province to be eventually united by force if necessary. Many in Taiwan are concerned that closer economic ties with China would expand Beijing's economic and political influence on Taiwan. They are

FIGURE 11.2 University students protesting against CSSTA and urging the occupation of the Legislative Yuan

Source: Ketty W. Chen

apprehensive that the government's active pursuit of economic ties to China would eventually undermine their democratic way of life. Already, pro-China Taiwanese businesses now own or have major stakes in several media companies including newspaper and cable television. Companies with major investments in China have also sided and contributed significantly to the pro-China KMT Party. In addition, police brutality against protesters has escalated in recent years, particularly during visits of Chinese officials.

The lack of proper oversight for the signing of the trade agreement was also a sign of eroding democracy and accountability that concerned many activists. Waves of protests around Taiwan against the trade agreement eventually forced the government to compromise by agreeing to hold 16 public meetings to review the agreement. Eight of the meetings would be presided by KMT legislators, and the other eight by the opposition DPP legislators. Academics, NGOs, and members of the sectors potentially affected by the CSSTA were all supposed to participate in the public hearings. At the time, a group of young activists formed the Black Island Nation Youth Alliance ("Black Island" hereafter).[6] Members of Black Island submitted a list of names to participate in the "public" hearings. However, their request was rejected by the government.

The KMT legislators held their portion of the hearings in a matter of one single week by holding two hearings per day. Many academics, civil groups, and industry representatives complained that they were either notified too late to participate or not notified at all, making such hearings all the more prejudiced in the eyes of the activists. In contrast, the activists were able to participate in the public hearings presided by DPP legislators, who according to the KMT, took their time to hold the hearings in order to delay the process. The persistent protests over the CSSTA made it impossible for the government to implement the CSSTA in 2013, and the legislative session resumed in March of 2014 to continue deliberation on how the government should implement the trade agreement. Eventually, a DPP legislator secured the right to preside over the legislative session, and decided to evaluate the CSSTA clause by clause through a compromise between DPP, KMT, and a smaller, pro-independence party, the Taiwan Solidarity Union (TSU). But KMT legislators blocked the podium to prevent the evaluation.

On March 17, 2014, KMT legislator Chang Ching-Chung brought a personal microphone to the legislative session. Chang was directed by the administration to pass the CSSTA to the legislative floor for voting as soon as possible. The DPP legislators attempted to block Chang, while the KMT legislators surrounded Chang to protect him. Chang quoted Article 61 of the Legislative Yuan's Functions Act, announcing that the review process had gone beyond the 90-day review period, and that the CSSTA should therefore be considered as reviewed and ready for submission to a plenary session on March 21 for the final vote. Chang's effort to send the CSSTA for a vote took half a minute. The sudden announcement of the committee's passage of CSSTA angered the activists who were already participating in a sit-in outside the Legislative Yuan. The sit-in soon drew a much larger crowd in the evening of March 18.

Occupy Legislature

For many academics, political analysts, and journalists in and outside Taiwan, the eruption of the Sunflower Movement seemed spontaneous. In fact, however, the movement has been the outcome of a series of attempts by activists through legal means but with no avail. For more than a year, the young activists exhausted all means within the legal framework. They received no response from any government institution in response to their objection of the trade agreement. In fact, on at least two occasions, activists submitted a list of names to attend the public hearings at the Legislative Yuan, only to be rejected. Furthermore, the activists were prevented from entering the Legislature all together.

The initial attempt to "occupy" the Legislature happened after the activists were prevented from attending the public hearings on the trade agreement. The activists reached the courtyard of the Legislature, sat on the ground, locked arms, and chanted slogans until police officers expelled them from the Legislature premises. After several attempts to occupy the Legislative Yuan's courtyard without much impact, a decision was then made by the protesters' leadership to escalate their actions. In the evening of March 18, 2014, during the "Safeguard Democracy" rally, participants of the rally surprised the guards and entered the Legislative Yuan. This time they did not stop at the courtyard. The protesters stormed into the legislative chamber. The students and young activists managed to climb over the gates and went inside the Legislature through the underground garage and the exterior windows. They managed to bypass the police and successfully secured the main chamber of the Legislature by piling chairs and furniture at the eight entries of the chamber to block law enforcement from entering. The extraordinary occupation of the legislative chamber surprised the authorities, as there was no precedent for such action. According to the Sunflower Movement participants, they were also surprised that they were able to enter and secure the legislative chamber without much resistance. They also did not expect the occupation to last 23 days. In fact, they were expecting to be expelled during the first or second night.[7]

Despite the extraordinary action, the administration under President Ma Ying-Jeou refused to respond to the demands of the occupiers, prompting some activists to try to further escalate the resistance by making an attempt to occupy the Executive Yuan on March 23 and 24, 2014. The confrontation sparked one of the bloodiest crackdowns in Taiwan's recent history. Special police officers were dispatched with the identification numbers on their armor covered, disguising their identity. Water cannons were deployed against the unarmed crowd causing many injuries. As the

FIGURE 11.3 A student climbing over the gate to take over the Ministry of Interior

Source: Ketty W. Chen

protesters sat, locked arms, and chanted slogans, police officers began beating their legs and knees with shields and even hit their bodies and heads with batons. Numerous protesters were seen bleeding from the head as they exited the Executive Yuan building. Furthermore, law enforcement blocked medical personnel and lawyers from entering the Executive Yuan premises to assist the protesters. The "Siege of Executive Yuan" remains one of the most contentious political events in Taiwan to date, alongside incidents of the Martial Law era from 1949 to 1987.

When one examines the series of persistent protests from those by Black Island youths to the rally of half a million individuals during the Sunflower Movement, the sudden increase of participants and the shift in public support has been nothing but extraordinary. Every evening during

FIGURE 11.4 Citizens and students occupying the street between the Ministry of Interior and the Legislative Yuan

Source: Ketty W. Chen

the occupation of Legislative Yuan, thousands of citizens answered the call from the activists to come to the Legislature to show their support. They came to the surrounding streets to show solidarity and to guard the area and protect those who remained inside the Legislative Yuan building from eviction by the police. The movement's activists also hoped the numbers of bodies taking up the space outside of the Legislature would demonstrate broad public support for halting the CSSTA. During the 23-day occupation, thousands of supporters continuously gathered outside of the Legislative Yuan. The level of public support as demonstrated by the persistent presence of a large crowd on the streets, even during harsh weather conditions, was one of the reasons that the occupation lasted for as long as it did.

On the Streets: Cliques, Tribes, and Splinter Groups

The 23-day occupation brought together people from all walks of life in Taiwan. While the Sunflower activists occupied the legislative chamber, the streets surrounding the Legislative Yuan were occupied by different civil society organizations as well as ordinary citizens, including some parents of the students inside. In different areas of the streets and even spaces within the Legislative Yuan, the occupation exhibited different characteristics as the occupiers formed cliques and tribes among themselves. For example, those who guarded the windows and doors on the second floor of the Legislative Yuan eventually called themselves the "Guardian Angels of the Second Floor," and were the last ones to exit the Legislative Yuan premise when the occupation ended. The streets of Qingdao East Road along the northern side of the legislative complex became "The Small Fortress," with tents and booths erected by various organizations to sort through the

FIGURE 11.5 The Guardian Angels of the Second Floor

Source: J. Michael Cole

supplies, food, water, and medical equipment donated by the public. The area was also used as a resting hub for the security guards, a makeshift library, and outdoor classrooms. Professors from major universities in Taipei moved their classes to the streets, lecturing to students and others who participated in the sit-in. The educators called their open classroom, the "Democracy Classroom." A "Citizenship Forum" was set up to host open discussions on government policies, including the CSSTA, widespread land expropriation, and the proposed textbook adjustments to create a more Sino-centric curriculum.

When one approached the Legislative Yuan, the visitor could see not only demonstrators sitting in, but also students reading books and doing homework. One could also find food stands, cellphone charging stations, free tutoring of high school students by college students, and booths occupied by media personnel lining along the streets. EMT Tough, an animal rescue organization consisting of tall, muscular men wearing leather pants, black T-shirts, and bikers' outfits, protected the students from pro-China gangsters, who often emerged in the middle of the night to harass the students. Aboriginal students also formed their respective groups on Qingdao East Road. Besides the government's China-leaning policies, they were also protesting against a long history of imposed cultural practices and political control on the indigenous tribes. Toward the end of the occupation, an independent musician, Indie Dadee, created a live broadcast and invited participants of the Sunflower Movement, including the popular student leaders, professors, and even celebrities, to sit with him and air their grievances (and profanities) on anything they wish to address. The wildly popular event was known as the "Large Intestine Flower" Movement, mocking the "official" Sunflower Movement.[8] Altogether, the highly self-organized form of street demonstration bore resemblances to the global Occupy movement, something that has not been observed at previous demonstrations in Taiwan.

While the formation of different cliques and tribes on the grounds surrounding the Legislature constituted an interesting and lively phenomenon during the Sunflower Movement, these cliques and tribes also illuminated the Sunflower Movement as a conglomerate of multiple social movements and civil society groups concerned with issues ranging from human rights and anti-eviction, to judicial reform, military reform, women's rights, workers' rights, animal rights, anti-free-trade and globalization, and pro-Taiwan independence. While these groups congregated at the premises of the Legislature and united in their opposition against the CSSTA, the motivations of their participation were dissimilar, leading to tensions and disagreements between the groups and amongst movement members on protest tactics and strategies. Such disagreements have proven divisive among the decision makers of the protest within the chamber of the Legislative Yuan, as well as the groups outside on streets. The most visible example was the formation of the "Downtrodden's Area," which bore the slogan "We are not rioters; we are just downtrodden. We are against elitism and the CSSTA!" It became a place at the protest site where members of advocacy groups would go and air their complaints about other organizations, the protest leaders, or other protest members.

These disgruntled activists branded themselves as "downtrodden" to mock the "elite" decision-making activists inside and outside of the Legislature. Specifically, they were dissatisfied with the movie-star-like attention and popularity that only a few movement leaders received and the fact that only a small group of individuals were included in the decision-making group. Tensions also arose between the movement leadership and the downtrodden when the groups disagreed on the focus of their protest—whether one should focus on the government's disregard of democratic procedure in reviewing and rectifying the CSSTA, the impact of the trade agreement and globalization, or the opposition to Chinese influence. Furthermore, argument also ensued regarding when and on what condition should the activists end the occupation and exit the legislative chamber as the protest went on.

The movement leadership, consisting of student leaders and their senior advisors, ultimately decided to end the occupation after an agreement was reached with then-Speaker of the Legislative Yuan, Wang Jyng-Ping, with the agreement that the lawmakers would not proceed with rectifying the CSSTA until an oversight bill was first passed by the Legislature. Some occupiers disagreed with the decision. To them, the promise from Speaker Wang was not sufficient, as there was no repercussion if the Legislature did not follow through with the promise. The "exit" from the legislative chamber was momentarily delayed due to minor disruption at the formal announcement by the protest leaders. Eventually, the group of more than 100 remaining students and youths did set aside their differences and exit the Legislative Yuan. They were surrounded by about 20,000 supporters in a rally outside of the Legislature. Nevertheless, the ideological divide among the protesters subsequently caused what the activists called "movement injuries."[9] The disagreements among the protesters would also later translate into a split among the so-called Third Force, a third-party political movement, resulting in the emergence of multiple small political parties following the Sunflower Movement rather than a unified political front.

After the Sunflower: Engagement with Electoral Politics

As of the 2015 legislative session in Taiwan, the oversight bill was still on hold in the Legislature, and the CSSTA also continued to be stalled in the Legislature. The political scene in Taiwan, on the other hand, was re-energized and profoundly transformed by the Sunflower Movement. Building on the wave of discontent against the government, the opposition party DPP won by a landslide during the local election in November 2014, capturing the seats of a large majority of cities and counties. The transformation also included the mobilization and political awakening of a large segment of the younger generations that had been seen as apathetic to politics and social issues.

Another important contribution of the Sunflower Movement has been the reinvigoration and reconciliation of Taiwan's civil society organizations that had been otherwise combative toward each other over the years. According to Fan Yun (2004), Taiwan's democratic transition and democratization is owed to the active civil society and their role in bringing important political and social issues to the fore. The Sunflower Movement, comprising of 54 different civil organizations and social groups, also assumed the task of informing the public of various issues, from land expropriation and energy policy to textbook adjustments. Before the movement, civil society groups in Taiwan, other than the formation of the DPP as Taiwan's largest opposition party, have not been able to create a political instrument that activists need to affect changes within the system. The young activists have realized that staying on the street to protest is one thing; however, protests cannot and do not last forever. The Sunflower Movement could only have a lasting effect if the young activists and their supporters learned how to transform their activism into forces that could influence the existing political structure and politics. Although some have chosen to stay outside of the political system, a large portion of the young activists and their supporters now believe, in order to summon change to the current political situation, they, too, have to participate in the political system.

By the beginning of 2015, a number of small political parties were established by the activists and their advisors. The New Power Party (NPP) and the Social Democratic Party are two prime examples. The New Power Party has introduced several legislative candidates, including Freddy Lim, the politically active lead singer from the death metal band Chthonic who also served as the Board Chair of Amnesty International Taiwan. All NPP candidates have been active on the social movement scene and have popular followings. On the other hand, the Social Democrats vowed to be the genuine leftist party. They have also vetted their own candidates for the 2016 legislative election. Though less known, the Social Democrats had hoped to gather enough party votes to receive seats to nominate legislators at large. In addition, Green Party Taiwan, established in 1996, also presented several candidates to compete in the 2016 legislative election. Several other small parties that advocate for Taiwan independence joined the ranks of new political parties as well.

On Election Day on January 16, 2016, Taiwan voters elected their first female president, Tsai Ingo-Wen, representing the DPP. Furthermore, the Legislature experienced the first peaceful transition of power in Taiwan's political history. Many of the Sunflower activists who once occupied the Legislature were elected now as legislators. For example, Huang Kuo-Chang, a legal scholar and adviser to the Sunflower youths and also the Chair of the New Power Party, successfully defeated a KMT incumbent. Freddy Lim, too, claimed victory and dethroned a seven-term KMT opponent. Lin Fei-Fan and Chen Wei-Ting, two popular student leaders of the Sunflower Movement, also joined the campaign respectively as a campaigner and a campaign manager. Chen's candidate did not win, however, and the activists have learned that elections and sustaining a political party are not as easy as they might seem. Running an election campaign was different from protesting on the streets or occupying the Legislature.

Nevertheless, practices and tactics learned during the Sunflower Movement did migrate beyond the movement itself. Specifically, the effects of the Sunflower Movement could be seen pollinating recent student movements in Hong Kong and Macao. During the Umbrella Movement in Hong Kong, one could observe students in Hong Kong utilizing some of the mediums used by the Taiwanese youngsters in the protests leading up to the Sunflower Movement. These included the utilization of social media (such as Telegram, Facebook, LINE, or WhatsApp) to organize and mobilize, the use of drones to video document the protest, the organization of security and cleaning crews during and after the protest, and open classrooms organized by teachers and professors. More recently, some of the Umbrella activists have also come to observe the election activities in Taiwan and plan to form their own political party in Hong Kong.

Conclusion: Democracy and the Occupation of Public Space

Street protests have been a common sight in Taiwan's political history; however, the occupation of government buildings and public space for such an extended period during the Sunflower Movement was unprecedented. Through occupying the Legislative Yuan, the Sunflower Movement not only was the longest occupation of a government building by civilians in Taiwan, it was also an escalation of occupation as a protest tactic in Taiwan's social and political movements. With the occupation of government buildings as a form of protest, the Sunflower Movement also brought to the fore a debate concerning the politics of public space protests in Taiwan, i.e., whether government buildings constitute a form of public space, and whether the act of occupying government buildings can be justified in social and political movement in a democracy.

Setha Low and Neil Smith (2006) contend that 2006 was the pivotal moment for examining the politics of public space and the definition of public space. A decade later, in Taiwan, the important task of defining what should be considered as private and public space continues. For the protesters and most Taiwanese,[10] the definition of public space refers to, as Low and Smith (2006, p. 3) defined, "the range of locations offered by the streets, the park, the media, the Internet, the shopping mall, [. . .] national governments and local neighborhoods." In an active democracy, these are spaces for political assemblies and expression. However, this view was not shared by everyone, including the KMT legislators and some conservative commentators who saw the occupation as violating the laws.

Regardless of the sustained contention, by taking over the floor of the legislative chamber and drawing overwhelming public support for the occupation, the Sunflower protesters eventually succeeded in achieving their goal to block the CSSTA. According to J. Michael Cole (2015), the Sunflower Movement's greatest accomplishment was to remind the authorities that there were certain invisible lines that Taiwanese would not allow them to cross, one of which was their way of life under a democratic institution. With the success of the Sunflower Movement, Taiwanese politics and democracy have entered a new phase in which social movement is represented directly by the independent political parties formed by movement activists. Meanwhile, the general public in Taiwan is becoming more aware of social and political issues affecting their life and the lives of others. As a result of the Sunflower Movement, the quality and substance of democracy in Taiwan have risen through active engagement of its citizens in the broader political process, an engagement that began in the streets and through the occupation of public space.

Notes

1. Cross-Strait Service Trade Agreement (CSSTA), a sub-agreement to the Economic Cooperative Framework Agreement (ECFA) signed between Taiwan and China in 2010.
2. Legislative Yuan is the legislative branch of the Taiwan government.
3. The Sunflower Movement was named after a florist contributed 1,000 sunflowers to the students outside the Legislature. Some of the flowers were brought inside the chamber and became a symbol of the protest.
4. "Dangwai" in Chinese means "outside of the party." Under the authoritarian rule of the Kuomintang from 1945 to 1987, no other political parties were permitted in Taiwan; therefore, the opposition movement was then dubbed the "outside of the party" movement.
5. Executive is the executive branch of the Taiwan government.
6. Black Island was named after an organization from the Japanese colonial era, which advocated against colonial rule.
7. *Liberty Times*, March 18, 2015, One Year Anniversary of 318: Lin Fei-fan: Being in the Spotlight Can Be Troublesome [318滿週年 林飛帆坦言：成鎂光燈焦點是衝擊]. Available at: http://news.ltn.com.tw/news/politics/breakingnews/1260447 [Accessed 18 March 2016].
8. Indie Daadee dubbed his event the "Large Intestine Flower" to mock the ideological pureness of the Sunflower Movement.

9. "Movement injuries" (運動傷害) was the term used by social movement activists who spent 2012–2014 on the streets protesting various social issues. Subsequent to the Sunflower Movement, the frequency of social movement dwindled due to the participants' fatigue.

10. *Liberty Times*, October 16th, 2015, Academia Sinica Academic: Sunflower Changed the Public's Attitude Toward Politics [中研院學者：太陽花改變民眾政治態度]. Available at: http://news.ltn.com.tw/news/politics/breakingnews/1477280 [Accessed 18 March 2016].

References

Cole, J. M., 2015. *Black Island: Two Years of Political Activism in Taiwan*. Taipei: CreateSpace Independent Publishing Platform.

Fan, Y., 2004. Taiwan—No Civil Society, No Democracy. *In*: M. Alagappa, ed. *Civil Society and Political Change in Asia: Expanding and Contracting Democratic Space*. Stanford: Stanford University Press, 164–190.

Jang, S.L., 2014. Cross-Strait Service Trade Pack: Guidelines and Recommendations for Renegotiation [online]. Available from: www.slideshare.net/ntuperc/englishok [Accessed 17 March 2016].

Low, S. M. and Smith, N., 2006. *The Politics of Public Space*. London and New York: Routledge.

McAdam, D., McCarthy, J. D., and Zald, M. N., 1996. Introduction: Opportunities, Mobilizing Structures, and Framing Processes: Toward a Synthetic, Comparative Perspective on Social Movements. *In*: D. McAdam, J. D. McCarthy, and M. N. Zald, eds. *Comparative Perspectives on Social Movements: Political Opportunities, Mobilizing Structures, and Cultural Framings*. New York: Cambridge University Press, 1–20.

Moore, S., 2013. Taking Up Space: Anthropology and Embodied Protest. *Radical Anthropology* 7, 6–16.

12

SHIFTING STRUGGLES OVER PUBLIC SPACE AND PUBLIC GOODS IN BERLIN

Urban Activism Between Protest and Participation

Henrik Lebuhn

Since the fall of the Wall in 1989, Berlin has experienced a dynamic process of neoliberalization (Bernt et al. 2013). Over the course of the 1990s and 2000s, over 50% of the city's public housing stock has been sold to private investors, and the city has become a highly desirable destination for international property investment (Holm 2007). State-owned properties and buildings have been sold to private parties through a special property trust (Liegenschaftsfonds) and important parts of the city's infrastructure, like water and electricity, have been (partially) privatized as well. Public expenditures have been cut significantly, leading to understaffed district administrations, the closure of neighborhood libraries, and prolonged emergency response times of firefighters and ambulances (due to lack of staff and equipment) to name just a few examples.

In response to this process, protest groups increasingly frame their actions and campaigns around questions of gentrification, privatization, and the city government's accountability for public space and resources (Lebuhn 2015). Interestingly, activists not only rely on a classical protest repertoire including rallies and occupations, but also make use of the city's participatory instruments such as round tables and referenda to pursue their goals. In particular, the citywide referendum has become an important vehicle for demands like the re-municipalization of electricity and the strengthening of the democratic accountability of the public utility agency (2013), the prevention of residential and commercial development on the closed inner-city airport Tempelhof (2014), and most recently for the expansion of Berlin's public housing program (2015).

These observations stand somewhat in contrast to the literature and the debates on participatory politics and urban protests. Among urban scholars, protest and participation are usually discussed separately. Similarly, activists often draw a clear line between the two and think of participatory instruments as something that either co-opts movement politics or can be co-opted by political interests. According to this understanding, resistance to neoliberal urban development can only take place outside participatory politics; round tables or referendums can still be used by activists as instruments, at best, but do not create insurgent dynamics themselves and remain external to the notion of resistance.

On one hand, there are good reasons to keep protest and participation conceptually separate. Most importantly, it would be imprudent for critical urban researchers to ignore the antagonistic character and transformative potentials of radical protests and simply incorporate them as an effect of urban neoliberalism with its armor of participatory and activating social technologies (Rose and Osborne 2000, Blokland et al. 2015). On the other hand, the development of participatory

channels and instruments that allows residents to influence planning and policy-making processes clearly changes the ground for social movements and leads to new forms and unexpected
dynamics of urban activism. But attention is rarely paid to the intersection between protest and
participation, and to the question of what forms of resistance may develop within or be facilitated
through participatory practices.

Against this background, the article uses Berlin as an exemplary case to explore two questions:
How have struggles over public space and public goods shifted under the conditions of neoliberal urban governance, and specifically in the context of participatory politics? And what are
the dynamics that (can) unfold when activists enter participatory processes in order to advance
"right to the city" claims? The article's first section offers an introduction into the debates that
provide the framework for my analysis. In the second section, I present a short overview of recent
struggles over public space in Berlin and the shift towards new forms of activism at the intersection between protest and participation. In the third section, I will look in more detail at two
examples of recent participatory processes in order to identify some of the dynamics through
which movement building and the advancement of claims can be either furthered or blocked. In
the concluding section, I will summarize the arguments and outline some of the implications for
further research as well as for urban activism.

Protest and Participation in the Neoliberal City: Perspectives and Debates

Like in most other Western democracies, cities in Germany have developed place-specific forms
of "neoliberal urbanism" (Theodore et al. 2011) roughly since the 1980s. This process has been
characterized by two elements: first, urban politics have shifted towards entrepreneurial strategies
(Harvey 1989). Urban governments emphasize the development of local and regional economic
resources and forcefully stimulate private sector investments in order to maneuver increasing
inter-urban competition (Aalbers 2013, Brenner and Theodore 2002, Hubbard and Hall 1998). In
the case of Berlin, this process is closely entangled with fundamental changes in urban planning
approaches and economic policies (Knierbein 2010) and processes of state territorial restructuring
(Brenner 1997) that started in the late 1970s and early 1980s as well as with Berlin's new role as
the German capital after the fall of the Wall in 1989 (Häußermann and Strom 1994, Lehnhardt
1998, Heeg 1998, Lebuhn 2015). Secondly, cities have developed strategies of "soft neoliberalism."
Famously coined by Nikolas Rose as a means of "governing through community" (Rose 1996,
Rose and Osborne 2000), these consist of local and area-based policies that aim at activating and
integrating civil society actors, communities and so-called third sector organizations into cooperative governance structures (Evans et al. 2005, Swyngedouw 2005). In Berlin, the development
of such strategies can be traced back to the so-called careful urban renewal policy of the 1980s
(Holm and Kuhn 2011) and gained momentum in the late 1990s and 2000s (Holm and Lebuhn
2013, Kemp et al. 2015, Lanz 2013, Lanz 2008).

It is within this "double movement" that the dynamics at the intersection between urban protest and participatory politics become increasingly relevant. On one hand, the commodification
of urban space and goods has led to a new cycle of protest and contestation (Künkel and Mayer
2011). On the other hand, the process of "rolling out neoliberalism" (Peck and Tickell 2002) has
opened up the political arena for civil society actors and invites them to participate in various
areas ranging from planning and budgeting procedures to neighborhood revitalization programs
and profit-oriented public-private partnership projects. As a result, social movement organizations and grassroots groups are presented with new opportunity structures, but also confronted
with the financial and political constraints of "real politics."

Scholars critical of neoliberalism have provided a pointed analysis of the changing role of the so-called third sector (Mayer 1994, 2000). And there also seems to be a growing interest in the potential of deliberative democracy and participatory politics for urban justice (see for example Fung and Wright 2001, Fung 2004, Silver et al. 2010). However, this work does not necessarily focus on the role that urban social movements play within formal participatory processes. The planning literature, in turn, provides insightful analyses of participatory and community planning procedures (Arnstein 1969), but focuses more on the quality and development of the instruments themselves rather than on their contextualization within dynamics of urban contestation (see Hou and Hammami 2015; for a critical introduction to urban planning see Marcuse 2011).

Finally, activists themselves often state that participatory instruments like referenda, round tables, and community planning procedures represent strategies to co-opt and neutralize social movements; others, however, argue that movements can actually make good use of them in order to advance their claims for social justice. Neither one of these assumptions is completely right or wrong, as I shall argue. Rather the question is: How do political agency and participatory structures shape each other? And what kind of dynamics (can) unfold when grassroots groups enter participatory processes?

Shifting Struggles Over Public Space and Goods in Berlin

When it comes to struggles over public space and public goods, Berlin turns out to be a peculiar latecomer. Although early signs of urban neoliberalization can be traced back to the 1980s (Knierbein 2010), Berlin's unique situation as a "divided city" between socialism in the East and capitalism in the West generally protected it from market-driven forms of privatization, gentrification, and encroachment of "the public" until 1989. Before the fall of the Wall, cultural and political dissidents in East Berlin were often confronted with an authoritarian government and rigid regulations when maneuvering in the public realm. But the state economy and a strong public housing sector provided social security for all citizens. Gentrification, the privatization of public space through capital, and speculative investment in public infrastructure were basically unknown. West Berlin in turn was surrounded by "enemy land" and only accessible to/from West Germany by air-traffic or by a narrow rail and highway corridor of approximately 100 miles length. As a result, private investors shied away from West Berlin with its unfavorable geographical location and unpredictable political situation throughout the Cold War.[1] Generous subsidies from the West German central government compensated for the lack of private capital and maintained the capitalist part of Berlin as a "display window of the Golden West" (Hoff and Krüger 2004). Although West Berlin experienced intense neighborhood protests against top-down urban renewal policies, rising rents, and housing shortages in the 1970s and 1980s, protests were often framed vis-à-vis the state and not the market: The strong squatter movement of the early 1980s, for example, was struggling for "autonomous space" rather than defending "public space." In summary, the struggle for public space wasn't on top of the agenda for most urban activists in Berlin until 1989.

This changed dramatically with the fall of the Wall. With the (alleged) defeat of socialism and German reunification, Berlin's political elite explicitly subscribed to an entrepreneurial strategy. Germany's new capital[2] was expected to quickly attract investment from major transnational corporations and turn into a control center for the European, if not for the global, economy. In addition to the ideological discourse that dominated Berlin during the years after the reunification, significant economic pressure weighed on the city's urban development: the federal government decided to cut its Cold War subsidies, increasing inter-urban competition appeared on the horizon, and outdated industrial structures continued into a steep decline. Between 1989 and 1998,

Berlin lost about 270,000 manufacturing jobs, which amounts to about 67% of the industrial workforce of that time (Krätke and Borst 2000).

The early 1990s, then, can be interpreted as a landmark period for Berlin's ongoing process of neoliberal restructuring and its increasing orientation towards international investment in the real estate and in the service sector, large-scale commercial developments, and the decisive promotion of tourism, the health industry, and the new economy (on the pitfalls of economic restructuring in Berlin, see Krätke 2004). Early measures included the decision to privatize large parts of Berlin's public housing stock (Holm 2007), an urban renewal policy for East Berlin's Prenzlauer Berg neighborhood, followed by a brutal wave of gentrification and displacement (Holm 2006) and the partial privatization of public space (Knierbein 2010) and infrastructure, such as electricity in 1997 (Monstadt 2007) and water in 1999 (Beveridge and Naumann 2013).

However, over the course of the 1990s, urban protests against Berlin's entrepreneurial turn remained relatively weak. Among the many factors that account for this dynamic, two seem crucial: First, living costs and rental prices continued to be relatively low, and due to the prolonged and often chaotic process of restructuring in the East, urban spaces often remained noncommodified and not overly regulated well into the 2000s—making Berlin especially attractive for artists, bohemians, and subcultural activities (Bader and Scharenberg 2010).[3] Second, the fall of the Wall had taken everyone by surprise, including the Left. Many grassroots groups in East and West didn't even know of each other, and political activism was highly fragmented. In East Berlin's Prenzlauer Berg neighborhood, tenants were among the first ones in the city to battle post-Wall gentrification and displacement. The "Innenstadtaktion" (Central City Action) addressed privatization and surveillance of public spaces in the central city. And the NOlympia campaign of the 1990s mobilized against Berlin's run for the 2000 Olympic Games. But overall, activists were lacking common ground. They did not recognize shared problems or a shared vision, which could have served as a framework to build a citywide movement against the neoliberal agenda of the 1990s.

In 2001, Berlin's economic downfall combined with fiscal mismanagement lead to a severe financial crisis followed by fierce austerity policies (Krätke 2004). At the same time, large-scale investment projects that had been in the planning or construction stages began to materialize. The effects of neoliberal policies became much more noticeable and started to work as a catalyzer for urban protests. One of the first major mobilizations that combined a number of crucial elements characterizing Berlin's neoliberal restructuring and drew citywide attention was the Mediaspree Versenken! (Sink Mediaspree campaign) of 2006 to 2009 (see Dohnke 2013). "Mediaspree" refers to one of Berlin's largest investment projects. Its goal is to develop the banks of the river Spree southeast of the city center in an area where the Wall used to divide the neighborhoods of Kreuzberg and Friedrichshain. It especially aims at attracting media and telecommunication companies as well as luxury apartments, and it includes wide-ranging urban renewal policies for the adjacent neighborhoods.

Eventually the Sink Mediaspree campaign only achieved a modification of the original development plan. But interestingly, the large and persistent mobilization against Mediaspree—and against the expected effects of gentrification, privatization, and neighborhood change—developed "a kind of unintended division of labor" (Kuhn 2011): it combined creative and radical direct actions by activists, the protests of local clubs and beach bars that had temporarily occupied the river banks and were now being evicted, and the use of participatory channels, namely the referendum (on the district level) and a round table that included activists and local politicians. In this regard, Sink Mediaspree set an example that has since been replicated by several campaigns.

Today, fragmentation is still a challenge for urban social movements in Berlin. But in comparison to the 1990s, activists in East and West have managed to establish a shared discursive framework and better coordinate their actions. More and more, grassroots campaigns mobilize under the banner of anti-gentrification and anti-privatization and for the democratic control of urban resources. The encroachment of public space and public goods has become a major concern for many residents. As I will argue in the next section, activists' use of participatory channels has played an important, yet ambivalent role in this process. On one hand, participatory politics have reframed urban conflicts by focusing on particular "issues" rather than on fundamental questions of social justice and they have integrated movements into Berlin's governance structures; on the other hand, they have given movements a strong public voice, supported the construction of a counter-hegemonic discourse, and, at times, even facilitated successful interventions into neoliberal development projects.

At the Crossroads Between Protest and Participation

In Berlin, urban protests and the development of participatory politics are historically closely entangled. Many of the participatory instruments the city uses today in order to integrate residents and non-state actors into urban planning and development processes are rooted in the urban struggles of the New Left of the 1960s and 1970s. In West Berlin, the '68 movement and the neighborhood struggles that nurtured and evolved from it created political dynamics characterized by militant urban protests, bottom-up demands for participation in local politics, and top-down strategies to incorporate grassroots groups into urban planning and policy-making procedures (Kemp et al. 2015). The squatter movement of the early 1980s played a particularly important role for Berlin's shift from top-down to so-called careful urban renewal policies and for the development of participatory instruments that mediate conflicts between various stakeholders on the neighborhood and city level (Holm and Kuhn 2011).

The fact that participatory instruments represent rather ambivalent victories of struggles against top-down modernist planning, large-scale demolition, and the displacement of local communities in the 1960s and 1970s seems to be true for other cities as well (for Hamburg see Rinn 2016, for Tel Aviv see Alexander 2008, Kemp et al. 2015). However, it was usually not until the 1990s and 2000s that participatory practices were formalized and routinely applied by local administrations and city planners. Berlin, for example, published its first official Handbook of Participation in 2011, a 340-page-long "hands-on" guide for the city's administrative staff that provides "step-by-step" information on how to get residents and actors involved and mediate claims and conflicts "on the ground" (Senatsverwaltung 2011). Another recent development has been the introduction of the referendum on Berlin's district level. The respective law was passed in 2005 and, in comparison to other German cities, the procedure is regarded as relatively transparent and accessible to residents.[4] The referendum at the state level has been part of Berlin's constitution for much longer, but was hardly ever used by the city's residents.[5] It underwent significant reforms in 2006, 2008, and 2010, and is now also regarded as a best-practice model for how the referendum is applied in other German states.[6]

As Adriana Kemp, Galia Rattner, and I have argued elsewhere, the strengthening of participatory instruments yields ambivalent effects when it comes to grassroots politics (Kemp et al. 2015). On one hand, participatory channels create new democratic opportunities. They are designed to solve specific "problems" and mediate residents' particularistic interests in preformatted ways. By doing so, they give residents the opportunity to influence urban policy-making and planning processes. At the same time, participatory politics can obstruct exactly those elements that Manuel Castells identified as crucial for the successful development of broader urban social movements (Castells 1983). Most importantly, this concerns three elements: the ability to make the connection between a particular issue and the underlying political and economic roots and dynamics; the formation of broad alliances with groups and organizations beyond the particular issue; and the connection of various fundamental problems (poverty, ecology, nationalism) with each other and with universal claims on recognition and redistribution. However, depending on the context, participatory channels create ambivalent and sometimes unintended results. In what follows, I will take a closer look at two recent cases in which activists engaged in participatory processes, and I will argue that—despite the structural problems mentioned above—we can also identify dynamics that create favorable conditions for the advancement of bottom-up demands. These dynamics deserve explicit attention in order to explore the potentials of participatory politics for the struggle over public space and goods.

The Referendum on the Re-Municipalization of Berlin's Electricity Grid

Over the course of 2013, Berlin experienced an intensive grassroots campaign for a referendum on the re-municipalization of the city's electricity grid. The campaign aimed at bringing the grid back into the public domain and at strengthening regional and renewable energy. While many of Berlin's politicians actually agreed that the city should consider buying the electricity grid back from the Swedish company Vattenfall, a more far-reaching demand of the campaign turned out to be highly contested: Activists also argued that the public utility agency, which would administer the grid, should be brought under popular control. They made several suggestions how to strengthen the democratic accountability of the agency; for instance, they proposed that some of the members of the agency's board should be elected directly by residents rather than being parachuted into their management positions by the city's political class.[7] The latter demand did not find much support among Berlin's politicians. Opponents argued "that there are dangers in putting complex management and construction jobs in the hands of local authorities with little experience,"[8] and eventually the Berlin Senate as well as the city parliament officially recommended to vote against the proposed reforms.[9] The referendum was held on November 3, 2013, but fell slightly short of the required 25% voter participation. Of Berlin's voters, 24.1% went to the polls with 83% of them voting in favor of the grassroots proposal.[10] Despite the defeat of the grassroots campaign, two important dynamics unfolded: First, under the wing of the Berlin Energy Table, the campaign for the referendum brought a coalition of 50 organizations together including environmental advocate groups, trade unions, tenant unions, anti-globalization activists, as well as local chapters of political parties ranging from Social Democrats to the Green Party and the Left Party.[11] For several months, activists and residents with various political affiliations worked closely together. They got to know each other, created new political networks, and jointly organized numerous public actions and events promoting the campaign and gathering residents' signatures for the referendum. Secondly, the campaign triggered a strong public counter-discourse about the democratic control of the city's resources: local newspapers, radio stations, and television channels reported on the proposed reform to strengthen the democratic accountability of the city's public utility agency and invited politicians, journalists, and experts to discuss the subject. Even though the political class tried to discredit the proposed reform, the referendum was an important step in the process of advancing and shaping anti-privatization protests and focusing them onto the question of democratic control rather than on a simple, binary private-public dichotomy.

The Referendum Against the Development of the Airport Tempelhof

In 2011, residents and activists working within the organizational framework of "Tempelhof 100 Percent"[12] initiated a campaign for a referendum to prevent the city of Berlin from developing the closed inner-city airport Tempelhof.[13] Since the closure of the airport in 2008, the future of the former airfield had been subject of heated debates and actions. In 2009, the grassroots coalition Tempelhof for All (Tempelhof für alle) called for a coordinated effort to open the field to the general public. The climax of that campaign was the endeavor to open the fences and literally squat the field (Roskamm 2014, p. 65): "A massive police force prevented the squat and the curious image of 2,000 constables guarding a huge empty meadow was broadcasted in the news" (ebd.). In view of the immense public pressure as well as changing planning approaches, the city eventually decided to open the field up to the public and allow interim use until further development of the area would begin. Residents' ideas for the future use of the field were surveyed by the city, and temporary projects like urban gardening were facilitated through the public service company Grün Berlin GmbH.

Once the field was open, tens of thousands of urbanites "appropriated" the huge empty space by simply "doing things" there on a day-to-day basis (Kaschuba and Genz 2014). In this context, Roskamm stresses that "the field is completely unchanged. It is not more (and not less) than an almost 400 hectare big open field, meadows with almost no trees and two runways, an airport without airplanes. And exactly this condition seems to fascinate people" (Roskamm 2014, p. 67). When it became clear that the Senate of Berlin planned to develop part of the former airfield for commercial and residential use, a network of grassroots groups, neighbors, and activists started the above-mentioned campaign, Tempelhof 100 Percent. Working against a massive counter-campaign run by private interest groups, much of the media, and the Berlin government itself, activists managed to collect more than 185,000 valid signatures to launch a referendum. For several months, the referendum and the discussions around it—namely issues of public space, affordable housing, and democratic accountability of Berlin's government—dominated Berlin's public debate. In May 2014, 46.1% of Berlin's voters went to the polls, and 65% of them voted in favor of the bill proposed by the Tempelhof activists.[14] The successful referendum prevents the city from developing the airfield and ensures that the entire area will be kept open as one huge park for the public.

Similar to the case of the electricity grid discussed above, activists' efforts to organize the referendum created an enormous amount of grassroots activity, coordinated actions, and communication. A particularly interesting aspect of this process is that the procedure of the referendum requires activists to condense their demands to a clear proposal, which can be voted on, and turned into legislation, if successful. As a result, Tempelhof activists from diverse backgrounds as well as numerous individual residents entered a complex dialogue to agree on a simple claim, which would have to establish a compromise among the various interests at stake, meet the formal criteria of the referendum, and have the potential to mobilize tens of thousands of voters toward a single issue: no permanent constructions on the former airfield. Finally, the insurgent effect of spatial everyday practices on the field itself can hardly be underestimated (Roskamm 2014, Hilbrandt 2016). An unattributed quote from an urban planner working for the city states that it was "the biggest mistake to open the field up in the first place." In other words: Once people had actually experienced the freedom of the open and undefined space of Tempelhof, you could no longer take it away from them.

Conclusions

The case of Berlin reveals that struggles over public space and public goods are shifting under the conditions of neoliberal urban governance. First, questions of privatization, gentrification, and the government's accountability of public goods and resources have become crucial in urban politics, and they are particularly important as a conceptual framework that unites Berlin's fragmented protest movements. Second, the struggle over public space and public goods is closely entangled with the strengthening of participatory politics. Grassroots groups increasingly make use of participatory instruments in order to advance right to the city claims, which results in new and hybrid forms of urban activism.

It is important to note that urban activism, participatory planning, and deliberative democracy should not be simply equated with each other. However, the strengthening of various participatory channels beyond the electoral arena has transformed the terrain on which grassroots groups operate. This in turn presents particular challenges for activists, especially as participatory instruments are not designed for movement politics, but to solve specific "problems" and mediate residents' particularistic interests in preformatted ways. Nevertheless, a close examination of recent cases, in which activists in Berlin made use of instruments like the referendum suggests the possibility that participatory processes create dynamics favorable to movement politics. This includes the bundling and focusing of (fragmented) discourses, the development of new activist and cross-actor networks, socio-spatial practices and encounters in public space facilitated through participatory practices, and the strategic adoption of grassroots claims to an administrative and political logic.

In Berlin it is noticeable, though, that urban protests entangled with participatory procedures seem to remain relatively contained and focused on specific issues. This becomes especially obvious when we compare Berlin to cities with weak or underdeveloped participatory channels like Istanbul and Tel Aviv, where anger and outrage over top-down urban development projects, gentrification, rising rents, and exploding living expenses have turned into forms of massive civil disobedience, and where urban activists have expanded their local agenda to fundamental questions of justice and inequality.

How exactly, then, do participatory ensembles like those in Berlin shape activists' strategies and collective identities, and what is their impact on the types of claims that can be advanced? So far only few scholars have taken on the invitation to study the intersection between protest and participation. Future research should focus more on the question of how participatory structures and political agency mutually constitute and shape each other, and what forms of resistance can emerge within participatory processes. Obviously, there will not be a one-size-fits-all answer. Instead, we need a historically informed perspective as well as a comparative one in order to explore the impact of different urban settings (e.g. different political coalitions, different instruments, different institutions, etc.) on participatory processes (for example concerning the weakening versus strengthening of radical claims); but also to understand the different dynamics that unfold around partnership-oriented participatory instruments, such as the round table or participatory planning procedures, versus antagonistic forms of participation, such as the referendum. Eventually, a better empirical analysis and theoretical understanding of the dynamics at work will also help activists to maneuver the shifting terrain of urban governance and strengthen the struggle for urban justice.

Notes

1. Some scholars point out that early forms of public space investment and commodification of public space and public furniture took place in West Berlin already in the 1980s (Knierbein 2010).
2. After WWII, West Germany relocated its capital from Berlin to Bonn. In 1991, the national parliament decided to move the capital back to Berlin.
3. Legal instruments to regulate these spaces existed, but were often not applied. Later on, private companies lobbied to deregulate and re-regulate public spaces to support their own type of market exploration, especially through the modification of Berlin's street and building regulations.
4. See the website of the NGO Mehr Demokratie! Berlin-Brandenburg, http://bb.mehr-demokratie.de/berlin-buergerbegehren.html [Accessed 14 September 2015].
5. Berlin has a two-level governance system: The city as a whole holds the status of a state (Land) while its districts (Bezirke) are regarded as municipalities. Compared to other German cities, this gives Berlin (along with Bremen and Hamburg) more legislative and fiscal autonomy from the federal government.

6. See the website of the NGO Mehr Demokratie! Berlin-Brandenburg, http://bb.mehr-demokratie.de/berlin-volksbegehren.html [Accessed 14 September 2015].

7. For the complete text of the referendum, see the campaign website of the *Berliner Energietisch* at http://berliner-energietisch.net/images/gesetzentwurf%20und%20begrndung.pdf [Accessed 15 September 2015].

8. Der Spiegel Online, *Energy Referendum: Public Buy-Back of Berlin Grid Fails*, November 4, 2013. Available at: www.spiegel.de/international/germany/berlin-referendum-on-buying-electricity-grid-from-vattenfall-fails-a-931609.html [Accessed 18 August 2015].

9. See the official statement at www.wahlen-berlin.de/abstimmungen/VE2013_NEnergie/Broschüre_Energie.pdf [Accessed 15 September 2015].

10. The citywide (state) referendum consists at its core of a two-step procedure: In the first phase, activists need to collect 175,000 signatures (7% of the registered voters). If they manage to do so, the city government has the opportunity to respond by considering the proposal. Otherwise the second phase kicks in, which consists of the actual public referendum. If successful, it forces the city parliament to pass the proposed bill.

11. See the campaign website of the *Berliner Energietisch* at http://berliner-energietisch.net [Accessed 15 September 2015].

12. For more information, see the website of *Tempelhof 100* at www.thf100.de/start.html [Accessed 4 June 2015].

13. See *Volksbegehren gegen Tempelhof-Bebauung*, October 19, 2011. Available at: http://taz.de/taz-Serie-Schillerkiez-Buergerprotest/!80255/ [Acessed 10 November 2015].

14. See *Berlin Voters Claim Tempelhof*, May 27, 2014. Available at: www.dw.de/berlin-voters-claim-tempelhof/a-17663944 [Accessed 3 June 2015].

References

Aalbers, M. B., 2013. Neoliberalism Is Dead . . . Long Live Neoliberalism! *Journal of Urban and Regional Research (IJURR)*, 37 (3), 1083–1090.

Alexander, E., 2008. Public Participation in Planning—A Multidimensional Model: The Case of Israel. *Planning Theory & Practice*, 9 (1), 57–80.

Arnstein, S. R., 1969. A Ladder of Citizen Participation. *Journal of the American Institute of Planners*, 35 (4), 216–224.

Bader, I. and Scharenberg, A., 2010. The Sound of Berlin: Subculture and the Global Music Industry. *International Journal for Urban and Regional Research (IJURR)*, 34 (1), 76–91.

Bernt, M., Grell, B., and Holm, A., eds., 2013. *Berlin Reader: A Compendium on Urban Change and Activism.* Bielefeld: Transcript.

Beveridge, R. and Naumann, M., 2013. The Berlin Water Company. From "Inevitable" Privatizatin to "Impossible" Remunicipalization. *In*: M. Bernt, B. Grell, and A. Holm, eds. *Berlin Reader: A Compendium on Urban Change and Activism.* Bielefeld: Transcript, 189–203.

Blokland, T., Hentschel, C., Holm, A., Lebuhn, H. and Margalit, T., 2015. Urban Citizenship and the Right to the City: The Fragmentation of Claims. Symposium. *International Journal for Urban and Regional Research (IJURR)*, 39 (4), 655–665.

Brenner, N., 1997. State Territorial Restructuring and the Production of Spatial Scale: Urban and Regional Planning in the Federal Rebublic of Germany, 1960–1990. *Political Geography*, 16 (4), 273–306.

Brenner, N. and Theodore, N. 2002. Cities and the Geographies of "Actually Existing Neoliberalism." *Antipode*, 34 (3), 349–379.

Castells, M., 1983. *The City and the Grassroots.* Berkeley: University of California Press.

Dohnke, J., 2013. Spree Riverbanks for Everyone: What Remains of "Sink Mediaspree"? *In*: M. Bernt, B. Grell, and A. Holm, eds. *Berlin Reader, a Compendium on Urban Change and Activism.* Bielefeld: Transcript, 261–274.

Evans, B., Richmond, T., and Shields, J., 2005. Structuring Neoliberal Governance: The Nonprofit Sector, Emerging New Modes of Control and the Marketisation of Service Delivery. *Policy and Society*, 24 (1), 73–97.

Fung, A., 2004. *Empowered Participation: Reinventing Urban Democracy.* Princeton, NJ: Princeton University Press.

Fung, A. and Wright, E. O., 2001. Deepening Democracy: Innovations in Empowered Participatory Governance. *Politics & Society*, 29 (1), 5–41.

Harvey, D., 1989. From Managerialism to Entrepreneurialism: The Transformation in Urban Governance in Late Capitalism. *Geografiska Annaler. Series B, Human Geography*, 71 (1), 3–18.

Häußermann, H. and Strom, E., 1994. Berlin: The Once and Future Capital. *International Journal for Urban and Regional Research (IJURR)*, 18 (2), 335–346.

Heeg, S., 1998. "Vom Ende der Stadt als staatlicher Veranstaltung": Reformulierung städtischer Politikformen am Beispiel Berlins. *Prokla—Zeitschrift für kritische Sozialwissenschaft*, 110, 5–23.

Hilbrandt, H., 2016. Insurgent Participation: Consensus and Participation in Planning the Redevelopment of Berlin-Tempelhof Airport. *Urban Geography*. doi: 10.1080/02723638.2016.1168569.

Hoff, B. I. and Krüger, M., 2004. Die Finanzierung der Hauptstadt Berlin im europäischen Vergleich. *In*: E. Z. f. F.-F. Tübingen, ed. *Jahrbuch des Föderalismus 2004. Föderalismus, Subsidiarität und Regionen in Europa.* Baden-Baden: Nomos, 109–122.

Holm, A., 2006. Urban Renewal and the End of Social Housing: The Roll Out of Neoliberalism in East Berlin's Prenzlauer Berg. *Social Justice*, 33 (3), 114–128.

Holm, A., 2007. Faces of Resistance: Housing Privatisation in London, Berlin and Amsterdam. *PRESOM (Privatisation and the European Social Model) Newsletter*, 3 (November 2007), 1–3.

Holm, A. and Kuhn, A., 2011. Squatting and Urban Renewal: The Interaction of Squatter Movements and Strategies of Urban Restructuring in Berlin. *International Journal for Urban and Regional Research (IJURR)*, 35 (3), 644–658.

Holm, A. and Lebuhn, H., 2013. Die Stadt politisieren. Fragmentierung, Kohärenz und soziale Bewegungen in der "Sozialen Stadt." *In*: M. Kronauer, and W. Siebel, eds. *Polarisierte Städte. Soziale Ungleichheit als Herausforderung für die Stadtpolitik.* Frankfurt and New York: Campus, 194–215.

Hou, J. and Hammami, F., 2015. On the Entangled Paths of Urban Resistance, City Planning and Heritage Conservation. *PlaNext*, 1 (July), 9–16.

Hubbard, P. and Hall, T., 1998. Introduction. *In*: P. Hubbard, and T. Hall, eds. *The Entrepreneurial City: Geographies of Politics, Regime and Representation.* Chichester: Wiley, 1–27.

Kaschuba, W. and Genz, C., eds., 2014. *Tempelhof. Das Feld—Die Stadt als Aktionsraum.* Institut für Ethnologie (Selbstverlag), Berlin. Available from: http://issuu.com/tempelhof/docs/tempelhof_-_das_feld?e=13219644/9000413.

Kemp, A., Lebuhn, H., and Rattner, G., 2015. Between Urban Governance and the Right to the City: Participatory Politics in Berlin and Tel Aviv. *International Journal for Urban and Regional Research (IJURR)*, 39 (4), 704–725.

Knierbein, S., 2010. *Die Produktion zentraler öffentlicher Räume in der Aufmerksamkeitsökonomie. Ästhetische, ökonomische und mediale Restrukturierung durch gestaltwirksame Koalitionen in Berlin seit 1980.* Wiesbaden: VS Verlag.

Krätke, S., 2004. City of Talents? Berlin's Regional Economy, Socio-Spatial Fabric and "Worst Practice" Urban Governance. *International Journal for Urban and Regional Research (IJURR)*, 28 (3), 511–529.

Krätke, S. and Borst, R., 2000. *Berlin. Metropole zwischen Boom und Krise.* Opladen: Leske and Budrich.

Kuhn, A., 2011. The Citizenship of Urban Social Movements. Participation as a Point of Reference for Social Struggles in Berlin. Unpublished paper presented at the International Symposium, Urban Citizenship Revisited. Rights, Recognition and Distribution in Berlin and Tel Aviv, 15–16 September 2011. Berlin: Humboldt University Berlin.

Künkel, J. and Mayer, M., eds., 2011. *Neoliberal Urbanism and Its Contestations—Crossing Theoretical Boundaries.* London: Palgrave Publishers.

Lanz, S., 2008. Powered by Quartiersmanagement: Füreinander Leben im Problemkiez. *dérive. Zeitschrift für Stadtforschung*, 31, 28–31.

Lanz, S., 2013. Be Berlin! Governing the City Through Freedom. *International Journal for Urban and Regional Research (IJURR)*, 37 (4), 1305–1324.

Lebuhn, H., 2015. Neoliberalization in Post-Wall Berlin: Understanding the City Through Crisis. *Critical Planning, UCLA Journal of Urban Planning*, 22, 99–118.

Lehnhardt, K., 1998. "Bubble-Politics" in Berlin. Das Beispiel Koordinierungsausschuß für innerstädtische Investitionen: eine "black box" als Macht-und Entscheidungszentrale. *Prokla—Zeitschrift für kritische Sozialwissenschaft*, 110, 41–66.

Marcuse, P., 2011. The Three Historic Currents of City Planning. *In*: G. Bridge, and S. Watson, eds. *The New Blackwell Companion to the City.* Malden, Oxford, Chichester: Wiley-Blackwell, 643–655.

Mayer, M., 1994. Post-Fordist City Politics. *In*: A. Amin, ed. *Post-Fordism: A Reader*. Oxford: Basil Blackwell, 316–337.

Mayer, M., 2000. Urban Social Movements in an Era of Globalization. *In*: P. Hamel, H. Lustiger-Thaler, and M. Mayer, eds. *Urban Movements in a Globalizing World*. London and New York: Routledge, 141–157.

Monstadt, J., 2007. Urban Governance and the Transition of Energy Systems: Institutional Change and Shifting Energy and Climate Policies in Berlin. *International Journal for Urban and Regional Research (IJURR)*, 31 (2), 326–343.

Peck, J. and Tickell, A., 2002. Neoliberalizing Space. *Antipode*, 34 (2), 380–404.

Rinn, M., 2016. *Konflikte um Stadtentwicklungspolitik in Hamburg. Eine Analyse von Akteur_innen, Praktiken und Dynamiken*. Münster: Westfälisches Dampfboot.

Rose, N., 1996. The Death of the Social? Refiguring the Territory of Government. *Economy and Society*, 25 (3), 327–356.

Rose, N. and Osborne, T., 2000. Governing Cities, Governing Citizens. *In*: E. Isin, ed. *Democracy, Citizenship and the City: Rights to the Global City: Routledge Studies in Governance and Change in the Global Era*. London: Routledge, 95–109.

Roskamm, N., 2014. 4,000,000 m2 of Public Space: The Berlin "Tempelhofer Feld" and a Short Walk with Lefebvre and Laclau. *In*: A. Madanipour, A. Knierbein, and A. Degros, eds. *Public Space and the Challenges of Urban Transformation in Europe*. New York and London: Routledge, 63–77.

Scharenberg, A. and Bader, I., 2009. Berlin's Waterfront Site Struggle. *City: Analysis of Urban Trends, Culture, Theory, Policy, Action*, 13 (2–3), 325–335.

Senatsverwaltung, 2011. *Handbuch zur Partizipation*. Berlin: Senatsverwaltung für Stadtentwicklung und Umwelt Berlin.

Silver, H., Scott, A., and Kazepov, Y., 2010. Participation in Urban Contention and Deliberation. *International Journal for Urban and Regional Research (IJURR)*, 34 (3), 453–477.

Swyngedouw, E. 2005. Governance Innovation and the Citizen: The Janus Face of Governance-Beyond-the-State. *Urban Studies*, 42 (11), 1991–2006.

Theodore, N., Peck, J., and Brenner, N., 2011. Neoliberal Urbanism: Cities and the Rule of Markets. *In*: G. Bridges, and S. Watson, eds. *The New Blackwell Companion to the City*. Oxford: Blackwell, 15–25.

13

OCCUPIED OAKLAND, PAST AND PRESENT

Land Action on the New Urban Frontier

Marcus Owens and Christina Antiporda

When the Occupy movement emerged in 2011 as a critique of Wall Street bailouts following the Great Recession, New York City's Zuccotti Park enjoyed "flagship" status given its proximity to New York's financial sector. However, occupiers in Oakland, California also garnered attention as the nation watched violent protests and radical actions such as the dramatic closure of the Port of Oakland. These reactions were compounded by strained police-civilian relationships stemming from the high-profile acquittal of police officers in the killing of Oscar Grant, a young black man handcuffed and lying facedown on a train platform during New Year's celebrations the previous year, depicted in the award-winning feature film *Fruitvale Station* and resonating in today's Black Lives Matter movement. Lesser-known actions included attempts to permanently occupy vacant buildings in downtown Oakland, leading to pitched battles with the police and a proliferation of political squats across the city.

In this chapter, these occupations serve as an opportunity to consider a genealogy of occupying land in the US west, as well as broader questions of public space and political resistance within contemporary forms and processes of urbanization. Specifically, we consider how the material emphasis of "the land question," pivotal to 19th century politics as the US expanded westward, may inform contemporary politics of urban resistance since the new left focus on cultural symbolism and identity beginning in the 1970s. An account of collaboration with the Oakland-based squatter's advocacy group Land Action illustrates this political turn.

Formed in the years leading up to Occupy Oakland, Land Action uses "adverse possession" to advance goals of housing equality and environmental justice. Adverse possession, the legal procedure for acquiring property through squatting, has its roots in the settling of the west. A focus on how these practices shift over time reflects a genealogical consideration of occupying space as a political act, derived from Foucault's analysis of Nietzsche. Through this interpretation, genealogy differs from history in that it does not seek to demonstrate that the past actively exists or continues to animate the present in some essential, predetermined form (Foucault 1980). Rather, genealogy identifies the accidents, deviations, errors, false appraisals, and faulty calculations that gave birth to things that have value to us. This genealogy of squatting and occupations in San Francisco Bay Area is far from complete or exhaustive, but allows for preliminary exploration of shifting power relations and changes in the production of space and political resistance behind recent movements such as Occupy Oakland and Land Action.

As a tool for understanding the power relations engendered by practices of squatting, we draw upon the idea of the *parazone* (Rabinow 2014). Developed in Paul Rabinow's Anthropological

Research on the Contemporary Collaboratory (www.anthropos-lab.net), the parazone describes the permeable and contestable zones adjacent to legal domains. In the parazones of the old west, legal frameworks for squatting land established in the Preemption Acts outlined the bounds between public and private and provided a bulwark against the collective masses in specifying how (and which) settlers could claim private ownership. Settlers staked out and communicated occupation of tracts of federal land, defending them with what was known as a "shotgun title," and then economically *improved* wilderness land for five years (Pisani 1994). Today, legal frameworks for occupying land give form to a new parazone with a different set of parameters for occupying vacant urban lots in contemporary California. As suggested by Neil Smith (1996), economic restructuring creates new urban frontiers and new urban wilderness imaginaries ripe for improvement. Continuing to trace this genealogy affords a better understanding of how these practices travel across time and shape the spaces of resistance in the contemporary urban landscape.

Oakland, the East Bay, and the San Francisco Bay Region

First, an overview of the landscapes and spatial dynamics of the Bay Area region provides a context for Land Action's work. While many readers may associate the San Francisco Bay Area with the eponymous city, only a small fraction of the region's population lives in the city on the tip of the Peninsula. As urban geographers Walker and Schafran (2015) describe it, the Bay Area shares a similar brand of urbanism with its sprawling rival to the south, made famous by the "Los Angeles School" of urban studies (Dear 2001). Both metropoles are characterized by a polycentric network of vast suburban sprawl, as well as a relationship between topography and class. Inner-core "flatland" areas ringing the bay shore are traditionally the most densely populated and industrialized, where the working classes occupy the oldest housing stock, and the wealthy gradually move higher and higher up the hills (Figure 13.1). This class topography also

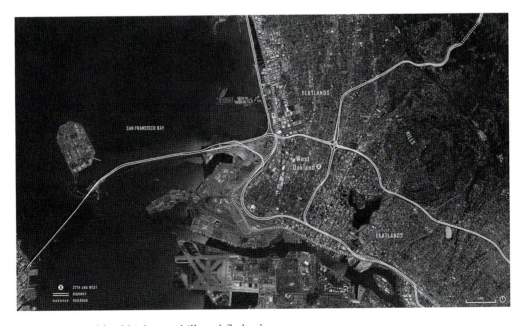

FIGURE 13.1   Oakland highways, hills and flatlands

Source: Authors, 2015

FIGURE 13.2 Bay Area regions and historical infrastructures

Source: Authors, 2015

intersects with the economic geography of the area's three primary urban cores surrounding the bay. Generally speaking, the bay shore flatlands struggled in the wake of post-Fordist restructuring while San Francisco remained a center for finance and tourism (see Maharawal, this volume). While venture capital washes over Silicon Valley, a familiar cycle of vanishing union jobs replaced by low-wage service positions unfolds in the East Bay (Benner 2002, Self 2005). As a result of this uneven development, the region has some of the most extreme economic inequality in the country. These factors, in conjunction with bottlenecks in the housing delivery system, make for skyrocketing rents across the region as downtown Oakland and the East Bay flatlands sit on the verge of transformation (Walker and Schafran 2015).

In terms of demographics, the East Bay historically attracted diverse working populations of Chinese, Japanese, Filipinos, and Mexicans, as well as the Irish, German, and southern European immigrant groups that arrived in large numbers to other US urban centers in the years before the Great Depression. A significant influx of African Americans from the American South also landed in Oakland, first as railroad porters, then seeking wartime manufacturing jobs. This "second great migration" during WWII firmly positioned Oakland as a thriving center for Black Californian culture and politics (Murch 2010). However, the Black California dream was deferred in a way similar to Langston Hughes's famous depiction of Chicago in *Raisin in the Sun*. Discriminatory lending practices such as redlining and blockbusting limited Blacks, as well as Asians and Mexicans, to disinvested and isolated ghettos, while freeways sliced through flatland neighborhoods like West Oakland in the late 1960s (Self 2005, Rhomberg 2004).

Concurrent to the emergence of radical and reformist black power movements, suburban housing developments followed highways out of town into the tri-valley area, leapfrogging nature conservation zones in the hills ringing the bay. By the 1970s, a majority of affluent white residents exited the inner East Bay, taking a substantial portion of the tax base with them, and were eventually joined by middle-class Blacks, Asians, and Latinos as housing desegregated (Walker 2009, Walker and Schafran 2015). A key piece of legislation indicative of the shift from governance *because* of the market to governance *for* the market is the infamous Proposition 13 of 1978. The legislation exacerbated this draining of public funds by freezing property taxes, effectively ending an era of progressive planning that built the infrastructure of 20th-century California. In addition to decimating public services, Proposition 13 fiscalized land-use decisions by operating according to costs (such as schools for children) and tax-role benefits (such as sales tax), further inscribing in space the uneven development of the 1990s (Schafran 2013). By the 1990s, inner-core neighborhoods lining the bay shore began to gentrify as Bay Area municipalities competed to attract tech companies and a highly paid workforce that skews young and childless in contrast to the previous blue-collar industries situated there. Despite its reputation for crime and disinvestment, Oakland, especially West Oakland, gradually became appreciated for its Victorian housing stock, multicultural diversity, and ten-minute train ride to downtown San Francisco.

Beyond instituting Prop 13, state and municipal government played an active role in accelerating this process. The completion of a large ecological restoration of Lake Merritt, a central outdoor social space in town, opened up a parcel of land which the city then sold in a no-bid, sub-market-rate deal to a private developer for luxury housing, sparking public outcry. The prolific California politician Jerry Brown was mayor of Oakland during this period, transforming downtown with his plan to bring 10,000 new residents to the core at prices unaffordable to 80% of existing Oakland households (Rhomberg 2004). In a cruel twist of irony, as residents were priced out of the flatlands, the bulk of affordable housing was constructed in distant suburbs up to 100 miles from San Francisco. The sub-prime mortgage crisis of 2008 played an important part in accelerating this process, with Bardhan and Walker (2011) arguing that California was "the fountainhead of the Great Recession," with the hardest hit working-class families in the gentrifying flatlands and the far-flung suburbs of the valley.

This change in the state's relation to the market occurred alongside what Neil Smith (1996) identified as "revanchist" tendencies along the new urban frontier. For example, the award-winning environmental restoration of Lake Merritt that resulted in a controversial sale of public land also served as pretext for racialized crackdowns on barbeques, DJs, and drumming at Lake Merritt, which had been common practices for decades. Realtors rebranded a number of traditionally working- and middle-class black neighborhoods (where Land Action also operates) along the northern border of Oakland and in Berkeley and Emeryville as "NOBE" (North Oakland-Berkeley-Emeryville). Phat Beets, the environmental justice organization that organized gardens and markets in the area, lashed back at the realtors' ad campaign.[1]

During the nationwide protests against police killings in 2014 that sparked the Black Lives Matter movement, neighborhoods and businesses that remained suspect of these transformations appeared to be targeted in Oakland protests. In each of these cases, it is impossible to decouple market-driven environmental "improvements" from the political implications of urban processes that displace residents in a privatized housing market.

Land and Publics in California

This paradox of improvement and displacement may be traced to the imposition of a public/private spatial binary and the process of enclosure described in Marx's concept of *ursprüngliche Akkumulation*. For Marx, enclosure creates a dispossessed, proletariat wage class marking the transition from feudalism to capitalism (Sevilla-Buitrago 2013). From the spatial perspective of landscape and urbanism, this corresponds to the enclosure of common lands by the English manors and the rise of "landscape picturesque" as an aesthetic category. The modern practice of landscape architecture soon followed as public parks from Hyde Park to the Tiergarten, and later Golden Gate Park, were created in the landscape garden style of these English manors. These new public spaces functioned as both economic tools as well as spatial technologies for the state to mold the character of an urbanizing nation (Young 2004, Meyer 2002). However, this process cannot be so easily transposed onto California. Prior to the ascent of the private property regime in California, the Catholic Church's missionary agenda and the Spanish military imposed a configuration of the sacred and the secular through colonial processes. In what is modern-day San Francisco, this process began with the Presidio military installation on the northwest corner of the peninsula in 1776, which provided security to the Pueblo settlement and Mission, a node in the linear network separating a day's travel on Camino Real. In the Pueblo, the Spanish crown imposed spatial regulations following the 1573 Law of the Indies (McMurray 1915). These guidelines are most well known for their *cuadrícula* grid system, establishing precedents for today's conceptions of public space such as the construction of a plaza for pasturing livestock and trading goods in what is now Portsmouth Square Plaza in San Francisco. These formal aspects underpinned a racial hierarchy and conceptual transformation of space in sparsely settled California according to the ecclesiastical cosmology of the mission rather than native ways of life on the land (Haas 1995, Moore 2003).

A center for this transformation was San Francisco's Mission Dolores, a few miles southeast of the Presidio in more hospitable bayside climates away from the ocean. Here, representatives of the ecclesiastical order such as recently beatified Junipero Serra forcefully acculturated the resident Ohlone Indians into laboring within the Spanish mercantilist system. As reflected in the writings of Serra's 18th-century contemporary Rousseau in the 1754 *On the Origins of Inequality*, people such as the resident Ohlone of the Bay Area lacked a recognizable system of property and therefore understood living in terms of the mythic "state-of-nature." Deemed *gente sin razon* (people without reason), for the colonizer, the Ohlone resided on the boundaries of humanity and required salvation (Moore 2003). Administrators of the Mission system saw the process of imposing agro-pastoralism, restricting mobility, and assigning individual identifiable Christian names not merely as divine labor but a wrenching *unnatural process* akin to breaking a wild animal (Hackel 1997). Like the people, the *land* in the eyes of the colonizer was seen as being in an unimproved, wild, and natural state that required partitioning or remapping through a sacred and secular cosmology. The notion of improvement is an important one; historians of colonialism (Pratt 2007, Drayton 2000) link "improvement" of the land and its people as a spatial reflection of the imperialist idea that surplus-oriented societies were inherently more advanced than subsistence ones. Hence the frontier dynamics used by Neil Smith (1996) to describe the contemporary phenomenon of gentrification, with the "rent gap" or the difference in current rent and potential rent following improvement of a given neighborhood or property—often entailing the racialized displacement and erasure of previous residents.

The decline of Spanish mercantilism and conflict in Europe led to Mexican independence in 1821 and the secularization of the Mission system in the 1830s, relieving the Church of its role as primary arbiter of land and labor. Outside of the Pueblos and Presidios, the Mexican state supported a gentry of mostly *Californios*, people born in California of Spanish descent, through the transfer of large private land grants, or *Ranchos*. However, some 25 years later, US expansionism in Texas triggered the outbreak of the Mexican-American War. In the Mexican backwater of *Alta California*, Anglo-American militia men, roughnecks, settlers, and would-be squatters seized the unmanned Sonoma Presidio north of San Francisco, giving birth to the short-lived California Republic before the annexation of the territory by the US. The 1848 Guadaloupe-Hidalgo peace treaty between Mexico and the United States respected the property rights of the Californios in theory, but land that could not be legally accounted for by the *Californino* gentry in arcane Spanish records became de facto public domain administered by the Public Land Commission. As dictated by the Preemption Acts at work in other western territories, this land was eligible for settlement by white men using methods of "shotgun title," whose labor would improve it and bring the land into the market.[2]

A year later, the gold rush of 1849 positioned San Francisco as a pressure control valve, siphoning excess labor from the slums of Europe and industrial centers on the east coast, through its port and into the foothills of the Sierra Nevada Mountains. This led to violent conflict with Indians in remote areas, but also the mobilization of squatters as a political force. Ideologically, "the land question" emerged from a Jeffersonian belief in a direct relationship between democracy and land tenure in the vast United States. As argued by the historian Tamara Shelton (2013), for many squatters the Ranchos and other recipients of large land grants appeared too similar to the European aristocracies many squatters had fled, contradicting Jeffersonian ideals of white free-holding agrarianism as a bedrock of the republic. Squatters' political movements pushed for regulating the favored "actual settlers," those living on the land versus speculators and absentee landlords who employed low-pay landless laborers, often Chinese, Mexican, and native peoples. Along these lines, squatter politics aligned against slavery in California not out of solely abolitionist fervor, but to prevent the large-scale plantation slave economies and caste system seen in the American South or Caribbean. Such a system would force poor landless whites to compete with African Americans, who, like the Chinese, were perceived to be biologically predisposed to servility and hard labor.

As the mythical lone gold prospector of 1849 gave way to large-scale mechanized extraction and industrial manufacturing facilitated by railroads after the US Civil War, squatters connected with a growing urban labor movement opposing industrial monopoly. The political philosopher Henry George articulates this transition in popular texts such as *Our Land and Land Policy* (1871) and *What the Railroad Will Bring Us* (1868), arguing land monopolies diminish wealth by withholding land from production, even in nonagrarian or "urban" contexts, and identifying land as the foundation of the industrial structure and the source of all wealth from which all society should benefit. As such, all rents on a given plot of land should be captured as tax and returned to society or the community that generated value from the place (Shelton 2013, p. 100). It is this adoption of the "urban land question"—where value generated from rents must be returned to society—that we will use to reconsider contemporary urban contestations and the issue of decolonization.

It must first be noted, however, that George was not a socialist, and this squatter–worker political alliance succumbed to the xenophobia and race-baiting of the Workingmen's Party of California, who targeted Chinese workers as scapegoats or proxies for the large land-holding industrial monopolies associated with the Republican Party. Rather than attempting to bridge a very real cultural divide between landless or yeoman whites and exploited Chinese workers by targeting industrial capital to organize for land reform, opportunistic labor organizers and politicians scored cheap political points by targeting Chinese people. "Yellow Peril" or the fears of an inassimilable, largely male Chinese population led to discriminatory local and state ordinances across California and the US west (Lee 2007, Shelton 2013). State and municipal codes ghettoized the population in Chinatowns and targeted everyday Chinese life in California through restrictions of sidewalk activity, living space, and businesses such as laundries, finally culminating with the federal government passing the Chinese Exclusion Act of 1882 barring immigration from China. In some sense, the afterlives of Henry George's political theories reverberate on the right wing as "sagebrush rebellion" movements springing up in the late 1970s as ranchers fought environmental regulations and targeted large federal landholdings in the US west (Culhane and McGreggor 1994). These backward-looking conservative movements advocate a return to a mythical pastoralism, a lifestyle only available to white settlers, divorced from technological development underpinning the contemporary production of urban space. These reactionary movements also correspond to the "culture wars" of the late 20th century, as evidenced by the following discussion of the occupation of Alcatraz.

Cultures of Resistance: From Alcatraz to Oscar Grant Plaza

The 1969 to 1971 occupation of Alcatraz Island by Native Americans represents an important turn in the genealogy of occupying land in California, specifically, a turn from occupation as a settler tactic for appropriating land to a resistance tactic with outcomes related to postcolonial cultural politics. Citing treaties that called for the transfer of decommissioned federal land to tribal authorities, a group of identified as Indians of All Tribes occupied the federal prison on Alcatraz Island in San Francisco Bay following the Department of Justice's decision to close it. This occupation occurred against the backdrop of late 1960s opposition to the Vietnam War, fights for pluralist representation embodied in movements to establish ethnic studies departments at local universities, and broader movements for third-world liberation and national self-determination that questioned euro-centric conceptions of modernity and progress.

As a result of assimilationist policies that relocated Indians from rural areas to urban centers, prominent leaders joining the Alcatraz occupation hailed from as far away as Iroquois Confederacy of the Great Lakes rather than solely local tribal groups such as the Ohlone (Johnson 1996). For many historians the occupation serves as an important marker of the rise of "Red Power," pan-Indian cultural identity, and symbolic politics of representation (Nagel 1997). This approach embraced the broader construct of race rather than specific tribal identity as a source of political mobilization and empowerment. To be sure, the physical occupation of Alcatraz depended on elaborate and sophisticated logistical planning. However, rather than using piles of rocks and shotguns to defend the land by force, these occupations largely relied on press conferences and slogans with support networks reaching across increasingly global public spheres thanks to broadcast TV and radio.

Ultimately, the occupation fragmented. While it failed to achieve the goals of returning the island to Indian authority, it did help spark a movement that ended assimilationist Indian termination policies. When the new left used culture and identity as points of mobilization rather than territorial or material demands, the former could be hollowed out into politically choreographed, symbolic gestures, as in the case of Alcatraz, redesigned as a park-museum by Lawrence Halprin.

The preservation of the Indians of All Tribes militant graffiti by the US National Park Service illustrates the power of aesthetics and the landscape gaze. With San Francisco shifting from a military-industrial economy to financial services and tourism, the market subsumes ostensibly territorial claims, such as "You Are Now on Indian Land," as a historic capital-generating visual asset (Strange and Loo 2001) for a space managed as a public-private partnership. Like the transition from agro-pastoralism to industrial-scale mining and manufacturing, this phenomenon represents an important development in the production and extraction of value from spaces of urbanization that shapes not only practices and politics of squatting and occupying, but also landscape and urban design. To consider how land generates and distributes wealth and power in contemporary urban contexts, we turn to Land Action and the Occupy movement.

Occupy Oakland and Land Action

Rooted in the punk rock culture of the East Bay, Land Action founder Steven DeCaprio became acquainted with squatting while on tour with his band in 1999, performing at squats across Europe, notably La Scintilla in Modena, Italy. By the time DeCaprio returned to the Bay Area he found himself homeless, and after several years navigating the dizzying legal process and an arrest for trespassing, he successfully defended his own residence at an abandoned duplex in Oakland. As DeCaprio legally and structurally secured the occupation, he came to be considered by many an expert on squat law and adverse possession, and his house served as a sort of headquarters and material depot while the nascent group organized with other squatters in the area. Occupy Oakland provided a platform to expand Land Action as a skill-share network, where occupiers would exchange tactical and legal knowledge, contributing their own skills and labor in the many efforts required by occupying buildings left vacant and disintegrating by the racialized economic restructuring described in the opening of this chapter. DeCaprio delivered presentations at Occupy Oakland on occupying buildings with the goal of providing permanent space for activists and organizers of Occupy Oakland.

Through trial and error, Land Action attempted to design a process to systematically deploy adverse possession as a direct action technique. The current process begins with site selection, researching tax-defaulted property auction listings or inquiring with government officials on the legal and financial status of other prospective sites. Once a prospective site is selected, physical and spatial qualities such as presence of buildings or quality of the soil become important indicators for the possible use of the site and the potential for signifying its "improvement," while the location of sewer pipes might dictate the placement of additional structures such as a "water house" with shared kitchen and bathroom. Major impediments to taking action can include intimidation from police or red tape from municipal officials in acquiring building permits. To anticipate these obstructions, structures were constructed with a maximum footprint of 11.15 square meters, spaced 15 meters apart, thus not requiring a building permit in California. An occupation can be evicted at any time, especially in the early stages, so inexpensive and modular designs were adopted that could be easily and cheaply constructed using commonly salvaged or off-the-shelf materials. As Land Action physically secures an occupation they create a paper trail tying themselves to the property by paying back taxes, which will name Land Action on the assessor's tax roll, filing a homestead declaration that recognizes the property as the primary residence of the occupiers, and so on. DeCaprio has found that as this paper trail of innocuous bureaucratic requests snowballs, the occupation becomes more secure as claimants will require lengthier legal proceedings to win evictions and therefore become more willing to negotiate with occupiers.

In many respects, these design tactics—salvaged materials, condensed structures that activate the landscape as a sort of outdoor room—intersect with the "tiny home" or "small house" trend burgeoning in the largely affluent northern reaches of the Bay Area (Anson 2014). Following this typology, the proper design of a small dwelling can serve to activate the landscape as a dwelling space. However, in contrast to the Thoreau-inspired dogma prevalent in the tiny house movement, occupying urban land means working with people, building coalitions and commons, and most importantly, realizing that spatial politics in Oakland cannot be reduced to building codes.

Occupy to Decolonize?

Returning to Occupy Oakland, several accounts of race and racism within the Occupy movement exist (Maharawal 2011, Anglin 2012) and have important implications for understanding the material and cultural aspects of decolonization. Specific to the dynamics of publics and counter-publics of occupation, general assemblies in Oakland, like other western US and Canadian cities, debated proposals to change the name from Occupy Wall Street to Decolonize Wall Street (Brady and Antoine 2012, Barker 2012, Kilibarda 2012). This debate was particularly contentious in Oakland, occurring in the context of the port blockade and mounting police repression. Similarly, debate broke out over the symbolic renaming of the site of the Occupy encampment. Many took to calling the plaza after Oscar Grant, the young black man killed by police earlier that year. For others, however, this new name slighted civil rights advocate Frank Ogawa, Oakland's first Japanese City Council member and survivor of the WWII internment camps for whom the city dedicated the plaza in 1998.

Once evicted from the plaza, a subsequent wave of post-Occupy Oakland squats continued to encounter mutually exclusive assertions of rights rooted in cultural conflicts between publics and counter-publics. Land Action faced difficulty coordinating with occupiers and reciprocating through skill shares, which in part stemmed from the lack of a cohesive structure at many of the occupations. In the worst cases, individuals or groups of individuals would strong arm their way into an occupation, what DeCaprio would call "squatting a squat," ultimately leading to conflicts at numerous squats in Oakland, including the "Hot Mess Squat" which was rendered uninhabitable due to severe fire damage in the spring of 2014. At this point Land Action shifted its focus to vacant lots around Oakland produced by the city's anti-blight campaign that demolished rundown tax-defaulted properties.

Land Action's project of occupying these vacant lots as "urban micro-farms" addressed multiple issues that arose in working with collectives occupying vacant buildings. The urban microfarm project tapped into existing community garden networks, sustainability politics, and slow and local food movements sweeping the country, which already had a strong presence in the Bay Area. Many in Land Action felt gardening made the organization more broadly appealing than squatting vacant buildings, which was associated with Occupy Wall Street, vandalism, riots, and violent clashes with the police. While squatters generally viewed community gardening as volunteerism and therefore unsustainable in the long-term outside of those with disposable time and income, the micro-farming project incorporated housing into the action. Adopting a stewardship-housing model for individuals or small groups of people also bypassed the long-term social difficulties presented by squatted buildings. The idea was that these individuals or smaller collectives would be bound to the land, laboring upon it as required by the adverse possession process, with support from Land Action. Following this model, Land Action even reached an agreement with the city of Oakland where Northern California Community Land Trust would take ownership of the land once occupations were legalized through the adverse possession process. Because of the Land Trust's stewardship mission, adverse possession became a means to de-commodify land through the labor of occupation, returning it to the commons rather than enclosing it as private property as in the days of the frontier.

FIGURE 13.3 West Oakland landscape resulting from decades of racialized disinvestment. This building, the "Hot Mess Squat," was squatted in collaboration with Land Action shortly after Occupy Oakland.

Source: Marcus Owens

However, significant hurdles remained as occupiers turned to green and sustainability politics in their desire to distance themselves from the radical politics and racial divisions of Occupy Oakland. A summer crowd-funding campaign was not as successful as hoped, likely due to the fact that a localized community garden project with no connection to broader political resistance failed to resonate beyond the immediate milieu of Bay Area gardeners and local food advocates. Worse, soliciting donations under the banner of "a garden on every corner" replicated the colonial ideology of "improvement" and risked appearing obtuse to the reality of displacement in the context of extreme gentrification. While an apolitical sustainability approach saved Land Action gardens from displacement by city authorities, it offered little aid to the very real fears of neighbors who may view tiny homes sprouting up on abandoned lots as harbingers of gentrification and react with hostility.

Like the broader Occupy movement, Land Action is not a black-led group of multigenerational Oaklanders but a hodge-podge anarchistic affinity group, with a heterogeneous mix of racial and class backgrounds, but broadly leaning towards queer, punk youth. While DeCaprio emphasizes that many of the group are not white, they are nonetheless often racially labeled as outsiders. This labeling also has political connotations, placing them outside of the West Oakland Black community's long-established social and political hierarchies, cultural norms, and power brokers. These dynamics allowed for power brokers within racial and cultural affinity groups to mobilize against occupations or other challenges to entrepreneurial urban development. The group clashed with Elaine Brown, former leader of the Black Panthers, as well as local clergy and investors looking to cut deals with the city on undeveloped property in West Oakland. In February of 2016, the Alameda County district attorney cracked down on one of Land Action's occupations, charging

FIGURE 13.4 Land Action's "proof of concept" micro-garden squat in West Oakland

Source: Marcus Owens

not only the occupiers but also DeCaprio and another organizational board member with felony, conspiracy, and fraud. DeCaprio and three other group members now face up to 8.5 years in prison. DeCaprio believes these charges to be politically motivated, stemming from his dispute with the California State Bar Association's refusal to grant his law license over issues of "moral character." While these charges are serious, they also present an opportunity to make visible the role of the state in the contemporary crisis of housing and access to land in the Bay Area.

Conclusion

Reflecting on the genealogy of squatting land in California, it is clear that racism and the trauma of colonialism continue to drive urban resistance and contestation over urban space. However, the purpose of this genealogy is not to propose a postcolonial fundamentalism that seeks an essentialist, overdetermined relationship between gentrification and settler colonialism. Rather, it is imperative to understand how past accidents and false appraisals of "the land question" persist in politics while allowing for the design of new actions. Clearly, developments in capitalism transform the stakes, tactics, and modes of spatial production. In the 1960s and 1970s, the new left justly rose up to challenge the Euro-centric assimilationist violence of the nation-state and racial and gendered exclusions of the traditional labor movement, but separated from the materiality of "the land question," they are easily recuperated as symbolic, representational issues or "lifestyle" politics manipulated by the cultural industries.

Similarly, when squatting and urban gardening becomes an end to itself, detached from an overarching framework for connecting individual land actions to the broader dynamics animating contemporary space, little differentiates these occupations from the nouveau City Beautiful "parklets" popping up in front of cafes in gentrifying neighborhoods. As Jeffrey Hou (2012) argues, neither formal public spaces nor symbolic cultural inclusion is sufficient to challenge the commodification of social relations as result of fiscalized spatial planning. Institutionalized

FIGURE 13.5 "Ohlone Land"—graffiti on a freeway overpass in Oakland

Source: Marcus Owens

"greening" or multiculturalism in public space, lacking material and structural demands, will not solve the problem of displacement, and may even accelerate gentrification by increasing the cultural capital of a given place.

In closing, what might it mean to reconsider the "land question" as a practice of decolonization? In a 21st century context, perhaps this may be a means to ground the material outcome of cultural work within the production of contemporary late-capitalist, hyper-branded urban space. Designers and urban planners should think critically about "everyday life" as a broader site of production and how this value circulates within contemporary regimes of urban governance. In doing so, we can aim to generate not merely welcoming or culturally appropriate spaces, but practices that challenge structures of landlordism and settler-colonial regimes of private property. This may lead not only to more vibrant public spaces, a prime goal of planners and designers after the Congrès Internationaux d'Architecture Moderne (CIAM), but also a more equitable society.

Acknowledgements

The authors would like to thank Steven DiCaprio and Land Action, as well as Paul Rabinow, Jeffery Hou, Sabine Knierbein, and the editors for their patience and thoughtful feedback in helping convert this collaboration into writing.

Notes

1. See Phat Beets' video on NOBE, *Neighbors Outing Blatant Exploitation*. Available at: www.youtube.com/watch?v=JneAYdmDGCE [Accessed 26 July 2016].
2. Historians note that this was anything but a clear-cut process, with major Squatter's Riots breaking out in 1850. Upwards of 40% of California land was lost (Hackel 1997), in no small part due to lack of resources to contest land claims in court (McWilliams 1999, Chandler 2003).

References

Anglin, R. V., 2012. Whose Voice: The Limited Participation of People of Color in the Occupy Movement. *In:* R. Shiffman, R. Bell, L.J. Brown, and L. Elizabeth (eds), *Beyond Zuccotti Park: Freedom of Assembly and the Occupation of Public Space.* Oakland: New Village Press, 125–132.

Anson, A., 2014. "The World is My Backyard": Romanticization, Thoreauvian Rhetoric, and Constructive Confrontation in the Tiny House Movement. *In:* W.G. Holt (ed), *From Sustainable to Resilient Cities: Global Concerns and Urban Efforts.* Bingley: Emerald Group Publishing, 289–313.

Bardhan, A., and Walker, R., 2011. California Shrugged: Fountainhead of the Great Recession. *Cambridge Journal of Regions, Economy and Society,* 4 (3), 303–322.

Barker, A. J., 2012. Already Occupied: Indigenous Peoples, Settler Colonialism and the Occupy Movements in North America. *Social Movement Studies* 11(3–4), 327–334.

Benner, C., 2002. *Work in the New Economy: Flexible Labor Markets in Silicon Valley.* 1st edition. Malden, MA: Wiley-Blackwell.

Brady, M. J. and Antoine, D., 2012. Decolonize Wall Street! Situating Indigenous Critiques of the Occupy Wall Street Movement. *American Communication Journal* 14(3), 1–10.

Chandler, R. J., 2003. An Uncertain Influence: The Role of the Federal Government in California, 1846–1880. *California History,* 81 (3/4), 224–271.

Clary, R. H., 1980. *The Making of Golden Gate Park: The Early Years: 1865–1906.* San Francisco, CA: California Living Books.

Culhane, P. and McGreggor Cawley, R., 1994. *Federal Land, Western Anger: The Sagebrush Rebellion and Environmental Politics.* Lawrence: University Press of Kansas.

Dear, M., 2001. *From Chicago to LA: Making Sense of Urban Theory.* Thousand Oaks, CA: SAGE Publications.

Drayton, P. R. and Drayton, R., 2000. *Nature's Government: Science, Imperial Britain, and the "Improvement" of the World.* New Haven: Yale University Press.

Ethington, P. J., 1994. *The Public City: The Political Construction of Urban Life in San Francisco, 1850–1900.* New edition. New York: Cambridge University Press.

Foucault, M., 1980. *Language, Counter-Memory, Practice: Selected Essays and Interviews.* Ithaca, NY: Cornell University Press.

Haas, L., 1995. *Conquests and Historical Identities in California, 1769–1936.* Berkeley: University of California Press.

Hackel, S. W., 1997. Land, Labor, and Production: The Colonial Economy of Spanish and Mexican California. *California History,* 76 (2/3), 111–146.

Hou, J., 2012. Beyond Zuccotti Park: Making the Public [online]. *Places Journal.* Available from: https://placesjournal.org/article/beyond-zuccotti-park-making-the-public/ [Accessed 28 July 2016].

Johnson, T.R., 1996. *The Occupation of Alcatraz Island: Indian Self-determination and the Rise of Indian Activism.* Chicago: University of Illinois Press.

Kilibarda, K., 2012. Lessons from #Occupy in Canada: Contesting Space, Settler Consciousness and Erasures within the 99%. *Journal of Critical Globalisation Studies* 5, 24–41.

Lee, E., 2007. The "Yellow Peril" and Asian Exclusion in the Americas. *Pacific Historical Review,* 76 (4), 537–562.

Maharawal, M., 2011. Standing Up. *In:* T. Astra, ed. *Occupy!: Scenes from Occupied America,* London: Verso Books, 34–40.

McMurray, O. K., 1915. The Beginnings of the Community Property System in California and the Adoption of the Common Law. *California Law Review,* 3(5), 359–380.

McWilliams, C., 1999. *California: The Great Exception.* Berkeley: University of California Press.

Moore, S. A. W., 2003. "We Feel the Want of Protection": The Politics of Law and Race in California, 1848–1878. *California History,* 81 (3/4), 96–125.

Murch, D. J., 2010. *Living for the City: Migration, Education, and the Rise of the Black Panther Party in Oakland, California.* Chapel Hill, NC: UNC Press Books.

Nagel, J., 1997. *American Indian Ethnic Renewal: Red Power and the Resurgence of Identity and Culture.* Oxford: Oxford University Press.

Pisani, D., 1994. Squatter Law in California, 1850–1858. *The Western Historical Quarterly,* 25(3), 277–310.

Pratt, M. L., 2007. *Imperial Eyes: Travel Writing and Transculturation.* London and New York: Routledge.

Rabinow, P., 2014. Minor Vices: Disparagement [online]. *Anthropological Research on the Contemporary*. Available from: http://anthropos-lab.net/bpc/2014/04/minor-vices-disparagement-rabinow [Accessed 31 August 2015].

Rhomberg, C., 2004. *No There There: Race, Class, and Political Community in Oakland*. Berkeley: University of California Press.

Rothman, H., 2004. *The New Urban Park: Golden Gate National Recreation Area and Civic Environmentalism*. Lawrence, KS: University Press of Kansas.

Schafran, A., 2013. Origins of an Urban Crisis: The Restructuring of the San Francisco Bay Area and the Geography of Foreclosure. *International Journal of Urban and Regional Research*, 37 (2), 663–688.

Self, R. O., 2005. *American Babylon: Race and the Struggle for Postwar Oakland*. Princeton, NJ: Princeton University Press.

Sevilla-Buitrago, A., 2013. Urbs in Rure: Historical Enclosure and the Extended Urbanization of the Countryside. *In*: N. Brenner, ed. *Implosions/Explosions: Towards a Study of Planetary Urbanization*. Berlin: Jovis, 236–259.

Shelton, T. V., 2013. *A Squatter's Republic: Land and the Politics of Monopoly in California 1850–1900*. Berkeley: University of California Press.

Smith, N., 1996. *The New Urban Frontier: Gentrification and the Revanchist City*. London and New York: Routledge.

Strange, C. and Loo, T., 2001. Holding the Rock: The "Indianization" of Alcatraz Island, 1969–1999. *The Public Historian*, 23 (1), 55–74.

Walker, R., 2009. *The Country in the City: The Greening of the San Francisco Bay Area*. Seattle: University of Washington Press.

Walker, R. and Schafran, A., 2015. The Strange Case of the Bay Area. *Environment and Planning A*, 47 (1), 10–29.

Young, T., 2004. *Building San Francisco's Parks, 1850–1930*. Baltimore: JHU Press.

PART 4

Contesting

Against Backlashes, Criminalization,
Co-optation, and Anti-Pluralism

14

OPERATION 1DMX AND THE MEXICO CITY COMMUNE

The Right to the City Beyond the Rule of Law in Public Spaces

Silvano De la Llata

> When injustice becomes law, resistance becomes duty.
>
> *—Thomas Jefferson*

#1DMX:[1] December 1, 2012, Mexico City, date and time of a call for action. President Enrique Peña Nieto is to be inaugurated by the Congress in the Palacio de San Lazaro. This day represents the return to power for the authoritarian Institutional Revolutionary Party (PRI), which ruled Mexico with an iron hand for more than seven decades, signaling a moment where power is reproduced, ritualized, and transferred. But, as power is delivered and received, it risks being lost, recaptured, and reappropriated. For over one week, the Congress complex was fenced off from the rest of the city with 9-foot-tall solid-steel plates within which 1,200 riot policemen waited, armed with clubs, plastic shields, tear-gas launchers, and rubber-bullet rifles. The surroundings were heavily policed, too. People going to schools, stores, office buildings, and their own houses within the perimeter of the blockade were stopped and identified by the police. One subway station and three bus stations were closed, and streets and public spaces in a one-kilometer radius were blocked from pedestrian and vehicular circulation (Figures 14.1 and 14.2). Beyond this perimeter a multitude of thousands were ready to break into San Lazaro and protest against—and potentially stop—a presidential inauguration based on an election considered to be undemocratic and fraudulent.

The protest turned into a riot that spread across the city and resulted in 100 (mostly random) arrests, 20 people wounded, one person in a coma, and several cases of alleged torture. The repression was largely justified via a law against purported "attacks on public peace." The 1DMX was the beginning of the criminalization of protest and public assembly amidst a wave of police repression, infiltration, co-optation, and disruption of public demonstrations; but it was also a seminal moment for the constitution of a social movement challenging this repression by linking university students' assemblies, neighborhood associations, human rights organizations, indigenous activists, as well as teachers, workers, and trade unions—an articulation of insurgent publics without precedent since 1968 in Mexico. The energy of the protest and the level of repression reveal both an oppressive yet potentially emancipatory moment.

The 1DMX is illustrative of the tensions between legitimacy and legality that were present in most of the uprisings and protests in 2011 and 2012. These kinds of movements have been described as *movements of movements* (Mertes 2004), *non-movements* (Bayat 2010), and *social mobilizations* (Rebelaos.net 2012), rather than social movements. During this period, I undertook participant fieldwork in the Occupy Wall Street movement in New York City and the Indignados

FIGURE 14.1 Protestors run away from the blockade of San Lazaro as the riot police shoot tear gas. Mexico City, Mexico, December 1, 2012

Source: Pedro Anza/Cuartoscuro

FIGURE 14.2 A truck rams into the metal plates fencing San Lazaro (the Congress). Mexico City, Mexico, December 1, 2012

Source: Guillermo Perea/Cuartoscuro

Movement in Barcelona, and was also able to interview activists in Paris and Mexico City. In general assemblies I participated in—online and offline—there was a sense of global solidarity, especially in regard to struggles to defend human rights. There was a generalized feeling that human rights were systematically violated in different ways. For example, the privatization of the public sector was seen as violating the right of access to basic services. The destruction of the environment and the privatization of natural resources were perceived as violating the right to have access to common goods. Generalized corruption was perceived as violating the right to be properly represented by the government. The criminalization of protest is perceived as violation of the right to free assembly. Thus, a significant sector of the population perceived that when basic rights are at stake, violating of the law via acts of urban resistance is justified. Conversely, governments saw themselves as entitled to the use of force—even when this represents the violation of people's rights—to maintain a general order. In short, one side justifies the violation of law to defend human rights; the other justifies the violation of human rights to defend law and order.

The 1DMX constitutes part of a paradigm shift in activism in the last 20 years, and similar uprisings around the world (i.e. Occupy Wall Street, the Indignados). They used direct action and direct democracy as a means of expression and communication, both on site and through the Internet. The target of the protests and the selection of the sites and moments also reflect a key change. By targeting sources of money and power, protests pinpoint temporal and spatial nodes where transactions happen. In the logic of financial capitalism, in which not only accumulation but also flows and transactions become the source of money and power, protests target the temporal and spatial nodes in which this happens. Historically, protest focused on sites in which power *resided*; today it targets sites in which it *transfers*. The 1DMX cleverly targeted not only the place of power transference but also the very moment when it happened.

This chapter explores the potential of public space as catalytic of extreme and controversial manifestations of the right to the city: the right of resistance to oppression. More specifically, it examines tensions between the right to the city and the rule of law in public spaces, i.e. between the state's justification of the use of force and violation of human rights in defense of public space, and an insurgent citizenship calling for the exceptional right of breaking the law to defend human rights and democracy in public space. The 1DMX is key to understanding how cycles of repression operated in the ongoing criminalization of protest in public space in the aftermath of 2011 and how, or if, this tendency can be reversed by civil society.

In the next section, I analyze the right to the city by examining the right of resistance to oppression and what this means in an era of nonviolent insurgencies that use public space to highlight political struggle and democratic assembly. Here, I explore the notion of *destituent power* as an alternative to transcend the legitimacy-legality tension. Later, I provide a brief description of how protest and repression operate in the Mexican political system, and make a detailed account of the events of presidential inauguration in Mexico City to illustrate different forms of tension between the right to the city and the rule of law. I describe three scenarios: (1) the right to the city (beyond the rule of law), (2) the rule of law (beyond human rights), and (3) the use of the law (against human rights). In the last section, I describe that, even though there are challenges to face with the ongoing criminalization of protest, there is also opportunity to overcome these processes through thinking of protest as a creative—but nevertheless transgressive—process, and of resistance as the exercise of destituent power and insurgent articulation.

The Right to the City as Resistance to Oppression

The Mexican Constitution describes that, "national sovereignty resides essentially and originally in the people. All public power originates in the people and is instituted for their benefit. The people at all times have the inalienable right to alter or modify their form of government"

(Constitution of Mexico, Art. 39, 2015).[2] The call to depose an authoritarian, but nominally democratic, government on the 1st of December implicitly echoes Article 39. This right, based on the notion of the "right of resistance to oppression," is not unique to Mexico's Constitution, as many other countries have constitutions that mention the right of rebellion or resistance to oppression. The Universal Declaration of Human Rights (1948) also mentions the right of "rebellion against tyranny and oppression [as] [. . .] human rights [that] should be protected by the rule of law." However, the first time this right was explicitly cited was in *The Declaration of the Rights of Man and the Citizen* (1793), redacted as a result of the French Revolution: "When the government violates the rights of the people, insurrection is for the people, and for every portion thereof, the most sacred of rights and the most indispensable of duties."

The right to resistance of oppression is in fact a modern concept originating in the Enlightenment. Thinkers such as Locke, Jefferson, and Lafayette propounded that rights are inherent to human nature and are therefore inalienable. At the time, the right to resist and alter the government was thought of as the right to bear arms to overthrow an oppressive regime. However, the nonviolent struggles of the 20th century that were successful in overthrowing or reforming oppressive regimes (e.g. the Indian Independence Movement, the Civil Rights Movement, the Anti-Apartheid Movement) have changed perspectives about the means to transform society. In recent peaceful uprisings, such as the Argentinazo in 2001 and the Arab Spring, the occupation of urban space through blockades, pickets, protest actions, or democratic assemblies aimed at altering governments have demonstrated that the right to the city is inherently linked to the right of resistance of oppression.

The concept of the *right to the city* has been explored from different perspectives (Purcell 2002, Mitchell 2003, Harvey 2008, Blomley 2008, Kafui 2011) since Lefebvre's influential essay was published in the context of 1968. The right to the city is not only the right to change the city, but also the right to transform and alter social relations (when they are oppressive) through the democratic reappropriation of urban space. This way of exercising the right to the city creates tension: occupying urban space (even illegally) as the means for political transformation is perceived as legitimate by a sector of the population, while the government defends itself by violating human rights.

The legitimacy/legality tensions of the 1DMX link the concept of the right to the city with four key notions about the politics of public space. Firstly, it alludes to Rancière's (2010) descriptions of *politics, the political*, and *the police*. *Politics* is the arena in which two antagonistic concepts play out: *the police*, which structures everything in its "right" place and sets what is allowed and what is not, and where, and how, and *the political*, which are the processes of emancipation and dissent. The police order technically operates *within* the legal framework, while the political operates *beyond* it. This tension also echoes Negri's (1999) notions of *constituent* and *constituted power*. Departing from Marx's idea that capital is dead labor Hardt (1999), commenting on Negri's concepts, describes that the purpose of The State is to contain the fluid character of democracy and revolution: The State is dead democracy. *Constituent power* is democratic, deliberative, and revolutionary processes in flow; *constituted power* is consolidated power in the form of The State and government institutions. They exist in a dialectic. Thirdly, it reminds of Abensour's (2011) notion of "democracy against The State" as there were insurgent publics using direct democracy and direct action to transform the government. Finally, it is crucial to analyze the notion of *destituent power*[3] (Agamben 2014, De la Llata 2014, 2016) which arose directly from conversations in the protest encampments of 2011 and 2012. Inevitably framed in Negri's explorations, we can think of destituent power as a political force that moves in the opposite direction of constituent and constituted power. It seeks to disperse—and in the process recapture rather than consolidate power. The 1DMX protest can be understood as an expression of destituent power, as it sought to contest, and potentially, depose the state's power.

Context: Resisting the "Perfect Dictatorship"

The Mexican political system is a complex one. For the most part of the rule under the PRI, dissent has been treated with a combination of repression and co-optation. Mario Vargas Llosa (1990) did not call it the "perfect dictatorship" for nothing. The Mexican system "is a camouflaged dictatorship," and the PRI

> is an immovable party, which allows enough space for criticism to the extent that it is useful to it (because that confirms that it is a "democratic" party), but suppresses by all means— even the worst ones—criticism that puts its permanence at risk [. . .] So much it [Mexico] is a dictatorship that all the other Latin American dictatorships have tried to create something similar to the PRI in their own countries.
>
> *(Vargas Llosa 1990, 1:37–3:07)*

In this simulated democracy, the transference of power is really the moment and way in which the regime perpetuates. The government often tries to domesticate dissent and strip its revolutionary potential.

Since the past 20 years, demonstrations have been frequent and massive in Mexico—by 1996, for example, there were on average more than ten demonstrations a day (Irazábal 2008). However, repression is not as explicit as it was in the 1960s and 1970s. While there is obvious repression in the form of physical coercion, there is also repression through the infiltration and disruption of demonstrations by secret government agents. Furthermore, there are random arrests and blithe guilt by association in demonstrations and protesters. The objective is to make an example and discourage people from protesting or even approaching protests. Torture and forced confessions are common tactics. Amnesty International warned that torture is "out of control" and is "tolerated by authorities" (Amnesty International 2014). Lastly, the press usually misrepresents protesters as criminals. All this is made easier thanks to one of the most infamous legal principles in Mexican law: guilty until proven otherwise.

Operation 1DMX and the YoSoy132 Movement

Operation 1DMX—as it was called in social media—was chiefly planned by the YoSoy132 Movement. This was a massive and self-declared, nonviolent student movement that included most of the largest universities in Mexico. The movement demanded radical reforms, such as changes in neoliberal economic policies; a transformation in scientific, education, and technology policies; a revision of the security strategies related to the highly militarized war on drugs; the end of criminalization of protest; and, most uniquely, the democratization of the media—largely accused of "manufacturing" and "imposing" Peña Nieto (especially Televisa). Televisa has been historically perceived as not just uncritical, but also an ally of the government.[4] In Mexico, although there is technically free press, a de facto censorship exists through underrepresentation of dissident voices, overrepresentation of the government's achievements, and threats and punishments from corrupt politicians and organized crime.

The origin of the name YoSoy132 implicitly addresses the issue of legitimacy. After Peña Nieto's disastrous campaign visit to the Universidad Iberoamericana ended with protests against police brutality during his tenure as state governor, Televisa portrayed the protesters as "a small group of agitators," and Peña Nieto himself said, "Those kind of expressions were not legitimate." The next day, 131 students posted a video online showing their university IDs to prove they were in fact students, and therefore legitimate activists. The following days, students across the country showed solidarity by saying they would join the cause, hence the name YoSoy132 (I Am the 132nd).

Similar to the Occupy and Indignados Movements, YoSoy132 adopted direct action, direct democracy, and leaderless organization, and made broad use of the Internet as an organizational platform. Some outstanding actions of YoSoy132 included the creation of observer's brigades, which recorded and published the election's irregularities, and the organization of the first independent, online presidential debate in Mexican history (which Peña Nieto did not attend).

Mexico Has No President: Destituent Power and the Right to the City (Beyond the Rule of Law)

The 1DMX protest was announced a month before the presidential inauguration after a long debate in a general assembly in Atenco. Throughout the presidential campaign, YoSoy132 shifted from being only a student movement to becoming a social mobilization. In several online inter-university assemblies that I participated in, one of the central topics of discussion (which I personally raised in online forums) was that of articulation. After five months of discussions, the movement loosely articulated (or acted in solidarity) with unions, peasant organizations such as San Salvador's Atenco activists and the Zapatistas, and dissident sections of teachers' and electrician's unions, among others.

The movement called for the occupation of San Lazaro based on the idea that the elected president—and the regime in general—was illegitimate and, therefore, called for his deposition. This was manifest in one of the most widely re-tweeted hashtags in the days previous to the inauguration: #MexicoNoTienePresidente (#MexicoHasNoPresident). The protest was in the spirit of resistance against oppression. It implicitly claimed a right to the city beyond the rule of law. The movement concluded that,

> the electoral process was corrupted in its origins, and institutions were deliberately incapable of preventing and sanctioning the countless anomalies. Therefore, we [the #YoSoy132 Movement] state that the elections showed enough irregularities as to assert that it was not a democratic election [. . .] The #YoSoy132 Movement declares itself against the processes of imposition that brought candidate Enrique Peña Nieto to the Presidency of the Republic [. . .] [So] It is not accepted, and it will not be.
>
> *(#YoSoy132 General Assembly Minute 2012)*

The sealing of the inauguration was interpreted as the return of a corrupt and authoritarian regime that violates the rights to life, free press, free passage, and public assembly. The "Occupation of San Lazaro" would include artistic activities, the reading of a manifesto (CNN Mexico 2012), and a national political strike (Redacción Aristegui Noticias 2012c). The event sought to be the last demonstration of indignation against the election process, Peña Nieto, Televisa, and the regime in general. It was quickly endorsed by other dissident groups across Mexico City and the country.

There were four broad sectors that participated in the 1DMX (Rea and Martinez 2013): (1) The Frente Oriente, a self-described communist organization with a proletarian perspective based on neighborhood and popular assemblies; (2) the Acampada Revolucion (Encampment Revolution), which, similar to the Zuccotti Park, Plaza del Sol, and Tahrir Square encampments, occupied the esplanade of the Monument to the Mexican Revolution; (3) the (self-declared) Anarchists, which were composed of many organizations, who justified the use of direct action and black-block tactics to protect protestors from the riot police; and (4) the largest sector of all, the civil society, consisting of loose articulation of the participants of the YoSoy132 Movement and a wide variety of dissidents, unionists, and citizens.

The Sealing of San Lazaro: The Rule of Law
(Beyond Human Rights)

Peña Nieto was officially declared the winner of the election even when more than a thousand irregularities were documented (including the alleged distribution of money cards and groceries packages to buy votes, among others) (Redacción Sin Embargo 2012). The Presidential Guard, in collaboration with Mexico City's Secretary of Public Safety, announced the "sealing" of San Lazaro (the Congress) from November 25 to December 2 (Redacción Aristegui Noticias 2012a) based on the legality of the election, regardless of the irregularities. The police described these measures as "preventive," but many regarded them as excessive and denounced not only the alleged fraudulent elections and irresponsible media coverage, but also the evident police-state-like management of public space.

The protest began at 7:30 a.m. and mainly targeted two places: the Plaza de la Constitución (better known as the Zocalo), where the National Palace is, and San Lazaro. The former is the seat of power, and the latter is where power transfers—and actually resides. The demonstration began with a march towards the Congress blockade. As soon as the first column arrived, they were received with rubber bullets, water cannons, and tear gas. About half an hour later, Juan Francisco Kuykendall, a director, playwright, and activist, was hit by a tear gas can in the head and fell into a coma; he died a year later. As the clashes intensified, the march briefly stopped to read a manifesto and detoured towards the Zocalo (Mas de 131 2012). The march was generally peaceful and included music, chants, and theatrical performances. However, one of the protest contingents decided to continue marching towards the fence. As the police shot rubber bullets, they threw rocks and Molotov cocktails. A small group took a seven-ton dump truck and rammed it against the metal plates. They continued engaging in confrontation with the police using black-block and urban-guerrilla tactics (see Figure 14.3).

These kinds of groups were difficult to identify and according to the rest of the protesters they represented a fifth group: the *infiltrated*. In videos distributed by activists and people passing by, they appear on the police's side of the fence, being let in and out freely. This was broadly documented in the nonmainstream and social media (Redacción Aristegui Noticias 2012b). Allegedly, they constituted what is infamously known in Mexico as *hawks*, or people who infiltrate protests and attack the police to provoke repression of protesters. One of the tactics used by YoSoy132 against the hawks was to call people to sit whenever violent acts arose, in order to spot potential hawks. However, it was often confusing to identify if the actions towards the police were actually direct action or violence coming from hawks. There was also a significant group of independent protesters and passersby who spontaneously joined the riots and clashes with the police. There was a sentiment of legitimacy in the face of the violation of rights, and therefore people largely felt the breaking of the police blockade was justified in that context. On the other hand, the evident sentiment of the police was that, as the protests turned into riots, the rights of people should be violated in order to protect the state.

The human rights situation of the 1DMX was widely covered in social media and by human rights organizations. Mexico City's Human Rights Commission (CDHDF 2012) reported that there were random arrests, beatings, humiliations, and torture. According to them there were 88 arrests, of which 70 were detained. YoSoy132 published a list of 106 arrestees (Bolaños 2012). The CDHDF reported that people doing shopping, taking pictures and video, or just passing by were arrested, beaten, and transported in trucks. Most of these arrests were carried out by policemen in

FIGURE 14.3 Protestors (or perhaps infiltrators) took a dump truck and rammed it against the metal plates blockading the Congress

Source: Eneas de Troya

civilian clothes who "encapsulated" the protesters and later beat them (CDHDF 2012). In Mexico City, this practice became widely used and sometimes included the beating of the protesters with clubs, anti-riot shields, and trooper boots. There were also at least four documented cases of torture, in which the detainees reported having been either beaten in the head and eyes, spit at, sexually molested, and/or electrocuted. The Commission reported that the rights of freedom and personal safety, of personal integrity, and of not being tortured were violated in the context of the 1DMX (CDHDF 2012).

These violations suggest that the police were not protecting the law per se, but a third entity: the official version of order in everyday urban life. The government broke the law because they did not perceive it as an instrument to protect people's rights, but rather to protect power. This leads to the third form of legitimacy-legality tension: the use—and abuse—of the law, regardless of human rights.

The Backlash: The Use of Law (Against Human Rights)

The aftermath of the 1DMX revealed not only an explicit violation of human rights via the violation of the law, but also a restructuring and use of the existing legislation to enable repression (Figure 14.4). One week after the wave of arrests of the 1DMX all but 14 detainees were set free. The "1DMX's 14" were charged with controversial charges of "terrorism" and "attacks on public peace." Mexico City's Civil Code describes that, "penalties of 5–30 years of prison and suspension of political rights for up to 10 years will be imposed on those who [. . .] disturb public peace or undermine the authority of the Government of the Federal District" (Codigo Civil del DF, Art.

FIGURE 14.4 Protestor waves a Mexican flag with black ribbons in front of the blockade of San Lazaro after the protests of the 1DMX

Source: Eneas de Troya

362, in Redacción Animal Político 2012a). Based on this law the detainees faced long sentences for their participation in the 1DMX. According to civil and human rights organizations, none of those engaged in street combat were arrested, only people who were protesting peacefully. Nevertheless, the city government embarked on an intense media campaign against those whom they indistinctly called "anarchists." As response to that, a strong social media campaign not only pushed for the liberation of the 14 but also brought to the table discussion about the illegitimacy of the law on "attacks on public peace." The pressure from social media eventually played a role in the liberation of the detainees three weeks after and pushed the government to reform the law, reducing penalties to 2 to 7 years (instead of 5 to 30 years) (Redacción Animal Político 2012b). Nevertheless, a debate about how to regulate protests in general began in the city congress. The discussion focused on criminalizing protest and public assembly.

One year later, when a protest to commemorate the 1DMX's anniversary resulted in clashes with the police, Mexico City's Legislative Assembly approved a law that became informally known as the "Anti-Protest Law." Economic sanctions may be imposed on those who violate the law, and authorities were allowed to dissolve protests if they interfere with traffic (Sotomayor Chávez 2013). The law and *the police*—as referred to by Rancière—structure a spatial order by saying when, where, and how to protest. Anything outside this order is considered disorder and any voices coming from "disorder" are considered noises (Dikeç 2005). The anti-protest laws and the presumption of guilt are legal instruments that give the regime room to repress, disband, and discourage public protest. Therefore, legality is expanded in order to prevent social organization and change, rather than to protect rights. Conversely, resistance also moves across—and beyond—the legal spectrum, as it becomes clear that there is a "sense" of right (both in the sense of *what is correct* and in the sense of *human rights*) based on the respect for human life and freedom that transcends the official order.

The backlash to the social movements of 2011 and 2012 came in many forms across the world, and it was not unique to Mexico. Evidence of "encapsulation" tactics suggests that police forces learn from each other to control public space. In Spain, there were laws that were approved to prevent citizens from video-recording policemen and to impose strong economic sanctions to protesters without trial. Anti-protest laws were also approved in Egypt and North African countries after the Arab Spring (Nachawati 2013). Similar laws were also approved in Greece, Quebec, the United Kingdom, and the United States (Seymor 2013) in direct response to the protests of 2011 and 2012. In New York City, the rules of privately owned public spaces (such as Zuccotti Park) were changed to ensure the "use and enjoyment by the general public in passive recreation." However, while this global backlash exposes de facto powers and power dynamics, it also invites creative ways to resist oppression.

Conclusion: Destituent Power and Creative Resistance

The tension between the right to the city and the rule of law reveals the paradox of any modern state aspiring to be democratic: a government's legitimacy is only attained to the extent that it is revocable. Identifying how repression (and oppression) operates and how it can be contested is key to transcend this paradox. For the purpose of this chapter, we can identify three steps in a cycle of repression that are illustrative of the post-2011 and 2012 backlash: (1) The government approves a series of laws and policies that are perceived as the legalization of violations of human rights; (2) an insurgent public perceives such laws as illegitimate, and therefore acknowledges the right to resist oppression, and if necessary break the law; and (3) the state, rather than reforming, expands the repressive scope of the law by criminalizing public assembly. In this cycle, public space is key, as it is the realm for potential social change through nonviolent organization and articulation, and also the site in which the state exercises the power to control what is allowed, where, and what is not allowed. This, however, does not mean that power in public space only moves in one direction. The relationship between legitimacy and legality is unstable and the right to the city is one in a constant redefinition. The third stage of this cycle makes oppression visible. Revealing this condition is perhaps the first step towards emancipation. This exposure is what pushed the government to release political prisoners and what forced them to reduce the penalties on the issue of "attacks on public peace." This exposure was only possible because of shared articulation between different sectors of society.

1DMX provides lessons about our understanding of the right to the city and public space. First, it reveals that the legal status of the right to the city is plastic. Laws can either protect human rights (i.e., legal and legitimate) or legalize the violation of rights (i.e., legal and illegitimate). The right to the city situates in the realm of legitimacy regardless of its legal status: *the right to the city is potentially a destituent power.* Second, it shows that social movements have to protect themselves by both making sure that the existing laws that *do* protect human rights are enforced, and by pushing the government to derogate laws that prevent public assembly. Third, and most importantly, the 1DMX teaches us that protest cannot be constrained by what is legal and what is not. It has to be creative to operate beyond the law *and* remain nonviolent. Transgressiveness is needed to resist oppression. But transgression does not necessarily mean violence.

Creativity and articulation are conditional to resistance, and are the most important challenge and opportunity to exercise the right to the city. As Stephen Hessel (2010) points out, "to create is to resist, to resist is to create." This creativity was evident in two arenas in the 1DMX as protesters identified the place and moment of power transference and as they made themselves ungraspable to power. These two aspects are the result of the fact that power no longer only *resides* and is kept in space, but instead *flows* and creates a network. As such, it is permeable—and vulnerable. Resistance may potentially operate like that as well.

The 1DMX was potentially emancipatory as it situated itself in a moment in which power can be potentially recaptured, but as power acknowledges this potential, it seeks to cancel it. Power is forced to "seal" these moments and therefore falls into a contradiction. Destituent power ultimately exposes this contradiction and by doing so strips the state from its legitimacy. Creative, nonviolent actions are key to put legitimacy on the side of resistance so the only thing they are left with is the use—and abuse—of the law. Exposing power is the first step towards emancipation. The 1DMX could be considered a first iteration of the Mexico City Commune. Its future iterations can be staged and sustained by articulating a creative resistance and solidarity across society. This is the true challenge for an effective destituent power that resists oppression.

Notes

1. #1DMX refers to the date of the event planned for the 1st of December in Mexico City. This Twitter format (#DayMonthPlace) was probably adopted from the Indignados Movement (also known as #15M) in Spain, which used it in most calls for action.
2. All original Spanish texts translated to English by the author.
3. The term *destituent* does not exist in English, as it comes from Latin *destituens*: "abandoning"—*destituente* (It.), *destituyente* (Sp.), *destituent* (Cat.), and *destituant* (Fr.). As a verb, the closest translations would be to depose, to overthrow, or to cease from power.
4. The founder of Televisa once described himself as "a soldier of the PRI." The network explicitly glorified Peña Nieto during his presidential campaign, and a year after he was elected his government condoned 90% of Televisa's owed taxes, which totaled almost one quarter of billion dollars (Redacción Aristegui 2013).

References

#YoSoy132, 2012. #YoSoy132 General Assembly Minute [online]. July 14, San Salvador Atenco, Mexico. Available from: www.lahaine.org/convencion-nacional-contra-la-imposicion [Accessed 1 August 2015].

Abensour, M., Blechman, M., and Breaugh, M., 2011. *Democracy Against the State: Marx and the Machiavellian Moment.* Cambridge: Polity Press.

Agamben, G., 2014. What Is Destituent Power? *Environment and Planning D: Society and Space*, 32, 65–74.

Amnesty International, 2014. *Torture and Other Ill-Treatment in Mexico.* London: Amnesty International.

Bayat, A., 2013. *Life as Politics: How Ordinary People Change the Middle East.* Stanford: Stanford University Press.

Blomley, N., 2008. Making Space for Law. *In*: K. Cox, M. Low, and J. Robinson, eds. *Handbook of Political Geography.* London: SAGE, 155–168.

Bolaños, C., 2012. #YoSoy132 presenta lista de 106 detenidos [online]. *El Universal*, December 1, 2012. Available from: http://archivo.eluniversal.com.mx/notas/887244.html [Accessed 10 July 2015].

CNN Mexico, 2012. #YoSoy132 anuncia marchas contra la toma de posesión de Peña Nieto [online]. *CNN Mexico*, November 28, 2012. Available from: http://mexico.cnn.com/nacional/2012/11/28/yosoy132-anuncia-marchas-contra-la-toma-de-posesion-de-pena-nieto [Accessed 12 August 2015].

Comisión de Derechos Humanos del Distrito Federal (CDHDF), 2012. Informe Preeliminar de la Investigación Relacionada con las Detenciones del 1o [online]. Full report published in *Animal Político*, 2012. Available from: www.animalpolitico.com/2012/12/hubo-tortura-y-detenciones-arbitrarias-contra-manifestantes-cdhdf/#axzz2Eky3zyir [Accessed 1 August 2015].

Constitution of Mexico. Available from: www.oas.org/juridico/mla/en/mex/en_mex-int-text-const.pdf [Accessed 15 August 2015].

The Declaration of the Rights of Man and Citizen. Available from: www.columbia.edu/~iw6/docs/dec1793.html [Accessed 1 August 2015].

De la Llata, S., 2014. Spaces of Becoming: Destituent Power and the Protest Encampments. Paper presented at the Conference of the Association of American Geographers (AAG), Tampa, FL.

De la Llata, S., 2017. *Becoming others: Refusal, Destituent Power and Creative Resistance (Three radical ideas from the protest encampments of 2011–12)*, Manuscript submitted for publication (copy on file with author).

Dikeç, M., 2005. Space, Politics, and the Political. *Environment and Planning D: Society and Space*, 23 (2), 171–188.

Hardt, M., 1999. Foreword: Three Keys to Understanding Constituent Power. *In*: A. Negri (ed), *Insurgencies: Constituent Power and the Modern State.* Minneapolis: University of Minnesota Press, vii–xii.

Harvey, D., 2008. The Right to the City. *New Left Review*, 53.

Hessel, S., 2010. *Indignez-Vous.* Montpellier, France: Indigène.

Irazábal, C., 2008. *Ordinary Places, Extraordinary Events: Citizenship, Democracy and Public Space in Latin America.* London: Routledge.

Kafui, A., 2011. What Kind of Right Is the Right to the City? *Progress in Human Geography*, 35 (5), 669–685.

Mas de 131, 2012. *Operación #1Dmx (San Lázaro y Centro Histórico DF)* (documentary) [online]. December 6, 2012. Available from: www.youtube.com/watch?v=HY5AeTkBrHk [Accessed 9 August 2015].

Mertes, T. and Bello, W.F., 2004. *A Movement of Movements: Is Another World Really Possible?* London: Verso.

Mitchell, D., 2003. *The Right to the City: Social Justice and the Fight for Public Space.* New York: Guilford.

Nachawati, L., 2013. El Año de las Leyes Antiprotesta [online]. *ElDiario.es*, December 16, 2013. Available from: www.eldiario.es/desalambre/leyes-anti-protesta-Espana-Mexico-Bahrein-Egipto-Reino_Unido-Quebec-represion-protestas_0_206829322.html [Accessed 26 July 2016].

Negri, A., 1999. *Insurgencies: Constituent Power and the Modern State.* Minneapolis: University of Minnesota Press.

Purcell, M., 2002. Excavating Lefebvre: The Right to the City and Its Urban Politics of the Inhabitant. *GeoJournal*, 58, 99–108.

Rancière, J. and Corcoran, S., 2010. *Dissensus: On Politics and Aesthetics.* London: Continuum.

Rea, D. and Martinez, P., 2013. ¿Quienes protestaron en el 1Dmx y por qué? (Primera y Segunda Parte) [online]. *Animal Político*, November 25–26. Available from: www.animalpolitico.com/2013/11/un-ano-del-1dmx-quienes-protestaron-y-por-que-primera-parte and www.animalpolitico.com/2013/11/quienes-protestaron-el-1dmx-y-por-que-segunda-parte [Accessed 3 July 2015].

Rebelaos.net., 2012. Rebelaos! y germinemos la semilla de la revolución integral [online]. Available from: http://rebelaos.net/fitxers/rebelaos-cat.pdf [Accessed 11 March 2017].

Redacción Animal Político, 2012a. Publica GDF reforma sobre "ataques a la paz" [online]. *Animal Político*, December 27, 2012. Available from: www.animalpolitico.com/2012/12/publica-gdf-reforma-sobre-ataques-a-la-paz-entra-en-vigor-hoy/ [Accessed 3 July 2015].

Redacción Animal Político, 2012b. #YoSoy132 convoca marcha contra el delito de "ataques a la paz pública" [online]. *Animal Político*, December 12, 2012. Available from: www.animalpolitico.com/2012/12/yosoy132-convoca-a-marcha-contra-el-delito-de-ataques-a-la-paz-publica/ [Accessed 3 July 2015].

Redacción Aristegui Noticias, 2012a. Blindan San Lázaro, como en 2006, por "asunción" de EPN [online]. *Aristegui Noticias*, November 25. Available from: http://aristeguinoticias.com/2511/mexico/blindan-san-lazaro-como-en-2006-por-asuncion-de-epn/ [Accessed 3 July 2015].

Redacción Aristegui Noticias, 2012b. Denuncias ciudadanas por los disturbios del 1 de diciembre 2012 [online]. *Aristegui Noticias*, December 4, 2012. Available from: http://aristeguinoticias.com/0412/mexico/denuncias-ciudadanas-por-los-disturbios-del-1-de-diciembre-2012/ [Accessed 20 July 2015].

Redacción Aristegui Noticias, 2012c. Advierte #YoSoy132 manifestaciones en toma de protesta de EPN [online]. *Aristegui Noticias*, 4 December 2012. Available from: http://m.aristeguinoticias.com/0411/mexico/advierte-yosoy132-manifestaciones-en-toma-de-protesta-de-epn/ [Accessed 8 March 2017].

Redacción Aristegui Noticias, 2013. Condona Hacienda 2.9 mil millones de pesos a Televisa [online]. *Aristegui Noticias*, May 11. Available from: http://aristeguinoticias.com/1105/mexico/condona-hacienda-2–9-mil-millones-de-pesos-a-televisa/ [Accessed 3 July 2015].

Redacción Sin Embargo, 2012. #YoSoy132 documenta mas de mil irregularidades en la elección presidencial; presenta informe [online]. *SinEmbargo.mx*, July 5. Available from: www.sinembargo.mx/05-07-2012/287507 [Accessed 20 July 2015].

Seymor, R., 2013. From Quebec to Spain Anti-Protest Laws Are Threatening True Democracy [online]. *The Guardian*, November 25, 2013. Available from: www.theguardian.com/commentisfree/2013/nov/25/quebec-spain-anti-protest-laws-democracy [Accessed 1 August 2015].

Sotomayor Chávez, J. F., 2013. Proyecto de Ley del Grupo Parlamentario del Partido Acción Nacional de Manifestaciones Públicas del Distrito Federal [online]. Available from: http://sil.gobernacion.gob.mx/Archivos/Documentos/2013/10/asun_3013511_20131003_1380814630.pdf [Accessed 20 August 2015].

Universal Declaration of Human Rights, 1948. Available from: www.un.org/en/documents/udhr/ [Accessed 10 August 2015].

Vargas Llosa, M., 1990. Participación de Mario Vargas Llosa en el "Encuentro Vuelta," organizado por Octavio Paz y moderado por Enrique Krauze el 30 de agosto de 1990. Available from: https://www.youtube.com/watch?v=kPsVVWg-E38, 1:36–3:07 [Accessed 8 March 2017].

15

PUBLIC SPACE IN A PARALLEL UNIVERSE

Conflict, Coexistence, and Co-optation Between Alternative Urbanisms and the Neoliberalizing City

Elina Kränzle

On May 15, 2011, Puerta del Sol in Madrid became the center of the Indignados' protest against austerity, which had palpable effects on Spanish society and everyday life. Facing foreclosures, cuts in welfare spending, and the intensified privatization of public goods, and thus of public spaces, activists occupied the most physically and culturally central square in the capital, Puerta del Sol, to demand "Democracia Real YA!" (Real Democracy Now!). The square was transformed into a camp for weeks where protesters expressed their discontent with the political and economic model which had brought about the crisis and tested alternative models of self-governance (Walliser 2013, p. 329). The image of a cross-section of the Spanish public turning public space into a political sphere where rules and values of a different politico-economic system were reimagined became linked with Puerta del Sol. One month later, as the police "cleared" the square of activists, discontentment spread into the neighborhoods of Madrid, where alternative imaginaries of the city and its public spaces were publicly practiced in empty lots and undeveloped lands. This "making, producing, participating, moving, sharing, spreading, enhancing, inventing, and rekindling" (Tonkiss 2013, p. 233) of public space has become a familiar image of the new Madrid. These alternative urbanisms, alternative both in their formation (from the grassroots) and their values (for people, not for profit) from hegemonic urbanism, received attention and approval from practitioners and academics.

Two years later, Puerta del Sol no longer looks like a symbol of the Indignados' protests. The city's metro station at Puerta del Sol has been renamed "Vodafone Sol" in a €3 million deal with the British mobile giant in 2013, rebranding the focal point of the anti-austerity protests with the name of a global phone company scrubbing its history out with global capitalism (Rushton 2013). The utilization of a historical square's name for corporate branding is just the beginning of the intensified commercialization and privatization of central public spaces in Madrid. Against this backdrop, I will analyze how the alternative public spaces that emerged around the 15M Movement have transformed Madrid's neighborhoods, at the same time as the neoliberalization of public space re-intensified. In her chapter on Barcelona in this volume, Melissa García-Lamarca explores the Platform for Mortgage Affected People (PAH) as an insurgent practice with the most emancipatory potential in Spain after the 15M Movement. While her case points out the role of PAH in disrupting the capitalist order of the city, the grassroots public space initiatives in Madrid are characterized by a more ambivalent role in relation to urban capital accumulation. The macroeconomic restructuring of Madrid's political economy after the crisis led to the outsourcing of public service and public space provision to architectural collectives through funding by the cultural sector, rendering civil society initiatives dependent and in danger of being exploited for capital accumulation (Knierbein 2014, p. 12).

With urban activists retreating to niches of democratically run spaces, do we see new excess in commercial occupation of the most central public spaces? Have non-consumer-oriented squares been usurped by cultural gentrification strategies aimed at attracting creative industries and tourism (Sequera and Janoschka 2015, p. 381, Méndez et al. 2012, p. 6)? Have spaces representing cities for people, not for profit (Brenner et al. 2011) actually played a significant role in the increased neoliberalization of Madrid after the anti-austerity politics? Based on fieldwork conducted in Madrid in 2015, comprised of interviews with public space activists and academic experts, as well as participatory observation, this chapter addresses the stark contrasts marking the development of public spaces in Madrid as long-term consequences of austerity politics and its contestations, and delineates the ambiguous role of alternative austerity urbanisms as contrasting parts of the neoliberalizing city. It questions if alternative urbanisms are capable of disrupting the political order and discusses alternative ways to advance political change.

Excess

The financial crisis affected Madrid in a variety of ways both temporally and spatially due to an immediate past "full of excesses," a present "dominated by a deep recession," and a future "faced with major challenges and uncertainties" (Fernández-Güell 2015, p. 53). From the 1980s onwards, discourse on a competitive metropolitan region and the development of Madrid into a global city was pushed by politicians from all factions (Díaz Orueta 2007a, p. 186). A strategic plan was developed, to transform Madrid into a hub for advanced global services and finances, prompting the development of a high-capacity airport. Another goal was to establish Spain's capital as a center of science and technology, culture and tourism (Fernández-Güell 2015). Fernández-Güell (2015, p. 56) describes the key conditions to implement these goals as "a favorable economic context, a friendly planning framework for urban development, and a managerial political style to push complex projects forward." All these conditions were met with Spain's access to cheap loans as an EU member, a new city plan facilitating urban growth, and the leadership of Ruiz-Gallardón, who implemented several large-scale projects as a conservative politician (Partido Popular) during his 15-year career. One of the biggest mega-projects was the development of Madrid Rio from 2003 to 2007, a large recreational and cultural area on the bank of the Manzanares. For some years, Madrid's strategy to become a global city seemed to be on a successful path with high global city rankings and rising economic activity in the capital (Fernández-Güell 2015).

Crisis

The boom of the real estate industry led to optimistic investment, including by many private households. Spain's real estate sector formed an enormous part of the country's gross national product and the construction of thousands upon thousands of new flats led to an explosion of real estate and rent prices. The bursting of the city's real estate bubble led to the downfall of the real estate sector's profits and employment in 2007. The real estate market collapse dragged the economy down as a whole (Klein and Rumpfhuber 2014), leading to skyrocketing unemployment rates, declining incomes, and fiscal debts rising from approximately 1 billion euros in 2001 to about 7 billion euros in 2013 (see Fernández-Güell 2015). A vicious cycle was revealed, as "the real estate market crashed, the financial sector became entrapped, the construction sector collapsed, industrial output decreased, unemployment went up, consumption went down, fiscal revenues diminished, social needs augmented, fiscal debt skyrocketed, and so on" (Fernández-Güell 2015, p. 66).

The hegemonic discourse on austerity policies was discussed in abstract political terms—budget deficits, state restructuring, and default risk—but such policy abstractions fail to account for the material effects on people (Benach 2015). Urban populations became "major victims" of economic crises, due to the significance of the construction sector and housing and infrastructural development for the urban economy, as well as consumption and commerce (Sevilla-Buitrago 2015, p. 42). The crisis was visible in the physical fabric of the city, with unfinished building projects marking many failed real estate projects in the metropolitan area. The most severe effects of the austerity policies imposed on the crisis-shaken societies by national governments and the European troika were cuts in welfare just as more and more people became dependant on social security. Lastly, many private households were stuck with paying off their exorbitant mortgages and facing foreclosures and eviction from their homes.

Discontent

The discontent of the Spanish population suffering from the austerity measures became palpable in the political movement 15M and its protest camps in cities all over the country. Both the form, the occupation of central public spaces, and the content of these movements, primarily the call to end neoliberal and austerity policies and implement a solidarity and egalitarian political-economic system, have been central to a "new transnational geography of dissent" (Vasudevan 2015, p. 317). There, "autonomous geographies" were created in protest against neoliberalization and austerity, as spaces where people aimed to "constitute non-capitalist, egalitarian, and equitable forms of political, social, and economic organization through a combination of resistance and creation" (Pickerill and Chatterton 2006, p. 730).

In discussing urban occupations from a perspective of the right to the city, various scholars have presented it as a right to occupy and reimagine public space (Mitchell 2003) as well as a right against urban revanchism (Smith 1996). In Madrid, activists first practiced their right to resistance by targeting securitization and surveillance strategies implemented by the city in Puerta del Sol. Through social networks, the group Democracia Real YA! called for all those indignant with the political and economic situation they faced to protest in Spain's major cities starting on May 15, 2011.

The various factions of counter-hegemonic activism for the first time came together under one claim and intervened in the political discourse with one voice, "claiming equality in, over and through space" (Janoschka 2015, p. 87). On June 12, three weeks after the national elections, the protesters at Puerta del Sol decided to leave the camp. Fernández-Savater (2012) interpreted the closure of the camp as a consequence of the composition of the protesters, who were not just "professional" activists, but people without previous political engagement, and thus termed the occupation of Plaza del Sol as an exceptional period. As soon as the protesters left, police stormed Plaza del Sol and dismantled all remnants of the 15M Movement.

Contestation

After the clearance of the camp, activists continued their engagement in neighborhood projects, through a network of public spaces all over the city. This decentralization correlates to a political culture strongly based on the neighborhood level: Since the end of the Franco regime in 1975, neighborhood associations have taken up a significant role in representing local claims in urban development in Madrid, and have paved the way for the democratization of the local councils in 1979 (Blanco et al. 2011, p. 331). Manuel Castells asserted that "the social mobilization on urban issues that occurred in the neighborhoods of most Spanish cities throughout the 1970s was [. . .] the largest and most significant urban movement in Europe since 1945" (Castells 1983, p. 215). The neighborhood projects analyzed in this chapter, which came into being around 2011, represent long-term "occupations" where the right to the city was lived as a right to reimagine public space (Mitchell 2003), to "reclaim and reconfigure urban space as an oeuvre and to maximise use value for residents rather than to maximise exchange value for capital" (Purcell 2003, p. 587). The following will introduce two exemplary projects where activists reclaimed unused public spaces for neighborhood needs as a way to contest existing models of urban public space.

Esta Es Una Plaza (EEUP)!

Behind a high wall, "Esta Es Una Plaza!" (This is a square!), a large, blooming garden full of interesting little constructions, is hidden in the neighborhood of Lavapiés, with colorful mural art, toys for kids, and benches and tables in the shade. The project has become a prominent example for occupying an empty lot and transforming a deserted urban field into a green refuge. The cultural center La Casa Encendida organized a workshop on the production of space with the permission for temporary constructions in the lot of Calle Doctor Fourquet for two weeks, after it had been empty for more than 30 years. During the workshop, participating neighbors came up with the idea to extend the use of the space beyond the two weeks. However, authorities expelled participants and destroyed their constructions, closing off the unused plot of land once again. Some workshop participants then organized public breakfasts in front of the fence, inviting the neighborhood for debates on public space, local participation, and especially possible uses of this empty lot. With every breakfast there was growing citizen support to reclaim the space. While the initial workshop started as an academic discussion on urban development by mostly architects and planners, more and more neighbors got involved and made the repeated manifestations successful. Finally, the initiative obtained another temporary permit of one year to use the space. Since then the permit has been renewed every year.

In the course of more than five years, the neighborhood association of EEUP, counting about 80 members, has brought life to the empty lot with garden beds, playgrounds, a tool library, etc. The association's main goal is to develop the lot as an accessible public space based on principles of social responsibility and self-management. Everyone who agrees to the statute of the association can become a member and have the right to vote. The association is organized in a horizontal, democratic manner, and decisions are made by the members in the scheduled assemblies. The objective is to find consensual solutions to all issues and include all opinions in a commonly agreed upon decision. The association's main principle is to maintain its independence of any other actors and their interests, and thus donations are not accepted. The main values defining the program of the space are social, ecological, and economical sustainability in the creation of an open public space which offers alternative ways to spend leisure time, engage in communal education, or enjoy intergenerational and intercultural exchange. The discrete aims of the associations stem from the activation and participation of citizens in the management of public space: the upkeep of the garden, which was created in 2008, allowed for the promotion of an economy based on exchange and reuse, and the promotion of ecological and do-it-yourself practices ultimately culminated in the development of cultural, educational, and creative activities to enhance social exchange between neighbors.

El Campo de Cebada

El Campo de Cebada (the Barley Field) is an occupation and reinvention of a public space located in the center of La Latina, a working-class neighborhood in Madrid. From 2007 on, the authorities conceived a plan with the aim to renovate the public market halls and a sports center and privatize their management. An extravagant architectural design covering the whole area of the market by Rubio and Alvares-Sala won the international competition for the city of Madrid (Pluch 2014). However, after having demolished the sports facilities in 2009, the project came to a halt and the authorities left behind an empty, sunken space of about 5,000 square meters, surrounded by an opaque fence. As part of the White Night festivities, the empty lot was transformed into a "rain forest" and a swimming pool for ten days, sparking the neighbors' interest in claiming the space that had been neglected by the government. While the temporary installations were dismantled, a diverse group of neighbors formed El Campo de Cebada. Led by several architects, the group worked to discuss the future use of the space before the construction works would begin and the authorities would begin leveraging claims to the space. With the general goal to create a self-managed, collaborative public space to foster meaningful social relations in La Latina, the group came to an agreement with the authorities to temporarily utilize the space (Bravo 2012).

Weekly assemblies for programming the space took place: basic installations for water and electricity were implemented, furniture was collectively built, sports equipment was installed, and walls were decorated with street art. In the ensuing years, the square hosted diverse events from concerts to dancing lessons and debates, all open and free for everyone. The program was conceived through consensus rather than a top-down curation and selection of events and projects, reflecting the communal, grassroots, radical-democratic character of the square which has been saved from its abandoned existence by citizens, transforming it into one of the most lively noncommercial sites in the city.

FIGURE 15.1 Peeking through a loophole in the opaque fence that still surrounds Campo de Cebada

Source: Eva Maria Mitterwieser, 2015

FIGURE 15.2 "Llena la vida de color" reads a graffiti covering the market hall's facade at Campo de Cebada: "Fill life with color"

Source: Eva Maria Mitterwieser, 2015

Repercussions

Despite the legacy of many public space initiatives led by citizens in Madrid, the city government has continued to transform central public spaces according to market principles. When neoliberal governance transformed the concept of public services through the privatization of health care and public transport, for example, it also transformed the concept of public space, into "an empty space between buildings which has to be formed according to the objectives of developers and the government" (Urquiaga 2014, p. 2, translated by author). Thus, public authorities have turned public spaces into a new target for investment and urban renewal with the goal of revitalizing declining neighborhoods to stimulate gentrification, turning citizens' neighborhoods into spaces of speculation (Urquiaga 2014, p. 2). The analysis of the production of public spaces in an attention economy (Knierbein 2010) has pointed to the ways through which the state in coalition with the market reinforces post-Fordist territorial capital accumulation. Public space is developed into a central object of capitalist appropriation with cities aiming to render public goods profitable by renting out public spaces temporarily or selling out inner-city areas for private development. In addition to physical transformations of public space, cities apply intensive security or surveillance strategies, not obviously linked to crime control but rather as a means to achieve citizen obedience (Sequera and Janoschka 2015). In that manner the neighborhoods of Lavapiés and Triball, as well as Puerta del Sol, have been equipped with CCTV as well as around-the-clock police patrols. Public authorities and business owners have transformed public space "to foster circulation and commercial appropriation and prevent people from appropriating open spaces by implementing municipal ordinances that hamper everyday use" (Sequera and Janoschka 2015, p. 386) (e.g. drinking in public or playing music), consequently forbidding its traditional meaning as a truly common space. Commercial and cultural gentrification and the renting out of central squares exemplify the ongoing neoliberal strategies guiding hegemonic urban development.

Commercial Gentrification in Triball

Plaza de la Luna has been a recent target of urban renewal due to the deteriorated state of the neighborhood presenting both the possibility for intervening not only architecturally but also for the manipulation of the social and commercial life of the neighborhood (Urquiaga 2014, p. 5). The process was initiated when an investor bought and renovated buildings, turning them into shops and hotels, and further founded a business association to politically safeguard the investment (Asociación de Comerciantes ACtriBall, ca. 170 members). The association took over many older businesses in the area and gained a strong regional influence. The commercial gentrification of the area was supported by the authorities through financial subsidies as well as the renovation of Plaza de la Luna (Sequera and Janoschka 2015, p. 383). Rather than going through the full circle of gentrification with the expulsion of old residents, the neighborhood was recharacterized by social polarization, where the new gentries lived next to a more vulnerable population. Sex work, drug consumption, and the presence of homeless people led to the stigmatization of the square resulting in physical and economic degradation (Urquiaga 2014). Neighbors and businesses collectively called for the municipality to solve these issues.

At first, a participatory process involved the neighbors in the new design for the square, but neoliberal entrepreneurial disposition won significant influence with a vision for the renovation of Plaza de la Luna. Described by the architects as "an authentic scenery for urban living," Urquiaga describes it as a cold and imprecise space (Urquiaga 2014, p. 7, translated by author). The square is now mainly used for commercial and sports events due to its wide-open design. The undefined and plain center of the square mostly stays empty, and in spite of the new design, its most visible users are still the stigmatized sex workers, immigrants, and beggars (Urquiaga 2014, p. 9).

With an understanding of public space as a space without private domination, accessible for everybody, many conflicts arise at Plaza de la Luna. Due to temporary occupation for festivals, markets, and sports events, the square is no longer accessible for everyone equally. At the same time the local population of the neighborhood itself practices a strategy of excluding unwanted groups seen as outsiders of not just the community but society as a whole. This problem has not become part of the redevelopment discourse of the square. This aspect shows that bottom-up practices can also reproduce exclusions based on a moral depreciation of sex work, homelessness, and drug consumption.

Plaza Callao, or "Plaza Alquilada"

"Plaza Alquilada" (Rented-Out Square) as the author Urquiaga calls it, refers to Plaza Callao. It is located at the crossing of Madrid's main shopping streets of Gran Vía and connected to Puerta del Sol through Preciados street. Callao was once a highly used traffic node used by pedestrians and motorized traffic alike. The main objective for the renovation of Plaza Callao in 2009 was to create a pedestrian zone and eliminate car and bus traffic. The city promoted the renovation with the promise to plant 48 new trees, adding to the existing 28, as well as to refurbish streetlights and urban furniture. In the end the renovation turned out very differently from that vision. The new plaza was characterized by a large and empty hard surface without any ornament or urban furniture provided, and shade could only be found under the few cafes' terraces on the edges of the

FIGURE 15.3   An impression of Plaza de la Luna in Triball: At the same time as the square was renovated, a police station was installed

Source: Elina Kränzle 2015

square. The renovation of the square was not centered on neighborhood demand, but on the business interests of many big brand commercial stores and hotels around it (Urquiaga 2014, p. 11).

After the renovation, Callao became a purely transitory space due to unfavorable heat in the summer and cold and wind in winter. Huge screens were installed on nearby facades through a project called Escena Encendida, transforming Callao into a copy of New York's Times Square. Instead of turning the square into a pedestrian zone, it is now mostly used for private events. Instead of providing for the basic functions of a public square, it is designed as a privately rentable parcel, profitable for the municipality, rendering a public space a commodity (Urquiaga 2014).

The two examples above demonstrate the recent transformation of public space in Madrid into an object of and for consumption (Urquiaga 2014). Their physical design is aimed at keeping the space free of any "disturbances": large open spaces that are easy to clean and control both physically and socially. At Plaza de la Luna the aim was to give a new meaning to the quarter and push forward the revaluation of the area to push out unwanted users. Both examples show the combined efforts of (1) security and control achieved through wide, open, hard surfaces producing inhospitable space, and (2) in "Plazas Alquiladas," financial value gained from private events. In the context of recent political and economic development of Madrid, the first of these could be interpreted as an answer to the 15M occupations, and the second as a strategy of creating new markets in the face of an economic recession.

Cultural Gentrification in Lavapiés

However, the city center has not been the only target of urban renewal. The central neighborhood of Lavapiés is known for its dense urban fabric, lack of green spaces, and its diverse population, with the highest percentage of foreigners (25%, Madrid Estadística 2014). In 1997 the area was declared an Area de Rehabilitación Preferente (ARP, prioritized renovation area) (Díaz Orueta 2007b, p. 171). The aim of this plan was to renovate the building stock, in many cases destroying the architectural heritage. At first, basic infrastructure was renovated, for example the construction of an underground parking lot below the square of Agustín Lara and at the same time the renovation of the square itself, constituting the largest public space in the area. After these investments authorities focused on placing new cultural institutions in Lavapiés. An associate center and a library for the Universidad Nacional de Educación a Distancia (UNED) and a new hall for the National Institute for Performing Arts and Music (INAEM) in Plaza Lavapiés were built; the Casino de la Reina was renovated as a social center; and the old neo-Mudéjar building was converted into the cultural center La Casa Encendida (Díaz Orueta 2007b).

While some understand the construction of cultural centers and policies to attract a new middle class and tourism as the best way to develop the area, others emphasize that Lavapiés is threatened by gentrification and the risk of having its working-class population pushed out. The needs of the middle class and tourism were prioritized over vital existing neighborhood needs for schools and healthcare centers (Díaz Orueta 2007b, p. 185). Sequera and Janoschka (2015) support the stance that Lavapiés is being gentrified, arguing that this gentrification process can be linked to a strategy of cultural production triggered by public investments in the cultural economy. One of the reasons they see behind the gentrification of Madrid's city center is the municipality's aim to attract a creative class and creative industries using "policies that explicitly track and demand qualified human capital to relocate to the city in general, with a specific emphasis on the historical city center" (Méndez et al. 2012, p. 6, Sequera and Janoschka 2015, p. 381). According to the authors, the authorities made specific interventions to shape the identity of Lavapiés as a neighborhood filled with innovative art and culture, adding to its exotic image of an immigrant neighborhood with ethnic shops and restaurants. Activists recently reoccupied an empty lot, the so-called Solar de Lavapiés, after having been evicted from it some years ago. In their speech they criticized exactly this strategy of cultural production (García 2015):

> When we talk about the Solar de Lavapiés, we're not only talking about the fact that the city of Madrid and the IVIMA (Madrid's social housing agency) are abandoning the spaces meant for housing, we're also talking about the fact that, in a systematic manner, the inhabitants of a neighborhood are expelled with different strategies: Forced expropriation, no relocation, fines, persecutions, threats and lies. Today the colonization of a territory is no longer pursued with big deeds, but with instigating speculation, with expropriations, cultural institutions placed top-down and through a propagated exotic image attractive for tourism.
>
> *(Translation by author)*

Although one of the stated aims of the prioritized renovation area is to enhance citizen participation, the developments in Lavapiés have effectively not included the inhabitants in the planning process, presenting them with only the finished plans. A neighborhood organization comprising different associations of Lavapiés was founded in 1997 to demand that the needs of Lavapiés' inhabitants should be met first in the renovation of the area. After fighting with the authorities for many years for spaces to be used by neighborhood associations (Díaz Orueta 2007b), their demands were met in 2009, when they could move into the publicly owned building of an old

FIGURE 15.4   The mural at Esta Es Una Plaza! criticizes the city's approach to urban development

Source: Elina Kränzle 2015

tobacco company, now called La Tabacalera. However, except for their independence from the city government, the public and cultural spaces of Esta Es Una Plaza! and La Tabacalera involuntarily enhance exactly the image of Lavapiés that the authorities have pursued with their upgrading strategy.

Contentment?—"Wrong Life Cannot Be Lived Rightly"?[1]

The mural at EEUP in Lavapiés represents a strong critique of urban development in the city. The artist manipulated the coat of arms of Madrid: a bear leaning against a strawberry tree. In a new version of the city symbol, two construction workers are shown about to cut the strawberry tree down, putting up a construction fence and carrying building materials to the site. However, the mural's argument, manifest in 15M activists' continued fight for more public spaces that are truly representative of their economic and political claims on all scales, seems to have waned. These groups now seem content with their niches of democratically run public spaces. With the occupation of Madrid's symbolic center, Puerta del Sol, the Indignados' camp addressed the specific site of urban restructuring exemplary of all the "wrongs" in global and Spanish economic and political development. After the encampment the activists continued their work in the neighborhoods, where they created testing grounds for a solidary, egalitarian, sustainable and democratic society. While these alternative publics became more or less institutionalized, the sites of the 15M protests underwent increasing surveillance and privatization, increasing their value not only as a public good, but as a marketable commodity. Moreover, the areas of alternative urbanisms themselves have also become targets of the city's marketization strategies. The cultural gentrification in Lavapiés exemplifies how "city governments and urban development actors have begun to institutionalize making use of countercultural actors for their purposes" (Mayer 2013, p. 11), creating an image of the creative city fit for tourism and consumerist lifestyles. Alternative urbanisms have become an essential part of the marketing of urban neighborhoods, and while political empowerment is practiced in these safe havens, they have become a "generative force of neoliberalizing cities," encouraging self-responsibility while the austerity state keeps on cutting public spending (Mayer 2013, p. 9, 12).

As Hou (2012, p. 97) points out,

> the root cause of diminishing public resources and the privatization of public space in our cities today is precisely the privatization of our political system, a deeper crisis, that cannot be addressed by creating more public spaces alone or by making public space simply more inclusive and accessible.

As the 15M activists claim to go beyond making space and demand change in the political and economic system as a whole, have they been successful in bringing about the change in the political and economic system they demanded in 2011? Looking at alternative urbanisms in Madrid, and their origins in the 15M movement in 2011, the activists seemed to have left the conditions, whose change was at the heart of the Indignados' demands, unchanged. More so, they might have inadvertently fueled the processes of cultural gentrification.

While this chapter points to the ambiguity of alternative urbanisms in a city that increasingly pursues commercialization and securitization by transferring alternative urbanism into revaluation strategies, the achievements of EEUP and Campo de Cebada, who created inclusive urban spaces, should in no way be discounted. Nevertheless, we need to reflect on both the constraints and pitfalls of bottom-up placemaking in a context of intensifying cultural gentrification. We also need to reflect on ways that mobilization can foster political and economic change beyond the boundaries of the *plaza*.

The political engagement at the neighborhood level in Madrid did contribute to change for the city as a whole. After 24 years of conservative rule, the Podemos-supported platform Ahora Madrid's candidate Manuela Carmena became the capital's new mayor in 2015 in coalition with the Spanish Socialist Workers' Party. For many, the former judge, who was actively supported by various social movements, stands for the end of corruption, and a focus on the "social city." It remains to be seen, however, if the new coalition will rewrite the rules for the bottom-up making of public spaces, and more importantly, prioritize equal access and local needs instead of value-creation and governmental hegemony in the development of public space. This political change has a chance to not just address the needs of alternative urbanisms, but also to actively counter urban development strategies of gentrification and commodification. The government's decision to end the corporate sponsorship of the metro station Sol, which lost the Vodafone tag in May 2016, is a sign of hope.

Note

1. Original "Gibt es ein richtiges Leben im falschen," a well-known saying based on Theodor W. Adorno, *Minima Moralia* (Gesammelte Schriften 4, Frankfurt/M. 1997, p. 43). Due to the societal consequences of late capitalism, we cannot but be usurped by the societal system: either through inadvertently helping to maintain it, or through our direct contribution.

References

Benach, N., 2015. Contest Discourses of Austerity in the Urban Margins (A Vision from Barcelona). *In*: F. Eckardt, and J. R. Sanchez, eds. *City of Crisis: The Multiple Contestation of Southern European Cities.* Bielefeld: Transcript-Verlag, 71–88.

Blanco, I., Bonet, J., and Walliser, A., 2011. Urban Governance and Regeneration Policies in Historic City Centers: Madrid and Barcelona. *Urban Research & Practice*, 4 (3), 326–343.

Bravo, D., 2012. *The Barley Field* [online]. Available from: www.publicspace.org/en/works/g362-el-campo-de-cebada [Accessed 27 July 2016].

Brenner, N., Marcuse, P., and Mayer, M., 2011. *Cities for People, Not for Profit: Critical Urban Theory and the Right to the City*. London and New York: Routledge.

Castells, M. 1983. *The City and the Grassroots: A Cross-Cultural Theory of Urban Social Movements*. Berkeley and Los Angeles: The University of California Press.

de la Fuente, R., Walliser, A., Velasco, M., and Alguacil, J., 2014. Redefining Governance in the City: New Urban Activism and Public Space in Madrid. Paper presented at EURA Conference: Paris.

Díaz Orueta, F., 2007a. Madrid: Urban Regeneration Projects and Social Mobilization. *Cities*, 24 (3), 183–193.

Díaz Orueta, F., 2007b. Los grandes proyectos de desarrollo urbano y la reconfiguración socio-especial de la ciudades: El barrio de Lavapiés (Madrid). *Cuaderno Urbano*, 6, 169–194.

Fernández-Güell, J. M., 2015. Madrid, a Tale of an Ambitious City That Failed to Fulfil Its Global Vision. *In*: F. Eckardt, and J. R. Sanchez, eds. *City of Crisis: The Multiple Contestation of Southern European Cities*. Bielefeld: Transcript-Verlag, 53–70.

Fernández-Savater, A., 2012. Como se organiza un clima? *Publico.es*, January 9, 2012. Available from: http://blogs.publico.es/fueradelugar/1438/%C2%BFcomo-se-organiza-un-clima [Accessed 13 April 2016].

García, T., 2015. Medio centenar de vecinos recupera el solar de Lavapiés [online]. *Diagonal*, July 18, 2015. Available from: www.diagonalperiodico.net/libertades/27386-medio-centenar-vecinos-recupera-solar-lavapies.html [Accessed 21 August 2015].

Hou, J., 2012. Making Public, Beyond Public Space. *In*: R. Shiffman, R. Bell, L. J. Brown, and L. Elizabeth, eds. *Beyond Zuccotti Park: Freedom of Assembly and the Occupation of Public Space*. Oakland, CA: New Village Press, 89–98.

Janoschka, M., 2015. Politics, Citizenship and Disobedience in the City of Crisis: A Critical Analysis of Contemporary Housing Struggles in Madrid. *DIE ERDE—Journal of the Geographical Society of Berlin*, 146 (2–3), 100–112.

Klein, M. and Rumpfhuber, A., 2014. Knappheit, Austerität und die zeitgenössische Stadt. *Dérive Zeitschrift für Stadtforschung* 55. Available from: www.derive.at/index.php?p_case=2&id_cont=1232&issue_No=55 [Accessed July 27, 2016].

Knierbein, S., 2010. *Die Produktion zentraler öffentlicher Räume in der Aufmerksamkeitsökonomie: Ästhetische, ökonomische und mediale Restrukturierungen durch gestaltwirksame Koalitionen in Berlin seit 1980*. 2010 edition. Wiesbaden, VS: Verlag für Sozialwissenschaften.

Knierbein, S., 2014. Reflection Seminario Abierto Urbanismo Reflectivo. *In*: Knierbein, S., Krasny, E., and Tihomir, V. (eds), *Concepts and Critique of the Production of Space. Urbanismo Afectivo*. Interdisciplinary Centre for Urban Culture and Public Space, TU Wien.

Madrid Estadística, 2014. Estadística del Ayuntamiento de Madrid. Available from: http://www.madrid.es/portales/munimadrid/es/Inicio/El-Ayuntamiento/Estadistica?vgnextfmt=default&vgnextchannel=8156e39873674210VgnVCM1000000b205a0aRCRD [Accessed 21 August 2015].

Marcuse, P., 2009. From Critical Urban Theory to the Right to the City. *City*, 13 (2–3), 185–197.

Mayer, M., 2013. First World Urban Activism. *City*, 17 (1), 5–19.

Méndez, R., Michelini, J.J., Prada, J. and Tébar, J. 2012. Économía creative y desarrollo urbano en Espana: una aproximación a sus lógicas espaciales. *EURE (Santiago)*, 38 (113), 5–32.

Mitchell, D., 2003. *The Right to the City: Social Justice and the Fight for Public Space*. New York: Guilford Press.

Mitchell, D. and Heynen, N., 2009. The Geography of Survival and the Right to the City: Speculations on Surveillance, Legal Innovation, and the Criminalization of Intervention. *Urban Geography*, 30 (6), 611–632.

Pickerill, J. and Chatterton, P., 2006. Notes Towards Autonomous Geographies: Creation, Resistance and Self-Management as Survival Tactics. *Progress in Human Geography*, 30 (6), 730–746.

Pluch, K., 2014. *Community Centre Cebada* (Master's Thesis). Faculty of Architecture and Planning, TU: Wien.

Purcell, M., 2003. Citizenship and the Right to the Global City: Reimagining the Capitalist World Order. *International Journal of Urban and Regional Research*, 27 (3), 564–590.

Rushton, K., 2013. Madrid rebrands metro in Vodafone deal [online]. April 24. Available from: www.telegraph.co.uk/finance/10016166/Madrid-rebrands-metro-in-Vodafone-deal.html [Accessed 13 April 2016].

Sequera, J. and Janoschka, M., 2015. Gentrification Dispositifs in the Historic Center of Madrid: A Reconsideration of Urban Governmentality and State-Led Urban Reconfiguration. *In*: L. Lees, H. B. Shin, and E. Lopez-Morales, eds. *Global Gentrifications: Uneven Development and Displacement*. Bristol, UK: Chicago Policy Press, 375–393.

Sevilla-Buitrago, A., 2015. Crisis and the City: Neoliberalism, Austerity Planning and the Production of Space. *In*: F. Eckardt, and J. R. Sanchez, eds. *City of Crisis: The Multiple Contestation of Southern European Cities*. Bielefeld: Transcript-Verlag, 31–52.

Smith, N., 1996. *The New Urban Frontier: Gentrification and the Revanchist City*. London and New York: Routledge.

Tonkiss, F., 2013. Austerity Urbanism and the Makeshift City. *City*, 17 (3), 312–324.

Urquiaga, A. A., 2014. Madrid. Espacio público confiscado. La privatización y resignificación del espacio público en los procesos de transformación material de las plazas del centro de Madrid. XIII Coloquio Internacional de Geocrítica—El control del espacio y los espacios de control. Barcelona.

Vasudevan, A., 2015. The Autonomous City: Towards a Critical Geography of Occupation. *Progress in Human Geography*, 39 (3), 316–337.

Walliser, A. 2013. New Urban Activisms in Spain: Reclaiming Public Space in the Face of Crises. *Policy & Politics*, 41 (3), 329–350.

16

MIYASHITA PARK, TOKYO

Contested Visions of Public Space in Contemporary Urban Japan

Christian Dimmer

In summer 2010 a small urban park in Tokyo's iconic Shibuya shopping district became the scene of an occupation that lasted nearly half a year. Homeless citizens, artists, youth activists, unionists, and public intellectuals congregated not only around the physical space of Miyashita Park but also catalyzed heated debates among planning professionals, or social movement scholars, in which the nature of public space in urban Japan was broadly discussed (Dimmer 2010, OurPlanet-TV 2010, Nikkei Architecture 2011, Tsukamoto and Nakatani 2011). These intensive debates were fomented by a controversial deal brokered between the Shibuya local government and Nike Japan, who agreed to buy the naming rights for a period of ten years and install rental sports facilities in parts of the park. These plans were leaked to the public only after major decisions had been made behind closed doors. The ensuing protests against what the activists called the "Nike-fication of public space" (Ogawa 2012) utilized a new cultural repertoire of protest in which expressive means like graphic design, visual art, and music played a central role.

In this context, it is tempting to depict the struggle around Miyashita Park in line with global trends within a supposedly universal meta-narrative of state and local governments yielding to uniform globalizing and neoliberalizing forces, and broad sections of civil society claiming their right to the city. However, while the global struggles discussed resemble one another, the debates around the remaking of Miyashita Park followed a distinct local logic, at a time when conceptual histories of public and private were reexamined in Japan (Kim and Sasaki 2001), when the politics of place in Tokyo became more confrontational (McNeill 2009), and an increasing number of actors began to assume active roles in place-making and place governance (Dimmer 2014, 2016).

The "Nike-fication" (*Naiki-ka*) of Miyashita Park has been extensively discussed in popular media and among social movement scholarship circles. The accounts are sympathetic to the struggle of the activists, focusing mostly on the activists and their elaborate means of protest (Mōri 2009, OurPlanet-TV 2010, Cassegård 2011, 2013, Hirabayashi 2010, Shiraishi 2011, Kindstrand 2012). Less is said about the wider socio-spatial conditions on which the developments were contingent. Furthermore, the focus on the activists tends to bracket other important actors as complicit in the renovation, cooperative with the government or big business or to depict them simply as proxies of the forces of capitalism or neoliberalism. While the protests against the Nike-fication fit nicely into the global iconography of recent public space struggles, they failed to similarly galvanize the broader public. The struggles at Miyashita Park did have, however, some indirect effects on the protest tactics during the large anti-nuclear mass protests of summer 2012 against the government's plans to restart Japan's nuclear power plants after the Fukushima disaster, and the peace protests of summer 2015 that sought to protect Japan's pacifist constitution, but these protests quickly ebbed off after a few weeks, without disrupting the sociopolitical status quo. Meanwhile, recent positive social change and empowerment is coming in a less confrontational, quiet form (Kingston 2004), represented by a new breed of social entrepreneurs, community innovators, and socially engaged artists that collaborate at times with government and big business but pursue socially emancipatory agendas, without being openly political (Dimmer 2017).

To examine the case of Miyashita Park, this chapter adopts a relational view of place-making as socially negotiated, constantly changing, and contingent upon "networked politics of place" (Pierce et al. 2011) that emerge at the intersection of national, metropolitan, and local urban scales. Together, the place-making efforts of a powerful global sports and lifestyle corporation, diverse local community-building initiatives, social movements, professional place-makers, and everyday users of public space embody not only the "complex weave of *competition*, and *struggle*," but also "*cooperation*" (Harvey 2001, p. 116). The architects, politicians, and other local civil society actors who collaborated with Nike and Shibuya ward can be depicted, on one hand, as co-opted for a subversive brand strategy of a global corporation. On the other hand, phenomena like neoliberalism or entrepreneurialism are seldom monolithically imposed from above, or travel neatly from one policy context to another (McCann and Ward 2011). Instead, local actors consciously strategize and pursue their own, often more diverse, ambiguous agendas by exploiting opportunities that emerge in the cracks of a changing governance landscape. Thus, as shown below, a coalition of local politicians and designers welcomed the opportunity to work with Nike because it would allow them to create a new kind of active public space that simply couldn't be designed and managed within Japan's hitherto state-centered, highly bureaucratic, and inflexible institutional framework (Uno 1998, Tsukamoto and Nakatani 2011).

Remaking of Miyashita Park

The Nike-fication of Miyashita Park didn't come out of the blue. As we will see, entrepreneurial, independent, local politicians like Ken Hasebe and Takeshi Ito and social innovators like Motokazu Terai were already working to transform Shibuya's public spaces in *cooperation* with government and businesses. During the Football World Cup in Japan and Korea in 2002, Nike installed a temporary "Nike Park" in and around the iconic gymnasiums that Kenzo Tange had designed for the 1964 Tokyo Olympics, which became a significant publicity success and convinced local policy and place-makers of the importance of popular sports for urban branding.

In 2003 the prolific Ken Hasebe came across a Nike program for which recycled sneakers were reused to create sports facilities. In an interview with the investigative, independent news outlet OurPlanet-TV (2010), he explains how he contacted Nike Japan to invite them to collaborate on a similar project in Shibuya and how the sneaker maker keenly courted him. Hasebe convinced a reluctant, elderly mayor to accept the donation of a basketball court by Nike by having Michael Jordan open it in May 2004 during a Tokyo visit. While Hasebe negotiated with the authorities, city councilor Takeshi Ito was in contact with members of the local community, and when complaints emerged about the noise the new court caused, Ito suggested to relocate it to nearby Miyashita Park. Here he saw the opportunity to create a new, comprehensive sports park to attract young people to Shibuya, to take the skaters from the public sidewalks, where they had angered pedestrians, and to "push out the homeless people, who littered the area and spoiled the cityscape" (OurPlanet-TV 2010). In June 2006 two rental futsal courts were completed inside the park that Ito had lobbied for. In an interview, he appears somewhat disappointed that this reduced the homeless population "only" by half and he goes on to insinuate that as the remaining homeless continue to cause a risk for public safety, he would push for the full conversion of Miyashita into a park for trendy street sports (OurPlanet-TV 2010).

The events leading up to the naming rights deal between Shibuya and Nike Japan are meticulously detailed by the hour-long documentary *Miyashita Park, Tokyo/Shibuya—Can the Democracy Be Bought for Money?* (OurPlanet-TV 2010). In an impressive display of investigative journalism, the film stitches together the dubious circumstances that led to the conclusion of a naming agreement between Nike Japan and Shibuya ward. The documentary indicates that local politicians, park administrators, and Nike Japan have scrambled to create the illusion of a democratic planning process: fabricated petitions and citizen requests are compiled and hurriedly submitted in order to meet deadlines and formal requirements.

In June 2007 Nike Japan hired the prominent architectural practice Atelier Bow-Wow to develop a concept plan. Nike hoped to open the park in autumn 2008, just in time to capitalize on the renewed sports boom expected from the Beijing Olympics (Tsukamoto and Nakatani 2011). In September 2007 the plans were presented to the planning authorities and at the end of November the design was finalized. In February 2008 Nike Japan and two other companies formally submitted naming rights proposals, but OurPlanet-TV (2010) suggests that the competing bids were fabricated to create the fiction of a fair tendering process. As part of the deal, Nike promises to foot the ¥465 million (about USD$4.1 million as of March 2016) bill for the renovation of the derelict park that includes a rental skateboarding area and a climbing wall. The company would additionally pay a yearly sum of ¥17 million (USD$150,000) until 2020 for the naming rights (Shibuya-ku Miyashita Park Naming Rights Agreement 2009). On May 10, 2008 local newspaper *Just Times Shibuya* revealed to the general public and the city council that Shibuya ward was to conclude a naming rights agreement with Nike Japan.

Japan's cash-strapped municipalities had begun selling naming rights of public facilities in the 2000s. In 2006 Shibuya ward sold the naming rights to its public auditorium for five years to a soft-drink brand and in 2009 it began even to brand public toilets. However, these processes were transparent and followed proper procedures.

Shortly after, the Coalition to Protect Miyashita Park from Becoming Nike Park (Miyashita Kōen wo Naikikakeikaku kara mamoru kai; hereafter the "Coalition") formed to protest both in physical public space as well as in virtual forums including blogs, Twitter, Facebook and YouTube. Cassegård (2011, 2013), Kindstrand (2012), and Mōri (2009) detail the struggle. The activists themselves also commented substantially on the issue (Ogawa 2012, Nikkei Architecture 2011). Furthermore, abundant material published on websites including Artists in Residence Miyashita Park (http://airmiyashitapark.info/wordpress), and Everyone's Park (http://minnanokouenn. blogspot.com) allowed the public to follow the conflict and provided templates for activists elsewhere. The site Miyashita Improvement (http://miyasitaseibi.blog71.fc2.com) contains many classified documents that the activists forced the ward to disclose by invoking the fairly recent Administrative Information Disclosure Act (2001). Campaigners carried out sit-ins in the park and protest marches in the streets of Shibuya and in front of Nike shops and the Nike headquarters. The vocal protest and skillful use of social media brought the issue to the attention of international media and even the 'UN Special Rapporteur on Adequate Housing as a Component of the Right to an Adequate Standard of Living, and on the Right to Non-Discrimination' confronted the government of Japan on the issue.

In June 2009 the Shibuya mayor informed the ward assembly for the first time about the plans for Miyashita Park without offering details. On August 27, 2009, a naming rights agreement was concluded for Miyashita Nike Park. Although construction was originally to begin in autumn 2008, then September 2009, the protests and the relocation of the homeless delayed the process. Meanwhile, the Coalition attempted to initiate a dialogue with politicians and the general public through street demonstrations, petitions, and demands for negotiations, which failed (Cassegård 2013, p. 168). The struggle intensified when authorities visited the park on March 16 to close public access and prepare the site for construction. This episode took place during a three-day occupation by a group of activists who had joined the last remaining homeless people. Encouraged by driving away the officers with anti-gentrification and anti-privatization slogans (Kindstrand 2012, p. 41), they stayed in the park, leading to a six-month occupation that turned the park into a "Temporary Autonomous Zone" (Bey 2003) or an experimental common, where new alternative forms of life were prefigured. As an equivoque on ubiquitous government-sponsored residency programs and Nike sneakers, the activists called themselves A.I.R. (Artists in Residence).

Cassegård describes (2013) how the park was filled with imaginative dolls, banners, sculptures, and a variety of other art objects assembled from the garbage that happened to be at hand (Figure 16.1). The activists cooked together and organized workshops, rock concerts, film screenings, outdoor karaoke, and poetry readings (Figure 16.2). A library and a community garden were also created. Along the park fence, banners were hung, stating "Everyone's Park" or "Miyashita Park is our common future." The place also served as a base for campaigns into the surrounding public spaces through sound demos in which dozens of homeless, activist musicians and other participants paraded or danced through the streets while drumming, blowing trumpets and trombones, or beating frying pans, metal cans, or other sound-making items (Figure 16.3). "Outside Nike's new boutique in Shibuya a three-day 'no Nike fashion show' was arranged during which activists dressed up in rags and other things they had found in the park" (2013, p. 169). However, as imaginative and playful as these actions were, they remained insignificant in scale compared to

FIGURE 16.1 During the half-year occupation, DIY-style art objects expressed that the park belonged to everyone, not just to those who can pay for it. However, although the sign stated that the park remained open, the aesthetics of the installations repelled regular park users.

Source: Christian Dimmer

FIGURE 16.2 During the occupation, concerts, raves, poetry readings, film screenings, discussion rounds, and many other events were held by A.I.R. These however weren't aimed at, or failed to attract, members of the wider public.

Source: Christian Dimmer

FIGURE 16.3 The activists also frequently protested outside of the park. At the 'homeless mayday' in May 2010, a large puppet was carried through the streets of Shibuya, expressing the soul of Miyashita Park that rebels against "privatization."

Source: Christian Dimmer

FIGURE 16.4 Protesters approaching the iconic Shibuya Crossing. The image shows how small the number of protesters is, how little attention the protest attracts, and how heavily it's cordoned off by police.

Source: Christian Dimmer

the everyday consumerist activities in Shibuya (Figure 16.4), and were largely ignored by main-stream media.

On September 15, the occupation was forcefully ended when over 100 private security guards, riot police, and municipal park staff invaded the park at 6:30 in the morning (Figure 16.5). By then, however, the movement had already lost its vigor due to exhaustion in the weeks before. Nine days later properties of the artists and of the remaining homeless in the fenced-off park were removed, and shortly thereafter construction began. The Coalition continued to stage sit-ins on the sidewalk and outside the construction site to no avail. On April 30, 2011, the new Miyashita Park opened with high-ranking representatives of Nike Japan and local politicians present, while a handful of Coalition members protested outside the park.

Crowd Control and Public Space as Afterthought

In order to better understand the diverse motivations of actors involved in the case of Miyashita Park and why the protests failed to connect to the general public, it is important to look at the evolution of public space in urban Japan. For most of post-war Japanese history, engineering and infrastructure-based thinking dominated the making and management of public spaces (Dimmer 2012). Generally speaking, engineers and administrators would often conceive of public space as facilitator for effective pedestrian circulation or an element in elaborate disaster response strategies (Uno 1998). After the violent student protests of the late 1960s many public places were designed

FIGURE 16.5 On September 15, 2010 over 100 private security guards and riot police ended the Miyashita Park occupation and sealed off the park with construction fences

Source: Christian Dimmer

to prevent easy assembly and are controlled through top-down, standardized management routines that emphasize management efficiency, crowd control, and smooth pedestrian circulation.

In 1969 anti-Vietnam War protesters and student groups pushed outside the campuses and cheerfully formed discussion groups in front of major Tokyo transportation hubs. Most famous was the iconic occupation of a multi-layered modernist transportation node that traffic engineers had dreamed up for the west exit of Shinjuku Station (Eckersall 2011, Sand 2013). Shinjuku Station Underground Square (*Shinjuku Eki Nishiguchi Chikahiroba*) attracted thousands, who sang folk songs peacefully together and afterwards engaged in animated public debates. These performances of the 'Shinjuku folk guerrillas' convened diverse public spheres in physical space, evolving around just as many different discussion circles. Later, in order to frustrate such non-state-sanctioned assemblies, the authorities relabeled the underground *plaza* (chika *hiroba*) into underground *passage* (chika *tsūrō*). Thus, the space was redefined into a circulation space, which would be governed by the Road Traffic Act (Toshi Dezain Kenkyūtai 2009). This was more than just a symbolic act, since redefining it as transitory space allowed the application of traffic regulations that could be used to prevent any form of stationary activity or assembly.

As a result of this and of many other, more violent protests of the 1960s, what remains today is a strong bias on the side of authorities to control political assemblies in public space through design and strict regulations. In addition, deliberately vague notions of public safety (*kōan*) or nuisance (*meiwaku*) help administrators invoke strict control over public spaces where and whenever deemed necessary. It is this negative notion of public space as a highly restricted space that contemporary place-makers are struggling against to this day. Many established regulations, design standards, and maintenance regimes still frustrate easy change and more people-centered design. Furthermore, despite an often-lamented, quantitative lack of public open space in urban Japan, parks like Miyashita Park are rarely used. Paradoxically, if a space is privately owned, fewer regulations apply and more design and management experiments are possible. Most designers in Japan embrace the idea of greater design choice with the aim to increase the quantity of users (Tsukamoto and Nakatani 2011). Thus, for Shibuya councilor Ken Hasebe and park designer Yoshiharu Tsukamoto of Atelier Bow-Wow, the opportunity to collaborate with Nike offered the prospect to experiment with new, more flexible funding and management schemes.

Miyashita Park: From Engineering Marvel to Alternative Space

Like many other public spaces in Japan, Miyashita Park's origins are utilitarian: the long, narrow stretch of land along the city's Yamanote Line was cleared from housing before WWII and served as a fire break during the Allies' incendiary bombing campaigns. Owing to its unfavorable layout, it miraculously survived as open space during the years of reconstruction followed by rapid economic and urban growth. To beautify the city for the 1964 Olympic Games, a polluted creek running through the site was rerouted and a one-story parking palette was erected here with Japan's first elevated park on its roof. In his famous 1966 metabolism-inspired redevelopment plan for Shibuya, Le Corbusier's student Junzo Sakakura envisioned Miyashita Park as clean, no-nonsense space, part of an area-wide, independent, elevated pedestrian circulation system above the car-invaded street level.

Due to its location away from major pedestrian thoroughfares, the former showcase of modernist planning faded from public memory, while an intensive competition between the two rival retail and railway corporations Seibu and Tōkyū turned Shibuya into Tokyo's glossy epicenter of conspicuous consumption. By the late 1990s, the park was mostly perceived as an unsightly place and avoided by most. After the burst of Japan's infamous asset bubble in the early 1990s and the "two lost decades" of economic stagnation it became a temporary home to over 70 homeless people at peak times (Figure 16.6). From the late 1990s on, activities such as a weekly soup kitchen

FIGURE 16.6 Before plans for the renovation of Miyashita Park surfaced, the park was only used by few passersby and was home to a significant homeless population

Source: Christian Dimmer

and a summer festival were hosted here, where the 'Shibuya Free Association for the Right to Housing and Well-Being of Homeless People' (*Shibuya Nojukusha no Sonzai to Seikatsu wo kachitoru Jiyu Rengo*) sought to "(re-)politicize the city's homeless constituencies and establish solidarity networks with similar organizations" (Kindstrand 2012, p. 19). It also served as an important rallying point for political protests around Shibuya station.

Vij (2012, p. 138) sees places occupied by homeless people like Miyashita Park as spaces of temporary dislocation, occasioned as Foucauldian heterotopic counter-sites that enable an emergent alternative sociopolitical imaginary, in which homelessness "delineates a different sociality, one not predicated on a progressivist narrative of [. . .] home ownership or shelterization." For Cassegård (2011, p. 405) the old Miyashita Park is a "vacant lot" (*akichi*) that allows activists and subaltern groups to convene outside the constraints of mainstream society, where communication, action, and a recovery of political commitment seem possible. But for Tsukamoto of Atelier Bow-Wow, such space is seen as a failure, as "the most important thing for a park is to be used by a large number of people" (Tsukamoto and Nakatani 2011).

Homeless people in Japan are frequently regarded "as an eyesore by pedestrians and neighboring residents" and occasionally violently harassed (Aoki 2003, p. 365). This might be one reason why the Coalition's protests and their DIY-style aesthetic didn't resonate with mainstream society. The figure of the "homeless" is a frequent trope in urban planning in Japan with the consequence that public spaces are fortified against such "undesirables." The so-called homeless problem in Miyashita Park was only one of many symptoms of a perceived general decline in Shibuya. In the 1960s, Shibuya flourished in the proximity of Tange's Olympic gymnasiums in nearby Yoyogi

Park. During the 1970s the area became the epicenter for the emergence of Japan's post-modern consumer culture. With the advent of the economic crisis in the early 1990s and Japan's growing global integration, more and more chain stores moved into the area, diminishing the once classy area image. From the mid-1990s on, Shibuya had also become the locus of intense media debates and moral panics about different groups of youths who staged their deviance from the rigid mainstream society in prominent public spaces like Centergai, the town's main shopping street (Morris 2010, Kindstrand 2012, p. 13–14). Control and removal of these deviant youth subcultures (*datsugyaru*) and the creation of a new market for more "mature," well-funded audiences (*otona na macho wo*) therefore became the primary objectives for revitalizing Shibuya.

Shibuya Policy Entrepreneurs

Paul Waley (2007, p. 1470) notes that under Tokyo governor Ishihara an "exhortatory entrepreneurial urbanism began," which aimed to increase international competitiveness and "retain a top-ranking world city status." Competitiveness and free market principles are narratives that are interpreted by local actors and translated into concrete local place-making activities. The case of Miyashita Park shows how in the above-discussed climate of crisis, opportunities opened up for new kinds of local policy entrepreneurs, who played a crucial role in city branding and place-making.

The Zero-Tolerance/Pro-Sports Politician

Independent Shibuya councilor Takeshi Ito is one such policy entrepreneur and a power broker behind the Nike-fication. He presents himself as a racing cyclist, marathon enthusiast, and straight talker who tirelessly advocates for more sports facilities for better public health. To distance himself from conventional politics in Japan marked by noncommittal language, the populist prides himself in using clear language. His slogans are "Clearly 'yes'!" (*hakkiri 'yes'!*) to sports facilities and public safety, while he says "Clearly 'no'!" (*hakkiri 'no'!*) to homeless people in parks and skaters on sidewalks. Early on, Ito campaigned with the promise to clean up public space and in his election manifestos suggests that the futsal courts in Miyashita Park he had lobbied for "removed" at least half of the homeless.

The Street Art Activist and Social Entrepreneur

In Shibuya, the nonprofit organization Komposition was formed by social entrepreneur Motokazu Terai in 2002 to promote freedom of artistic expression, including graffiti, support young artists, strengthen community, and create a "society that maximizes the possibilities of young people" (Komposition 2016). Their first project, Legal Wall, sought to transform Shibuya into a gallery by obtaining permissions from public and private property owners to first clean illicitly scribbled walls and then allow graffiti artists to fill these new canvases with street art. While graffiti is generally perceived as a social problem and even a crime, Komposition managed to enlist the support of the Shibuya government as well as local businesses under the label of art. Nike Japan also supported Komposition. Kindstrand (2012) and Von Borries (2004) suggest that such assistance is part of Nike's guerrilla marketing strategy to co-opt innovative street art and streets sports actors and use them for their guerilla-style marketing campaigns. It is clear, however, that groups like Komposition also skillfully used the prestige of large corporations to realize their own objectives.

The Political Artists and Social Activists

In October 2007, students from the nearby Japan Designers School were invited by the Shibuya government to "beautify" a gloomy underpass of Route 246 near Shibuya station, from which the resident homeless community was displaced. As reaction, a group of activists, critical scholars, and artists called '246 Conference of Expressive Artists (*246 Hyougensha-kai*)' gathered to protest against the "instrumentalization and appropriation of artistic practice by state and corporate power" (Kindstrand 2012, p. 22). The group formed around the socially engaged political artists Tetsuo Ogawa and Misako Ichimura, who also formed the core of the 'Coalition to Protect Miyashita Park'. The group not only protested but also assembled "small temporary autonomous zones on the streets, [like] the Kitchen 246 street picnics" in order to prefigure a more inclusive society where the homeless are no longer marginalized (Cassegård 2013, p. 148). Ogawa and Ichimura had become famous for running a community cafe for many years, living together with the homeless in a tent village inside of Yoyogi Park.

The Creative City Advocate and Community Innovator

Another key player behind the remaking of Miyashita Park is former councilor, now-mayor Ken Hasebe. The 43-year-old independent Hasebe represents a new type of entrepreneurial politician/ community innovator. After quitting his job at an ad agency, Hasebe, a Shibuya native, became a community activist and began engaging in the regeneration of his city into a "cool" (*kakkoi*) place (Hasebe 2016). One of his first endeavors was the establishment of the NPO Greenbird in 2003, with the aim to clean up and beautify public space where the maintenance performance of the city was lacking. Utilizing the resources of his former job, Hasebe savvily enlisted the support of Nike Japan and other corporations, who sponsored the uniforms of the volunteer organization. Greenbird was extensively covered by media and quickly expanded across Japan and even worldwide, with over 60 local chapters today and over 30,000 citizen volunteers taking care of the public spaces of their cities. After becoming elected as councilor in 2003, Hasebe introduced a different kind of entrepreneurial politics that "the city hall could have never imagined" (Hasebe 2016). He pitched, for example, the idea of Shibuya University to the mayor, which started in 2006 as a new kind of community college that offers free, community-based, lifelong learning. Classes are taking place in the streets, community gardens, parks, record shops, and museums, and citizens are directly teaching other fellow citizens.

Direct and Indirect Outcomes of the Protests

The direct outcomes of the anti-privatization protests and the occupation were mixed, as parts of the park such as two futsal courts, a climbing wall, and the skating area were eventually turned into rental sport facilities, and the homeless population was displaced. On the other hand, the displacement was neither complete, nor was Nike able to brand the space as initially planned. When the naming rights agreement was concluded in August 2009, the park was to be named Miyashita Nike Park. After the activists' eviction, which caused a considerable public stir, Nike claimed they never had the intention to rename the park and thus the old name remained (Ogawa 2012, p. 3). Nike's plan to use the park for sponsored events for 200 days a year was reduced to 10. The design of the park also became less conspicuous. Initially highly visible in bright orange colors and with a towering advertisement structure, the final design was far more subdued, in part due to the protests as well as structural and cost reasons. With a homeless person injured during the eviction, the Coalition sued Shibuya ward. After repeated appeals by the ward against earlier decisions, the court ruled on a rather symbolic compensation of ¥110,000 (USD$1,000) for personal suffering. However, it ruled that the naming rights agreement was illegal because no legitimate tendering process had taken place and the city assembly had not been properly involved.

At Miyashita Park, the creative occupation of public space, the importance of digital media, and tactical spatialization neatly fit into the global iconography of recent protests. Indeed, Cassegård (2011, 2013) and Gonoi (2012, p. 159–160) gesture at the empowering aspects of recent youth protests that emerged around contested public spaces like Miyashita Park. Both are drawing more or less direct lines from what Mōri calls "new cultural forms of protest" (2009) that they see helping to create affordances for subsequent mass protests in Japan in 2012 and 2015. For the first time since the turbulent 1960s, large masses of protesters rallied in the streets of Tokyo in summer 2012 in order to protest against the restart of nuclear power plants that had been idle since the Fukushima nuclear disaster. The demonstrators occupied strategic locations in Tokyo's Kasumigaseki government quarter and in front of the prime minister's office to create "temporary autonomous zones" (Bey 2003). Slater et al. (2015) link these anti-nuclear protests to the more widely reported SEALDs (Students Emergency Action for Liberal Democracy) peace protests against Prime Minister Shinzo Abe's attempt to dismantle Japan's pacifist constitution in summer 2015. In both cases, creative, cultural forms of protest were enacted similar to those at Miyashita Park. The new cultural movements consciously distance themselves from earlier political activism with an open and loose network structure, and ideologically diverse, more egalitarian and individualist forms of organization, with a preference for art, performances, and fun (Mōri 2009).

Wider Effects

In their book *Catalyst Architecture*, Danish urban theorists Kiib and Marling (2015, p. 175) laud Miyashita Park as "a 'new pocket public'—a modest urban space that offers scope for development to young people in the street and to vulnerable homeless people of the neighborhood." They claim that "in Miyashita Park, it has been possible to bring different social groups together in the same arena," and they suggest that "the design has created what Richard Sennett calls a true democratic place. Different social and age groups can actually stay right next to each other, observing each other according to mutual agreement" (Kiib and Marling 2015, p. 205). Leaving aside the question whether homeless people agree to be stared at, they are right to point out the factual coexistence of homeless people who continue to use the renovated park. Comparing the current park with its prior condition before the renovation, the spectrum of different user groups (Figures 16.7 and 16.8) has widened indeed, but one has to ask if this is sufficient to call the new park "a democratic place." Lyn Lofland (1998, p. 204) remarks, "where there are no people, of course, there can be no public realm." However, the old Miyashita Park only appeared empty to those who didn't recognize it as a heterotopic counter-site for subaltern groups such as homeless and political activists.

Current Shibuya mayor Hasebe continues to see projects like the Shibuya University and Greenbird as clearly empowering and activating new aspects of society. They give greater choice to citizens and cater to rapidly diversifying lifestyles in hitherto uniform and inflexible Japan. However, as Sennett (2006) warns, "the cunning of neoliberalism [is] to speak the language of freedom whilst manipulating closed bureaucratic systems for private gain by an elite." How much can politics cooperate with big business without being co-opted, particularly in regard to public space—one of the most socially vulnerable fields of urban policy? When is the promise of greater freedom and choice only a pretext to advocate the retreat of the welfare state for corporate gains?

Lastly, the case of the Miyashita struggle shows how difficult collaboration between different protest movements is, and how little understanding there is for a public realm that is shared by all.

FIGURE 16.7 After the renovation, homeless people are still allowed to continue using the park; they are not prevented from entering

Source: Christian Dimmer

FIGURE 16.8 At the foot of Miyashita Park homeless people who were displaced for the renovation are allowed to live in cardboard houses. The sports facilities are not overly commercial. Schoolchildren pay ¥100 (USD$.90) for two hours of skating, or ¥200 for two hours of climbing.

Source: Christian Dimmer

While the Coalition was battling against the Nike-fication of Miyashita Park, other activists were simultaneously fighting against the construction of a privately run aquarium in Kyoto's Umekoji Park and the construction of a large road project that would eradicate the bustling alleyways in Tokyo's Shimokitazawa area. While all these groups were fighting for the right to *their* public space, they were not able to connect their respective public space struggles, nor even see that they were part of the same struggle. When asked, activists in Umekoji and Shimokitazawa would not be concerned about the homeless issue in Miyashita. They were not able to conceive their disparate struggles as protecting a larger public realm. In the end, all three movements failed.

Postscript

While the newly renovated park only opened in 2011, a strong pro-development coalition is already similarly depicting it as shabby and in urgent need of renovation. At the end of March

2015, when the coalition won its victory against Shibuya ward in court, new plans surfaced for a complete remodeling of a New Miyashita Park. With the 2020 Tokyo Olympics looming ahead, Shibuya ward aims to remove the old parking deck and replace it with a three-story shopping and gourmet structure with a park on its roof. As the city perceives a shortage of lodging space for Olympic visitors, a 17-story hotel is planned at the northern end of the park. If approved, the Mitsui Estate Corporation would lease this part of the park for 30 years and pay an annual rent of approximately ¥600 million (USD$5.3 million) (Penn and Tolsma 2015). The Coalition is protesting against this. Thus, the struggle for Miyashita Park and for public space in metropolitan Japan continues.

References

Aoki, H., 2003. Homelessness in Osaka: Globalisation, Yoseba and Disemployment. *Urban Studies*, 40 (2), 361–378.

Bey, H., 2003. *TAZ: The Temporary Autonomous Zone, Ontological Anarchy, Poetic Terrorism.* 2nd edition. New York: Autonomedia.

Cassegård, C., 2011. Public Space in Recent Japanese Political Thought and Activism: From the Rivers and Lakes to Miyashita Park. *Japanese Studies*, 31 (3), 405–422.

Cassegård, C., 2013. *Youth Movements, Trauma and Alternative Space in Contemporary Japan: Global Oriental.* Boston: Leiden.

Dimmer, C., 2010. Plans for Public Space Need the Public's Input. *The Japan Times*, October 26, 2010.

Dimmer, C., 2012. Re-Imagining Public Space: The Vicissitudes of Japan's Privately Owned Public Spaces. *In*: C. Brumann, and E. Schulz, eds. *Urban Spaces in Japan: Cultural and Social Perspectives.* New York: Routledge, 74–105.

Dimmer, C., 2014. Evolving Place Governance Innovations and Pluralising Reconstruction Practices in Post-Disaster Japan. *Planning Theory & Practice*, 15 (2), 260–265.

Dimmer, C., 2017. Place-Making Before and After 3.11: Emergence of Social Design in Post-Disaster, Post-Growth Japan. *Review of Japanese Culture and Society* (Josai University) XXVIII.

Eckersall, P., 2011. The Emotional Geography of Shinjuku: The Case of Chikatetsu Hiroba (Underground Plaza, 1970). *Japanese Studies*, 31 (3), 333–343.

Gonoi, I., 2012. *What Is a "Demonstration"? Transforming Direct Democracy* (「Demo」 to wa nani ka? Henbō-suru Chokusetsu Minshu Shugi). Tokyo: NHK Shuppan.

Harvey, D., 2001. *Spaces of Capital: Towards a Critical Geography.* New York: Routledge.

Hasebe, K., 2016. Achievements of the Past 12 Years (*12-nenkan de, jitsugen dekita shigoto*) [online]. Available from: http://hasebeken.net/#past [Accessed 3 September 2016].

Hirabayashi, Y., 2010. Activism in Defense of Freedom in Public Space: Anti-"Miyashita Nike Park" Movement (Kōkyo Kūkan no Jiyū wo mamoru Akutibizumu—Miyashita Nike Pa-ku Hantai Undō). *The Tsuru University Review*, 72, 77–88.

Kiib, H. and Marling, G., 2015. *Catalyst Architecture—Rio de Janeiro, New York, Tokyo, Copenhagen.* Aalborg: Aalborg University Press.

Kim, T. C. and Sasaki, T., eds., 2001. *Public Philosophy: Public and Private in Comparative Intellectual Histories* (Kōkyō Tetsugaku: Kō to Watakushi no Shisōshi). Tokyo: Tōkyō Daigaku Shuppankai.

Kindstrand, L., 2012. *Ghosts against Nikeification: Spaces of Representation in Tokyo's Miyashita Park* (Master's Thesis). Sophia University, Tokyo.

Kingston, J., 2004. *Japan's Quiet Transformation: Social Change and Civil Society in the 21st Century.* New York: Routledge Curzon.

Komposition, 2016. What is Komposition? (*Komposition ha*) [online]. Available from: http://komposition.org/#komposition.org/about/komposition/ [Accessed 3 September 2016].

Lofland, L. H., 1998. *The Public Realm: Exploring the City's Quintessential Social Territory.* New York: Aldine de Gruyter.

McCann, E., Ward, K., and Cochrane, A., 2011. *Mobile Urbanism: Cities and Policymaking in the Global Age.* Minneapolis: University of Minnesota Press.

McNeill, D., 2009. Mean Streets Feared Under Tokyo's New Safety Law. *The Japan Times*, May 5, 2009.

Mōri, Y., 2009. *Street Thought: The 1990s as Turning Point* (Sutorito no Shiso—Tenkanki toshite no 1990 Nendai). Tokyo: NHK Bukkusu.

Morris, B., 2010. Un/Wrapping Shibuya: Place, Media, and Punctualization. *Space and Culture*, 13 (3), 285–303.

Nikkei Architecture, 2011. Why Is There No Discussion About the Renovation of Miyashita Park—Asking Tetsuo Ogawa (Giron naki Miyashita Kōen no Kaishū—Ogawa Tetsuo-shi ni kiku) [online]. Available from: http://kenplatz.nikkeibp.co.jp/article/knp/column/20110927/552963/ [Accessed 3 September 2016].

Ogawa, T., 2012. Critique of the Entire Text of the Interview About Miyashita Park by Tsukamoto Yoshiharu of Atelier Bow-Wow (Atorie Wan Tsukamoto Yoshiharu no Miyashita kōen intābyū zen-bun hihan) [online]. Available from: www.dropbox.com/s/8icebzxbkweag9f/tukamoto%EF%BC%882012116%EF%BC%89.pdf [Accessed 3 September 2016].

OurPlanet-TV, 2010. *Miyashita Park, Tokyo/Shibuya—Can the Democracy Be Bought for Money?* (Miyashita Kōen Tokyo/Shibuya). OurPlanet-TV.

Penn, M. and Tolsma, J., 2015. Battle Over Shibuya Park Heats Up as Tokyo Olympics Loom. *The Japan Times*, Issues: The Foreign Element, April 1, 2015.

Pierce, J., Martin, D. G., and Murphy, J. T., 2011. Relational Place-Making: The Networked Politics of Place. *Transactions of the Institute of British Geographers*, 36, 54–70.

Sand, J., 2013. *Tokyo Vernacular: Common Spaces, Local Histories, Found Objects*. Berkeley, LA and London: University of California Press.

Sennett, R., 2006. *The Open City* [online]. Available from: https://lsecities.net/media/objects/articles/the-open-city/en-gb/ [Accessed 3 September 2016].

Shiraishi, H., 2011. Commodifying Public Space: Nike's Take-Over of Miyashita Park, Shibuya (Ichibaka sareru Kōgyō Kūkan—Nike ni baishū sareru Shibuya Miyashita Kōen). *Sekai*, 813, 131–138.

Slater, D. H., O'Day, R., Uno, S., Kindstrand, L., and Takano, C., 2015. SEALDs (Students Emergency Action for Liberal Democracy): Research Note on Contemporary Youth Politics in Japan, *The Asia-Pacific Journal*, 13 (27), 1–21.

Toshi Dezain Kenkyūtai, 2009. *Japan's Public Plazas* (Nihon no Hiroba). Tōkyō: Shōkokusha.

Tsukamoto, Y. and Nakatani, N., 2011. *The Existence of Architects and the Role of Historians at a Turning Point: A Conversation* (Daiwa: Tenkanki ni okeru Kenchikuka no Sonzai, Rekishka no Wariai). 10+1 [online]. Available from: http://10plus1.jp/monthly/2012/04/post-37.php [Accessed 3 September 2016].

UN, 2009. Report of the Special Rapporteur on Adequate Housing as a Component of the Right to an Adequate Standard of Living, and on the Right to Nondiscrimination [online]. Available from: www.ohchr.org/Documents/Issues/Housing/A-HRC-19-53_en.pdf [Accessed 3 September 2016].

Uno, M., 1998. The Urban Space We Are Heading from Now (Korekara no Toshikūkan ni mukete), *Zokei*, 17, 24–25.

Vij, R., 2012. Time, Politics and Homelessness in Contemporary Japan. *Proto Sociology*, 29, 117–142.

Von Borries, F., 2004. *Who's Afraid of Niketown?: Nike-Urbanism, Branding and the City of Tomorrow*. Rotterdam: Episode Publishers.

Waley, P., 2007. Tokyo-as-World-City: Reassessing the Role of Capital and the State in Urban Restructuring. *Urban Studies*, 44, 1465–1490.

17

WORLDED RESISTANCE AS "ALTER" POLITICS

Train of Hope and the Protest Against the Akademikerball in Vienna

Sabine Knierbein and Angelika Gabauer

This chapter touches upon severe backlashes against democratic culture through exclusionary appropriations of public spaces that reflect growing nationalisms, racisms, and narrow cultural and ethnic perspectives in Europe (Ajanovic et al. 2015). We first develop a conceptual framework to investigate anti-democratic tendencies in public spaces, before providing empirical research regarding two forms of resistance seeking to overcome exclusionary spatial practices in Vienna. The analysis offers a conceptual approach to distinguish exclusionary activism from inclusive activism, as well as a more nuanced understanding of the altering potential of two different forms of inclusive activism.

Austria has long witnessed political struggles over national identities, with Vienna being the most "worlded" spot in an otherwise conservative alpine nation. Vienna's central public spaces have historically served as places for disputes over mono- or multicultural identities. Analysis of public space is often focused on moments of insurgence where body politic spatiality is part of face-to-face politics aimed at reclaiming the political through dissent and the formation of more egalitarian politics of difference (Kaika and Karaliotas, this volume). Such investigations are critical, but in contemporary Europe, scholarly inquiry on increasingly anti-democratic phenomena in public space remains under-emphasized, yet urgently needed. As actually existing neoliberalism increasingly pushes forward "culturalized" and "ethno-racist" lenses of urban development (Palumbo 2014), research is needed that tackles ways through which collective organization can overcome racist appropriations of public space, research that depicts possible paths of self-organization that foster an egalitarian understanding and attitude towards refugees, migration, and geopolitical mobility.

Public space and racism studies share a conceptual link where infringements on public space are understood as grounds for the contestation of hegemonic urban restructuring through protest or alternative social practices by counter-publics and insurgent cultures (Knierbein 2015). Contributions from postcolonial (Roy 2011) and refugee studies (Brun 2001) criticize essentialist notions of cultures and places which suggest "that all people have a natural place in the world" (Brun 2001, p. 15). Such essentialist conceptions understand refugees as "being torn loose from their place and thus from their culture and identity" (Brun 2001, p. 15). Lanz (2015) similarly criticizes essentializing cultures as ethno-national and homogeneous "cultural circles," an approach which denies the representational character and precludes exchange processes of cultural practices. Roy and Ong (2011) use the concept of "worlding" to retrace patterns of (neo)colonialization within urban studies, and their hegemony over "truth." Worlding and urban everyday practices "creatively imagine and shape alternative social visions and configurations—that is 'worlds'" (Roy 2011, p. 314). The necessary, dual importance of the plurality of everyday urban life and ways of knowing provides important connections for equity in debates about city publics, refugees, and postcolonial urbanism.

In urban politics, forms of essentialization are frequently employed in the political programs of far-right-wing parties such as the Freiheitliche Partei Österreich (FPÖ, Freedom Party of Austria) (Ajanovic et al. 2015). The anti-pluralism that the FPÖ fosters in Austria's public sphere is now steadily accompanied by increasingly violent, racist, and anti-pluralist attacks organized by a political movement called the Identitäre Bewegung Österreich (IBÖ, Identitarian Movement of Austria) which actively discourages Islam (Ajanovic et al. 2015). They support assaults in many different realms: on the street, in the theatre, on campuses, and in front of or even inside refugee shelters.[1] In 2013, for example, 40 to 50 refugees—some of them on hunger strike to protest against the poor asylum conditions in Austria—sought asylum in the Vienna Votivkirche, a church adjacent to Vienna's Ring Road. On February 10, 2013, "activists" entered the church to "occupy the occupation" in order to bring xenophobic thought into daily mainstream media discourse through "right-wing activism." Their tactics abused the exposed humanity of the protesting refugees as a way to render themselves superior and "the other" (i.e. the refugees) inferior. This performative essentialization of a racist notion of "culture" is one of the most psychologically violent forms of racist expression towards one of the most vulnerable groups. Despite its political origins, the IBÖ has self-organized as an activist movement by using traditional left-wing tactics of disturbance.

In April 2016, the IBÖ occupied Nobel Laureate Elfriede Jelinek's "The Wards," a theatrical play criticizing the Austrian refugee policy. Refugees in the Audimax at the University of Vienna performed the play. The activists used artificial blood to scare off the event's actors and visitors. Less than two weeks later, professional artists performed the play in the Burgtheater, a nearby Imperial Court Theater, under the aegis of the President of the Austrian National Council. Activists of the IBÖ again disturbed the event by climbing the theater, unfolding a banner at the top, and throwing flyers from the façade's roof.

IBÖ's basic strategy is to mirror left-wing activists' spatial resistance tactics and to turn the core concepts of anti-racist discourse against the practices and strategies of migration-friendly and pro-refugee parties and groups, thus crippling the effectivity of tactics made viable by their political opponents. They attempted to mock and humiliate their opponents by pretending that they share the same values and ideas. This is a military strategy known to seduce "the enemy" with the illusion of joint values in order to neutralize their strategies, claims, and goals through intentionally contrived mimicry.

Programs of these parties and movements articulate narrow visions of spatiality as they frequently essentialize cultures, religions, and places, and emphasize the potential loss, or scarcity of (essentialized) space. Research has addressed the rise of new far-right-wing parties and movements through different lenses, including racist, Islamophobic, fascist, xenophobic, or anti-pluralist (Ajanovic et al. 2015, p. 76). However, critical debates regarding anti-pluralist practices rarely engage with public staging of civic dissent to protect and support the rights of migrants, refugees, and displaced populations against all forms of discrimination, nor have they offered reason for the successes of protests against exclusionary and racist practices relating to public space. This is why this chapter will first focus on perspectives on racism (Krzyzanowski and Wodak 2008) and anti-pluralism (Ajanovic et al. 2015) as they have recently been discussed in regards to Austria.[2] The second part will deal with a way forward in contesting racial and anti-pluralist instrumentalization of public space through what we call "worlded resistance."

Racist and Anti-Pluralist Expression in Public Space

"Racial discrimination includes all acts—verbal, nonverbal, and paraverbal—with intended or unintended negative or unfavorable consequences for racially or ethnically dominated groups" (Essed 1991, p. 45). In many European countries, current shifts away from traditionally overt racist discourses towards more nuanced forms of racism highlight a key shift away

> from the older kinds in that [they are] usually not expressed [. . .] in the terms of neo-fascist discourses, for instance by reference to some notion of biological or racial superiority, white supremacy, or skin color. Instead, the repertoires of justification that are typically employed use social characteristics [. . .] (e.g., protecting jobs, concern about welfare benefits) or cultural incompatibilities or differences)
>
> *(Krzyzanowski and Wodak 2009, p. 1)*[3]

What unifies far-right-wing positions is their anti-pluralism: their pursuit of homogeneity, the denial of plurality, and their use of binary antagonisms between "us" and "them" (cf. Ajanovic et al. 2015, referring to Laclau 2005). Research on "anti-pluralism" seeks to criticize and disable homogenizing discourses and practices directed against a whole set of differences: ethnicity, nationality, culture, religion, and gender. Right-wing extremism employs a twofold anti-pluralism: it works (a) in an excluding way towards the outside and (b) in an internally homogenizing way towards the inside. This anti-pluralism deploys binary antagonisms on both horizontal and vertical levels: A "we" is vertically confined against "the top brass" in a people-state binary as well as it is horizontally defined in dissociation from "the others," those who are "not-we" (cf. Ajanovic et al. 2015, p. 76). In this way, "the people" is delineated as "ordinary people" equipped with a "uniform will" and is brought into position against "the elites" (e.g. the national government). The invocation of "the people" also serves the exclusion of "the others," particularly of marginalized groups. Far-right-wing members argue plurality in society is always forced upon "the people" in a top-down fashion and is therefore unwanted. "The people" is understood as "our people," meaning that ethnic, religious, and national belonging becomes a central shared reference point. Anti-pluralist discourses rely on the premise of "a collective idea of homogeneity accompanied by the allegation of inequality among human beings. In such a conception pluralism can only be considered as a danger" (cf. Ajanovic et al. 2015, p. 76).

Exclusionary spatial practices are not new, as scenes of German-laden folkish and racial rituals persist in collective memory.[4] This history has been key to despots over the last century, for instance, Hitler's staging in Munich's public space through massive parades as expansive expressions of Nazi propaganda that enacted a broader Nazi narrative of cultural achievements, political triumphs, and militant nationalism. It is therefore no coincidence that uses of public space play a key role in promoting far-right-wing positions, as "the ordinary people" find space to flesh out their discursive identification strategies in a public realm such as the street. The public realm typically serves as the main gathering ground for public protest and consequently carries the potential of bringing democratic and anti-democratic discourses into the affective realm of face-to-face politics, through either specific inclusion mechanisms (Madanipour 2003) or through exclusionary "boundary drawing" (Gurtner and Sauer 2014). In the latter case, translating reason into passions might show the radical right's attempts to co-opt face-to-face politics, by cultivating a politics of fear inimical to a pluralist future. Space (as discourse, as practice, as experience) is key to visualizing and enacting boundary drawing as a practice that impedes access of undesired groups. The social production of public space therefore is not innocent, but deeply entangled in power structuration and hegemonic cultures.

After having depicted the features of far-right-wing expressions in public space, our inquiry in anti-racist and pluralist resistance seeks to deconstruct such narrow perspectives as an attempt (1) to "essentialize" space and culture and (2) to diminish the democratic and pluralist meanings that public spaces carry in democratic societies.

Accounts in radical anthropology have distinguished the role of the body in protest from discursive claims. Moore has emphasized that "the body is central to the work occupations do in shifting from 'politics' to the 'political,'" while stating that "politics" (including oppositional politics) "allows for contention within certain parameters" (of the institutionalized state), whereas "the political" "challenges the very foundations of these parameters" (2013, p. 12). Rather than understanding insurgent acts of resistance as "anti"-politics, Hage (2012) suggests unraveling the embodied action of resistance through occupation by recognizing its full mobilizing potential as "alter" politics.

While a great deal of work remains to unravel the dark sides of public space, i.e. the instrumentalization of public space by racist and anti-pluralist populism and extremism, this chapter takes a step forward and maps acts of resistance against these appropriations in Vienna. The study draws upon qualitative social research consisting of a qualitative content analysis of social media postings, daily and weekly newspapers, and online journals, as well as interviews and ethnographic observation realized during (1) mobilization against the Akademikerball at Hofburg (Vienna's Imperial Palace) with its adjacent Heldenplatz (Heroes Square) and (2) the emergence of Train of Hope, a new refugee-friendly movement at Hauptbahnhof (Vienna Main Station) in late summer 2015.

Akademikerball—Protest Against Racial Discrimination

Since 2008, the Ball des Wiener Korporationsrings (WKR-Ball, a Ball of Viennese student associations) has annually provoked massive anti-racist protests in Vienna (Figure 17.1).[5] The WKR-Ball is the umbrella organization of mainly ultra-conservative, German-nationalist laden student fraternities practicing academic fencing (the Mensur).[6] The WKR-Ball has been part of a proud formal ball tradition that has been annually organized during the carnival season for over four centuries. Hosted since 1952, the WKR-Ball is the most contested ball as it serves as a European gathering of far-right-wing political figures in one of the most iconic palaces of the Austrian Republic. The WKR-Ball is an essential link between institutionalized right-wing politics in Europe, student fraternities (as perpetuators of institutionalized modes of discrimination), and the organized neo-Nazi scene. Activism against the gathering thus often includes critique of student fraternities' networks, focusing on how such networks act and reproduce themselves mediated through public and private forms of formal and bureaucratic institutions.

The first protests against the WKR-Ball occurred in 2008 through the radical left-wing (student) scene, the so-called Autonome (noWKR, an alliance of different autonomous groups), and have grown to broader demonstrations involving a wider range of social groups. The Offensive Gegen Rechts (OGR, Offensive Against the Right) joined in 2012, founded by primarily socialist groups who followed another mobilization strategy attempting to implement larger demonstrations to address a broader public. Thirdly, another alliance called Jetzt Zeichen Setzen (JZS, Settings Signs Now) emerged in 2012 as an even broader movement consisting of several civil society organizations, such as the Austrian Students' Association, holocaust survivors, and different religious groups, as well as more institutionalized political parties including Austrian Green Party and Social Democratic Party of Austria.

While the protests initially took place as a spontaneous demonstration of a few hundred protestors in 2008, the year 2009 witnessed around 1,500 people taking to the streets to demonstrate

FIGURE 17.1 Protests against the WKR–Ball in 2014; the building of the Austrian Parliament is visible in the background

Source: Christopher Glanzl

against the Ball (Foltin 2011, p. 158). In 2010, the police stated it would be a danger to public security and order and consequently prohibited the overall demonstration. Yet, roughly 700 people still gathered at the initial meeting point. The police surrounded ("kettled") several hundred protestors. Some were accused of "participation in an illegal demonstration" and were later sentenced (Foltin 2014, p. 272). In 2011, on the day before the actual Ball, a spontaneous demonstration against a newly issued demonstration ban served as pretext for the police to ban a proposed substitute demonstration in the nearby Sigmund Freud Park. The day of the Ball, however, several hundred protestors moved through the city despite the bans. The police blocked whole areas of the inner city for public and private transport and again, several protestors were arrested (Foltin 2011, 2014). Two years later, the Austrian Constitutional Court found—referring to a jurisdiction of the European Court of Human Rights—that the prohibition of the demonstration in 2011 was unconstitutional.

The year 2012 marked a turning point in the (inter)national and urban reception of the WKR-Ball as it had been scheduled for January 27, the date of the Holocaust Remembrance Day. On this occasion, large counter-demonstrations with approximately 8,000 participants were for the first time independently organized by all three groups and accompanied by an increasingly critical public debate. By December 2011, the Hofburg's operating company had announced the end of the WKR-Ball tradition: "Because of the actual political and medial dimension, which have grown around the celebration of the WKR-balls [we have] decided not to offer [our] services as administrative authority for the WKR-Ball after the ball season of 2012" (Hofburg Vienna 2011). This cancellation did not emerge by coincidence: The Vienna Ball was removed from the UNESCO Index of Intangible Cultural Heritage due to the controversy around the WKR-Ball.

In 2013, the FPÖ's Vienna section started to host the Ball as Wiener Akademikerball (Vienna Academics Ball), spurring continued protest. Hofburg's operating company justified the glaring discrepancy to allow for a shadowy rebranded continuation of the Ball by arguing that the Hofburg is a central House of the Republic and therefore needs to open its gates for Austrian political parties. Even though 2014 demonstrations were marked by impressive police measures including a sealed off area which stretched over large parts of Vienna's first district (Figure 17.2) and a ban on face-covering for the whole inner city (Figure 17.3), showing a new sort of repression towards the demonstrators, thousands still protested the far-right event (Foltin 2014).

Demonstrations against the Ball have become increasingly accepted and supported by broader publics over the years while simultaneously retaining a high degree of heterogeneity within the group itself. Since 2012, the three groups have independently mobilized protest marches with the protest organizers finally being "evicted" from organizing any protests. Bolstered by the Austrian Minister of the Interior, the police prohibited demonstrations organized by noWKR in 2015 as the organizers—according to the police—would have incited violence in their mobilization campaign and public statements, putting public order and national security at risk. However, the protests hosted by OGR and JZS still took place.

Despite legal setbacks including temporary criminalization of protests as well as competing mobilization strategies of the involved groups, these continued acts of urban resistance against the Akademikerball exemplify a broad willingness to stand up against (institutionalized and informal) racism and anti-pluralist expression in Austria. The importance of the Ball diminished and the number of visitors decreased (Goetz 2014). The success of the protestors can be seen in the abolition of the WKR-Ball, the popularization of protest against racism, a (partly) shared agenda of pluralism, the UNESCO decision to withdraw the Ball from the list, and the juridical reinstatement of the freedom of expression in Vienna's public space. In addition, the City of Vienna started to host its own counter-ball in the municipality halls in 2015—the Vienna Ball of Science, an institutional strategy following a worlded and inclusive conception of the ball as an intercultural event.

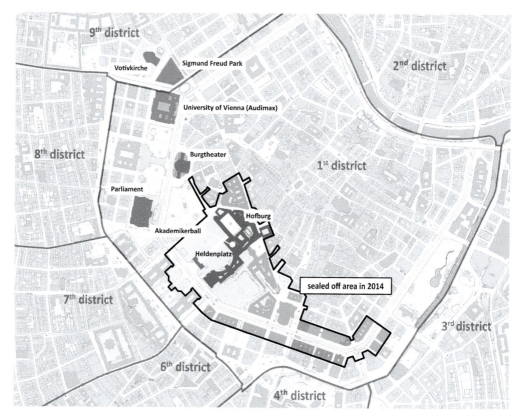

FIGURE 17.2 The police cordoned off large parts of Vienna's first district during the Akademikerball in 2014

Source: Angelika Gabauer

Train of Hope—Egalitarian Support at Wien Hauptbahnhof

In 2015, Vienna became entangled in the massive geopolitical upheavals related to the so-called "refugee crisis" in Europe and the wider region, thus producing a paradigmatic shift from using Vienna's public space as stage of *protest against* anti-democratic instrumentalization towards developing forms of *resistance to "alter"* prevailing post-political conditions through direct action in support of refugees.

The city has developed a generally refugee-friendly culture throughout the last century, which resulted in an outburst of solidary action when the first large groups of refugees arrived in summer 2015. Public criticism against national state politics gained momentum during recent events highlighting the damaging consequences of a disposition of disenfranchisement: Amnesty International's complaint about the "inhumane" living conditions in Austria's first emergency refugee camp, Traiskirchen (July 2015); the discovery of 71 dead refugees whose bodies were found lined up in a truck on the Austrian motorway (August 2015); the March of Hope of numerous refugees on the motorway from Budapest towards Austria (September 2015); and during the prelude to Vienna's contested municipal elections, including political struggles over the main issue of the refugee crisis (October 2015).

After being deeply affected by the harrowing humanitarian conditions and in response to the first trains full of refugees arriving in Vienna on August 31, a group of eight young volunteers met on September 1 at the Hauptbahnhof to begin the relief effort for arriving refugees in a corridor of the train terminal's east wing. Once they realized there was no humanitarian organization

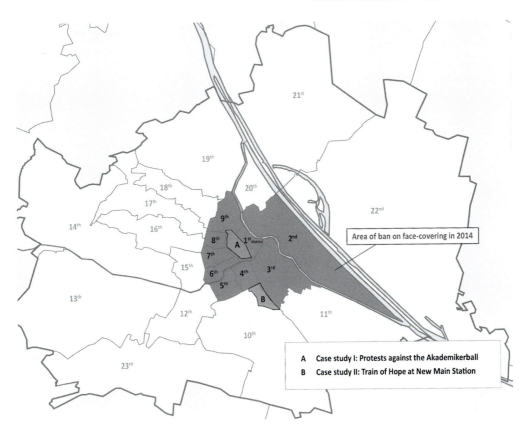

FIGURE 17.3 In addition to a large sealed-off area, a ban on face-covering was imposed for the whole inner city in 2014

Source: Angelika Gabauer

present at the Hauptbahnhof they decided to remain and offer the humanitarian support themselves. The emancipatory act blossoming in the public space of a train station represents the initial spark for the March of Hope, in which approximately 1,000 refugees participated.

On Friday, September 4, a small group of refugees stuck in Hungary decided to mobilize others and start marching on the central motorways between Budapest and Vienna. While moving their battered bodies through the sunset of the Pannonian landscape that Friday afternoon, Austrian and German governments successfully negotiated and finally welcomed the refugees at their borders the following night, hoping to prevent a humanitarian crisis. In the wake of these incidents, a new insurgent and networked solidarity movement emerged: Train of Hope Vienna (ToH), where the young helpers had managed to mobilize hundreds of voluntary helpers and later, over a thousand voluntary helpers in Vienna to *provide* humanitarian support in the stations' underpasses and to *instantiate* pro-refugee practices in public space (Figure 17.4).

Volunteers first took donations and provided people with basic supplies of food, clothing, and electricity, as well as information about further steps and legal advice regarding asylum possibilities. The number of arriving refugees skyrocketed in the days after the March of Hope and ToH started to offer help more systematically through "learning by doing":

> There is a lot of hustle and bustle at [. . .] Hauptbahnhof at the moment [. . .] What is really happening here is what Julian Pöschl calls civil society. The 22-year-old is one of the people

FIGURE 17.4   Volunteers at the Hauptbahnhof organized the care of thousands of refugees

Source: Christopher Glanzl

here [. . .] organizing the care of thousands of refugees [. . .] Yet the astounding thing is that none of this is the product of an institution or state organization, but a network that has virtually formed itself [. . .]. Volunteers are asked what they can do to help—and will then be given a suitable task [. . .] There is even a team for social media, which is [. . .] the back-bone of the movement. [. . .] The hierarchies are flat. Admission is possible for everyone.

(Presse 2015)

Some days later, they started a professional medical treatment area and a childcare area (including professional therapists for traumatized children), and organized a series of steps for receiving ref-ugees. A new subgroup searched internationally for people who went missing during migration and helped reunite them. Within just two weeks, ToH developed into a horizontally networked group of approximately 1,000 local youths, residents, tourists, migrants, former refugees, and all those willing to offer a helping hand, financial support, a shower, or a shelter. Student unions and the organized humanitarian players networked with the movement while arranging other reception points (e.g. the Caritas at Westbahnhof) or transfers between emergency humanitarian aid and the provision of emergency dorms and shelters throughout the whole country.

ToH's main goal is to provide refugee travelers with what they need until further provisions are secured or they choose to proceed with their journey elsewhere, regardless of whether people decide to stay in Austria or seek to apply for asylum abroad (Train of Hope 2015). The movement "wishes to make the travelers feel welcome and to facilitate a moment of tranquility for them," with locally embedded and affectively embodied action being its key intervention. "It does not matter what language you speak, I tell volunteers," an activist emphasizes, "you have to be kind and loving to these people who have been through so much" (New York Times 2015). The fact

FIGURE 17.5   Route taken by the refugees; thousands went from Budapest through Vienna to Munich by train

Source: Angelika Gabauer

that many volunteers or their families have come to Vienna as migrants or refugees before is key to an understanding of the ways in which egalitarian difference is embodied and enacted in the composition of the movement.

Around 300,000 refugees traveled to and through Vienna in the weeks of early autumn 2015 (Figure 17.5), many of them spending days, weeks, or even months in train stations, emergency shelters, and converted office buildings, among them many families and unaccompanied children and youngsters.

Revisiting Resistance: Spatializing Anti- and Alter-Politics

We have previously portrayed two examples of spatial praxis characterized as (1) reactive and resistance-based and (2) active and propositional (García-Lamarca 2017). The enduring protests against the Akademikerball have succeeded in disclosing the informal networks of racist regimes, some of them rooted in right-wing circles and with frequent connections to the formal bureaucracies or institutions of Austria's political landscape. The student unions attending the Ball employed informal networks to disseminate and perpetuate anti-pluralist discourse. These networks reach broad distribution as graduates' networks extend into societal sectors and reproduce informal (ultra-conservative, partly racist) power structures.

Through the successful act of their humanitarian train station occupation, ToH managed to produce a positive reception of their work's intentions and actions. They have inspired the urban society to gather further and engage in positive face-to-face experiences with the subjects discriminated by racist anti-pluralist discourses in a public space of everyday importance. The Hofburg's problematic symbolism as an Imperial Palace sanctioning well-networked, anti-democratic voices was challenged by protestors. However, this challenge remains incomplete as protestors never actually entered the palace. The inability to imagine or transgress the palace's physical boundaries reflects historical power dynamics where true victory was never traditionally conceded until the competing party had physically crossed such thresholds. The lack of complete boundary crossing renders the palace a publicly contested institution unwilling to fully reject the racism and ardent nationalism of its past. The ostentatious dancing and dining of the anti-pluralists remained insulated from the protest by the castle's imposing physical structure and recalcitrance to engage with contemporary ways of thinking. This particular configuration of an utterly exclusionary realm of superiority makes the space inaccessible, thus complicating the mission of the protestors. Their protests are not sufficiently able to challenge racist and anti-pluralist locations of power through body politics, hampering their ability to call into question the nation's remaining pieces of imperialist "heritage."

Both forms of resistance can be understood as territorial struggles to disintegrate the spatial tactics of the far-right-wing and to contest essentializing "boundary drawing" which implicitly renders one user group in public space as superior and starts from the assumption that humans are unequal, thus attempting to justify their failure to respect human rights and the dignity of *all* humans regardless of their class, gender, religion, or ethnic background.

Activists concerned with the social and historical conditions of the Akademikerball organized through radical practice. Their goal was an oppositional form of politics—anti-politics—in order to both understand and find spaces where oppositional impact can be maximized (cf. Hage 2012, p. 292). In contrast, ToH activists have found a useful resource in alter politics—critical thought and action that "aims [. . .] at taking us outside of ourselves precisely to continuously remind us of the actual possibilities of being other to ourselves" (cf. Hage 2012, p. 292), that is, to overcome racism and anti-pluralism by *practicing* a distinct political project. They have resisted traditionally organized forms of protest in favor of a much more radical practice: to shape a new political presence through direct occupation and intervention in Hauptbahnhof instead of appealing to others (e.g., the government) to change political action and social intervention.

The analytical distinction amongst the motives, goals, and successes of various methods of inclusive resistance against the "dark side of public space" demonstrates that the actions of both ToH and the anti-Akademikerball protests empirically reflect Hage's finding "that the structure of the radical political imaginary at any given time is characterized by a certain balance between 'anti' politics and 'alter' politics" (2012, p. 292).

Inclusive Resistance Versus Exclusionary Mimicry

In the above sections, we have emphasized that both cases need to be understood as resistance to the dark side of public space. Therefore, we will now establish analytical crossovers between all sections in order to build an analytical and conceptual nexus to facilitate nuanced qualitative research of both (1) worlded resistance in public space, and (2) anti-pluralist and racist actions often equally framed as "resistance" by their agitators. We will refer to this latter type of resistance as "mimicry," as it distorts and perverts the original sense of resistance through mirroring and imitation.

Two working concepts are introduced as attempts aimed at empowering research to draw specific differences between antagonistic forms of resistance. First, *exclusionary mimicry* describes the anti-democratic nature of spatial appropriations that make use of public space in a racist or anti-pluralist way, or that use the embodied experience of public assembly as a means for the social and political sedition through a politics of fear (e.g. against newcomers). Second, *worlded resistance*, on the contrary, marks an implicitly postcolonial or pluralist self-conception of the collectives organizing inclusive and egalitarian resistance which allows an inclusive structure at the point when the movement emerges.

In contrast, the ToH constitutes a strong example for worlded resistance, whereas the actions of the far-right-wing IBÖ movement are examples of current types of exclusionary mimicry. Both groups pursue their antagonistic political goals through embodied forms of action (beyond discourse) in public space and gain their strength both through (a) the curation of a particular image of public space by influencing discursive counter-publics in the media (public sphere) and (b) the affective dimensions of face-to-face politics focused on the change of everyday experiences in the city (public space). Analytically speaking, both antagonistic movements produce their impact *because* they occupy space through embodied action: They fill spaces with their bodies and "occupy" every potential square meter of publicly accessible and medially and politically saturated space, thereby seeking to expand their understandings of the world. While the IBÖ plays on xenophobic fears wishing for the re-homogenization of Europe's historic squares and streets, ToH's emergence depends on a utopian vision of the present. ToH relies on a new insurgent geography of resistance through altering action, where a new spectrum of politics engages the rights and needs of humans, independent of their origins or cultures, culminating in the transformation of public space into an egalitarian realm.

From the Dark Sides of Public Space to Worlded Resistance

This chapter has worked to open a necessary academic debate on the "dark sides of public space" by addressing contemporary far-right-wing appropriations of public space, which represent core backlashes, pitfalls, and risks associated with resistance. Practices of "boundary drawing" are an instrument frequently used by far-right-wing parties and their related movements to push anti-pluralist and racist expressions into the public sphere. The literature in urban studies often tends to focus on the dazzling aspects of urban resistance where emancipatory acts of self-empowerment and self-organization are understood as the result of inclusive, open-minded worldviews. Scholars must find ways to challenge this academic pattern by engaging in research that also depicts and critically analyzes public space appropriations that exclude, mimic, and demean; research that unravels the dark sides to the right to public space and to the city. A more critical and nuanced understanding would mitigate a simplified conceptualization of public space as a sphere for reinstating democracy.

The protests against the Akademikerball, the actions of the ToH volunteers, and many other solidary movements in the wake of the March of Hope in September 2015 show that many people in Vienna are beginning to fight for a pluralist version of public space precisely because public space is beginning to be recognized as constitutive of democratic integrity. They do so because they realize that the basic pillars of pluralist democracy are at stake. ToH came into being as an implicit critique through the alteration of lived space via an explicitly worlded, pro-refugee position. Embodied space occupations, such as the ToH action, become key catalysts for producing alternative realities, or, as Roy and Ong (2011) state, "worlds." Worlded resistance, in this sense, is as an active and propositional form of social change through resistance that overcomes essentialized conceptions of space, place, and culture to achieve a truly global democracy on the premise of egalitarian difference and inclusive spatial practice: a new spectrum of radical politics. This new spectrum of radical politics is nurtured by a balanced awareness and attention to the spatial ramifications between "anti" and "alter" politics.

Notes

1. IBÖ is not restricted to Austria, but belongs to a wider European network of far-right-wing movements.
2. Whereas far-right-wing parties and movements have historically promoted strong xenophobic arguments and agendas, their new generation attempts to bring far-right-wing positions to the societal mainstream.

This is realized through a strategic widening of their agendas from a previously xenophobic and reduced political agenda to a wider program characterized by an opposition to many forms of plurality, including identities, sexual orientations, gender, and origin.
3. We identify a renewed interest at the interface between public space research and critical racism studies in Europe.
4. The term "folkish" (German *völkisch*) is a reference to an essentialized notion of culture. A folkish approach to (essentialized) German cultures has been central to how Hitler's party used public space for Nazi propaganda, e.g. through deployments in Munich (Hagen 2008).
5. The authors are aware of the fact that the focus on racism can help to analyze central parts, yet not the overall nature of the protests. The initial protests came into being out of the anti-fascist scene, which issued explicit critique of the (structural) anti-Semitism.
6. Even though not all fraternities belonging to the WKR can be considered as extreme right-wing, it has to be noted that in particular far-right associations have a crucial and leading position within WKR's umbrella organization.

References

Ajanovic, E., Mayer, S., and Sauer, B., 2015. Umkämpfte Räume. Antipluralismus in rechtsextremen Diskursen in Österreich. *Austrian Journal of Political Science*, 44 (2), 75–85.

Brun, C., 2001. Reterritorializing the Relationship Between People and Place in Refugee Studies. *Geografiska Annaler: Series B, Human Geography*, 83 (1), 15–25.

Essed, P., 1991. *Understanding Everyday Racism: An Interdisciplinary Theory*. Newbury Park: SAGE Publications.

Foltin, R., 2011. *Und wir bewegen uns noch. Zur jüngeren Geschichte sozialer Bewegungen in Österreich*. Vienna: Mandelbaum Verlag.

Foltin, R., 2014. Squatting and Autonomous Action in Vienna. *In*: B. V. D. Steen, A. Katzeff, and L. V. Hoogenhuijze, eds. *The City is Ours: Squatting and Autonomous Movements in Europe from the 1970s to the Present*. Oakland, CA: PM Press, 255–276.

García-Lamarca, M., 2017. From Occupying Plazas to Recuperating Housing: Insurgent Practices in Spain. *International Journal of Urban and Regional Research* [online]. Available from: http://onlinelibrary.wiley.com/doi/10.1111/1468-2427.12386/full [Accessed 20 March 2017].

Goetz, J., 2014. Ausgetanzt! Eine kritische Bilanz der Proteste gegen den WKR-Ball. *In*: Forschungsgruppe Ideologien und Politiken der Ungleichheit, ed. *Rechtsextremismus: Entwicklungen und Analysen—Band 1*. Wien: Mandelbaum, 200–224.

Gurtner, A. and Sauer, B., 2014. Der, andere Ort', die, andere Frau': intersektionale Raumkonstruktionen in der politischen Debatte über den Wiener Straßenstrich. *Feministische Studien*, 32 (2), 281–293.

Hage, G., 2012. Critical Anthropological Thought and the Radical Political Imaginary Today. *Critique of Anthropology*, 32 (3), 285–308.

Hagen, J., 2008. Parades, Public Space and Propaganda: The Nazi Culture Parades in Munich. *Geografiska Annaler: Series B, Human Geography*, 90 (4), 349–367.

Knierbein, S., 2015. Public Space as Relational Counter Space: Scholarly Minefield or Epistemological Opportunity? *In*: C. Tornaghi and S. Knierbein, eds. *Public Space and Relational Perspectives*. New York: Taylor & Francis Ltd., 42–63.

Krzyzanowski, M. and Wodak, R., 2008. Migration und Rassismus in Österreich. *In*: B. Gomes, W. Schicho, and A. Sonderegger, eds. *Rassismus. Beiträge zu einem vielgesichtigen Phänomen*. Wien: Mandelbaum Verlag, 256–278.

Krzyzanowski, M. and Wodak, R., 2009. *Politics of Exclusion: Debating Migration in Austria*. New Brunswick, NJ: Transaction Publishers.

Laclau, E., 2005. *On Populist Reason*. London: Verso Books.

Lanz, S., 2015. Über (Un-)Möglichkeiten, hiesige Stadtforschung zu postkolonialisieren. *sub\urban. zeitschrift für kritische stadtforschung*, 3 (1), 75–90.

Madanipour, A., 2003. *Public and Private Spaces of the City*. London: Routledge.

Moore, S., 2013. Taking Up Space: Anthropology and Embodied Protest. *Radical Anthropology*. 13 (11), 6–16.

Palumbo, M. A., 2014. Urban Transformation, Social Transition. Barbès, Paris. Where "Otherness" Takes (Public) Place. *In*: A. Madanipour, S. Knierbein, and A. Degros, eds. *Public Space and the Challenges of Urban Transformation in Europe*. New York: Taylor & Francis Ltd., 117–130.

Roy, A., 2011. Conclusion: Postcolonial Urbanism: Speed, Hysteria, Mass Dreams. *In*: A. Roy, and A. Ong, eds. *Worlding Cities: Asian Experiments and the Art of Being Global*. Malden: Wiley-Blackwell, 307–335.

Roy, A. and Ong, A., 2011. *Worlding Cities: Asian Experiments and the Art of Being Global*. Malden: Wiley-Blackwell.

(Social) Media Sources

Hofburg Vienna, 2011. Wiener Korporationsball 2012 zum letzten Mal in der Hofburg Vienna [online]. *ots.at*. Available from: www.ots.at/presseaussendung/OTS_20111201_OTS0283/wiener-korporationsball-2012-zum-letzten-mal-in-der-hofburg-vienna [Accessed 15 April 2016].

New York Times, 2015. Volunteers, Many Once Refugees Themselves, Help as Guides in Vienna [online]. Available from: www.nytimes.com/2015/09/25/world/volunteers-many-once-refugees-themselves-help-as-guides-in-vienna.html [Accessed 15 February 2016].

Presse, 2015. Erich Kocina: Die freiwilligen Helfer vom Hauptbahnhof [online]. Available from: http://diepresse.com/home/politik/innenpolitik/4820006/Die-freiwilligen-Helfer-vom-Hauptbahnhof [Accessed 19 October 2015].

Train of Hope, 2015. Train of Hope. Flüchtlingshilfe Wien Hauptbahnhof [online]. Available from: www.trainofhope.at/home/wer-wir-sind/ [Accessed 28 Oct 2015].

Conclusions

18

CITY UNSILENCED

Spatial Grounds of Radical Democratization

Sabine Knierbein and Jeffrey Hou

City Unsilenced has brought together contributions that detect, analyze, and reflect upon the relations between public space and urban resistance in an age of shrinking democracy. The objective of this work has been to advance urban research by focusing on recent urban acts of resistance, and to track their relations towards a deeper understanding of public space in the contemporary city. In this final chapter, we intend to further articulate the intersections between the recent resistance movements and the neoliberal conditions and processes that define today's global societies. We do so by highlighting a set of relationships emerging from the case studies that characterize the linkages between urban resistance, public space, and attempts to reinvigorate our democratic institutions and practices. Specifically, we examine four aspects in which public spaces serve as nodes of critical actions and reflections: public space as sites of mobilization and negotiation, public space as spaces of contestation and learning, public space as space of rescaling and re-politicizing, and public space as grounds of alter-politics.

Urban Resistance in the Global South and North

Although scholars tend to situate the ascension of global resistance to patterns of neoliberal urbanism in 2011, "the year of dreaming dangerously" (Žižek 2012), urban contestations against modes of neoliberal urban restructuring have been unfolding well *before* then. In Athens, civic uprisings against the upgrading, commercialization, and privatization of public space against the backdrop of beautifying the city for the Olympic Games in 2004 were already visible during the 1990s. The well-distributed documentary of Brazilian geographer Milton Santos titled "Por uma outra globalizacão" draws a strong reference to his book of the same title published earlier in 2000 in which he examines the resistance by citizens of Cochabamba, Bolivia's third largest city. Between December 1999 and April 2000, citizens successfully rallied against the privatization of water and the consequent increase in water consumption costs. The five-month resistance involved tens of thousands of protestors who ultimately succeeded in the de-privatization of a World Bank concession that was issued with the municipality in 1997 (Santos 2007 (2000)).

In South Africa, the Western Cape Anti-Eviction Campaign, initiated in 2001, served "as an umbrella body for a number of community organizations, crisis committees, and resident groups that emerge in Cape Town's poor townships to resist [. . .] evictions and service cut-offs and demand their rights to shelter and basic services" (Miraftab 2009, p. 36). In 2001, Argentina was heavily shaken by an economic crisis in which the Piqueteros Movement of unemployed factory workers (now unemployed due to flexibilization of labor patterns, e.g. in the global car industry) gained momentum, leading to massive acts of urban resistance and to the first signs of horizontal and collective organization against a neoliberal regime put in place under the military junta in the 1970s and 1980s (Rosa and Vidosa, this volume).

These earlier sparks of resistance against discriminatory, exclusive, and often racialized practices under neoliberal policy regimes have been globally recognized, but have not been systematically connected to the movements emerging later, nor to the main export product of the Western world: liberal democracy (Lorey 2014). The lack of more complete ontological understanding of the lineage, causes, and effects of urban resistance has distracted from our ability to analyze and problematize vertical integrations of Western democracies into other societies. Further, many Western scholars have stubbornly eschewed large tracts of scholarship in the Global South. This scholastic blind spot has disregarded broad ranges of urban scholarship, empirical evidence, and theoretical framing for understanding grassroots insurgency against neoliberal governance. It has resulted in challenges to neoliberal cultural or economic exports being poorly understood as growing pains to be overcome as a country undergoes neoliberalization. This two-pronged problem normalizes resistance in the context of a naturalized neoliberalism and significantly undercuts our collective ability to be critical practitioners and citizens.

In the light of these examples, 2011 can be conceived as a culminating point when resistance in the Global South spilled over to the North, reflecting the enhanced material inequalities related to the neoliberal policies. While this recognition is increasingly becoming a part of Western democracies' everyday life, it remains largely unconnected to events elsewhere in the world. In particular, the global economic crisis in 2008 had further exacerbated the decline of employment, continued the decay of welfare states, and posed serious challenges to the dismantling of speculative housing investments all around the world, including the North.[1] However, the impact of the neoliberal model cannot be framed in only economic or material terms, as its social, cultural, and political dimensions have reached far beyond what is calculable and palpable. Contemporary interpretations of neoliberalism argue it has actively produced a *political crisis* where its capacity for economic predation has hindered civic control and responsiveness. Such mitigations can be seen in the reduced ability of voting to change political course, the conflation of civic advancement with capitalistic advancement, and growing acceptance of neoliberalism across the political spectrum, which further enhances voter disenfranchisement and the exploration of viable alternatives (Monbiot 2016).

Unsettling Urban Routines and the Democratic Paradox

As a result of fundamental social, economic, and political restructuring, basic urban routines have become unsettled. Increasing urban inequalities in cities around the world is furthered by the de-politicization of politics through consensus-based liberal democracy; this has shut out citizens and left decisions to government managers, politicians, and specialists operating in a multilevel governance where actors who have not been democratically legitimated can increasingly assume power (Wilson and Swyngedouw 2015). Meanwhile, as economic stability plummeted, discontent directed at the commodified nature of public life and public space has increased, as more and more educated, formerly middle-class individuals and groups joined the so-called urban subaltern (Bayat 2010, Roy and Ong 2011). But, is this the primary narrative to understand why we currently witness increasingly public, space-based resistances? Hasn't public space always been a frontier between class interests, and a field for struggle against all sorts of repression?

Public space has come into focus during recent struggles where the restructuring of multiple interrelationships between civil society, state, and markets unfolds. As part of this restructuring, we see increased attention to the roles that cities play, as the (conception of) the modern nation-state faces a crisis (Appadurai 1996). With focus on the crisis facing the modern nation-state, the political formation of many Western liberal democracies is receiving more criticism. As Mouffe (2000) has stated, liberal democracy has always been based on a democratic paradox between the liberal and the democratic strands of political thought:

> On one side we have the liberal tradition constituted by the rule of law, the defense of human rights and the respect of individual liberty; on the other the democratic tradition whose main ideas are those of equality, identity between governing and governed and popular sovereignty. There is no necessary relation between those two distinct traditions but only a contingent historical articulation.
>
> *(Mouffe 2000, p. 2–3)*

The paradoxical dynamic between freedom (liberal tradition) and equality (democratic tradition), which the Keynesian welfare state was still able to generally maintain, contributed to the fact that sporadic civil unrest would not gain global momentum or permanence during more recent welfare-state provisions, as social and material well-being was still secured in the Western world. This sustained paradox has been accompanied by another dilemma (cf. Purcell 2009, p. 144–145), i.e., liberal democracies have long been adept at managing and legitimating social inequality. Their characteristic separation of the public and private spheres allows them to claim the existence of a formal political equality even when manifest social inequality is present. Under Keynesian policies, that equality deficit was mitigated by significant material redistribution and the meaningful inclusion of organized labor in public decision making (cf. Purcell 2009, p. 144–145). Yet those accommodations were central targets of the neoliberal agenda and were significantly eroded in post-war Germany (Foucault 2010), and sedimented into international and urban policies during the times of Reaganomics (USA) and Thatcherism (UK), and their successors (Tauss 2012). As a result, neoliberalism has increasingly exacerbated this democratic deficit that has long troubled liberal democracy (Purcell 2009).

With the rise of neoliberal policies, an imbalance between liberty and equality has been created with a strong focus on liberty, while issues of equality have been increasingly neglected (Mouffe 2000). In order to maintain its form of governance, the neoliberal political economy needs to actively modulate the political and social instability and crises it generates. That is why neoliberal policy agendas and their makers increasingly seek to link their goals and projects with democracy (Purcell 2009). To solve this frustration, community development with a focus on public space—the "soft spaces of neoliberalism" (Haughton et al. 2013; Lebuhn, this volume)—has in many cases operated as an essential enabling moment for the neoliberal project. In the field of planning and designing for public spaces in particular, formal participatory modes of communicative and collaborative planning have been applied that often tend to use consensus building and majority decisions, while (in)advertently flattening the contradicting voices (often of minority or marginalized groups) calling for a more radical and egalitarian democratic project and reality (Haughton et al. 2013; Lebuhn, this volume).

As more and more economic and political pressure is put on public space (Madanipour et al. 2014), accompanied by social and ethnic polarizations, it comes as no surprise that the realm of public life is the territory where one can witness intensified class reconfigurations, discrimination, and societal struggles. Tensions in public space, in this sense, need to be understood as seismographs of an over-accelerated and fragile neoliberal political economic model. This model has undermined the long history of urban commoning and has rendered public space a highly competitive field. In this field, political parties dominate representational space and access to voters; companies strive for higher revenues or civic legitimization; and civil society seeks reorientation in a landscape of power in which "the political" has become increasingly absent.

It is in this context that acts of public space based resistance become important to examine, as they not only disrupt the neoliberal taming of public life but also reinvigorate deep relationships between public space and lived democracy. It is also through this perspective that we attempt to highlight in the following specific processes as evident in cases included in the volume.

Public Space as Site of Mobilization and Negotiation

The use of public space as a site of mobilization and negotiation is one of the main processes that occurred in cases throughout this volume, from the Global South to the Global North. Cities are where the material impacts of neoliberal governance on the social lives of many dwellers become noticeable, as individuals and groups not only take actions but also engage in a deeper understanding of the changes occurring in their society and mobilize to find their voice. Recent acts of urban resistance have brought a new generation of protestors to the streets, people who have never before been active in street (or other types of) politics. Groups that usually would have moral values and positions quite opposite from one another (LGBT and conservative Muslims) (Yiğit Turan, this volume) and left-wing activists and right-wing protestors can find causes to walk side by side, and, in other cases, form political coalitions (Kaika and Karaliotas, this volume).

These recent instances of urban resistance combine a place-based and context-specific approach to protest with new ways of political identity formation (Yiğit Turan, this volume) through horizontal and worlded networks (Knierbein and Gabauer, this volume) and more global claims for egalitarian democracy (Kaika and Karaliotas, this volume). Meanwhile, a belief in the power of open dissent, civil disobedience, and active resistance against (quasi)authoritarian forms of governing is gaining force. Consensual solutions have found a smaller impact on changing the political landscapes as a new power balance between mainstream society and increasing minority power in diverse cities challenges consensual deliberation as a hegemonic tool of majorities to silence minorities and marginalized groups. Within pluralist and diverse groups consensus is practiced along with dissent as a valuable form of decision making. In some cases, power structures inherent in the group (formation) are explicitly reflected and reworked (Lorey 2014), indicating the active presence of negotiation.

Horizontality as a mode of mobilization, observed in the Latin American movements in 2001, has become a prevalent and effective strategy to self-organize and to develop new forms of resistance (Lorey 2014). It involves reflexive social regulations, new forms of organizing, and new modes of subjectivation, which might ideally lead to a collective and affective form of relations among protestors, while being used as an instrument for creating a social space in which participants feel empowered to speak and take part in common challenges. This is a space in which privileges and inequalities can be consciously addressed, and heterogeneity in the manner of speaking and in the opinions expressed has to be endured: Horizontal self-organization opens up a process in which conflicts and differences are not negated, but must be first recognized (Lorey 2014). It is important to note, though, that structural discrepancies are still enmeshed in these forms of horizontal mobilization. Specifically, there is a danger that horizontality and urban resistance mobilization might run a risk of nurturing types of mimicry resistance that are not progressive or striving for radical democratization at all (Knierbein and Gabauer, this volume). In these cases, urban resistance is instrumentalized by anti-democratic groups by fortifying boundaries between populations of different religions, cultures, ethnicities, classes, or genders (Chen and Szeto, Kaika and Karaliotas, Owens and Antiporda, all this volume).

Public Space as Space of Contestation and Learning

The heartbeat of neoliberal governance is crisis produced through austerity mechanisms and processes of de- and re-institutionalization (governance). This model constantly (re)produces social, political, and cultural divides, thus nurturing repetitive eruptions of urban resistance against increasing inequality, injustice, and imbalances. Crisis is the seemingly inherent necessity through which neoliberal measures are legitimized and produced politically, thus rendering it a self-fulfilling prophecy. As crises and impacts of neoliberal governance unfold and threaten the public life and public spaces of cities, these sites are also where the fissures and cracks of neoliberalism become visible and its continued evolution becomes contested.

The case studies in this volume exemplify the power of public space scholarship that utilizes hybrid combinations of micro, meso, and macro analytical techniques to carefully scrutinize urban life at a local level within the context of macro neoliberal politics and economics. Understanding that crises are increasingly happening in public spaces with unique local articulations of protest, prototypical post-structuralist critique risks oversimplification or generalization. In the cases of Berlin, Tokyo, Warsaw, and Poznań (Lebuhn, Dimmer, Domaradzka, all this volume) activists have used formal means of participation and/or formal rights and law to claim a citywide or neighborhood referendum, or to claim full information about legal and public authority-related procedures. Regardless of their results, the authors state that these processes have helped to facilitate learning in newly established political communities where the political claims had become more inclusive and focused, thus (a) trying to attract the wider city publics to engage with and support the activists' claims and (b) to make a clear message possible during the referendum campaign.

Meanwhile, other resistance groups have not allowed parties or formal procedures to entirely co-opt and conquer their mobilization dynamics, as shown in the cases of Athens, Istanbul, Hong Kong, and Taipei, whereas in Vienna, the emergence of a wider critique—and thus, of counter-publics—and more actively resisting groups was heavily supported by some political parties. The cases of Taipei, Hong Kong, Madrid, and Barcelona show that activists have made their way straight into the political system during times of elections, thus renewing the governing bodies and challenging long-established political practices. In Barcelona and Berlin, activist groups have stated their goal to perform as an incubator for democratic control of the governance regimes in place, and have actively organized policy and legal recommendations to revert the legal and economic hegemony of existing governance networks.

Public Space as Space for Rescaling and Re-politicizing

Chapters in this volume indicate that we are currently witnessing a moment in which the *spatial scales of crisis* require more complex ways to consider and engage the political through modes of urban resistance. Resistance tactics, goals, and claims need to connect and reorganize fragmented geographies of crisis, that is, resistance groups need to combine the quest for local human needs, urban equity struggles, regional justice mechanisms, national political contestations, supranational governance critique, and a struggle against the locally destructive impacts of global and virtual market forces, thus overcoming the "jumping scales of capital" (Swyngedouw 2003, referring to Smith 1984).

Urban public spaces are places where social densities and political identities meet, and where fragmented scales of resistance can be brought together, from local solidarity with peers within one's particular comfort zone towards a much more universal solidarity for egalitarian democracy. Some of the chapters in this volume have indicated that movements have occasionally shifted their focus from central public spaces to the neighborhood scale (and narrow comfort zone), consequently risking insufficiently addressing central political questions, and thus reducing the perseverance and universal impact of the movement (Kränzle, this volume). Certain local neighborhood interventions can even serve as a pretext for cultural regeneration and symbolic capital accumulation, and thus gentrification. Others, however, have stressed that there are certain central and politically symbolic places in cities where the quest for more genuine political reform or revolution has been repeatedly posed over centuries. These squares and streets have witnessed a new spark of radically democratizing the urban (Chen, Chen and Szeto, Kaika and Karaliotas, Yiğit Turan, all this volume), and inspired people to issue more fundamental political claims rather than engaging in narrow or local, interest-based politics.

Apart from this multi-scalar notion of resistance and the potential of resistance groups to reconnect and re-politicize the "jumping scales of capital," we also find resistance as counteraction, response, and contestation against all types of unsettling: economic, cultural, ecological, social, and political. Much of the debate in urban studies lingers on the role of resistance movements as a response to the economic crisis (through neo-Marxist approaches to understand the political economy of public space), and more recently, the political crisis (particularly through contributions to the post-foundational, post-political, and post-democratic debates) (Flesher Fominaya and Cox 2013). However, looking through the lenses of public space allows us to detect that neoliberal agendas have also been producing more severe cultural clashes, social polarizations, and ecological traumas. Contributions to this volume have shown that public space research links analysis at different levels, cross-cutting through diverse dimensions, reflecting the impact on the minutiae of everyday life. Many of the chapters emphasize attempts to re-politicize the many obvious as well as less visible relations between different scales and dimensions of crisis and resistance through radical dialectics (e.g. between housing and public space research, or between labor market and public space research, or between ecological struggles and their social selectiveness). For example, several chapters highlight the vulnerability of younger generations to evictions and displacement from their everyday places either as a result of commodified public spaces (Maharawal, this volume) or through racialized broken windows policing against communities of color (Cahill et al., Owens and Antiporda, all this volume). Such conditions provided in turn opportunities for engaged scholarship, participatory action research, and empowerment of disenfranchised actors to investigate and mobilize against such conditions and processes.

Insights from Hong Kong, Taipei, and Vienna also leave us more hopeful. In the first two cases the protests were very much student-led, with an active and politicized student generation trying to push through social and political reform and change, while in the case of Vienna, a group of youngsters issued state critique through humanitarian aid for refugees, thus calling for global human rights and solidarity with incoming refugees. In times of a decreasing consensus about the prevalence of human rights in our countries, urban resistance struggles are rooted in very material claims and goals as part of the everyday survival of those who have been dispossessed, disenfranchised, and disempowered (Knierbein and Gabauer, this volume).

Public Space as Grounds of Alter-Politics

The city has been historically understood as a collective actor (Bagnasco and Le Gàles 2000), where different parts of urban society constantly perform collaboratively, producing and using public space as urban commons. The neoliberal project, however, seeks to replace this collective and collaborative urban history with a new genealogy of competition: the city as a competitive space. As a result, competition has been rendered as a key aspect of current democracies, as it is linked to appearance of transparency, efficiency, and so forth, even though the actual linkages are weak and superficially constructed. Furthermore, in the construction of an exclusive politics and a moral climate, the narrative of competition renders those that are not able to or do not want to participate in such competition as outcasts (Tyler 2015). The various resistance movements presented in this book represent efforts to expose and intervene in the apparent cracks of this narrative and practice, not only to claim, but also to radically renew the democratic project.

As space is at the heart of the organization of changing political economies, it is worth reflecting on the spatial features of the acts of urban resistance and the role public space plays for different groups that have become increasingly disadvantaged and were ultimately mobilized by the ongoing outcomes of the neoliberal project. This work draws upon earlier thinkers who have coined those without a voice the urban subaltern, the disempowered, or disenfranchised (Roy 2011, Bayat 2010, Fraser 1990), and those who have articulated the collective production of spaces as truly democratic where constituents that previously had no part become now the key agents for renewing democracy (Rancière 2010, Kaika and Karaliotas, this volume). Through the case studies from different cities and continents, we have gathered results that enable us to (1) further differentiate those disempowered and disenfranchised and (2) to track how they relate (a) *to* public space and (b) *through* public space to make their claims (Figure 18.1).

The unemployed: Former workers protesting against labor market restructuring and job flexibilization take to the streets and reclaim public space as their medium of protest and a site for regaining public life, away from the site of production and employment.

The unsheltered: Individuals, groups, and families within the context of the anti-gentrification, anti-displacement, and anti-dispossession protests take to the streets to claim their human right for decent housing.

The indigent: People who have lost their belongings, social status, and security because of harsh austerity measures due to a recession, economic, or political crisis. They claim the human right for decent living conditions and urban equity.

The un(der)represented: All those who feel and think that the governing political representatives do not address their interests, and those who have been facing severe repression of their human right to protest and exercise freedom of speech against a repressive government. They take actions in public space as the last opportunity for defending and reinstating democracy.

The unattended: Those who are not offered adequate humanitarian aid, short-term shelter, affordable long-term housing, or other urban services including healthcare and pensions, fighting together with their supporters for an equitable urban social service delivery and just regulation for all.

The colonized: Those groups that have been disregarded, discriminated against, and oppressed by previous or present colonizing forces, or deprived of their humanity through present colonization by policing, disrespecting their legal status as citizens, and undermining their access to the (right to the) city. These resistance groups struggle for a de-colonization of urban space.

The nonconsumers: Those who claim consumption-free urban space to experience collective and individual rhythms and routines of urban everyday life and criticize politicians deciding primarily alongside the interests of global capital, having privatized means of collective consumption without democratic control of the service delivery, or influenced by the strong lobby of tech-led expert regimes.

City Unsilenced. Spatial patterns of urban resistance

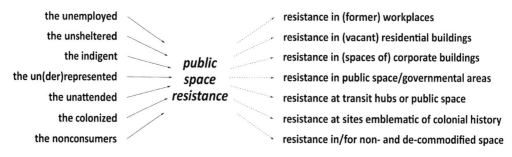

FIGURE 18.1 Spatial patterns of urban resistance. The classification of the aforementioned groups is not meant to be exclusive, as overlaps may exist before, during, or following acts of resistance in public space, where one actor can take an active role in more than one of the dimensions. This scheme shows that public space is where multiple concerns, frustrations, and motivations for change meet—a crossroads in the sense of political mobilization, where those disadvantaged by one dimension of neoliberal capitalism meet those hit by another.

Source: Sabine Knierbein, Graphic Design: Angelika Gabauer

For all these differently motivated resistance groups—the unemployed, the unsheltered, the indigent, the un(der)represented, the unattended, the colonized, and the nonconsumers—public spaces serve as the initial sites where many try to make their claim or state their dissent within their field, and to expand their political identifications to others (Bayat 2010). That way, they enable the embodied realm of public space becoming the key catalyst for the emergence of wider political dissent and the generation of new and alternative democratic projects. Public space is thus where the picture of multiple fragmentations, failures, and fractures of the current global capitalism become traceable, connected, and where the potential cracks and spaces that escape neoliberalism's spatial conquering expeditions can be protected, analyzed, and explored. It is here where different types of publics and counter-publics meet and collide in cities worldwide where supporters and affected groups intermingle and develop solidarity despite differences. Public space, thus, represents both an opportunity and a challenge, as on the one hand it makes their struggle become (globally) visible to gain supporters; on the other hand, public space is where their vulnerability is exposed, with a high risk of being further stigmatized, marginalized, dispossessed, criminalized, or menaced. At times, this includes the risk of losing ones' lives.

Urban resistance tactics have connected public space assemblies with direct actions into the private, public, or hybrid territories of capital accumulation to disrupt, offset, or interfere with the productive space of the competitive neoliberal economy. *The unemployed*, for instance, have reappropriated vacant factories, container terminals, and office space to set up new labor markets or collective industrial cooperatives, which in turn finance their protest. *The unsheltered* have de-privatized and rehoused empty buildings or have de-commodified private property through land action and adverse possession. *The indigents* have blocked banks and reclaimed bank assets into public and collective property. *The un(der)represented* have blocked parliament buildings and emblematic public squares and streets. *The unattended* have used train stations as local hubs to show a worlded resistance, to stand together in global solidarity and to get what is needed on the ground. *The colonized* have occupied former prisons emblematic of long histories of colonialism, thus symbolically unchaining themselves from a colonizing genealogy of oppression and inferiority. *The nonconsumers* have developed new alternative modes of being in-common and living and sharing common resources, while using both private and public properties. These resistance tactics link:

- public space with the workplace and labor markets;
- public space with housing;
- public space with the places of resource transfer and (missing) material redistribution;
- public space with the places where democracy ideally should be made (e.g. parliament, fora, agora);
- public space with mobility hubs and transport infrastructures;
- public space with places of oppression, terror, and imprisonment; and
- public space with actions of nonconsumption or commoning.

Urban research on these dialectical relations between the aforementioned fields can help to unmask the current neoliberal model as the principal producer of global modes of unsettling. Furthermore, there is a strong potential for counter-publics to develop acts, tactics, and strategies of resistance, not necessarily in the sense of anti-politics (demonstrations against certain issues), but more aligned with the idea of alter-politics (Hage 2012, Knierbein and Gabauer, this volume), the affective strive for a politics of change. Alter-politics aims at practicing a radical hope for a new democratic project that is stronger than the weak post-democratic model we witness today. It shows affective action for a collective and passionate capacity to long for alter-modernity (Hardt and Negri 2009, da Silva Andrade and Huguenin, this volume), to collectively produce the commons through an affective utopian project dwelling in present realities. Alter-politics in this context takes "us outside of ourselves to see how we can be radically other to ourselves." It "aims at finding a possibility of a different life outside a given [political] order of things," "generating new alter-modern spaces lying outside existing governmentalities" (Hage 2012, p. 294, 296, referring to Viveiros de Castro 2010, own insertion).

Unsilencing the Public and Public Spaces

Bayat has depicted public space in Western democracies as part of the institutions of the modern nation-state, to which many of the urban subaltern in the cities of the Global South have no access. He argues, "because modernity is a costly existence, not everyone can afford to be modern. It requires the capacity to conform to the types of behavior and modes of life [. . .] that most vulnerable people simply cannot afford" (Bayat 2010, p. 59). Public space as a highly formalized space is one of these institutions of the modern urban world. This is why many of the marginalized "quiet encroachers" tend to avoid public expression wherever possible. That way, they seek to escape the modern structure of law and order, which does not offer any resources or opportunities but confines their realm of everyday action (Bayat 2010). As we take a worlded, critical perspective in examining different forms of resistance (Roy and Ong 2011), it is also important to consider that silent, individual resistance, or "social non-movements" (Bayat 2010), can also contribute to the urban project to radically renew democracy.

This volume, however, is concerned with ways through which such silence has been dispelled, by seeing and using the city and public space as a site of resistance and a catalyst for political change, where people bang their pots and pans, use goggles, umbrellas, and flowers to disrupt political silence and renew—a democracy in which "the spaces of democracy (spaces for the practice of democracy) and the democracy of space (democratic relations in the production of space)" are inherently related (García-Lamarca, this volume, referring to Hoskyns

2014, p. 4). As Ober has put it, the original term "democracy" was meant to capture "power" as the "capacity to do things": "Demokratia" is not just "the power of the demos" in the sense of "the superior or monopolistic power of the demos relative to other potential power-holders in the state." Rather it means, more capaciously, "the empowered demos"—the regime in which the demos gains a collective capacity to effect change in the public realm, "the collective strength and ability to act within that realm and, indeed, to reconstitute the public realm through action" (Ober 2008, p. 7).

By better understanding the processes, actions, and implications of recent urban resistances, this volume aspires to contribute to the ongoing debates and renewed attention concerning the role and significance of public space in the practice of lived democracy and lived space. Specifically, we have argued that in the face of diminishing democratic institutions in cities and regions around the world, political resistance and demonstrations in public space have a greater role to play not only in holding the state and political establishments accountable to the interest of the society but in renewing and reinvigorating our democratic culture and institutions and pursuit for equity, egalitarian difference, and justice. Without resistance and public space agencies, mobilization of the masses, and continued public debates and social movements, democracy is at risk of becoming stagnant, narrow, and obsolete. The continued presence, contestation, and discourse of public space are fundamental to a renewed and lived democracy, a democracy that is worlded, open, and enacted through debates, dissent, contestation, and active participation—democracy that is fundamental to protecting and enhancing the welfare of citizens and communities against the encroachment of neoliberal interests and all forms of oppression.

Note

1. In Europe, for instance, the European GDP had dropped by 4% in 2009, reverting industrial production back to the levels of the 1990s, and left 23 million people, equivalent to 10% of the European Union's active population, unemployed, while erasing 20 years of fiscal consolidation (European Commission 2010, p. 7–8). In the USA, 19.9 million Americans now live in extreme poverty (DeNavas-Walt and Proctor 2015). Specifically, there are massive patterns of extreme poverty characterized by hunger or very low food insecurity (Worldhunger.org 2016).

References

Appadurai, A., 1996. *Modernity at Large: Cultural Dimensions of Globalization.* Minneapolis: University of Minnesota Press.
Bagnasco, A. and Le Gàles, P., 2000. *Cities in Contemporary Europe.* Cambridge: Cambridge University Press.
Bayat, A., 2010. *Life as Politics: How Ordinary People Change the Middle East.* Stanford: Stanford University Press.
DeNavas-Walt, C. and Proctor, B. D., 2015. US Census Bureau, Current Population Reports, 60–252. *Income and Poverty in the United States: 2014.* US Government Printing Office, Washington, DC. Available from: www.census.gov/content/dam/Census/library/publications/2015/demo/p60-252.pdf [Accessed 26 July 2016].
European Commission, 2010. *Europe 2020: A Strategy for Smart, Sustainable and Inclusive Growth.* Brussels: European Commission.
Flesher Fominaya, C. and Cox, L., 2013. *Understanding European Movements: New Social Movements, Global Justice Struggles, Anti-Austerity Protest.* London and New York: Routledge.
Foucault, M., 2010. *The Birth of Biopolitics: Lectures at the Collège de France, 1978–1979.* Lectures at the College de France, Picador.
Fraser, N. 1990. Rethinking the Public Sphere: A Contribution to the Critique of Actually Existing Democracy. *Social Text*, 25 (26), 56–80.
Hage, G., 2012. Critical Anthropological Thought and the Radical Political Imaginary Today. *Critique of Anthropology*, 32 (3), 285–308.

Hage, G., 2015. *Alter-Politics: Critical Anthropology and the Radical Imagination*. Carlton, Victoria: Melbourne University Press.

Hardt, M. and Negri, A., 2009. *Commonwealth*. Cambridge, MA: Belknap Press of Harvard University Press.

Haughton, G., Allmendinger, P., and Oosterlynck, S., 2013. Spaces of Neoliberal Experimentation: Soft Spaces, Postpolitics, and Neoliberal Governmentality. *Environment and Planning A*, 45 (1), 217–234.

Hoskyns, T., 2014. *The Empty Place: Democracy and Public Space*. Abingdon: Routledge.

Lorey, I., 2014. The 2011 Occupy Movements: Rancière and the Crisis of Democracy. *Theory, Culture & Society*, 31 (7–8), 43–65.

Madanipour, A., Knierbein, S. and Degros, A., 2014. *Public Space and the Challenges of Urban Transformation in Europe*. London and New York: Routledge.

Miraftab, F., 2009. Insurgent Planning: Situating Radical Planning in the Global South. *Planning Theory*, 8 (1), 32–50.

Monbiot, G., 2016. Neoliberalism—the Ideology at the Root of All Our Problems [online]. *The Guardian Online*, April 15, 2016. Available from: www.theguardian.com/books/2016/apr/15/neoliberalism-ideology-problem-george-monbiot [Accessed 7 September 2016].

Mouffe, C., 2000. *The Democratic Paradox*. New York: Verso.

Ober, J., 2008. The Original Meaning of "Democracy": Capacity to Do Things, Not Majority Rule, *Constellations*, 15 (1), 3–9.

Purcell, M., 2009. Resisting Neoliberalization: Communicative Planning or Counter-Hegemonic Movements? *Planning Theory*, 8 (2), 140–165.

Rancière, J. 2010. *Dissensus: On Politics and Aesthetics*, ed. and trans. Corcoran S. London: Continuum.

Roy, A., 2011. Slumdog Cities: Rethinking Subaltern Urbanism. *International Journal of Urban and Regional Research*, 35 (2) (March), 223–238.

Roy, A., and Ong, A., 2011. *Worlding Cities: Asian Experiments and the Art of Being Global*. Chichester, UK and Malden, MA: Wiley-Blackwell, 307–335.

Santos, M. 2007 (2000). Por uma outra globalição. Do pensamento único à consciência global. 14th edition. Rio de Janeiro and São Paulo: Editora Record.

Smith, N., 1984. *Uneven Development: Nature, Capital and the Production of Space*. Oxford: Blackwell.

Swyngedouw, E., 2003. Globalisation or "Glocalisation"? Networks, Territories and Re-scaling [online]. Available from: www.europaforum.or.at/site/Homepageifhp2003/downloads/Langfassung_swyngedouw1.pdf [Accessed 18 July 2016].

Tauss, A., 2012. Contextualizing the Current Crisis: Post-Fordism, Neoliberal Restructuring, and Financialization. *Colombia Internacional*, 76 (julio a diciembre de 2012), 51–79.

Tyler, I., 2015. Classificatory Struggles: Class, Culture and Inequality in Neoliberal Times. *The Sociological Review*, 63 (2), 493–511.

Viveiros de Castro, E., 2010. Introduction. *In*: P. Clastres, ed. *Archeology of Violence*. Cambridge, MA: MIT Press, 9–51.

Wilson, J. and Swyngedouw, E., 2015. Seeds of Dystopia: Post-Politics and the Return of the Political. *In*: J. Wilson, and E. Swyngedouw, eds. *The Post-Political and Its Discontents*. Edinburgh: Edinburg University Press, 1–24.

Worldhunger.org, 2016. Hunger in America: 2015 United States Hunger and Poverty Facts [online]. Available from: www.worldhunger.org/hunger-in-america-2015-united-states-hunger-and-poverty-facts [Accessed 26 July 2016].

Žižek, S., 2012. *The Year of Dreaming Dangerously*. London: Verso Books.

INDEX